COLLEGE READING AND
WRITING SKILLS

First Custom Edition

Humber College Institute of Technology and Advanced Learning

NELSON / EDUCATION

NELSON / EDUCATION

ISBN-13: 978-0-17-656289-2
ISBN-10: 0-17-656289-3

Consists of Selections from:

The Well-Crafted Argument: Across the Curriculum
White and Billings
ISBN-10: 1-133-05047-6

Mindscapes: Critical Reading Skills and Strategies
Second Edition
Carter
ISBN-10: 1-4354-6234-3

Dynamic Argument
Brief Second Edition
Lamm and Everett
ISBN-10: 1-111-84135-7

The New World Reader
Fourth Edition
Muller
ISBN-10: 1-133-31032-X

Perspectives on Contemporary Issues
Fourth Edition
Ackley
ISBN-10: 1-4130-1068-7

Writing Analytically with Readings
Second Canadian Edition
Rosenwasser, Stephen, and Babington
ISBN-10: 0-17-650446-X

Critical Thinking, Thoughtful Writing
Fifth Edition
Chaffee, McMahon, and Stout
ISBN-10: 0-495-89978-X

The Bare Essentials, Form A
Seventh Edition
Norton and Green
ISBN-10: 0-17-650034-0

Fusion: Integrated Reading and Writing, Book 2
Kemper, Meyer, Van Rys, and Sebranek
ISBN-10: 1-133-31249-7

Cover Credit:

Digital Vision/Thinkstock

ACKNOWLEDGMENTS

What is the purpose of a writing course in higher education? What do students need to learn, and why and how should they learn it? This textbook represents the collective response to these fundamental questions by the faculty in Humber's Department of English. It positions writing as the expression of one's critical engagement with an increasingly complex academy and world. As such, it focuses on building students' capacity not only to be successful in their studies and careers, but also to have agency to effect positive change.

The content you are about to experience is the result of a deeply reflective, iterative, and robust process of curriculum review taking place over more than a decade. It approaches the act of writing as interconnected with that of critical reading and reasoning. The first chapters, therefore, focus on developing students' ability to read texts critically and extract information purposefully. Further chapters concentrate on organizing ideas into coherent, informed, and audience-appropriate critical responses and arguments. Final chapters provide an overview of grammar and mechanics to assist students in deepening their understanding of language structures and how to use them to greatest effect.

This material is the result of a collaboration involving many faculty over time; however, I would like to thank particularly the following faculty who worked on this text: Trevor Arkell, Sarah Armenia, Dana Hansen, Anne Lyden, John Stilla, and David Wallace. Most of all, my thanks go to Prasad Bidaye, who steered this project from beginning to end and worked tirelessly to bring it to fruition. Lastly, I would like to acknowledge the wonderful support this project received from Nelson Education.

Vera Beletzan
Associate Dean, Department of English
Humber Institute of Technology and Advanced Learning

CONTENTS

PART 1

CRITICAL
READING

CHAPTER 1: METHODS OF CRITICAL READING   2

Active Reading   2

  Previewing   4

In-Depth Reading   6

Postreading   7

The Importance of Open-Mindedness When Reading   7

CHAPTER 2: RECOGNIZING PATTERNS OF ORGANIZATION   10

The Role of Transition Words   12

Supporting Details   13

  Major and Minor Details   13

Categories of Organizational Patterns   15

  Patterns That List   16

  Patterns That Explain   23

  Patterns That Analyze   27

Relationships Between Ideas   46

CHAPTER 3: HOW TO READ A VARIETY OF SOURCES   52

How to Read an Essay   52

How to Read a Newspaper Article   53

How to Read a Newspaper Editorial   54

How to Read a Visual   55

How to Read a Research Study   56

  The Structure of a Research Study   57

How to Approach Research Study Reading   57

How to Read Online Sources   58

Reading Controversial Text   60

Prescriptive Versus Descriptive Writing   60

Mapping Arguments   62

Fact and Opinion   66

Types of Support for Arguments   70

Recognizing Bias and Tone: Denotation, Connotation, and Loaded Language   82

Connotation and Denotation   82

Bias and Tone   83

Loaded Language   83

Evaluating Arguments   86

Recognizing Deductive and Inductive Reasoning   90

Evaluating Arguments   93

Intended Meaning: Euphemisms and Doublespeak   108

PART
2

PARAPHRASING AND
SUMMARIZING

CHAPTER 4: PARAPHRASING   116

Why Paraphrase?   116

Make Yourself the Main Speaker   116

Clarify When the Original Source Is Difficult to Understand   116

Add Stylistic Zest When the Original Source Is Worded Blandly   116

How to Paraphrase   117

Guidelines for Paraphrasing   118

Methods for Paraphrasing   118

CHAPTER 5: SUMMARIZING   126

Summarizing to Express Main Ideas and Supporting Details   126

How to Write a Summary   127

PART
3

CRITICAL
RESPONSE

CHAPTER 6: WRITING A CRITIQUE 142

The Connection Between Reading Critically and Writing a Critique 142

Writing a Critique 142

Determining Your Position 143

Introduction 145

Summary 145

Analysis 145

Assessing Persuasive Writing 145

Examining a Writer's Language 146

Examining a Writer's Evidence 146

Judging a Writer's Logic 146

Response 148

Conclusion 149

Illustration: Critique 153

PART
4

ARGUMENTATIVE
WRITING

CHAPTER 7: THE NATURE AND PROCESS OF ARGUMENT 162

Why Argue? 163

What Is an Argument? 163

A Formal Definition of Argument 164

Amplifying the Definition 164

What Is an Arguable Thesis? 165

Using Evidence in Argument 166

CHAPTER 8: GENERATING MATERIAL   168

Brainstorming   169

Critical Thinking   171

Discussing   173

Writing   174

Freewriting   174

Journaling   175

Blogging   176

Sketching and Scrapbooking   177

Discovering   177

Discovering Claims: What Are You Trying to Argue?   177

Discovering Evidence: How Will You Support Your Argument?   178

Researching   180

Primary Research   180

Secondary Research   180

CHAPTER 9: ORGANIZING MATERIALS   182

Charting   182

Diagramming   183

Clustering   183

Outlining   185

CHAPTER 10: THE WRITING PROCESS: DRAFTING ARGUMENTS   188

Structure of an Argument   188

Drafting an Introduction   188

Drafting Your Lead Sentences   195

Drafting the Body   198

What's Wrong with Five-Paragraph Form?   208

An Alternative to Five-Paragraph Form: The All-Purpose Organizational Scheme   210

Linking Evidence and Claims   212

Drafting the Conclusion   217

Tying It All Together 220

Using Qualifiers 220

Using Transitions 221

Student Essay 224

CHAPTER 11: THE WRITING PROCESS: REVISING AND EDITING ARGUMENTS 230

Revising an Argument 230

Revision Isn't Editing 230

Revision Guides, Checklists, and Rubrics 231

Using a Revision Guide 232

Using a Revision Checklist 235

Using Rubrics 235

Five Kinds of Weak Theses and How to Fix Them 238

Weak Thesis Type 1: The Thesis Makes No Claim 238

Weak Thesis Type 2: The Thesis Is Obviously True or Is a Statement of Fact 239

Weak Thesis Type 3: The Thesis Restates Conventional Wisdom 240

Weak Thesis Type 4: The Thesis Offers Personal Conviction as the Basis for the Claim 241

Weak Thesis Type 5: The Thesis Makes an Overly Broad Claim 243

Guidelines for Addressing Other Points of View 245

Giving and Receiving Feedback 248

Be Positive 248

Be Specific 250

Student Essay 253

Editing an Argument 257

Editing on a Word Processor 257

Editing Guides 261

Editing Marks 261

PART 5

GRAMMAR AND MECHANICS

CHAPTER 12: PARTS OF SPEECH   266

Nouns   266

Verbs   267

Pronouns   268

Adjectives   270

Adverbs   270

Prepositions   271

Conjunctions   271

Articles   272

Expletives   272

CHAPTER 13: SENTENCE BASICS   273

Subjects and Verbs (Predicates)   274

   Creating Subjects and Verbs (Predicates)   275

Special Types of Subjects   276

   Creating Special Subjects   277

Special Verbs (Predicates)   278

   Creating Special Predicates   279

Adjectives   280

   Using Adjectives   281

Adverbs   282

   Using Adverbs   283

Prepositional Phrases   284

   Building Prepositional Phrases   284

   Using Prepositional Phrases   285

Clauses   286

   Using Clauses   287

Real-World Application   288

CHAPTER 14: SIMPLE, COMPOUND, AND COMPLEX SENTENCES 289

Simple Sentences 290

Modifiers 290

Direct and Indirect Objects 290

Creating Simple Sentences 291

Simple Sentences with Compound Subjects 292

A Simple Sentence with Two Subjects 292

A Simple Sentence with Three or More Subjects 292

Using Compound Subjects 293

Simple Sentences with Compound Verbs 294

A Simple Sentence with Two Verbs 294

A Simple Sentence with Three or More Verbs 294

Using Compound Predicates 295

Compound Sentences 296

Compound of Two Sentences 296

Compound of Three or More Sentences 296

Creating Compound Sentences 297

Complex Sentences 298

Using a Subordinating Conjunction 298

Compound-Complex 298

Creating Complex Sentences 299

Complex Sentences with Relative Clauses 300

Relative Clauses 300

That and *Which* 300

Who and *Whom* 300

Using Relative Clauses 301

Real-World Application 302

CHAPTER 15: AGREEMENT 303

Subject-Verb Agreement 304

Correcting Basic Subject-Verb Agreement 305

Agreement with Two Subjects 306

Fixing Agreement with Two Subjects 307

Agreement with _I_ and _You_   308

Correcting Agreement with _I_ and _You_   309

Agreement with Singular Indefinite Pronouns   310

Correcting Indefinite Pronoun Agreement I   311

Agreement with Other Indefinite Pronouns   312

Correcting Indefinite Pronoun Agreement II   313

Pronoun-Antecedent Agreement   314

Correcting Pronoun-Antecedent Agreement   315

Other Pronoun Problems   316

Correcting Other Pronoun Problems   317

Real-World Application   318

CHAPTER 16: SENTENCE PROBLEMS   319

Common Fragments   320

Missing Parts   320

Incomplete Thoughts   320

Tricky Fragments   322

Absolute Phrases   322

Informal Fragments   322

Comma Splices   324

Correcting Comma Splices   325

Run-On Sentences   326

Correcting Run-On Sentences   327

Rambling Sentences   328

Correcting Rambling Sentences   329

Misplaced/Dangling Modifiers   330

Correcting Dangling and Misplaced Modifiers   331

Shifts in Sentences   332

Correcting Improper Shifts in Sentences   333

Real-World Application 1   334

Real-World Application 2   335

Real-World Application 3   336

CHAPTER 17: COMMA   339

In Compound Sentences and after Introductory Clauses   340

In Compound Sentences   340

After Introductory Clauses   340

Correcting Comma Errors   341

With Introductory Words and Equal Adjectives   342

After Introductory Phrases   342

To Separate Adjectives   342

To Determine Equal Modifiers   342

Correcting Comma Errors   343

Between Items in a Series and Other Uses   344

Between Items in Series   344

To Set Off Transitional Expressions   344

To Set Off Dialogue   344

To Enclose Explanatory Words   344

Correcting Comma Errors   345

With Appositives and Other Word Groups   346

To Set Off Some Appositives   346

With Some Clauses and Phrases   346

Using "That" or "Which"   346

Correcting Comma Errors   347

Real-World Application   348

CHAPTER 18: QUOTATION MARKS AND ITALICS   349

Quotation Marks   350

Using Quotation Marks   351

Italics   352

Using Italics   353

Real-World Application   354

CHAPTER 19: OTHER PUNCTUATION   355

Contractions and Possessives   356

Contractions   356

Possessives   356

Forming Contractions and Possessives   357

Semicolons and Colons   358

Semicolon   358

Colon   358

Using Semicolons and Colons   359

Hyphens   360

Using Hyphens   361

Dashes   362

Using Dashes   363

Real-World Application 1   364

Real-World Application 2   365

Index   366

CRITICAL
READING

iStockphoto/Thinkstock

CHAPTER 1 Methods of Critical Reading

CHAPTER 2 Recognizing Patterns of Organization

CHAPTER 3 How to Read a Variety of Sources

Methods of
CRITICAL READING

Considering the Disciplines

Most of us learned to read English so long ago that we don't even think about adjusting our reading to different texts—poetry, fiction, nonfiction, web pages. Sometimes, though, we may need to become more conscious of just how we read when we are reading for different purposes, just as we might watch a movie differently if we knew we were going to be quizzed about the movie afterwards rather than talking about our favorite parts with our friends. Especially when we read texts to see how we might incorporate ideas into our own arguments or to see how our own arguments are developing, we may benefit from thinking consciously about different methods of critical reading. Regardless of academic discipline, critical reading skills are necessary for determining the strength or weakness of an argument. The strategies this chapter presents can be adapted to your reading of a text in the social sciences as well as a newspaper, from an art exhibit to a web page, and you will learn from doing a critical reading of texts within your field what its conventions generally entail.

Reading and writing are intimately related modes of thinking—so intertwined that you really cannot do one without doing the other. Just as writers determine how to approach their subjects by considering their purpose and their readers, so too do readers determine how to approach *their* purpose for reading by considering how to approach the subject, often working along similar lines to those intended by the author.

ACTIVE READING

In the sense that to read means processing written language to understand it, all reading is "active." But some forms of reading represent a greater challenge to the comprehension process than others. A letter from a loved one may be processed relatively swiftly and efficiently, almost as a photograph would, whereas a demanding

> **"A READER MUST LEARN TO READ."**
> ALBERTO MANGUEL

legal or technical document of the same length may need to be processed in a much more methodical manner.

When we read primarily for pleasure—whether a novel, a work of nonfiction, or a friend's email—we are concerned primarily about content: What is going to happen to the characters in the novel? What is the author's premise in the work of nonfiction? What fun activities did the friend experience in London over the summer?

But when we read for a purpose besides (or in addition to) pleasure, we need to think more consciously of our reading process so that we can make necessary modifications. Such reading is task-oriented: to find out certain information, to summarize the work, to analyze the structure of the work, to assess the merits of the argument, to determine how the information coincides with our position on the issue.

You can adopt certain strategies to become a more active reader. It may seem strange to think of a "strategy" of reading. The only strategy that leaps to mind is moving our eyes across the page from left to right and top to bottom (for readers of most Western languages). But from a psychological and linguistic perspective, we are pulling off complex feats of cognition.

As students of writing, you read not just for understanding but for insight into the way in which an author organizes and develops an argument. This type of active reader needs to do the following:

1. Determine the *framework* of the author's argument. What are the claims, data, and warrants?

2. Evaluate the *data* (evidence) presented. Are they accurate? Sufficient? Appropriate? Relevant?

3. Evaluate the author's *organizational strategies*. Why does the author bring in X before Y and after W? Is the sequence beyond dispute, or is there no clear rhetorical purpose behind the sequence? Should the author have arranged things differently?

4. Speculate on the *significance* of what is being argued. What are the short- and long-term consequences of the author's views? If the author argues that student athletes are treated unfairly in the classroom, for example, and uses compelling evidence to back up that claim, then the significance of the argument is that it could persuade classroom teachers to be more flexible, say, in permitting student athletes to miss class to participate in out-of-town athletic competitions.

5. Analyze the *logic* of the argument. Has the writer inadvertently committed any logical fallacies?

Each of these cognitive acts works together to comprise active reading.

As you read to find sources of support for your argument, use the following strategies: previewing, in-depth reading, and postreading.

Previewing

Imagine Bob, a first-year student, trying to study for a political science quiz the next day. He's having trouble reading the textbook chapter being tested. It seems like more pages than he has time or inclination to absorb. So he finds his classmate Julie in the library and tells her he's having trouble motivating himself to do all that reading. Julie, who's already read the chapter, encourages him by saying, "Oh, Bob, the chapter essentially covers only four points about the economic conditions on the Greek islands comprising Santorini." Relieved that the chapter highlights only four main points, Bob returns to his room motivated to read but also with a sense of how to read the chapter productively. Julie has given him a *preview* of what to expect. Previewing is typically a two-stage process: (1) prereading, and (2) skimming.

Anything worth reading typically requires several readings, so you approach this previewing stage knowing that you will read the assignment more thoroughly later on.

To read as critical thinkers and writers, you must read to ensure that you

- understand the content and progression of the argument,
- can determine the rhetorical strategy (for example, the validity and significance of the claim), and
- are able to incorporate the author's views into your own.

PREREADING

You preread the text to determine its central purpose and approach. You may do this at the beginning of the term when, standing in line to purchase your textbook, you peruse the table of contents and the introductions to each of the chapters. You also preread when you read the topic sentences of the paragraphs in the introduction.

To preread an article or chapter from a work of nonfiction, you can rely on the structure that writers in the Western tradition have used for centuries and handed down to the modern college composition course:

- Introduction
- Thesis statement

- Topic sentences

- Transitional paragraphs

- Conclusion

Remember that the purpose of prereading is not to understand the whole piece but to identify the key points of the piece so that when you do read it in its entirety, you already have a clear sense of its framework.

After reading the introduction in full, read the topic sentences of the body paragraphs. These tend to be in one of three spots: first, last, or second. Topic sentences most frequently appear as the first sentences of the paragraphs, just where you have been taught to put them. But they also may occur as the last sentence in the paragraph when the writer has organized the content of the paragraph by presenting his or her evidence before the claim. And the topic sentence sometimes is the second sentence of the paragraph (the third most frequent position) when the first sentence is transitional, linking the paragraph before to the one that follows. In these cases, you will read both the transitional sentences and the topic sentences. You may need to read a bit of the article or essay to gain a sense of the writer's style—that is, where he or she tends to position the topic sentence.

Here is an example of a paragraph in which the topic sentence appears at the very end, a technique that this particular author, Carl Sagan, uses quite commonly in his writing. This selection is from Sagan's *The Demon-Haunted World: Science as a Candle in the Dark* (1995):

> What do we actually see when we look up at the Moon with the naked eye? We make out a configuration of irregular bright and dark markings—not a close representation of any familiar object. But, almost irresistibly, our eyes connect the markings, emphasizing some, ignoring others. We seek a pattern, and we find one. In world myth and folklore, many images are seen: a woman weaving, stands of laurel trees, an elephant jumping off a cliff, a girl with a basket on her back, a rabbit, . . . a woman pounding tapa cloth, a four-eyed jaguar. People of one culture have trouble understanding how such bizarre things could be seen by the people of another.

The pattern Sagan uses in this paragraph is this: He opens with a question, gives a string of examples to illustrate the basis of the question, and then answers the question, that is, posits the topic sentence. Such rhetorical patterning provides a coherence that enables readers to follow the strands of a complex discussion.

The final step in prereading is paying close attention to the concluding paragraph or paragraphs of the argument. Writers often summarize their main points here. They may also point out implications of the ideas or perhaps let readers know what steps they should take. To return to the chapter from *The Demon-Haunted World* that focuses on the difficulty of observing nature objectively, we arrive at Sagan's conclusion:

> By and large, scientists' minds are open when exploring new worlds. If we [scientists] knew beforehand what we'd find, it would be unnecessary to go [there]. In future missions to Mars or to the other fascinating worlds in our neck of the cosmic woods, surprises—even some of mythic proportions—are possible, maybe even likely. But we humans have a talent for deceiving ourselves. Skepticism must be a component of the

explorer's toolkit, or we will lose our way. There are wonders enough out there without our inventing any.

Sagan not only stresses his central idea about the need to maintain objectivity in the search for truth, but also assures us that the search for truth will reward us with discoveries every bit as wondrous as anything we could concoct.

By following a pattern of prereading, you may not yet fully understand the text, but at this stage you are just trying to provide yourself with an overview. You are also giving yourself a sense of how much energy you will need to invest before reading the piece fully.

SKIM-READING

At this stage, read the article in full, including the parts you have preread. But read swiftly, keeping alert for the key words in each sentence. To skim well, take advantage of your peripheral vision: You do not have to look directly at a word to see it; your eyes notice it just by looking in its general vicinity. Also, you already have an idea of the general parts of the article, and you are fleshing out those generalizations via the specifics that the writer provides. This enables you to grasp more readily the writer's logical progression of ideas and use of evidence.

By the time you reach the conclusion, you should feel more comfortable with whatever the author is summarizing or asking readers to do.

When skimming a page with visuals, return to the visual after skimming the text. First look for connections between the text and the visual; then, look for points of comparison and contrasts within the visual itself—for example, in a multiple-bar graph that shows changes in use of coal versus oil for heating in three different decades in the United States (represented by three different-colored bars), you want to notice the degree of difference between coal and oil, and whether such a difference is significant in arguing, say, that the United States has been doing a good job in becoming less oil-dependent from one decade to the next.

IN-DEPTH READING

The previewing strategies detail methods that you can follow if you wish to locate specific, brief information or to quickly scope out the gist of a piece. As a writer of arguments, you read for other reasons as well:

- **Summarizing** to demonstrate an ability and willingness to present another's ideas in a fair, unbiased way (see Chapter 5)

- **Analyzing** the structure of the piece to understand precisely the logic the writer uses, to determine whether the writer omits some important causal or temporal element, or whether the writer fairly and accurately represents all major viewpoints regarding the issue

- **Assessing** the strengths and weaknesses of the argument and determining the extent to which the writer's position influences your own

- *Annotating* in the margins to maintain an ongoing critical-response dialogue with the author as you are reading

POSTREADING

You follow the full reading with a postreading. Essentially, you read the same parts of the piece that you read for the preread. The purpose of a postread is to reinforce the framework of the whole in your mind and to distinguish between details and main points of a piece. In a postread, you cement in your mind the structure and logic of the piece by going back over it and reviewing its contents. During the postread, follow these steps:

1. Ask yourself, "What is the most important thing I learned from this piece, and where is it most clearly expressed?" At this stage, not any earlier, you begin to mark the text. Highlight this passage with a marker and make a marginal note briefly summarizing the passage in your own words. Summarizing helps you reinforce what you have read.

2. Now ask, "What evidence does the author use that supports the claim most convincingly?" Highlight and annotate this passage as well.

3. Finally, ask, "What concluding insight does the author leave me with?" Again, highlight and then annotate this segment of text in your own words.

Once you get into the habit of previewing, in-depth reading, and postreading articles and essays, you will find it an efficient and satisfying process.

THE IMPORTANCE OF OPEN-MINDEDNESS WHEN READING

One of the most important attributes that an education affords, along with self-discipline and attentiveness, is open-mindedness—the willingness to suspend judgment until one considers as many differing viewpoints as possible.

Learning to be truly open-minded takes effort. Everyone has deeply rooted beliefs, some of which even border on superstition. When these beliefs are challenged for whatever reasons, no matter how logical the reasons offered are, we resist—sometimes against our own better judgment. Beliefs often operate outside the realm of intellectual control and are entwined with our values and emotions. If, for example, someone in your family earns his or her livelihood in the Pacific Northwest logging industry, you may find it difficult to sympathize with environmentalists who advocate putting an end to logging in that region, even though a part of you wishes to preserve any species threatened with extinction due to continued deforestation.

Being predisposed toward a certain viewpoint is to be expected. Rare is the individual who goes through life with a neutral attitude toward all controversial issues. But one can be predisposed toward a certain view or value system and still be open-minded. For example, you might be highly skeptical of the existence of extraterrestrial creatures yet be willing to suspend that skepticism to give a writer a fair chance at trying to change your mind. Your willingness to be open-minded may increase, of course, if the author is a scientist or if the body of evidence presented has been shared with the entire scientific community for independent evaluations.

Sometimes we feel defensive when a long-held conviction is suddenly challenged. We may wish to guard the sanctity of that conviction so jealously that we may delude ourselves into thinking that we're being open-minded when we're not. When Galileo made his astronomical discoveries of the lunar craters and the moons of Jupiter known in 1610, he was promptly accused of heresy. We may think, from our enlightened perspective at the dawn of the twenty-first century, that the church was narrow-minded and intolerant, neglecting to realize that at the dawn of the seventeenth century, modern science had not yet come into being. Most people's conception of "the heavens" was literally that: The night sky was a window to Heaven. And celestial (that is, heavenly) objects like planets, stars, and the moon all occupied divine niches in that Heaven; they were called the *crystal spheres*. Galileo's modest telescopic observations revolutionized our conception of the universe, but it did not happen overnight, particularly because Galileo recanted his "heresy"—or, rather, was persuaded to recant by the threat of execution. We know that Galileo never wavered in his convictions because, even while under house arrest, he continued to write about his discoveries.

The moral of Galileo's story, and the stories of many other daring thinkers throughout history, is that open-mindedness is precious, despite its difficulties.

Recognizing
PATTERNS OF ORGANIZATION

By recognizing the structure of a reading passage, you will be able to recognize the organization that the author intends. In turn, you can use the pattern of organization to see the relationship between key ideas and to move the information from your working memory to your long-term memory and then retrieve and learn it most effectively.

Organizational patterns are important for a reader to recognize because they reveal how an author arranges the information in the passage, which allows you, the reader, to understand the "skeleton" of the piece of writing—the bones that support the "flesh" of the reading. To continue with this metaphor, the "skeleton" is how the author arranges ideas as a whole—the pattern of organization the author has used. The "flesh" is all the details that the author includes to elaborate on and explain more about his or her topic. You want to see the skeleton of the reading, so you can understand and remember what the author is trying to communicate about the topic. If you do not have much background knowledge about the topic of the reading, the pattern of organization will help you because if you can follow the author's train of thought more effectively, you will have less difficulty comprehending the reading and you can focus on the key points. Figure 2.1 summarizes the benefits of recognizing organizational patterns.

This "skeleton" is known by several names: *organizational patterns, patterns of organization, author's writing patterns, rhetorical modes,* and *writing structure,* depending on the class in which the topic is discussed. In reading classes, *patterns of organization* is the most common name.

Patterns of organization, like a topic, can apply to a whole reading (its structure), a subsection of a reading, or a paragraph. Patterns of organization can also help you see the relationships between ideas in sentences. There are four ways you can see a pattern of organization, from the larger to the smaller perspective, as you can see in Figure 2.2. Think of the bottom layer (the whole reading) as the most general, overall pattern. The top layer (between and among sentences) is the most detailed, or specific pattern.

Patterns of organization function to provide a structure to a reading, a subsection, a paragraph, or the interrelationship between ideas and sentences in a paragraph. Patterns of organization also help you determine the main details in a passage that support the main point. These main details within a reading are called **supporting details** because they support the author's most important point about the topic. These supporting details are arranged in the reading according to the pattern of organization. Stop and think about how logical this is: An author writes a passage about the causes of stress—this is the topic. What would be the main points the author would logically discuss? The author would discuss a series of causes or reasons that lead to stress. These causes or reasons are the major points that support the topic—the supporting details.

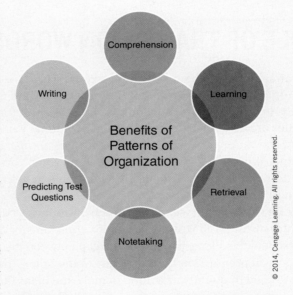

FIGURE 2.1 Learning How to Recognize Patterns of Organization in a Reading Will Help You in Many Ways

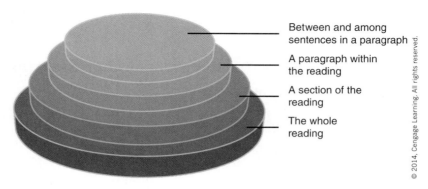

Between and among
sentences in a paragraph

A paragraph within
the reading

A section of the
reading

The whole
reading

FIGURE 2.2 Four Ways You Can See a Pattern of Organization

THE ROLE OF TRANSITION WORDS

What do you already know about transition words? They are not complicated words. You may not have considered before, however, how important they are to notice. For example, you look at transition words in order to figure out context clues. Many of the words to watch out for when you use context clues are also the clues used in organizational patterns. For example, consider these transition words for antonym or contrast context clues: *unlike, instead, but, however, on the other hand, rather,* and *conversely.* These words are helpful when you are trying to find out the meaning of a word you don't know. They also play the same role in helping you to understand the pattern of organization in a reading.

Transitions are words or phrases writers use to introduce a pattern of organization in the writing and between ideas within the writing. The prefix *trans-* means "across." When you make a *transi-*tion from high school to college, you bridge the gap between the two levels. *Transi*tion words, <u>then</u>, link ideas in a logical progression from one idea to the other. These words will look familiar to you <u>because</u> they are used frequently in writing to make the ideas flow together and to indicate important points. Transition words or phrases are <u>also</u> called signal words or phrases <u>because</u> they signal how the author is arranging ideas. Later, you will find lists of transition words for each type of pattern of organization.

<u>First</u>, transition words function to show the relationships within a sentence, a paragraph, a subsection, or an entire reading. Transition words <u>also</u> introduce supporting details. <u>In addition</u>, these words help ideas flow more smoothly in writing. <u>Furthermore</u>, transition words improve understanding between connected thoughts and provide and indicate a logical organization between the ideas in a reading. <u>In short</u>, they function to "lubricate" the parts of a reading to make them work smoothly together. <u>As a result</u>, your understanding of these ideas proceeds smoothly in your mind while you are reading.

SUPPORTING DETAILS

In the paragraphs about transition words and phrases, several main points were made, signaled by transition words and phrases. You could ask the question "What is the role of transition words?" and this would be your list of answers:

1. They show the relationships within a sentence, within a paragraph, or within a whole reading.

2. They introduce supporting details.

3. They help ideas flow more smoothly in writing.

4. They improve understanding between connected thoughts and indicate a logical organization between the ideas in a reading.

5. They facilitate the comprehension of these ideas to connect more smoothly in your mind while reading.

Points 1 through 5 are **supporting details** that back up the overall point of the paragraph about the topic—the role of transition words. Did you notice the underlined words in the above paragraphs? These are transition words that introduce the supporting details. Go back to these passages and notice how these words in the paragraphs help to make the ideas easier to follow. You would still be able to understand the two paragraphs without the transition words, but they make the ideas flow better, don't they? If so, the transition words are accomplishing their job. Their job, then, is to make the connections between supporting details flow smoothly.

Major and Minor Details

Supporting details can be classified as either major details or minor details. **Major details** are the main points to support the overall point in the reading. **Minor details** are more specific points that support the major points, usually by providing examples of the major details.

Read the paragraph below and underline the transition words as you read.

Combating Stress

There are several ways to minimize stress in your life. First, make exercise a regular habit at least three times per week. Exercise releases endorphins that improve mood. Exercise also improves vascular health and overall fitness. Another good preventative measure is taking stock of the internal stressors you can control. Use meditation techniques when overwhelmed and make sure to get sufficient rest to alleviate internal negative talk. Last, make sure to take time out of your busy schedule to do things that you enjoy. When stress builds up, time with family or friends can help reduce its effects. Similarly, regularly pursuing hobbies and other pleasurable interests serves to diminish the buildup of everyday stresses and strains.

Which of the sentences are major details? Which of the sentences are minor details? There are three major details, each indicated by a transition (*first, another,* and *last*). The first major detail is followed by two minor details that back it up. The second major detail is followed by one minor detail that supports it. The third major detail is followed by two minor details that provide examples. This is how the paragraph would look if the major and minor details were separated.

TOPIC . . . . COMBATING STRESS

Main Point . . . . There are several ways to minimize stress in your life.

   1st Major Detail . . . . <u>First</u>, make exercise a regular habit at least three times per week.

      1st Minor Detail . . . . Exercise releases endorphins that improve mood.

      2nd Minor Detail . . . . Exercise <u>also</u> improves vascular health and overall fitness.

   2nd Major Detail . . . . <u>Another</u> good preventative measure is taking stock of the internal stressors you can control.

      Minor Detail . . . . Use meditation techniques when overwhelmed and make sure to get sufficient rest to alleviate internal negative talk.

   3rd Major Detail . . . . <u>Last</u>, make sure to take time out of your busy schedule to do things that you enjoy.

      1st Minor Detail . . . . When stress builds up, time with family or friends can help reduce its effects.

      2nd Minor Detail . . . . <u>Similarly</u>, regularly pursuing hobbies and other pleasurable interests serves to diminish the buildup of everyday stresses and strains.

See how the minor details function to provide further information about the major details? The major details, in turn, provide support for the topic of the paragraph (Figure 2.3). Supporting details provide information to support the overall topic (Figure 2.4).

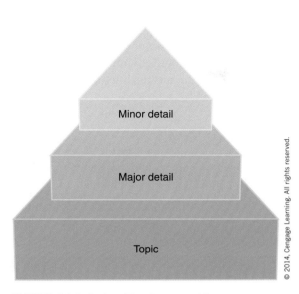

FIGURE 2.3 Relationships Between Ideas

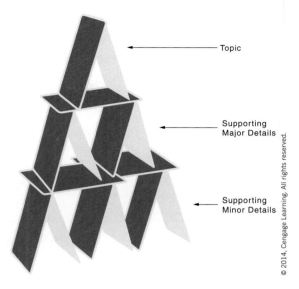

FIGURE 2.4 Support Details Work to Support the Topic

CATEGORIES OF ORGANIZATIONAL PATTERNS

There are three main categories of organizational patterns as shown in Table 2.1: patterns that list, patterns that explain, and patterns that analyze.

TABLE 2.1 Categories of Organizational Patterns

PATTERNS THAT LIST	PATTERNS THAT EXPLAIN	PATTERNS THAT ANALYZE
Random order list • Simple listing **Specific order list** • Order of importance • Chronological order • Sequence or process order • Spatial (or place) order	• Example/illustration or clarification • Definition and example • Description	• Division/classification • Cause and/or effect • Problem and/or solution • Compare and/or contrast

Patterns That List

Patterns that list include simple listing (or just list), order of importance, chronological order, sequence or process order, and spatial or place order. All of these patterns, except for simple listing, include items that must be in a certain order to convey the meaning that the author intends. In Table 2.2, review the transition words that indicate patterns that list.

TABLE 2.2 Transitions That Indicate Patterns That List

PATTERN OF ORGANIZATION	TRANSITIONS
Random Order	
Simple listing	Also, another, in addition, first, second, third, for example; punctuation (bullets, dashes); numbers (1, 2, 3); letters (a, b, c)
Specific Order	
Order of importance	Most important, finally, primarily
Chronological order	First, second, third, next, then, after, later, dates, after, afterward
Sequence or process order	First, second, next, then, after, later, finally, initially, follows, followed by, the first stage, stages, steps, the final step
Spatial (or place) order	To the left, to the right, above, below, next to, around, opposite, ahead, north, south, east, west, continuing from, near, beside, further, originate, endpoint

SIMPLE LISTING

Simple listing means that the items the author lists can be arranged in any order and still make sense. Every piece of writing is a list of something, whether causes, effects, similarities, differences, or steps in a process. So be careful not to oversimplify and see everything as a simple list. Always eliminate the other patterns of organization before you choose simple listing as the organizational pattern. Simple listing should always be your last choice, after you have eliminated all the other possibilities.

> **Example:** Memory tricks, <u>such as</u> mnemonic devices, word association, and visualization are used for studying information and learning it.

Note that these three memory tricks can be in any order and still make sense because the order does not change the meaning of the sentence. The signal phrase *such as* indicates a list of examples.

Next you'll read a passage from the National Institute on Alcohol Abuse and Alcoholism Web site targeted to parents. Read the passage, paying attention to the transition words that signal a supporting detail. Then, look at the visual that reflects how the ideas connect with one another.

Tips for Talking with Your Teen

Developing open, trusting communication between you and your child is essential to helping him or her avoid alcohol use. If your child feels comfortable talking openly with you, you'll have a greater chance of guiding him or her toward healthy decision-making. Some ways to begin:

- Encourage conversation. Encourage your child to talk about whatever interests him or her. Listen without interruption and give your child a chance to teach you something new. Your active listening to your child's enthusiasms paves the way for conversations about topics that concern you.
- Ask open-ended questions. Encourage your teen to tell you how he or she thinks and feels about the issue you're discussing. Avoid questions that have a simple "yes" or "no" answer.
- Control your emotions. If you hear something you don't like, try not to respond with anger. Instead, take a few deep breaths and acknowledge your feelings in a constructive way.
- Make every conversation a "win-win" experience. Don't lecture or try to "score points" on your teen by showing how he or she is wrong. If you show respect for your child's viewpoint, he or she will be more likely to listen to and respect yours.

SOURCE: From Make a Difference: Talk to Your Child About Alcohol, NIAAA website (National Institute on Alcohol Abuse and Alcoholism) NIH Publication No. 06-4314 Revised 2006, http://www.collegedrinkingprevention.gov/OtherAlcoholInformation/makeDifference.aspx#TeensWorld

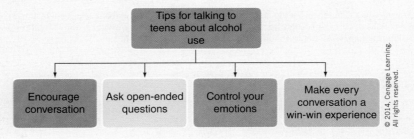

There are four tips for talking with your teen about alcohol use. These tips are indicated by bullet points. Ask yourself: Do these four techniques have to be in a specific order to make sense? These tips are in a random order—the tips could be rearranged and the meaning and intent of the passage would remain uncompromised. The pattern of organization, then, is simple listing.

ORDER OF IMPORTANCE

Order of importance (or emphatic order) means the items in the list need to be in a specific order to convey the author's point. Usually, the last point is the most important reason for, or example of, the author's main point.

Example: To remember learned information accurately, use memory tricks such as mnemonic devices, word association, visualization, and, <u>most importantly</u>, repetition.

The three memory tricks of using mnemonic devices, word association, and visualization can be in any order and still make sense, but the last item—repetition—is put at the end of the sentence because it is the most important point.

Here is a passage in order of importance from the National Institute on Alcohol Abuse and Alcoholism Web site on alcohol poisoning.

What Can Happen to Someone with Alcohol Poisoning That Goes Untreated?

- Victim chokes on his or her own vomit.
- Breathing slows, becomes irregular, or stops.
- Heart beats irregularly or stops.
- Hypothermia (low body temperature).
- Hypoglycemia (too little blood sugar) leads to seizures.
- Untreated severe dehydration from vomiting can cause seizures, permanent brain damage, or death.

Even if the victim lives, an alcohol overdose can lead to irreversible brain damage. Rapid binge drinking (which often happens on a bet or a dare) is especially dangerous because the victim can ingest a fatal dose before becoming unconscious.

Don't be afraid to seek medical help for a friend who has had too much to drink. Don't worry that your friend may become angry or embarrassed—remember, you cared enough to help. Always be safe, not sorry.

SOURCE: From Make a Difference: Talk to Your Child About Alcohol, NIAAA website (National Institute on Alcohol Abuse and Alcoholism) NIH Publication No. 06-4314 Revised 2006, http://www.collegedrinkingprevention.gov/OtherAlcoholInformation/factsAboutAlcoholPoisoning.aspx

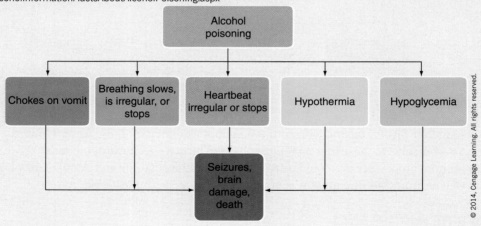

When you read the six bulleted points, which are the major supporting details, you can see that the worst outcome is placed last. In the visual, the first five points could be in another order and still make sense. For example, you could rank irregular heartbeat as worse than hypothermia. However, it is clear that seizures, permanent brain damage, or death are the most horrific possibilities. This outcome is the worst case scenario and, thus, is put last to make a point or emphasize the severity.

CHRONOLOGICAL ORDER

Chronological order (or time order) shows how something unfolds over time. The items in the list need to be in this order to make sense, such as events in history that occur over time.

> **Example:** First, take thorough notes during class. Then, review class notes immediately after class. Afterwards, as soon as you have a chance, rewrite your notes to aid in learning the main points.

Notice how you are advised to review notes first, right after class, and then to rewrite the notes later in the day. These events must occur in this order because you cannot review and rewrite your notes until you have actually taken the notes.

Here is a passage on the topic of heroin withdrawal. What is the timeline for withdrawal?

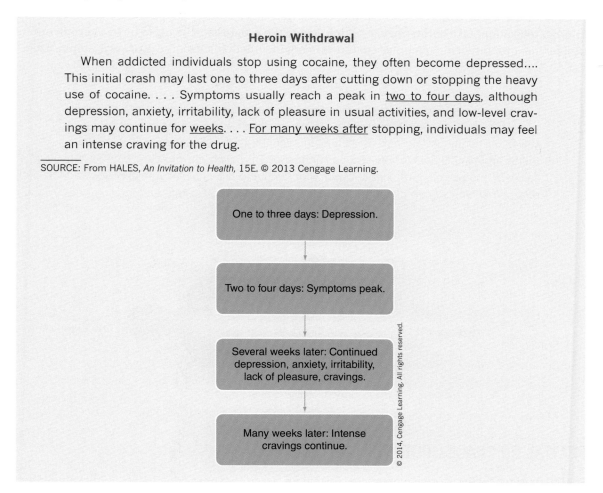

Heroin Withdrawal

When addicted individuals stop using cocaine, they often become depressed.... This initial crash may last one to three days after cutting down or stopping the heavy use of cocaine. . . . Symptoms usually reach a peak in two to four days, although depression, anxiety, irritability, lack of pleasure in usual activities, and low-level cravings may continue for weeks. . . . For many weeks after stopping, individuals may feel an intense craving for the drug.

SOURCE: From HALES, *An Invitation to Health,* 15E. © 2013 Cengage Learning.

One to three days: Depression.

Two to four days: Symptoms peak.

Several weeks later: Continued depression, anxiety, irritability, lack of pleasure, cravings.

Many weeks later: Intense cravings continue.

In this passage, the withdrawal symptoms are in an order according to time. Similarly, the information in the visual has to be in that order to make sense: it is a progression of symptoms. There are four major supporting details, characterized by the timeline and associated symptoms.

SEQUENCE OR PROCESS ORDER

Sequence or **process order**, like chronological order, indicates that certain steps need to be followed in a specific order for the result to make sense, such as the steps in a recipe or stages of growth or development. The difference between chronological order and sequence or process order is the subject matter. In sequence or process order, the author uses stages or steps rather than a clear timeline in hours, weeks, or days.

> **Example:** <u>Initially</u>, information goes into the sensory memory and, if accepted, information <u>then</u> is processed in the short-term memory. <u>Next</u>, information is stored in the long-term memory and can be learned if <u>followed by</u> repetitive study.

In this example, the steps or parts of the memory system are a process or must be in sequence to make sense. Following is a brief reading about the stages or steps in a process to relieve stress through relaxation. Like chronological or time order, the progression needs to be in a certain order. Unlike time order, specific references to time are not included. Instead, the process is emphasized.

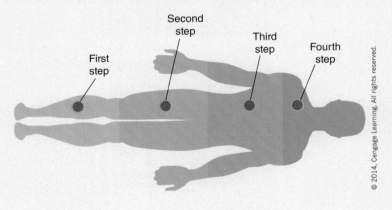

Relaxation is a powerful technique for reducing stress. To relax your body, lie on your back, breathe deeply and do the following exercise. <u>First</u>, tighten your toes and calves as tightly as you can, hold for ten seconds and relax. <u>Second</u>, tighten your thighs and hands, hold for ten seconds and relax. <u>Third</u>, tighten your core, hold for ten seconds and relax. <u>Fourth</u>, tighten your shoulders and face, hold for ten seconds and relax. When you've completed this exercise, your body will feel light and tension free.

SPATIAL OR PLACE ORDER

Spatial or **place order** shows an organized format for describing or making points about something, usually a three-dimensional space, such as a place. Descriptions may be organized from front to back, left to right, north to south, or bottom to top. This organization allows the points to be made in a coherent, structured fashion.

Example: <u>Continuing from</u> the brain stem at the back of the brain's structure and <u>near</u> the base of the spinal cord is the amygdala.

The organization of the information leads the reader to visualize the structure of the brain, from the brain stem at the back, moving upward.

Here is a map from BBC News showing the flow of opium and heroin to the United Kingdom.

Flow of Heroin to UK

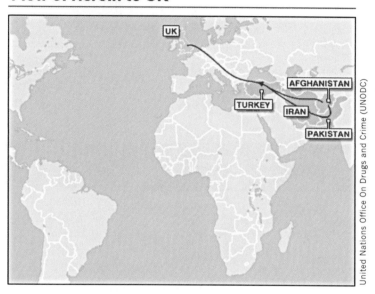

United Nations Office On Drugs and Crime (UNODC)

Heroin Trafficking into the United Kingdom

Here is a passage that illustrates the spatial order conveyed in the map.

The majority of the opium consumed in Western Europe and the world follows a typical trade route from origination to consumption. Most opiates <u>originate</u> in Afghanistan and make their way to Pakistan to the <u>south</u>. Then the drugs move to Iran to the <u>west</u>. Moved <u>farther west</u>, the drugs reach Turkey. At this point, the drugs are exported west over Europe and into the United Kingdom. In the United Kingdom the opiates are consumed or <u>further</u> shipped for distribution worldwide.

Notice how geographical connections are vital to the explanation of the map of the trade route. There are five major supporting details, arranged in order, according to the main geographical steps in the movement of opium from Afghanistan to the United Kingdom: Afghanistan to Pakistan to Iran to Turkey to the United Kingdom.

QUICK TIPS WHEN IS A LIST A LIST?

When you encounter a list of something, ask yourself, Do the items in the list need to be in a certain order to make sense? (See Figure 2.5.) If so, the pattern is order of importance, chronological order, sequence or process order, or spatial order. If not, the pattern is simple listing.

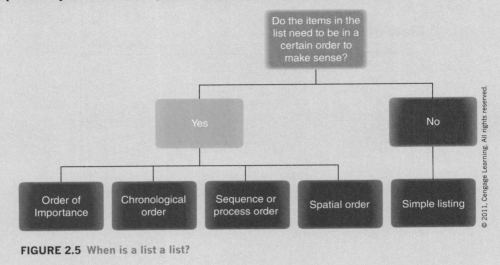

FIGURE 2.5 When is a list a list?

On Your Own PATTERNS THAT LIST

Identify the type of listing pattern used in each of the following paragraphs.

1.   Students often suffer from stress, especially during exams. However, there are several easy tips to alleviate the pressure and help. One useful tip is to learn and practice relaxation tips. Also be aware of the triggers for stress that alert you to taking action. If you can know yourself well enough to see the approaching stress response, you may be able to head off a full-blown stress meltdown. Furthermore, practice imagining a stressful situation when you are not stressed to strengthen your coping mechanisms and contemplate a stress-reducing solution.

2. Neurons

Your brain contains about 100 billion neurons—nerve cells that work nonstop to send and receive messages. Within a neuron, messages travel from the cell body down the axon to the axon terminal in the form of electrical impulses. From there, the message is sent to other neurons with the help of neurotransmitters.

—National Institute on Drug Abuse http://teens.drugabuse.gov/facts/facts_brain1.php

3.   Heroin is becoming more popular with teens and young adults than it has been in years. The use of this drug consists of the risk of drowsiness, slowed breathing, increased tolerance for the drug, physical dependence, psychological craving, and, worst of all, death.

4.   After the initial effects, abusers usually will be drowsy for several hours. Mental function is clouded by heroin's effect on the central nervous system. Cardiac function slows. Breathing is also severely slowed, sometimes to the point of death. Heroin overdose is a particular risk on the street, where the amount and purity of the drug cannot be accurately known.

—National Institute on Drug Abuse http://www.drugabuse.gov/publications/research-reports/
heroin-abuse-addiction/what-are-immediate-short-term-effects-heroin-use

5.   How Widespread Is Heroin Abuse?
    According to the Monitoring the Future survey, there was little change between 2008 and 2009 in the proportion of 8th- and 12th-grade students reporting lifetime, past-year, and past-month use of heroin. There also were no significant changes in past-year and past-month use among 10th-graders; however, lifetime use increased significantly among this age group, from 1.2 percent to 1.5 percent. Survey measures indicate that injection use rose significantly among this population at the same time.

HEROIN USE BY STUDENTS, 2009: MONITORING THE FUTURE SURVEY			
	8TH GRADE	10TH GRADE	12TH GRADE
Lifetime	1.3%	1.5%	1.2%
Past Year	0.7	0.9	0.7
Past Month	0.4	0.4	0.4

—National Institute on Drug Abuse http://www.drugabuse.gov/publications/infofacts/heroin

Patterns That Explain

Patterns that explain include example/illustration or clarification, definition and example, and description. These patterns allow an author to make a point, and then elaborate on or further explain that point to make sure the reader understands. These patterns are common in textbook readings because often a concept is introduced or a definition is stated, and then the next paragraph provides additional clarification of the concept or definition. In Table 2.3, review the signal words that indicate patterns that explain.

TABLE 2.3 Transitions That Indicate Patterns That Explain

PATTERN OF ORGANIZATION	TRANSITIONS AND TEXTUAL CLUES
Example/Illustration or Clarification	For example, to illustrate, to clarify, for instance, in other words, that is to say, to put it another way
Definition and Example	Punctuation following a boldfaced term (dash, comma, colon, parentheses), italics of term, is defined as, is known as, means, is
Description	Adjectives that describe (nice, colorful, misty, gloomy) to support the dominant impression (feeling) about the topic or describe or characterize and create a visual image.

EXAMPLE/ILLUSTRATION

Example/illustration or **clarification** occurs when an author makes a point—usually a complex point—and uses the rest of the paragraph to make sure the reader sees the importance of the point.

This organizational pattern is used most often in longer passages where an author makes a point in a paragraph, and then uses the following paragraph(s) to elaborate on and clarify the first point.

> **Example**: Spaced practice aids in learning. <u>For example</u>, imagine pockets of time during your day that could be used for study. You may find 10 minutes between classes to review vocabulary, or you may use the bus ride to or from school to preview a chapter.

The point about spaced practice is made, and then examples of using this time are provided. Here is another example of an example/illustration or clarification pattern of organization.

> Data from national and state surveys suggest that inhalant abuse is most common among 7th- through 9th-graders. <u>For example</u>, in the Monitoring the Future Study, an annual NIDA-supported survey of the nation's secondary school students, 8th-graders regularly report the highest rate of current, past-year, and lifetime inhalant abuse compared to 10th- and 12th-graders.

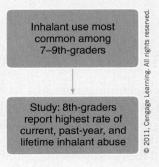

In this excerpt, the author states the point about the age group responsible for most inhalant use, and then gives a specific example to clarify and illustrate the concept. Notice how the phrase *for example* signals that an illustration or clarification of a previous point will be made. There is one major detail to back up the overall point about inhalant use among teenagers. This major detail is the findings reported in the NIDA study.

DEFINITION AND EXAMPLE

Definition (and **example**) is commonly used in concept-dense text, or writing with many complicated ideas. This pattern is useful for stating a concept or the meaning of a word and then providing examples to further explain the concept. The key term itself is often in special print, such as boldface, italics, or color. Definition patterns of organization always contain a definition vocabulary context clue.

> **Example:** To **preview** a reading <u>is</u> to assess the topic, structure, and overall point of a reading before reading the passage through in its entirety. <u>For example</u>, instead of reading from the first paragraph to the end, the reader previews the reading to determine important information first.

The term or concept *preview* is defined, and then an explanation of what previewing consists of is provided. Look at another excerpt.

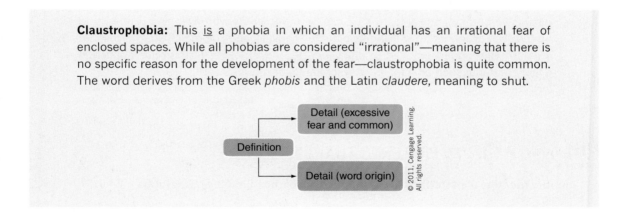

> **Claustrophobia:** This <u>is</u> a phobia in which an individual has an irrational fear of enclosed spaces. While all phobias are considered "irrational"—meaning that there is no specific reason for the development of the fear—claustrophobia is quite common. The word derives from the Greek *phobis* and the Latin *claudere*, meaning to shut.

Notice in the reading how the term to be defined (*claustrophobia*) is in bold print followed by a colon (:). This definition is then followed by additional information to explain the term. In the visual, the definition is indicated as the main piece of information on the left; the supporting details are leading from it on the right. There are two supporting details to back up the definition.

DESCRIPTION

Description is used when an author describes a person, place, or thing. With this pattern, the author uses sensory details to paint for the reader a mental picture of the subject to create a dominant impression. A sensory detail is a description that relates to one of the five senses: smell, sight, hearing, taste, touch. A dominant impression, the emotional mood or feeling of the passage, is created through the use of sensory details. If there are many adjectives (words that describe a person, place, or thing) that describe the topic of the passage, this would indicate description.

Example: Every year, after the lottery, Mr. Summers began talking again about a new box, but every year the subject was allowed to fade off without anything being done. The black box grew <u>shabbier</u> each year: by now it was <u>no longer completely black</u> but <u>splintered badly</u> along one side to show the original wood color, and in some places <u>faded or stained</u>.

—From "The Lottery" from *The Lottery* by Shirley Jackson. Copyright © 1948, 1949 by Shirley Jackson. Copyright renewed 1976, 1977 by Laurence Hyman, Barry Hyman, Mrs. Sarah Webster and Mrs. Joanne Schnurer. Reprinted by permission of Farrar, Straus and Giroux, LLC and Penguin Books Ltd.

In this passage, the author describes an object: a black box. She creates a visual image in the reader's mind of the object. Notice the descriptive words that detail the box's appearance. The dominant impression you get of the box is that it's shabby and old and has been in use for a long time, generations perhaps. Two supporting details back up the dominant impression of the shabbiness of the box. These supporting details are that the box is splintered badly and that it is faded or stained.

Here is another descriptive passage. Notice all the adjectives and descriptive phrases in the passage that make the description of the drug vivid.

PCP is a <u>white crystalline powder</u> that is readily soluble in water or alcohol. It has a distinctive <u>bitter chemical taste</u>. PCP can be mixed easily with dyes and is often sold on the illicit drug market in a variety of <u>tablet, capsule, and colored powder forms</u> that are normally <u>snorted, smoked, or orally ingested</u>. For smoking, PCP is often applied to a leafy material such as mint, parsley, oregano, or marijuana.

—National Institute on Drug Abuse http://www.drugabuse.gov/publications/infofacts/ hallucinogens-lsd-peyote-psilocybin-pcp

On Your Own PATTERNS THAT EXPLAIN

Identify the type of patterns that explain in each of the following paragraphs.

1.   Prescription drug abuse is the use of a medication without a prescription, in a way other than as prescribed, or for the experience or feelings elicited. According to several national surveys, prescription medications, such as those used to treat pain, attention deficit disorders, and anxiety, are being abused at a rate second only to marijuana among illicit drug users. The consequences of this abuse have been steadily worsening, reflected in increased treatment admissions, emergency room visits, and overdose deaths.

—National Institute on Drug Abuse http://www.drugabuse.gov/publications/research-reports/ prescription-drugs/what-prescription-drug-abuse

2.   Those who see marijuana as a harmless or even beneficial substance criticize studies as providing an inaccurate or incomplete picture of marijuana's effects. They argue, for example, that the same dopamine receptors activated by marijuana and heroin are also activated by sex and chocolate—and that few people would call for the criminalization of those pleasures. Moreover, the correlation between early marijuana use and later use of "hard drugs" could be due more to the people with whom marijuana users become involved than to any property of the drug itself.

—From BERNSTEIN/PENNER/CLARKE-STEWART/ROY, *Psychology*, 7E. © 2006 Cengage Learning.

3.   Peyote: The top of the peyote cactus, also referred to as the crown, consists of disc-shaped buttons that are cut from the roots and dried. These buttons are generally chewed or soaked in water to produce an intoxicating liquid.

—National Institute on Drug Abuse http://www.drugabuse.gov/publications/infofacts/hallucinogens-lsd-peyote-psilocybin-pcp

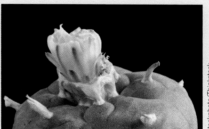
iStockphoto/Thinkstock

Patterns That Analyze

Patterns that analyze are division/classification, cause and effect, problem and solution, and comparison and contrast. Analysis is the act of looking at the parts of an entity and where they fit in to understand the big picture. Each of these patterns shows the relationship between two or more distinct features. In Table 2.4, review the signal words that indicate patterns that analyze.

TABLE 2.4 Transitions That Indicate Patterns That Analyze

PATTERN OF ORGANIZATION	TRANSITIONS
Division/Classification	Two (or more) types, groups, classified as, classes, category, kinds of, types of, characterized by
Cause	Is caused by, causes, for the reason, because, due to, being that, in that, inasmuch as, since, that is why
Effect	The effect is, consequently, as a result, results in, leads to, thus, as a consequence, hence, so, accordingly, therefore, for this reason
Problem and Solution	The problem is, can be solved by, the solution is
Comparison	Likewise, like, similar to, similarly, in the same way, equally, by the same token, in a like manner, comparable, in common
Contrast	However, but, in contrast, on the other hand, conversely, although, nevertheless, yet, while, whereas, still, though, otherwise, if not, neither . . . nor, some people, others

DIVISION AND CLASSIFICATION

Division/classification patterns simplify a difficult concept by breaking down the complex idea into manageable parts or categories. This type of pattern is common in college 100-level classes. Because introductory classes function largely to introduce you to the vocabulary of the discipline, patterns that provide terminology and put concepts into categories are common. Because classification involves introduction to the vocabulary of a discipline, this pattern also tends to contain definition clues. However, this pattern is different from definition and example patterns because the supporting details are specifically there to show the different categories or to divide a concept into different groups or types. Consider this passage where the author classifies, or divides, intermediate memory into two types.

> **Example:**   There are <u>two types</u> of intermediate memory processing: short-term and working memory.

Here is a passage that classifies phobias into different types. Notice that it begins with a definition of *phobia,* but it then goes on to classify phobias as one of two different types.

Types of Anxiety Disorders

Phobia

An intense, irrational fear of an object or situation that is not likely to be danger-ous <u>is called</u> a **phobia.** People who experience phobias usually realize that their fears are groundless, but that's not enough to make the anxiety go away. The continuing discomfort and avoidance of the object or event may greatly interfere with daily life.

Thousands of phobias have been described. . . . Phobias can be <u>classified</u> into specific, social, and agoraphobia <u>subtypes.</u>

SOURCE: From BERNSTEIN/PENNER/CLARKE-STEWART/ROY, *Psychology*, 7E. © 2006 Cengage Learning.

Phobia is defined as	The unrelenting fear of a situation, activity, or thing that causes one to want to avoid it

Social	Agoraphobia	Specific

Three supporting details back up the overall topic: What is a phobia? The three major details are the categories of phobias: specific, social, and agoraphobia. Notice how the word *phobia* is defined first. Definitions are often within classification patterns. This pattern is different from the definition pattern because the supporting details are specifically there to show the different categories of phobias.

CAUSE AND EFFECT

Cause and effect patterns show causes of a situation or phenomenon, or the effects or results of a situation or phenomenon to show the relationship between ideas. Some passages may show both causes and effects.

> **Example**: The human capacity for denial is boundless, and the <u>effects</u> of refusing to see the truth are overpowering.

The author provides a cause (self-denial) and the effect (being overpowered). A passage may explain both causes and effect, or one or the other.

Usually the focus of a passage is on either causes or effects. Notice the difference between the two in the following passages. The first passage explores the effects or consequences of college drinking, while the second example explores the causes of college drinking to excess.

A Snapshot of Annual High-Risk College Drinking Consequences

The <u>consequences</u> of excessive and underage drinking <u>affect</u> virtually all college campuses, college communities, and college students, whether they choose to drink or not.

- **Death:** 1,700 college students between the ages of 18 and 24 die each year from alcohol-related unintentional injuries, including motor vehicle crashes.

(Continued)

- **Injury:** 599,000 students between the ages of 18 and 24 are unintentionally injured under the influence of alcohol.

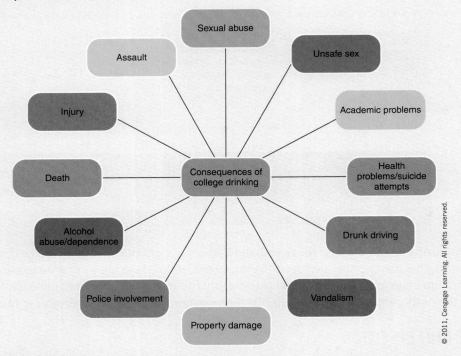

- **Assault:** More than 696,000 students between the ages of 18 and 24 are assaulted by another student who has been drinking.
- **Sexual Abuse:** More than 97,000 students between the ages of 18 and 24 are victims of alcohol-related sexual assault or date rape.
- **Unsafe Sex:** 400,000 students between the ages of 18 and 24 had unprotected sex and more than 100,000 students between the ages of 18 and 24 report having been too intoxicated to know if they consented to having sex.
- **Academic Problems:** About 25 percent of college students report academic consequences of their drinking including missing class, falling behind, doing poorly on exams or papers, and receiving lower grades overall.
- **Health Problems/Suicide Attempts:** More than 150,000 students develop an alcohol-related health problem and between 1.2 and 1.5 percent of students indicate that they tried to commit suicide within the past year due to drinking or drug use.
- **Drunk Driving:** 2.1 million students between the ages of 18 and 24 drove under the influence of alcohol last year.
- **Vandalism:** About 11 percent of college student drinkers report that they have damaged property while under the influence of alcohol.
- **Property Damage:** More than 25 percent of administrators from schools with relatively low drinking levels and over 50 percent from schools with high drinking

levels say their campuses have a "moderate" or "major" problem with alcohol-related property damage.

- **Police Involvement:** About 5 percent of 4-year college students are involved with the police or campus security as a result of their drinking and an estimated 110,000 students between the ages of 18 and 24 are arrested for an alcohol-related violation such as public drunkenness or driving under the influence.

- **Alcohol Abuse and Dependence:** 31 percent of college students met criteria for a diagnosis of alcohol abuse and 6 percent for a diagnosis of alcohol dependence in the past 12 months, according to questionnaire-based self-reports about their drinking.

It is very clear from the visual depiction of the passage that there are 12 major supporting details that back up the topic of consequences of college drinking. The supporting details are all effects of alcohol use. In the next excerpt, notice how the passage and graphic explore the *causes* of widespread college drinking.

Student Body as a Whole: The key to <u>affecting</u> the behavior of the general student population is to address the <u>factors</u> that encourage high-risk drinking. They include:

- Widespread availability of alcoholic beverages to underage and intoxicated students;

- Aggressive social and commercial promotion of alcohol;

- Large amounts of unstructured student time;

- Inconsistent publicity and enforcement of laws and campus policies; and

- Student perceptions of heavy alcohol use as the norm.

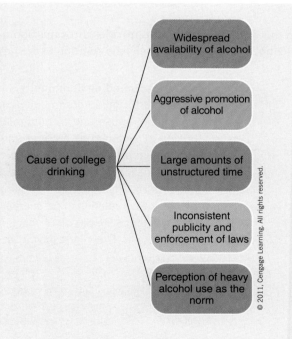

From 3-in-1 framework, from "College Drinking—Changing the Culture, NIAAA website (National Institute on Alcohol Abuse and Alcoholism) http://www.collegedrinkingprevention.gov/StatsSummaries/3inone.aspx

In this passage, there are five causes or influences that result in high-risk college drinking; these five factors lead to or promote the outcome of excessive drinking behaviors.

A specific type of cause and effect pattern is **problem and solution.** This subtype focuses on problems that lead to solutions, or a particular problem that has one or more solutions. Consider the passage on the next page.

What Should I Do If I Suspect
Someone Has Alcohol Poisoning?

- Know the danger signals.
- Do not wait for all symptoms to be present.
- Be aware that a person who has passed out may die.
- If there is any suspicion of an alcohol overdose, call 911 for help. Don't try to guess the level of drunkenness.

From from College drinking—changing the culture, NIAAA website (National Institute on Alcohol Abuse and Alcoholism) http://www.collegedrinkingprevention.gov/OtherAlcoholInformation/factsAboutAlcoholPoisoning.aspx#WhatHappens

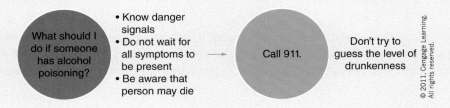

In this example, the author provides three tips about what a person should do if someone might have alcohol poisoning. Ultimately, the solution to the problem is to call for help.

College and the Surrounding Community: Mutually reinforcing interventions between the college and surrounding community can change the broader environment and help reduce alcohol abuse and alcohol-related <u>problems</u> over the long term. When college drinking is reframed as a community as well as a college <u>problem</u>, campus and community leaders are more likely to come together to address it comprehensively. The joint activities that typically result help produce policy and enforcement reforms that, in turn, affect the total drinking environment. Campus and community alliances also improve relationships overall and enable key groups such as student affairs offices, residence life directors, local police, retail alcohol outlets, and the court system to work cooperatively in resolving issues involving students.

—From "College Drinking—Changing the Culture, NIAAA website (National Institute on Alcohol Abuse and Alcoholism) http://www.collegedrinkingprevention.gov/StatsSummaries/3inone.aspx

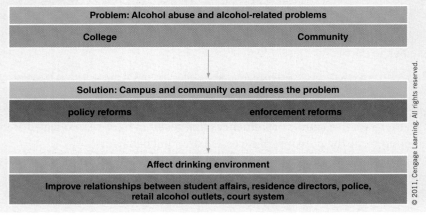

In the previous example, the problem is college drinking, and the solution to the problem is to combine both campus and community resources to effect change by improving community and campus relationships in the areas of student affairs, residency policy, police policy, enforcement at retail alcohol outlets, and within the court system.

COMPARISON AND CONTRAST

Comparison and **contrast** show similarities and/or differences between two or more concepts or entities. The paragraph or passage usually emphasizes similarities (comparisons) or differences (contrasts). The following passage contrasts methamphetamine and cocaine.

Methamphetamine is structurally similar to amphetamine and the neurotransmitter dopamine, but it is quite different from cocaine. Although these stimulants have similar behavioral and physiological effects, there are some major <u>differences</u> in the basic mechanisms of how they work. <u>In contrast</u> to cocaine, which is quickly removed and almost completely metabolized in the body, methamphetamine has a much longer duration of action and a larger percentage of the drug remains unchanged in the body. This results in methamphetamine being present in the brain longer, which ultimately leads to prolonged stimulant effects. And although both methamphetamine and cocaine increase levels of the brain chemical dopamine, animal studies reveal much higher levels of dopamine following administration of methamphetamine due to the <u>different</u> mechanisms of action within nerve cells in response to these drugs. Cocaine prolongs dopamine actions in the brain by blocking dopamine re-uptake. <u>While</u> at low doses, methamphetamine blocks dopamine re-uptake, methamphetamine also increases the release of dopamine, leading to much higher concentrations in the synapse, which can be toxic to nerve terminals.

Methamphetamine vs. Cocaine	
Stimulant	Stimulant and local anesthetic
Man-made	Plant-derived
Smoking produces a long-lasting high	Smoking produces a brief high
50% of the drug is removed from the body in 12 hours	50% of the drug is removed from the body in 1 hour
Increases dopamine release and blocks dopamine re-uptake	Blocks dopamine re-uptake
Limited medical use	Limited use as a local anesthetic in some surgical procedures

National Institute on Drug Abuse/
National Institutes of Health

In the previous passage, methamphetamine and cocaine are contrasted in terms of several criteria. Notice the transition or signal words that indicate points of comparison and contrast: *similar to, different from, similar, differences, in contrast, although,* and *both.* While there are some points of comparison made between the two drugs, the major focus of the passage is the differences between methamphetamine and cocaine. Notice also that the heading for the chart uses the abbreviation *vs.,* which is short for *versus,* indicating contrast.

In the following example about hypnotherapists, the author shows similarities or commonalities between these health care professionals. This example shows comparison.

Although hypnotherapists, <u>like</u> other health care practitioners, have their own style, expect some <u>common</u> elements:

- A typical session lasts from 30 to 60 minutes.
- The number of sessions can range from one to several.
- You generally bring yourself out of hypnosis at the end of a session.
- You can usually resume your daily activities immediately after a session.

SOURCE: From Hypnosis: An altered state of consciousness, from MayoClinic.com. Special to CNN.com
http://www-cgi.cnn.com/HEALTH/library/SA/00084.html

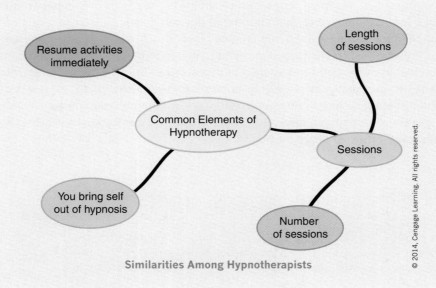

Similarities Among Hypnotherapists

In this passage and in the accompanying chart, the four major supporting details are clearly stated to support the topic of how hypnotherapists have these characteristics in common.

On Your Own PATTERNS THAT ANALYZE

Identify the type of pattern that analyzes in each of the following paragraphs. Choose classification, cause and effect, problem and solution, or compare and contrast.

1. The question of marijuana's long-term effects on memory and reasoning is also difficult to resolve, partly because studies of academic achievement scores and marijuana use tend to be correlational in nature. Cause and effect cannot easily be determined in such studies. Does marijuana use lead to poor academic performance, or does poor academic performance lead to increased marijuana use? Both possibilities are credible. The same can be said of the correlation between marijuana and mental disorder. Heavy use of marijuana could be a reaction to, or an early symptom of, mental disorder, not necessarily its cause.

    —From BERNSTEIN/PENNER/CLARKE-STEWART/ROY, Psychology, 7E. © 2006 Cengage Learning.

2. Hallucinogenic compounds found in some plants and mushrooms (or their extracts) have been used—mostly during religious rituals—for centuries. Almost all hallucinogens contain nitrogen and are classified as alkaloids. Many hallucinogens have chemical structures similar to those of natural neurotransmitters (e.g., acetylcholine-, serotonin-, or catecholamine-like).

    —National Institute on Drug Abuse, http://www.drugabuse.gov/publications/infofacts/
    hallucinogens-lsd-peyote-psilocybin-pcp.

3. Those who would decriminalize the use of marijuana argue that when marijuana was declared illegal in the United States in the 1930s, there was no evidence that it was any more harmful than alcohol or tobacco. Scientific evidence supports that claim, but more by illuminating the dangers of alcohol and tobacco than by declaring marijuana safe. In fact, although marijuana is less dangerous than, say, cocaine or heroin, it is by no means harmless.

    —From BERNSTEIN/PENNER/CLARKE-STEWART/ROY, Psychology, 7E. © 2006 Cengage Learning.

4. Marijuana easily reaches a developing fetus and should not be used by pregnant women; it suppresses some immune functions in humans; and marijuana smoke is as irritating to lungs as tobacco smoke. Further, because possession of marijuana is still a crime almost everywhere in the United States, as well as in many other countries throughout the world, it would be foolish to flaunt existing laws without regard for the legal consequences.

    —From BERNSTEIN/PENNER/CLARKE-STEWART/ROY, Psychology, 7E. © 2006 Cengage Learning.

QUICK TIPS STEPS TO DETERMINING ORGANIZATIONAL PATTERN

To determine organizational pattern or structure, follow these steps.

1. When determining the structural pattern of a reading, ask yourself, What is the author trying to do: list, explain, or analyze?

2. If your answer to Question 1 is list, does the reading list
   - items in a random order so that the details would make sense in any order?
   - items arranged according to importance?
   - events organized by time?
   - steps in a process?
   - items arranged according to space?

3. If your answer to Question 1 is that the passage is explaining something, is a
   - general point made with examples to make it clearer?
   - definition given along with examples?
   - description of a topic presented using adjectives?

4. If your answer to Question 1 is that the passage is analyzing something, does it
   - break a big concept into different parts, classifications, or categories?
   - show causes or effects?
   - outline a problem and its solution?
   - show comparison and/or contrast?

Thinking It Through MIXED PATTERNS

Sometimes an author uses more than one pattern of organization to express his or her points about the topic. Also, an author may use transition words that indicate more than one type of pattern within a reading. This can be confusing to readers because they do not know which pattern is the main pattern. The truth is there is a way to determine the main pattern, even if another one is also used to convey information within the paragraph. The rule of thumb is that the main pattern of organization is the one that is reflected in the author's most important point about the topic.

The following passage explores different types of inhalants. Can you determine more than one possible pattern of organization in this passage? Which pattern is the predominant or main pattern of organization?

What Are They?

Inhalants <u>are</u> breathable chemical vapors that produce psychoactive (mind-altering) effects. A variety of products common in the home and in the workplace contain substances that can be inhaled. <u>Examples</u> are some paints, glues, gasoline, and cleaning fluids. Many people do not think of these products as drugs because they were never meant to be used to achieve an intoxicating effect.

Although inhalants differ in their effects, they generally fall into the following <u>categories</u>:

Volatile solvents, liquids that vaporize at room temperature, present in:

■ certain industrial or household products, such as paint thinner, nail polish remover, degreaser, dry-cleaning fluid, gasoline, and contact cement

■ some art or office supplies, such as correction fluid, felt-tip marker fluid, and electronic contact cleaner

Aerosols, sprays that contain propellants and solvents, including:

■ spray paint, hair spray, deodorant spray, vegetable oil sprays, and fabric protector spray

Gases, that may be in household or commercial products, or used as medical anesthetics, such as in:

■ butane lighters, propane tanks, whipped cream dispensers, and refrigerant gases

■ anesthesia, including ether, chloroform, halothane, and nitrous oxide

—National Institute on Drug Abuse (NIDA)

Which two main patterns of organization are reflected in this reading?_____
_____
Which pattern is the predominant pattern? _____
Explain your reasoning. _____
_____

In this passage, the author begins with a definition of inhalants: *Inhalants are breathable chemical vapors that produce psychoactive (mind-altering) effects.* The author then continues with examples of different types of inhalants. So far, a definition and example pattern seems predominant. However, the passage then divides, or classifies, inhalants into three categories or types: volatile solvents, aerosols, and gases. What is the main pattern of organization, given both the characteristics of definition and example as well as classification? To answer this question, consider what the author's primary purpose is in writing this passage. If you think the author's primary purpose is to classify different types of inhalants, you are correct. The primary pattern of organization, then, is classification.

On Your Own MIXED PATTERNS

Read the following paragraph from a psychology textbook, and identify the two patterns of organization within it. Underline the transition words and phrases that indicate a pattern of organization. Be prepared to explain your answer.

We obviously need more definitive evidence about marijuana's short- and long-term effects, and it should be based on well-controlled experiments with large and representative samples of participants. Still, evaluating the meaning of even the best possible evidence will be difficult. The issues in the marijuana debate involve questions of degree and relative risk. For example, is the risk of marijuana dependence greater than that of alcohol dependence? And what about individual differences? Some people are at much greater risk than others for negative consequences from marijuana use. So far, however, we have not determined what personal characteristics account for these differences. Nor do we know why some people use marijuana only occasionally, whereas others use it so often and in such quantities that it seriously disrupts their ability to function. The physical and psychological factors underlying these differences have yet to be identified.

—From BERNSTEIN/PENNER/CLARKE-STEWART/ROY, Psychology, 7E. © 2006 Cengage Learning.

1. What are the two primary patterns of organization? _____
_____

2. Which do you think is the primary pattern and why? _____
_____

On Your Own IDENTIFYING THE MAIN PATTERN OF ORGANIZATION

Here are 10 practice exercises—some are textual and some are visual. For each, determine the topic and the main pattern of organization. Underline transition words or clues within the passage that help you decide on the main pattern. Then, list the major details that explain the topic. Be prepared to defend your answers.

1. **Where Do Hallucinogens Come From?**

   Some hallucinogens can be found in plants. Mescaline comes from a cactus called peyote. And certain mushrooms, also known as magic mushrooms, are hallucinogens. But many hallucinogens are chemicals that don't occur in nature. Some examples are:

   - LSD, also called acid
   - MDA, an amphetamine

- MDMA, an amphetamine, called ecstasy
- PCP (phencyclidine), often called angel dust

—National Institute on Drug Abuse (NIDA)

Topic: _____

Pattern: _____

Supporting details: _____

_____

2. Convert the following visual into written text. Use transition words in your paragraph, clearly indicating what pattern of organization is suggested by the information in the visual.

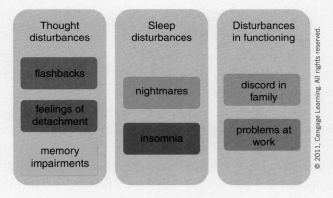

Symptoms of Post-Traumatic Stress Disorder

Your explanation of the visual: _____

_____

_____

_____

3. **Opiates Act on Many Places in the Brain and Nervous System**

The limbic system controls emotions. Opiates change the limbic system to produce increased feelings of pleasure, relaxation and contentment. (red)

The brainstem controls things your body does automatically, like breathing or coughing. Opiates can act on the brainstem to stop coughing or slow breathing. (blue)

The spinal cord transmits pain signals from the body. By acting here, opiates block pain messages and allow people to bear even serious injuries. (yellow)

—National Institute on Drug Abuse (NIDA)

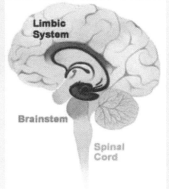

(Continued)

Topic: _____

Pattern: _____
_____

Supporting details: _____
_____

4. **What Is Drug Addiction?**

Addiction is defined as a chronic, relapsing brain disease that is characterized by compulsive drug seeking and use, despite harmful consequences. It is considered a brain disease because drugs change the brain—they change its structure and how it works. These brain changes can be long lasting, and can lead to the harmful behaviors seen in people who abuse drugs.

—National Institute on Drug Abuse (NIDA)

Topic: _____

Pattern: _____
_____

Supporting details: _____
_____

5. Convert the following visual into written text. Use transition words in your paragraph, clearly indicating what pattern of organization is suggested by the information in the visual.

Pain relievers
- Lessen chronic pain
- Allow individual to lead productive life

Central nervous system depressants
- Tranquilizers and sedatives
- Reduce anxiety and sleep disorders

Stimulants
- Help people with attention-deficit disorder to focus

Prescription Medications

Your explanation of the visual: _____
_____
_____

6.   MDMA was developed in Germany in the early 1900s as a parent compound to be used to synthesize other pharmaceuticals. During the 1970s, in the United States, some psychiatrists began using MDMA as a psychotherapeutic tool, despite the fact that the drug had never undergone formal clinical trials nor received approval from the U.S. Food and Drug Administration (FDA) for use in humans. In fact, it was only in late 2000 that the FDA approved the first small clinical trial for MDMA that will determine if the drug can be used safely with 2 sessions of ongoing psychotherapy under carefully monitored conditions to treat post-traumatic stress disorder. Nevertheless, the drug gained a small following among psychiatrists in the late 1970s and early 1980s, with some even calling it "penicillin for the soul" because it was perceived to enhance communication in patient sessions and reportedly allowed users to achieve insights about their problems. It was also during this time that MDMA first started becoming available on the street. In 1985, the U.S. Drug Enforcement Administration (DEA) banned the drug, placing it on its list of Schedule 1 drugs, corresponding to those substances with no proven therapeutic value.

—National Institute on Drug Abuse (NIDA)

Topic: _____

Pattern: _____

Supporting details: _____

_____

7.   **The brain continues to develop into adulthood and undergoes dramatic changes during adolescence.**

One of the brain areas still maturing during adolescence is the prefrontal cortex—the part of the brain that enables us to assess situations, make sound decisions, and keep our emotions and desires under control. The fact that this critical part of an adolescent's brain is still a work-in-progress puts them at increased risk for poor decisions (such as trying drugs or continued abuse). Thus, introducing drugs while the brain is still developing may have profound and long-lasting consequences.

—National Institute on Drug Abuse (NIDA)

Topic: _____

Pattern: _____

Supporting details: _____

_____

8.   Convert the following visual into written text. Use transition words in your paragraph, clearly indicating what pattern of organization is suggested by the information in the visual.

(Continued)

Your explanation of the visual: _____

_____

9. **How Science Has Revolutionized the Understanding of Drug Addiction**

Throughout much of the last century, scientists studying drug abuse labored in the shadows of powerful myths and misconceptions about the nature of addiction. When science began to study addictive behavior in the 1930's people addicted to drugs were thought to be morally flawed and lacking in willpower. Those views shaped society's responses to drug abuse, treating it as a moral failing rather than a health problem, which led to an emphasis on punitive rather than preventative and therapeutic actions. Today, thanks to science, our views and our responses to drug abuse have changed dramatically. Groundbreaking discoveries about the brain have revolutionized our understanding of drug addiction, enabling us to respond effectively to the problem.

—National Institute on Drug Abuse (NIDA)

Topic: _____
Pattern: _____
Supporting details: _____
_____
_____
_____

10. Convert the visual to the right into written text. Use transition words in your paragraph, clearly indicating what pattern of organization is suggested by the information in the visual.

Your explanation of the visual:

_____

_____

_____

_____

_____

_____

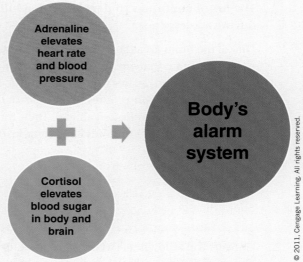

Understanding the Natural Stress Response

Thinking It Through   IDENTIFYING AN OVERALL PATTERN OF ORGANIZATION IN A LONGER READING

Now that you have had practice looking for patterns in shorter passages, apply what you have learned to a longer college-level reading. This reading passage is from a communications textbook. To understand the overall pattern of organization of the reading, take the following steps: preview the reading, determine the topic, and determine the pattern of organization based on the topic.

1. Who or what is the reading about? What is the topic? _____

2. With that topic in mind, and the overview of the structure you have gleaned from previewing, what is the pattern of organization?_____

3. How has the author organized information about this topic? Do they list, explain, or analyze? What specific pattern is used in this passage? _____

Next, turn your topic into a question. Read the passage to verify if your idea about topic and pattern was correct and to answer the question you created. Finally, read the explanation that follows the reading and compare it with your reasoning.

Gambling on Campus

1   Problem gambling has become more common among American adults than alcohol dependence. According to recent national surveys, levels of gambling, frequent gambling, and problem gambling increase during the teen years (even though underage gambling is illegal in most states), reach the highest point in the 20s and 30s, and decline after age 70. Men, who are more than twice as likely to be frequent gamblers as women, reach their highest gambling rates in their late teens. Whites are much more likely to report any gambling in the past year than blacks or Asians, but both African Americans and Native Americans report higher levels of frequent gambling.

2   Gambling also is becoming a more serious and widespread problem on college campuses. Many college students buy lottery or scratch tickets, bet on sporting events, or go to casinos. About half of those who gamble at least once a month experience significant problems related to their gambling, including poor academic performance, heavy alcohol consumption, illicit drug use, unprotected sex, and other risky behaviors. An estimated 3 to 6 percent of college students engage in "pathological gambling," which is characterized by "persistent and recurrent maladaptive gambling behavior."

3   Researchers identified key indicators associated with "pathological" gambling: gambling more than once a month, gambling more than two hours a month, and wagering more than 10 percent of monthly income. A combination of parental gambling problems, gambling frequency, and psychological distress also is associated with college gambling.

(Continued)

4   College students who gamble say they do so for fun or excitement, to socialize, to win money, or to "just have something to do"—reasons similar to those of adults who gamble. Simply having access to casino machines, ongoing card games, or Internet gambling sites increases the likelihood that students will gamble.

5   Although most people who gamble limit the time and money they spend, some cross the line and lose control of their gambling "habit." The term *problem gambling* refers to all individuals with gambling-related problems, including mild or occasional ones.

6   Researchers now view problem or pathological gambling as an addiction that runs in families. Individuals predisposed to gambling because of their family history are more likely to develop a problem if they are regularly exposed to gambling. Alcoholism and drug abuse often occur along with gambling, leading to chaotic lives and greater health risks.

SOURCE: From HALES, *An Invitation to Health*, 15E. © 2013 Cengage Learning.

Who or what is the reading about? What is the topic? *The title tells us that this passage is about gambling on campus. Also, the words gambling and college as well as students and problem are repeated numerous times throughout the passage. Try to narrow it down as you think the information through. So the topic is gambling on campus or problem gambling and college students.*

How has the author organized information about this topic?

a. **Is it a list?** *No, there are no strings of processes, steps, or information.*

b. **Does the passage explain?** *This is possible; the author seem to be providing information about the problems associated with gambling on campus.*

c. **Does the passage analyze?** *Is the author looking at parts and how they fit into the whole? Yes. The author considers the problem of gambling, specifically on college campuses.*

The author's chosen structure is to analyze the problem of gambling on college campuses. You could ask the question "What is problem gambling on college campuses?"

The pattern of this passage is problem and solution, as the author investigates the problems experienced by college gamblers. The author does not provide solutions for this problem in this passage, however; so, this is a problem passage.

Now, as you read the passage in its entirety, your brain is "primed" for the information that will be presented; your comprehension will be improved as a result of taking the time to see this skeleton first. Supporting points will make more sense because you understand what the author is trying to do.

Not only is it useful to determine the pattern of organization of a whole reading during the previewing stage, but it is also helpful to determine the structure of major sections and even paragraphs. While the overall structure of this passage is problem and solution, the author may also use different organizational patterns in paragraphs within the passage.

On Your Own ## IDENTIFYING AN OVERALL PATTERN OF ORGANIZATION IN A LONGER READING

Read the following passage and answer the questions about the overall topic and pattern of organization. As you read, circle the words that indicate the pattern of organization used in this passage.

Teens and Drugged Driving

1   According to the Centers for Disease Control and Prevention, vehicle accidents are the leading cause of death among young people aged 16 to 19. It is generally accepted that because teens are the least experienced drivers as a group, they have a higher risk of being involved in an accident compared with more experienced drivers. When this lack of experience is combined with the use of marijuana or other substances that impact cognitive and motor abilities, the results can be tragic.

2   Results from NIDA's Monitoring the Future survey indicate that in 2007, more than 12 percent of high school seniors admitted to driving under the influence of marijuana in the 2 weeks prior to the survey.

3   The 2007 State of Maryland Adolescent Survey indicates that 11.1 percent of the State's licensed adolescent drivers reported driving under the influence of marijuana on three or more occasions, and 10 percent reported driving while using a drug other than marijuana (not including alcohol).

SOURCE: NIDA, What Is Drugged Driving? http://www.drugabuse.gov/publications/infofacts/drugged-driving.

1. Who or what is the reading about? What is the topic? _____
    _____

2. How has the author organized the information about this topic? _____

QUICK TIPS PATTERNS OF ORGANIZATION FACTS

☑   There is an overall topic, structure, and point to a reading in its entirety.

☑   There is an overall topic, structure, and point to each subsection in a textbook chapter.

☑   There is an overall topic, structure, and point to each paragraph.

☑   When in doubt or if there seems to be two or more possible patterns in a section of text, go with the one that seems to be predominant.

RELATIONSHIPS BETWEEN IDEAS

Now that you have developed skills to see the "skeleton" or "big picture" or the patterns of organization in a reading, you will learn to see the relationships between ideas, or the "small picture," between sentences, and within a paragraph or section of a reading. The skills of seeing both the big picture and small picture are vital to understanding what you read. Developing these skills will make pinpointing the author's most important point, or main idea, far less perplexing.

Relationships between ideas can be defined as an author's arrangement of supporting details in a reading, often indicated by transition words or phrases that clarify, reflect, and support the most important point. Sometimes the author does not use transition words, but there is still a relationship between the ideas. In this case, you need to infer or make an educated guess about the relationships by applying what you already know. Just as the main pattern of organization of a reading dominates the different patterns used within subsections of paragraphs of a longer reading, so within a paragraph there are often mixed patterns, yet there is a dominant pattern that overarches the entire paragraph. Similarly, just as a good reader finds evidence of an overall pattern of organization in a reading, a good reader also notes relationships between ideas in a passage (Figure 2.6). Both approaches involve

- Identifying transitions that provide clues to the author's structure or pattern of organization.

- Determining a predominant pattern even though there may be other patterns in use.

- Making reasonable inferences, or educated guesses, about how the author is presenting information.

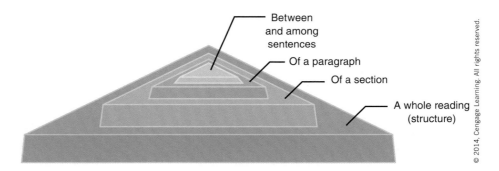

Between
and among
sentences

Of a paragraph

Of a section

A whole reading
(structure)

FIGURE 2.6 Determining an author's thought pattern is useful not only for understanding a whole reading or parts of a reading, but also for understanding how ideas connect between sentences.

Consider this passage:

> The United States has just experienced the greatest economic crisis since the Great Depression. People are likely to experience high stress levels and high unemployment rates this year.

What is the relationship between ideas in these two sentences?

a.   Sentence 1 restates the ideas found in sentence 2.

b.   Sentence 2 states the result of sentence 1.

c.   Sentence 2 gives an example of the point made in sentence 1.

d.   Sentence 2 describes the statement made in sentence 1.

Sentence 1 states that there has been an economic crisis of large proportion. Sentence 2 states that stress levels and unemployment will be high. Notice that there are no transition words to clarify the relationship between the ideas in the two sentences.

The answer to the question is *b.* The relationship between ideas is that sentence 2 *follows from* or is the *result of* sentence 1. In these sentences, there are no transitions to connect the ideas, but you could guess that words like *because of this, as a result,* or *for this reason* would fit at the beginning of the second sentence. Despite the absence of transitions, the ideas are very much connected: the connection is one of cause and effect. The first sentence states the cause and the second sentence states the effect. Understanding the relationships between ideas allows you, the reader, to connect and make sense of an author's ideas.

Thinking It Through FINDING RELATIONSHIPS BETWEEN IDEAS

Here is an abstract, or brief summary of main points, from an article on adolescents and gambling. Complete the following steps to become familiar with the reading.

1.   Preview the paragraph.

2.   Determine the topic.

3.   Determine the pattern of organization.

4.   Read the paragraph.

5.   Underline transitions or key words that show the relationship between ideas.

6.   Answer the questions following the passage about the relationship between ideas in the paragraph.

Gender <u>Differences</u> Among Adolescents with Gambling-Related Problems
By Stephen Ellenbogen, Jeffrey Derevensky, and R. Gupta

Abstract

[1]Data from five recent studies using self-reports were merged to explore gender <u>differences</u> in the characteristics of adolescent problem gambling, including comorbidity with other youth problems. [2]The sample consisted of 2,750 male and 2,563 female participants. [3]Male problem gamblers were more likely <u>than</u> females to report signs of psychological difficulties <u>while</u> females were more likely to note behavioural problems as a <u>consequence</u> of their gambling problems. [4]Males and females with severe gambling problems had remarkably <u>similar</u> prevalence rates

(Continued)

of depression, substance use and weekly gambling. [5]In the non-problem gambling group, depression was more likely to afflict females <u>whereas</u> substance use and frequent gambling were more prevalent among males.

SOURCE: Abstract from: http://www.ncbi.nlm.nih.gov/pubmed/17265189 Ellenbogen S, Derevensky J, Gupta R., Gender differences among adolescents with gambling-related problems.

The topic of this abstract is gender differences among adolescents with gambling-related problems. The title provides the clue as well as repeated words in the passage.

The pattern of organization is compare and contrast. The authors show similarities and differences between males and females with regard to gambling-related problems.

Now, consider the relationship between ideas among the sentences. Can you follow the author's reasoning and train of thought? How would you explain how each sentence's ideas connect to the next?

1. **What is the relationship between sentences 1 and 2?** *In the first sentence, the authors establish their topic and the subjects of the study. They expand on the problems related to gambling by using the language "comorbidity with other youth problems." What do you think comorbidity means, using prefix clues to determine a logical definition? If co- means "with" and morbidity refers to disease, comorbidity in this context means "a related disease or state that can occur alongside gambling." In sentence 2, the authors provide the numbers of participants or subjects in the study. The authors set up the contrast between the genders.*

2. **What is the relationship between sentences 2 and 3?** *Sentence 3, building on sentence 2, clearly contrasts males and females by clarifying the differences in how each attributes or categorizes the consequences of problem gambling. Note the transition words that indicate contrast.*

3. **What is the relationship between sentences 3 and 4?** *While sentence 3 provides a clear contrast between the genders, sentence 4 shows similarity. Both males and females with severe gambling problems encountered similar rates of comorbidity.*

4. **What is the relationship between sentences 4 and 5?** *Sentence 5 functions to contrast those with severe gambling problems with those adolescents described as "non-problem" gamblers. Sentence 5 also functions to contrast male and female "non-problem" gamblers.*

5. **What are the major supporting details in this paragraph?**

	PROBLEM GAMBLERS' REPORTED CONSEQUENCES	SEVERE PROBLEM GAMBLERS' REPORTED CONSEQUENCES	NON-PROBLEM GAMBLERS' REPORTED CONSEQUENCES
Male	Psychological difficulties	Depression, substance use, and weekly gambling	Substance use and frequent gambling
Female	Behavioral problems	Depression, substance use, and weekly gambling	Depression

- Male problem gamblers were more likely <u>than</u> females to report signs of psychological difficulties, <u>while</u> females were more likely to note behavioral problems as a <u>consequence</u> of their gambling problems.
- Males and females with severe gambling problems had remarkably <u>similar</u> prevalence rates of depression, substance use, and weekly gambling.
- In the non-problem gambling group, depression was more likely to afflict females, <u>whereas</u> substance use and frequent gambling were more prevalent among males.

On Your Own FINDING RELATIONSHIPS BETWEEN IDEAS

Read this passage from a college psychology textbook. Then answer the questions to uncover the relationships between the ideas.

What is the topic? _____

In Canada, it is legal to grow and use marijuana for medicinal purposes, and despite federal laws to the contrary, the same is true in ten U.S. states. Although the American Medical Association has recently rejected the idea of medical uses for marijuana, scientists are intent on objectively studying its potential value in the treatment of certain diseases, as well as its dangers (or lack thereof). Their work is being encouraged by bodies such as the National Institute of Medicine, and drug companies are working to develop new cannabis-based medicines. The United Nations, too, has recommended that governments worldwide sponsor additional work on the medical uses of marijuana. Ultimately, the most reasonable conclusions about marijuana use must await the outcome of this research.

    —From BERNSTEIN/PENNER/CLARKE-STEWART/ROY, Psychology, 7E. © 2006 Cengage Learning.

1. What is the relationship between sentences 1 and 2? _____
   _____
   _____
   _____
   _____
   _____

2. What is the relationship between sentences 2 and 3? _____
   _____
   _____

3. What is the relationship between sentences 3 and 4? _____
   _____
   _____

(Continued)

4. What is the relationship between sentences 4 and 5? _____
   _____
   _____

5. What are the major supporting details?
   ■ _____
     _____
     _____
   ■ _____
     _____
     _____
     _____
   ■ _____
     _____
     _____
   ■ _____
     _____
     _____

How to Read
A VARIETY OF SOURCES

A successful college reader adjusts his or her approach depending on the type of reading that is assigned. You are now familiar with the kinds of textbooks that make up the majority of assigned reading for college-level courses. You also have developed skills to enhance your understanding of literature. Reading essays, newspaper articles and editorials, and research studies from professional journals require specific reading strategies. Understanding and applying these strategies will help you understand the key points of each of these types of reading.

HOW TO READ AN ESSAY

Reading an essay is like reading a textbook in that the reader must determine the topic, main idea, structure, and relationships between ideas. In an essay, the main idea is called a **thesis.** Every detail in the essay functions to support the thesis. As you know, not every paragraph of an essay has an important point. Some paragraphs function to clarify or expand upon a point made in an earlier paragraph. In an essay, an author's purpose may be to inform, to instruct, to persuade, or even to entertain.

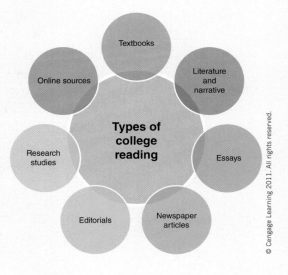

Types of college reading — Textbooks, Literature and narrative, Online sources, Essays, Research studies, Newspaper articles, Editorials

> *" READ NOT TO CONTRADICT NOR TO BELIEVE, BUT TO WEIGH AND CONSIDER. "*
>
> FRANCIS BACON

QUICK TIPS QUESTIONS TO ASK WHEN READING AN ESSAY

- ☑ Why is the topic important?
- ☑ Who wrote the essay?
- ☑ Where was it published?
- ☑ What is the author's thesis?
- ☑ What is the author's purpose: to inform, instruct, persuade, or entertain?

- ☑ What type of support does the author include to back up the thesis?
- ☑ How does the information in the essay affect your understanding of other information about the topic?
- ☑ Could the essay be biased as a result of who the writer is or where the essay was published?

HOW TO READ A NEWSPAPER ARTICLE

Newspaper articles provide excellent examples of highlighting the most important point. A newspaper article contains a **lead statement** that summarizes the most important points of the article in the first line. Journalists are taught to put the lead at the beginning of an article, so a reader immediately gets the key point at the very beginning of the story. The main idea, then, is explicitly stated in the opening of the article. The rest of the article functions to provide supporting details and explanation.

QUICK TIPS QUESTIONS TO ASK WHEN READING A NEWSPAPER ARTICLE

- ☑ Why is the topic important?
- ☑ Who wrote the article?
- ☑ Where was it published?
- ☑ What is the main point or lead statement?
- ☑ What type of support does the author include to back up the main point?

- ☑ What else has been done since this article was written or what else have you learned about this topic?
- ☑ How does the information in the article affect your understanding of other information about the topic?
- ☑ Could the article be biased as a result of who the writer is or where it was published?

HOW TO READ A NEWSPAPER EDITORIAL

An **editorial** is a commentary on an issue, usually placed in the op-ed section of a newspaper. In the op-ed (opinion-editorial) section, editors and commentators provide opinion articles expressing their points of view on the current topics reported by the press. Editorials attempt to persuade readers to accept a particular point of view. In contrast, news stories function to inform and present the information objectively, or without apparent bias. Because the intent of an editorial is to persuade, the author takes a side on a controversial issue. A **controversial issue** is one for which there are at least two primary points of view, or sides, a person can hold. Like reading essays, reading editorials requires you to find the thesis (if it is directly stated) and the supporting details, or supporting arguments, that support the thesis.

QUICK TIPS QUESTIONS TO ASK WHEN READING AN EDITORIAL

- ☑ Why is the topic important?
- ☑ Who wrote the editorial?
- ☑ Where was it published?
- ☑ What is the author's point of view?
- ☑ What type of support does the author include to back up his or her point of view?

- ☑ How does the information in the editorial affect your understanding of other information about the topic?
- ☑ Could the editorial be biased as a result of who the writer is or where the editorial was published?

HOW TO READ A VISUAL

You might be thinking, "Who needs to be shown how to read a visual? All you need to do is look at it!" Well, that might be true for the consumer—in fact, advertisers *hope* that consumers will simply look at their images so that the hidden persuasive appeals can work their alchemy. As writers of argument, however, you need to read visuals critically, just as you would read any book or article critically. But how does one read an image critically? Graphs and charts are virtually self-explanatory; their captions in effect tell you how to read them, so let's set this type of visual aside for the moment and focus instead on photographs and drawings.

As simple and unified as a photograph or drawing might be, it generates several different kinds of relationships: external, internal (that is, the interplay of particular visual elements within the whole image), and rhetorical (that is, what the different elements in the visual communicate or seem to communicate to the audience).

External Relationships

- The relationship of the visual to the text surrounding it and/or to the text referring to it
- The relationship of the visual to other visuals in the article, if any

Internal Relationships

- The interplay of figure and ground

The terms "figure" and "ground" refer to the object of focus (the figure), which dominates the photograph or drawing, and what is in the background. In a visual, everything in an image establishes a relationship of some sort with everything else, simply by its presence.

Before you choose to include a visual in your writing, ask yourself these two questions:

1. Do the figure and ground elements interconnect in ways that enhance the purpose of the image? Study David Plowden's photograph, "The Hand of Man on America" (see Image 3.1 on page 56). Notice how the foreground objects interact with the background object, the Statue of Liberty. One of the many ironies of this image is that the Statue of Liberty not only dominates the image, even though it's in the background (the telephoto lens used to take the photograph makes it appear larger than it would otherwise), but it also embodies the implicit conflict between the precious liberties it symbolizes and the ways in which those liberties are sometimes abused by environmentally damaging technology and industry.

2. Do all the objects in the foreground or background serve a unifying purpose? Are there extraneous elements in the ground that could prove to be distracting? Test the criterion of unity on Plowden's photograph. Can anything be deleted from the image without diminishing its impact? The cranes in the background? No; they, along with the telephone poles and the piles of refuse, contribute to the ironic contrast between the dark images of abuse and the bright image of liberty.

David Plowden, "The Hand of Man on America"

IMAGE 3.1 "The Hand of Man on America" by David Plowden.

HOW TO READ A RESEARCH STUDY

In college coursework, especially in the social and natural sciences, information is presented to the reader as a research study. For the general public, the results of a study often are condensed and abbreviated. The authors of these articles, from online magazines such as *Live Science* and other sources, report the main points of a study. These sources present material in a journalistic fashion and, therefore, do not bury the lead statement. Also, these summarized newspaper studies have an informative rather than persuasive purpose. To excel in college reading, it is necessary to know and understand the structure of research studies and how to find the details that support the key point.

Research studies follow a similar approach insofar as they usually begin with an **abstract** that is a summary of key findings. This general overview is followed by more detailed information in the method and results sections. The discussion section at the end of a study discusses the implications—what the results imply, or suggested outcomes of the research. In other words, the author draws conclusions for the reader based on the evidence presented from the research.

The Structure of a Research Study

Research studies for both the natural sciences and the social sciences have the same structure.

- The **abstract** is a summary of the key points of the study. The abstract contains the **hypothesis,** or the expected findings the researchers anticipated or predictions tested in the study, as well as their purpose for conducting the study.

- The **introduction** provides background knowledge for the reader and explains the motivation of the researcher or research team in conducting the study. This section also contains both a review of the results of previous research studies about the topic as well as the hypothesis (prediction to be tested).

- The **method** section outlines, in sequence, the steps of the process used in conducting the study; it also discusses the participants (subjects) who were involved in the study and how the data were gathered.

- The **results** section describes in detail what the researcher(s) found. It often presents data in statistical format and may feature charts, tables, or other graphics.

- The **discussion** section interprets the statistical information in the results section and discusses the findings of the study based on the hypothesis, previous research related to the topic, and implications and suggestions for further research to be conducted.

- The **references** section, which concludes the research article, lists the sources used actively in the study. Some research articles also include a bibliography (list of materials available in print, online, or in other media formats) of background readings related to the topic.

How to Approach Research Study Reading

1. Read the abstract to get an overview of the study. This allows you to preview the study.

2. Read the introduction to clarify the subject of the study. Focus on the last paragraph or so, where the hypothesis is usually discussed.

3. Read the discussion section to gain understanding of how the research concluded and the overall findings of the study.

4. Go back and read the methods section. This information is very detailed and contains all the steps in the research process.

5. Read the results for major findings. Unless you are proficient in statistics, this section is very dense; read for an overall grasp of the outcomes rather than for mathematical details, unless you are reading the study for a class that requires detailed knowledge of the results.

6. Carefully reread the discussion to solidify the information and implications (what the findings suggest) of the study.

7. If your purpose for reading the study is more specific, go back and read the entire document again. Take notes.

QUICK TIPS QUESTIONS TO ASK WHEN READING A RESEARCH STUDY

☑ Why is the study important?

☑ Who wrote the study?

☑ Where was it published?

☑ What is the hypothesis?

☑ Are the methods appropriate to the research?

☑ How does the information in the study affect your understanding of other information about the topic?

☑ Are the results significant?

☑ What are the implications of the study? (See the discussion section.)

☑ What else has been done since this study was conducted or what else have you learned about this topic?

☑ Could the data be biased as a result of the methods used, who the researchers are, or where the study was published?

How to Read Online Sources

Reading research suggests that reading online sources is different from reading print materials. Unlike reading print sources, reading online is "nonlinear." When you read a book or an article in print, you follow a reading sequence—beginning at the start of the text and progressing through the text systematically. However, when you read information online, you frequently jump around from source to source using hyperlinks that direct you to a different Web page. To read effectively online you need to be able to

- Use background knowledge to focus on the task.

- Locate information.

- Pose appropriate questions.

- Differentiate between fact and opinion.

- Think critically—analyze, synthesize and evaluate online material.

- Be familiar with changing technology and have some proficiency in navigating the Web.

Reading online and sifting between good and poor material requires some thought; not all online sources are created equal for academic reference. There is a difference between reading a blog on a certain topic and reading research conducted by an authority. How can you tell if an online source is reliable or not?

USING APPROPRIATE ONLINE SOURCES IN RESEARCH

To be an effective learner, you need to differentiate between academic and credible sources and those that express and opinion and are not necessarily factual or verifiable content. Just as you would assess the credibility of an author of a print source, you should also assess the credibility of an online source. These two considerations are important because they influence your judgment about whether the argument is a good source to cite for college research. If the author has authority by virtue of his or her background, experience, or expertise, then this authority lends some weight to the author's point of view and supporting arguments. If the author does not have the background, experience, or expertise to pass judgment on the issue, then this weakens the author's argument.

Here are the different types of sites you will find on the Internet:

- **.com sites:** These are commercial sites that may or may not provide reliable information.

- **.gov sites:** These are government Web sites that can be relied on to provide factual or reliable information.

- **.org sites:** These are sites originally intended for non-profit organizations. While these sites may provide reliable information, the information may be biased, as in a political Web site.

- **.net sites:** These sites were originally created for organizations involved in network technologies, such as an Internet service provider. Now, however, .net can include general-purpose domain sites. Verify the source.

- **.edu sites:** These sites are intended for educational institutions. These sites are of academic origin, but they may be biased.

However, just because you find a site that may look credible and reliable, you will need to critically evaluate the content of the site to make sure.

QUICK TIPS   FIVE STEPS TO EVALUATING AN ONLINE SOURCE FOR QUALITY

- **Type of site:** Check the type of site—is it a .com site, a .edu site, a .net site, or a .gov site? Is the publishing source reliable or not?

- **Author's credibility:** Check the author—is the author a credible voice?—is he or she an expert in the field or an authority whom you can believe? Is the author biased? Is there a biographical note about the author to help you make this judgment?

- **References:** Does the piece cite credible references? Credible sources cite reliable references.

- **Content:** Is the content reliable? Is the content accurate? Can the information be verified or proven?

- **Currency:** Is the information current? Can you find date references to verify the currency and accuracy of the information?

READING CONTROVERSIAL TEXT

You learned new strategies to read and determine what is important to learn in college-level texts across the disciplines. In this chapter, you will learn techniques to delve even further into a reading in order to make judgments about it rather than simply understand it. In order to do this, you must use everything you have learned so far in this textbook. To read critically, you learned to employ the following steps.

1. Determine the topic.

2. Determine the pattern of organization.

3. Determine the author's most important point, or thesis.

4. Determine the supporting points that back up the core idea.

Now you will apply this method to a controversial text—text in which a point of view about an issue is presented.

Prescriptive Versus Descriptive Writing

If the author's purpose is to persuade the reader to accept a particular position about an issue or to move the reader to a particular action, then that author gives the reader a *prescription,* so to speak. The author *prescribes* a stance, perspective, or course of action. This type of writing is called **prescriptive**—just as a doctor writes a prescription to make you better, so a writer outlines a *prescription* that, in her or his opinion, will address an issue in such a way as to make it better. You can recognize prescriptive writing from the use of phrases such as *we should, we ought to, we need to,* and so on. These are phrases that indicate a value judgment or opinion about an issue. Prescriptive writing is persuasive writing.

In contrast, if an author presents information about an issue without taking a particular side—presents just the facts and no personal opinion about the facts—he or she is *not* trying to convince or persuade. **Descriptive** or informative writing is used in a newspaper article or research study. The author writes to describe a situation or to inform the reader about something. There is no prescription for addressing the issue or proposal made for a course of action. The author may report on research that may lead to a point of view, but the author of the article writes objectively—without bias—and lets the results of the study speak for themselves. Discussion or interpretation sections of a research study, however, do present opinion, specifically that of the researcher or research team. Descriptive writing is informative writing.

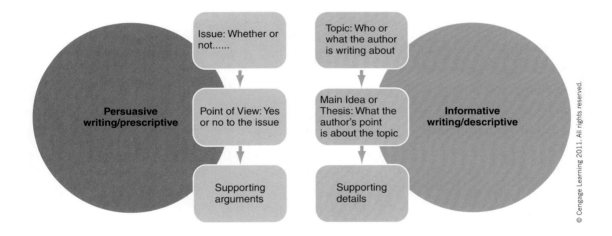

Some of the terms and concepts discussed thus far in this book are referred to differently in prescriptive writing. For example, the topic is called the **issue.** Similarly, the thesis or main idea is referred to as the **author's point of view.** Supporting details are called **supporting arguments** or **premises.**

An issue (or topic) is the subject of the debate. It is useful to use the phrase *whether or not . . .* when formulating the issue of a reading, so that the thesis, or author's point of view, is easier to identify. For example, if the issue at hand is whether or not gun control laws should be strengthened, an author's point of view is either (1) yes, gun control laws should be strengthened, or (2) no, gun control laws should not be strengthened. It is worth your time to carefully consider the issue in an argument to determine both the author's point of view and the support he or she presents for that point of view.

Mapping Arguments

To be a critical reader and thinker and to take your understanding of a reading to the next level, you need to develop skills to read and understand arguments. In an argument, the author's paramount purpose is always to persuade. The author's secondary purpose may be to inform, instruct, or entertain; his or her primary purpose, however, is to convince you to agree with his or her thesis or point of view. In arguments, the point of view has to do with the side the author takes on the issue, or what the topic of the argument is. The author then defends his or her point of view with supporting arguments.

To outline or represent the key point in an argument, follow this template.

Mapping Arguments

1. **Issue:** Whether or not . . . [summarize the topic of the argument]

2. **Author's Point of View:** the author's conclusion(s) about the issue

   Supporting Argument 1:

   Supporting Argument 2:

   Supporting Argument 3:

   Supporting Argument 4:

   Supporting Argument 5:

   Supporting Argument 6:

There may or may not be six arguments to back up an author's point of view; it is up to the reader to determine how many major supporting arguments the author makes to substantiate his or her point of view. Remember: The issue is like the topic; the point of view is like the main idea; the supporting arguments are like the supporting details.

Thinking It Through MAPPING AN ARGUMENT

The Innocence Project, started by lawyer Barry Scheck, uses law students to research criminal cases for death row convicts. The research uses DNA testing, previously unavailable when these inmates were convicted of their crimes, to exonerate, or to find those convicts not guilty, *after* conviction. The passage has been translated into an argument mapping format. Notice how clearly the major points and author's point of view or conclusion about the issue are represented in this method of note taking.

The Causes of Wrongful Conviction
by the Staff of the Innocence Project

1   As the pace of DNA exonerations has grown across the country in recent years, wrongful convictions have revealed disturbing fissures and trends in our criminal justice system. Together, these cases show us how the criminal justice system is broken—and how urgently it needs to be fixed.

2   We should learn from the system's failures. In each case where DNA has proven innocence beyond doubt, an overlapping array of causes has emerged—from mistakes to misconduct to factors of race and class.

Countless Cases

3   Those exonerated by DNA testing aren't the only people who have been wrongfully convicted in recent decades. For every case that involves DNA, there are thousands that do not.

4   Only a fraction of criminal cases involve biological evidence that can be subjected to DNA testing, and even when such evidence exists, it is often lost or destroyed after a conviction. Since they don't have access to a definitive test like DNA, many wrongfully convicted people have a slim chance of ever proving their innocence.

Common Causes

5   Here you will find further information about seven of the most common causes of wrongful convictions:

- Eyewitness Misidentification
- Unvalidated or Improper Forensic Science
- False Confessions/Admissions
- Government Misconduct
- Informants or Snitches
- Bad Lawyering

6   These factors are not the only causes of wrongful conviction. Each case is unique and many include a combination of the above issues. Review our case profiles to learn how the common causes of wrongful convictions have affected real cases and how these injustices could have been prevented.

7   To stop these wrongful convictions from continuing, we must fix the criminal justice system. The Innocence Commission is a reform that can help identify and address the fundamental flaws in the criminal justice system that lead to wrongful convictions.

SOURCE: http://www.innocenceproject.org/understand/

Example of Mapping Arguments
1. **Issue: Whether or not . . .** *we need to fix our justice system*
2. **Author's Point of View (conclusion about the issue):** *Our justice system needs to be fixed.* (first and last paragraph)

(Continued)

Supporting Argument 1: *We should learn from the system's failures.*

Supporting Argument 2: *Those exonerated by DNA testing aren't the only people who have been wrongfully convicted in recent decades.*

Supporting Argument 3: *Only a fraction of criminal cases involve biological evidence that can be subjected to DNA testing, and even when such evidence exists, it is often lost or destroyed after a conviction.*

Supporting Argument 4: *There are many other causes of wrongful convictions.*

All of these arguments directly support the conclusion (thesis) that the justice system needs to be reformed. All of these arguments rely on fact as a basis of support.

On Your Own MAPPING AN ARGUMENT

With a partner or individually as your instructor assigns, mark the text of the following passage from the Innocence Project Web site. Read to find and mark the author's point of view and the major arguments that support that point of view. Then use the mapping arguments template to outline the major arguments in support of the point of view.

Government Misconduct
by the Staff of the Innocence Project

1   Some wrongful convictions are caused by honest mistakes. But in far too many cases, the very people who are responsible for ensuring truth and justice—law enforcement officials and prosecutors—lose sight of these obligations and instead focus solely on securing convictions.

2   The cases of wrongful convictions uncovered by DNA testing are filled with evidence of negligence, fraud or misconduct by prosecutors or police departments.

3   While many law enforcement officers and prosecutors are honest and trustworthy, criminal justice is a human endeavor and the possibility for negligence, misconduct and corruption exists. Even if one officer of every thousand is dishonest, wrongful convictions will continue to occur.

4   DNA exonerations have exposed official misconduct at every level and stage of a criminal investigation.

5   Common forms of misconduct by law enforcement officials include:

- Employing suggestion when conducting identification procedures
- Coercing false confessions

  - Lying or intentionally misleading jurors about their observations
  - Failing to turn over exculpatory evidence to prosecutors
  - Providing incentives to secure unreliable evidence from informants

6   Common forms of misconduct by prosecutors include:

  - Withholding exculpatory evidence from defense
  - Deliberately mishandling, mistreating or destroying evidence
  - Allowing witnesses they know or should know are not truthful to testify
  - Pressuring defense witnesses not to testify
  - Relying on fraudulent forensic experts
  - Making misleading arguments that overstate the probative value of testimony

Necessary Oversight

7   We need to find solutions to fix these problems. One way to put checks on the enormous power of prosecutors and law enforcement officials would be to establish **criminal justice reform commissions**.

SOURCE: http://www.innocenceproject.org/understand/Government-Misconduct.php

1. **Issue:** _____

_____

2. **Author's Point of View (conclusion about the issue):** _____

_____

   Supporting Argument 1: _____

   _____

   _____

   Supporting Argument 2: _____

   _____

   _____

   Supporting Argument 3: _____

   _____

   _____

   Supporting Argument 4: _____

   _____

   _____

If you determined that the major arguments in this passage support the point of view that governmental misconduct in criminal prosecutions need reform, you are correct.

Fact and Opinion

Determining the issue, point of view, and supporting arguments is the first step to understanding persuasive writing. But to be a critical reader, you also need to recognize different types of supporting arguments and begin to evaluate their strengths and weaknesses. You need to consider the effectiveness of an author's argument by understanding the difference between fact and opinion.

On one level, fact versus opinion is an easy concept to grasp. After all, a **fact** is something that can be proven; an **opinion** is one person's belief, or something that cannot be proven. The truth is that statistics, or factual results in the form of numbers, so often used to back up an argument and support an author's perspective, can be used in a variety of ways and in a variety of forums, depending on how they are interpreted. For our purpose, facts are straightforward, provable, and documented pieces of information—facts exist, are known to exist, or can be verified, or proven, to exist. Statistics are facts; how they are interpreted is often a matter of opinion, as they are often used to convince a reader of a point of view.

Opinions, on the other hand, are someone's *interpretation* of facts. Opinion statements cannot be verified or proven. You may well agree with someone's opinion; you may even see the opinion as obvious and true. But an opinion *can* be debated. In other words, someone can argue the opposite point of view, or counterargue, and still, in his or her opinion, be "right."

Opinions involve a value judgment, and they are often signaled by words or phrases such as *in my opinion, the truth is, I think, we should, we must,* or *we ought to.* All of these phrases indicate an opinion, regardless of how convincing that opinion is. Furthermore, anything that has not yet happened must be opinion because it cannot be verified, even if it seems very likely. Thus, projections about population growth in the year 2050 are opinions, even if they are based on reasonable deductions and are mathematically probable. "Probable" is not fact, but opinion.

QUICK TIPS DIFFERENCES BETWEEN FACTS AND OPINIONS

Facts	Opinions
☑ Can be proven or verified	☑ Are someone's interpretation of facts
☑ May be statistics, but their *interpretation* is opinion	☑ Involve a value judgment
	☑ Are signaled by words and phrases like *the truth is, I think, we ought to, we should,* etc.

On Your Own RECOGNIZING FACT AND OPINION

Put an *F* next to the statements that are facts. Put an *O* next to the statements that are opinions. Put an *F/O* next to statements that contain both fact and opinion. The first three are done for you as examples.

F   1. Snitches contribute to wrongful convictions in 15 percent of cases.

O   2. Forensic scientists and prosecutors presented fraudulent, exaggerated, or otherwise tainted evidence to the judge or jury, which led to the wrongful conviction.

F/O 3. . . . more innocent people gain their freedom through postconviction testing. They are not proof, however, that our system is righting itself.

_____   4. The average sentence served by DNA exonerees has been 12 years.

_____   5. The common themes that run through these cases cannot be ignored and continue to plague our criminal justice system.

_____   6. Exonerations have been won in 31 states and Washington, D.C.

_____   7. These stories are becoming more familiar as more innocent people gain their freedom through postconviction testing.

_____   8. False confessions are another leading cause of wrongful convictions. Twenty-five percent of cases involve a false confession or incriminating statement made by the defendant.

_____   9. Whenever snitch testimony is used, the Innocence Project recommends that the judge instruct the jury that most snitch testimony is unreliable, as it may be offered in return for deals, special treatment, or the dropping of charges.

_____ 10. Prosecutors should also reveal any incentive the snitch might receive, and all communication between prosecutors and snitches should be recorded.

 UNDERSTANDING GRAPHICS

DISTINGUISHING FACT FROM OPINION IN VISUALS

When reading graphics, it is also important to determine what is fact and what is opinion. Any projection of a future trend is, of course, opinion, as it has not yet happened. However, a projection might be a *reasonable inference,* or an educated guess, based on facts that can be verified. To obtain future projection numbers, researchers use statistics to determine what is *likely* to happen (opinion) based on what has *already* happened (fact). To determine facts versus opinions in graphics, follow these steps.

1. Determine the topic, structure, and most important point of the visual.

2. Determine which part of the information is verifiable, or fact, and which part of the information is a projection, or a reasonable inference (therefore an opinion), based on already verified factual information.

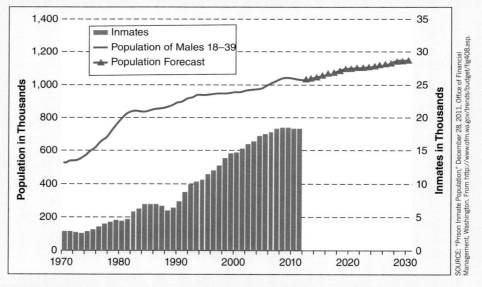

SOURCE: "Prison Inmate Population," December 28, 2011, Office of Financial Management, Washington. From http://www.ofm.wa.gov/trends/budget/fig408.asp.

FIGURE 3.1 Prison Inmate Population Compared to Age 18 to 39 Male Population

- From 1970 through 1988, the prison inmate population closely tracked the population group most susceptible to incarceration—males age 18–39.
- The Sentencing Reform Act stabilized and lowered the prison caseload in the mid- to late 1980s, while new policies, including an emphasis on drug crimes beginning in the late 1980s had a dramatic impact on the size of the prison population.
- 2007—Offender Reentry Initiative is implemented and expected to reduce future inmate caseloads through education, work force skills, and treatment programs.

—Office of Financial Management, http://www.ofm.wa.gov/trends/budget/fig408.asp

Look at Figure 3.1 tracing males in the population between the ages of 18 and 39 in the United States from 1970 to 2010, and the projected population up until 2030. Consider how this general population relates to the inmate population from 1970 to 2010. Keep in mind these facts related to Figure 3.1: two federal influential initiatives are cited following the graphic: The Sentencing Reform Act promoted consistency in federal sentencing and abolished federal parole, and the Offender Reentry Initiative provided multifaceted support for adults and juvenile offenders reentering society.

To determine fact versus opinion in graphics, follow these steps to answer the questions.

1. **What is the topic, structure, and most important point of the visual?**

    This is the prison inmate population from 1970 to 2010 as well as males aged 18–39 between the same years and projected through 2030. The pattern is compare and contrast as well as sequence. The most important point is that from 1970 through 1988, the prison inmate population mirrors the vulnerable population of males 18–39. After this point, the prison population rose disproportionately when compared with the population of males in the United States. According to the bulleted information, incarceration rates rose due to new laws.

2. **Which part of the information is verifiable, or fact, and which part of the information is a projection or a reasonable inference (therefore an opinion), based on already verified factual information?**

    Up until 2010, the information in the graphic is factual; from 2010 to 2030, the information is opinion.

3. **What can you infer regarding the future relationship between the young male population and that of the prison population, based on the bulleted information provided with the graphic?**

    It is reasonable to conclude that the prison population will decrease in relation to the rise of the population in this age group. According to the bulleted information, the Offender Reentry Initiative is likely to reduce the inmate population as alternatives to incarceration are implemented as well as improved rehabilitation methods.

Types of Support for Arguments

Recognizing a fact and an opinion as well as a mixed statement that contains both fact and opinion is the first step in evaluating an argument. However, understanding different ways that an author presents both facts and opinions to support his or her point of view will help you become a more informed critical reader. You know that an author can use facts to support his or her point of view, which is his or her opinion. An author will also use other types of support to lend credence or believability to his or her argument. When an author backs up the main idea (i.e., his or her point of view), one of these five types of support can be used.

1. **Facts.** As you learned, facts are supporting points that can be verified, or proved. Make sure the facts that are used to reinforce the point are directly related to the point. Statistics are a type of supporting fact. While these numbers or results could be verified (i.e., they can be traced to a study or report), do not always assume statistics prove the main idea without question. For example, statistics used out of their original context can be misleading. Often there are statistics from another source that could be used for equally verifiable counterargument! Furthermore, the *interpretation* of statistics blurs the line between fact and fiction or opinion. While textbooks appear to contain factual, objective information, be aware that the author may be biased if all opposing points of view on the subject are not mentioned.

2. **Reasons.** Authors also use *reasons* to support their point of view. Reasons are opinions based on facts. Reasons are logical arguments, although they are not usually verifiable (provable). In other words, a counterargument could use equally valid reasons to support the opposing point of view.

3. **Examples.** *Examples* are supporting points that illustrate or clarify the author's point of view. These may be logical and reasonable, but cannot be verified like facts or statistics. Examples often support reasons. Examples are usually found in a series of specific statements or descriptions that support an overall point.

4. **Testimony.** This type of support is used when an author cites an expert witness or someone seen to be an authoritative source to comment on, and back up, the overall point. Testimony can also be a quote from someone involved in an issue. Testimony may be based on facts to some extent, but it is *someone's opinion based on facts.* Testimony can also derive from eyewitness accounts that are not always accurate. While eyewitness testimony can carry substantial weight, particularly if the testimony was reported to an official source, this does not mean that the report is accurate or indisputable. The eyewitness could have misconstrued the event or misrepresented the information. An example of testimony is testimony in court, in which a person testifies by answering the questions of a prosecutor or defense attorney, or an expert witness passes judgment relevant to the trial proceedings.

5. **Counterarguments.** A writer can use counterargument (as do lawyers in court) to first outline what the opposing side argues and *then prove the opposing side wrong or point out errors in reasoning.* This is a very effective method of debate because it undercuts the arguments of the opposing side. To counterargue, an author can use facts, reasons, examples, or testimony.

In the following example, note how the author first reports a misconception on the side of those who are in favor of the death penalty, then goes on to argue why those in favor of the death penalty are wrong. Also note that the author is arguing *against* the death penalty, but saying what those *in favor of* the death penalty say and arguing that they are wrong.

> Those who argue for the death penalty cite that it costs tax payers less to execute an inmate than to incarcerate the inmate for life. Frankly, this argument is, at best, misguided and, at worst, wrong since it costs far more to finance the legal appeals process for a prisoner on death row whose life ends in execution than it does to finance a life sentence.

This example is one of fact and opinion.

> **Opinion:** This argument is, at best, misguided and, at worst, wrong . . .

> **Fact:** It costs far more to finance the legal appeals process for a prisoner on death row whose life ends in execution than it does to finance a life sentence.

However, the author does not provide specifics to support her saying that it costs more for taxpayers to support someone on death row than to keep that prisoner incarcerated for life. The author could provide some substantial or specific facts to support the claim that life-in-prison sentences cost taxpayers less money by citing documented costs of housing a prisoner for life in prison compared with the total cost of housing a prisoner, funding the legal appeals process, and, ultimately, executing the prisoner. As a critical reader, you do not want to accept what an author writes at face value. Table 3.1 lists some initial questions you can ask yourself regarding an author's point of view and supporting arguments to begin to delve beneath the surface of what is said and formulate your own opinion about an argument.

TABLE 3.1 Identifying the Type of Support for a Point of View

FACT	OPINION		FACT OR OPINION	
FACTS	**REASONS**	**EXAMPLES**	**TESTIMONY**	**COUNTERARGUMENT**
• Numbers • Statistics • Verifiable events	• Informed opinion • Logical arguments • Reasoned conclusions	• Lists in support • Names • Dates • Events • Specific cases	• Expert witnesses • Expert opinion	• Laying out the other side's points and finding fault with them
IS THE SUPPORT EFFECTIVE? ASK THESE QUESTIONS				
Are the facts verifiable? Are the statistics interpreted and, therefore, part opinion?	Are the arguments logical? Are the conclusions reasonable?	Are the lists or other examples directly relevant to the point being proven?	Are the experts qualified to pass judgment?	Are the opponents' points clearly and convincingly disproven?

Thinking It Through   IDENTIFYING FACT, OPINION, AND SUPPORT FOR POINT OF VIEW

Here is an excerpt from an article about an inmate who was exonerated (later found to be not guilty) well into his prison sentence. Notice the commentary that indicates whether a particular sentence or phrase is fact or opinion; also, note the types of support the author uses for his arguments.

Wrongly Convicted
by Terry Golway

1   Scott Fappiano spent more than 20 years in prison in New York. He was convicted of a brutal crime in 1985—the rape of a woman married to a police officer in Brooklyn.

Fact: can be verified

2   His trial was not exactly open and shut. Although the victim identified Fappiano as her attacker by looking at photographs, he was, in fact, about five inches shorter than the man she had described, and he had shorter hair. Extensive blood tests failed to establish any connection between Fappiano and the crime. Nevertheless, in 1985 he was convicted of the crime and sentenced to 50 years.

Opinion
Counterargument—citing the "other side's" perspective and then undercutting the argument

Fact—but this information is support for the opinion that the trial was not "exactly open and shut." Therefore, the support is examples.

3   He is free today because a group called The Innocence Project took up his case, demanded DNA testing, and proved what Fappiano had said all along: He was innocent. The State of New York, which had custody of him for nearly half of his 44 years on earth, released him earlier this year.

Fact that he is free and that he was backed by the Innocence Project and had DNA testing done; opinion that it is *because* of the Innocence Project that he is free. The author uses reasons to support his claim that the Innocence Project directly freed the inmate.

4   What do you say when you have spent more than 20 years in prison for a crime you didn't commit? Scott Fappiano simply said he was glad his ordeal was over and that the injustice had come to an end. His 69-year-old mother said she felt that her son had been kidnapped, but finally had returned.

While he may well feel this way, this is his opinion; the type of support for his claim that he is glad to be free is reasons.

That the mother said this may be a fact, but her feelings are an opinion; it is the mother's testimony or direct speech that she feels her son was "kidnapped."

5   In a sense, he was kidnapped—an innocent person taken away against his will by an imperfect justice system, imperfect because it is administered by flawed human beings who probably get it right most of the time but clearly not all of the time.

Opinion—the author uses reasons to support his claim that the justice system was imperfect.

6   Scott Fappiano received a long sentence for a crime he did not commit. How many prisoners in the United States today have received a far worse sentence—death—for crimes they did not commit? At a time when Americans have embraced the death penalty with unseemly enthusiasm, this question ought to haunt prosecutors, judges, and juries.

Fact that he received a long sentence.

Opinion—notice the phrase "ought to," which implies a value judgment; the support for the claim is a reason why society should rethink the death penalty.

SOURCE: "Wrongly Convicted," by Terry Golway of The Innocence Project. From *America*, 195. 15 (Nov 13, 2006): 8. Reprinted by permission of the author.

You can see from the example that finding facts and opinions can sometimes be straightforward; sometimes, it is complicated to separate what is a logical reason from a fact, since some statements can blur that line.

On Your Own **IDENTIFYING FACT, OPINION, AND SUPPORT FOR POINT OF VIEW**

Consider the rest of the "Wrongly Convicted" passage here. In the margins, note whether each passage is a fact or opinion. Highlight facts and underline opinions. Also, identify the type of support used in each section of the reading. The first two paragraphs have been completed as examples.

	FACT OR OPINION?	TYPE OF SUPPORT?
1 Death penalty advocates argue that the system has built-in checks and procedures that nearly eliminate the chance that an innocent person could be convicted of a capital crime and sentenced to death. But is that really the case?	Opinion	Testimony

(Continued)

	FACT OR OPINION?	TYPE OF SUPPORT?
2 In 1991 a man named Jeffrey Mark Deskovic was convicted of raping and murdering a young woman in Peekskill, N.Y. New York did not have a death penalty statute at the time because two successive New York governors, Hugh Carey and Mario Cuomo, vetoed death-penalty legislation annually. Had they not done so, Jeffrey Mark Deskovic surely would have received a death sentence.	Fact Fact/Opinion Opinion	Fact. Paragraph 2 is a counterargument to the statement in paragraph 1. Reason
3 But he did not commit that crime. He maintained his innocence for years and asked the local prosecutor, Jeanine Pirro, to examine DNA evidence that he believed would prove his case. The prosecutor's office declined to do so. But earlier this year, the Innocence Project took up Deskovic's case, a new prosecutor looked at the DNA evidence, and Deskovic was cleared of the crime after spending 15 years in prison.		
4 Without the support of the Innocence Project, Deskovic, Fappiano, and other wrongly convicted people in New York and elsewhere might still be in prison. The staff and lawyers of this not-for-profit legal clinic deserve the gratitude of all who pray for justice, for the clinic's mission is nothing less than the overturning of injustice. In the last year alone, the Innocence Project has helped free five prisoners wrongly convicted of murder in New York.		
5 The Innocence Project relies on DNA evidence to return the unjustly convicted to freedom. Since 1989, nearly 200 people have been released, because of DNA evidence, from prison for crimes they did not commit. The Innocence Project is pushing for the routine collection of genetic material from convicted felons. That seemingly sensible proposition, however, has drawn some opposition from civil libertarians, who fear the growth of government-maintained DNA databases.		

	FACT OR OPINION?	TYPE OF SUPPORT?
6 With two million people serving time in American prisons, the Innocence Project's mission could hardly be more urgent. How many of those two million have been wrongly convicted? The number certainly is small, but the presence of even one innocent person in prison mocks the very notion of justice. Once imprisoned, as Deskovic discovered, inmates and their continued pleas of innocence generally go unheard. Judges, prosecutors, and the public at large generally do not regard convicted felons as sympathetic or credible figures.		
7 All of this, of course, takes on even greater import when the death penalty becomes part of the equation. We know, thanks to the Innocence Project, that people have been wrongly convicted of crimes. Shouldn't that give death penalty supporters pause? Do they believe that the system is flawless, or do they believe that the occasional innocent executed in the name of justice is the tragic price we must pay for law and order?		
8 After Deskovic was released earlier this year, Barry Scheck, a lawyer who has been one of the driving forces behind the Innocence Project, directed his remarks to death penalty supporters. "This is the fifth man to be exonerated in a murder case in New York State in the past 10 months," he noted. "And for all those who are thinking that it might be a good idea to reinstate capital punishment in this state, please, please, please look at the evidence in front of you."		
9 The evidence in front of New Yorkers—in front of all of us—was a live human being wrongly sent to prison for murder he didn't commit. He lost 15 years of his life thanks to a miscarriage of justice.		
10 But at least he did not lose his life. Do we really wish to take that risk?		

SOURCE: Wrongly Convicted By Terry Golway of The Innocence Project. From *America*, 195. 15 (Nov 13, 2006): 8. Reprinted by permission of the author.

Thinking It Through   MAPPING AN ARGUMENT AND RECOGNIZING SUPPORT

After you have applied your skills of marking the text and annotating in the margins, consider the types of support the author uses for each argument he makes to back up his point of view. In this activity and the next, you will read two articles featuring opposing positions about harsh penalties for juvenile offenders. Should we allow life without parole for serious juvenile offenses, or should we take the position that juveniles deserve a second chance to show they can be rehabilitated?

Read the author's summary of the issue in the abstract preceding the argument against implementing life without parole (LWOP) for juvenile offenders. Think about what you already know about this issue, and then read the article and write the answers to the questions in the margin. Consider these questions as you read: What is the author's point of view? What are the key arguments the author uses to support his point of view? What types of support are used to back up each key argument? Are these supports fact or opinion? Afterward, read the explanation following the reading.

The types of support and whether the arguments are fact or opinion are indicated in the margin. The mapping of the argument follows the passage.

LWOP for Juveniles Is Morally Wrong
Should Juveniles Be Given Life Without Parole?
By John Coleman

1   The 1990s produced a rush of legislation to curb perceived crime, with lawmakers and politicians becoming tougher on crime to benefit their political agendas. States passed laws allowing juveniles to be tried as adults as well as habitual offender laws, allowing juveniles who repeatedly committed crimes to be given a sentence of life without parole (LWOP). The sentence is being tested before the Supreme Court. Those arguing against LWOP cite that giving a juvenile a life sentence with no chance of parole is cruel and unusual punishment, according to the Constitution. Juveniles are not as mentally capable as adults and are more likely to act on impulse and fall prey to peer pressure, which is why they should be treated differently than adults.

2   Currently, 109 prisoners in the United States are serving life-sentences without parole for non-homicide offenses, committed as juveniles; 77 of them are in Florida.

Fact

Many States Are Not Using This Sentence

3   A number of states (Texas, Colorado) have, legislatively, recently rescinded life-sentence without parole for juveniles, even in cases which involved homicide or felony murder charges. In these two states, however, there are provisions for life sentence for juveniles which only allow a possible parole after 40 years in prison. A bill proposing a similar outlawing of life-sentence without parole for juveniles is now pending before the California Assembly. California has 239 prisoners who were sentenced to life-sentences without parole as juveniles. Nationally the number runs to 1,755.

Fact

Fact

Fact

4   Every state permits life sentences for juveniles. Forty-five states allow life-sentences without parole for juveniles. In some cases of felony-murder, passive accomplices (e.g., "look-outs" in armed robberies) who had no idea a homicide was going to occur and did not directly wield any weapon have received life-sentences without parole.

Fact

5   Every other country has banned life-sentence without parole for juveniles.

Fact

Juveniles Can Be Rehabilitated

6   Juveniles have not developed in the same way as adults. They are more given to impulsivity, recklessness and are more susceptible to peer pressure. They are inherently less responsible—which does not mean entirely un-responsible! Neuroscientists have shown that brain regions and systems responsible for foresight, self-regulation, risk assessment, responsiveness to social influences continue to mature until early adulthood.

Opinion—reasons

Fact

7   Minors need to be considered differently than adults in sentencing due to differences in brain development, emotional maturity and their greater capacity for rehabilitation. As Alison Parker, Deputy Director of the U.S. Program at Human Rights Watch has put it: "Children are different than adults.

Opinion—reasons

(Continued)

They need to be punished for serious crimes but the punishment they receive needs to acknowledge their capacity for rehabilitation and life without parole does not do that."

Opinion—testimony

SOURCE: Adapted from: John Coleman, "Life Without Parole For Juveniles: Morally Wrong," America Magazine, April 13, 2010. Reproduced by permission of America Press. For subscription information, visit www.americamagazine.org.

Example of Mapping Arguments

1. **Issue: Whether or not . . .** *juveniles should be given life without parole.*

2. **Author's Point of View (conclusion about the issue):** *Life without parole for juveniles is morally wrong* (stated in the title and last paragraph)

   Supporting Argument 1: *Many states have rescinded (repealed) LWOP for juveniles.*

   Supporting Argument 2: *Forty-five states allow life-sentences without parole for juveniles. In some cases of felony-murder, passive accomplices (e.g., "look-outs" in armed robberies) who had no idea a homicide was going to occur and did not directly wield any weapon have received life-sentences without parole.*

   Supporting Argument 3: *Every other country has banned life-sentence without parole for juveniles.*

   Supporting Argument 4: *Juveniles' brain development is not mature, according to neuroscientists.*

   Supporting Argument 5: *Minors need to be considered differently than adults in sentencing due to differences in brain development, emotional maturity, and their greater capacity for rehabilitation.*

All of these arguments directly support the conclusion (thesis) that life without parole is morally wrong for juvenile offenders. Arguments 1 through 4 rely on fact as a basis of support. Argument 5 uses reasons and testimony for the point of view.

Notice how each of the supporting arguments functions to support the point of view directly. You should be able to say, "Therefore, life without parole for juveniles is morally wrong" after each argument is expressed. Double-check the arguments above. Does each argument logically lead to the conclusion?

On Your Own **MAPPING AN ARGUMENT AND RECOGNIZING SUPPORT**

As you read, note whether the arguments are fact or opinion. After reading, identify the major arguments and determine the type of support used for each by completing the chart that follows the reading. Follow these steps to guide your reading and mapping of the argument.

1. **What is the issue?**

2. **What is the author's point of view about the issue?**

3. **What are the key arguments the author uses to support his point of view?**

4. **Given the key arguments in support of the author's point of view, what type of support is used to back up each argument? Is each type of support fact or opinion?**

Harsh Punishment Is the Best Way to Prevent Juvenile Crime
by Kenneth W. Sukhia

1   Despite recent positive trends, our nation continues to record one of the highest violent crime rates in the world. Since 1960, the population of the United States has increased some 43%, yet the number of violent crimes has increased over 500%. While violent crime is a rarity in some countries, in America someone falls prey to a crime of violence every 17 seconds and one of us is murdered every 25 minutes.

2   No small contributor to this epidemic has been the astounding increase in juvenile crime. . . .

Swift and Certain Punishment

3   As discussed by [researcher] Eugene Methvin in the Summer of 1997 issue of *Policy Review*, studies at the University of Southern California and by criminologist Marvin Wolfgang in Philadelphia revealed that swift and certain punishment for convicted felons in the early stages of their criminal activity is a most effective means of suppressing crime.

4   In his *Policy Review* article, Methvin cited numerous studies confirming that society's failure to take punitive action in dealing with first-time youthful offenders is a primary factor contributing to the development of habitual criminals. As Mr. Methvin noted, "a troublesome youngster typically has ten or 12 contacts with the criminal-justice system and many more undiscovered offenses before he ever receives any formal 'adjudication,' or finding of guilt, from a judge. He quickly concludes that he will never face any serious consequences for his delinquency."

(Continued)

Recommendations for Improving the Situation

1. Long Term.

5   Given the disparity between the number of violent crimes committed by juveniles and the number of facilities available to detain them over the last decade . . . , juvenile offenders have been taught to believe through repeated brushes with the system that unless they commit murder, they stand little or no chance of being incarcerated for their crimes.

6   The long-term solution to the problem of juvenile crime clearly falls largely outside the law enforcement system. It requires strengthening of the basic institutions of family, schools, religious organizations and community groups which are responsible for instilling values and helping to raise law-abiding citizens. From a law enforcement perspective, however, there can be no meaningful deterrent to ongoing juvenile crime as long as juvenile offenders believe they will never be subjected to meaningful punishment for their crimes.

2. Build More Youth Detention Facilities.

7   Accordingly, we must commit to the building of a sufficient number of youth detention facilities to provide an adequate deterrent to those who would commit crime.

3. To Protect the Innocent, Violent Juvenile Offenders Must Be Punished and Removed from Society.

8   We must insure that violent and hardened juvenile offenders, who are responsible for a large share of the violent crime increase in Florida and our nation, are removed from society and punished. Increasingly, these violent criminals are being transferred to the adult system which seems incapable of imposing adequate punishment, and which fails to incarcerate 85 percent of the juveniles certified for adult treatment. . . .

9   A weak and indulgent response to juvenile crime serves an injustice to both the society which suffers from the effects of such crime and to the juvenile offender who is encouraged through repeated conduct which goes unpunished to escalate his criminal activity. To fail to act responsibly to address this crucial problem is to disserve both the law-abiding public and our state's youthful offenders.

SOURCE: Adapted from "TESTIMONY OF KENNETH W. SUKHIA BEFORE THE SUBCOMMITTEE ON CRIME OF THE UNITED STATES HOUSE JUDICIARY COMMITTEE," http://judiciary.house.gov/legacy/106-325.htm.

1. **Issue: Whether or not** . . ._____

2. **Author's Point of View (conclusion about the issue):** _____

_____

Now map the argument using the following chart.

SUPPORTING ARGUMENT	TYPE OF SUPPORT	FACT OR OPINION
1.		
2.		
3.		
4.		
5.		
6.		

Which of the two points of view about whether or not juveniles deserve harsh punishments do you believe provides the best support and the most convincing argument?

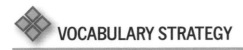 VOCABULARY STRATEGY

RECOGNIZING BIAS AND TONE: DENOTATION, CONNOTATION, AND LOADED LANGUAGE

A critical reader pays attention to the language an author uses to influence the emotions of a reader and that is, therefore, "high-inference" language. To draw these inferences as a critical reader, you need to understand the difference between denotative and connotative language. In addition, you need to understand how an author's use of language reveals his or her bias and tone.

Connotation and Denotation

The **connotative** meaning of words refers to the varied emotions, or references, a word may conjure in the mind of the reader. The connotation of a word has to do with the associations that are created in the mind of the reader. Many connotations of language can be attributed to culture or the learned associations passed on within a group of people from generation to generation.

The **denotative** meaning of a word is the straightforward, dictionary definition of that word. The denotative value of a word does not have anything "read" into it. Literal language and the denotative meanings of words are the same thing.

Consider the following example.

> The word *moon* on a denotative level means "a natural satellite revolving around a planetary body."

This is a dictionary definition of the word *moon*: the information is scientific, objective, detached. However, on a connotative level, the word *moon* may imply or symbolize several different meanings: Read the following examples that illustrate the connotative implications of the word *moon*.

- The word *moon* derives from the Greek word *luna.* We know this when we stop and think because the adjective for *moon* is *lunar.* From the same root comes the English word *lunatic,* an adjective, and the word *lunacy,* a noun—both indicating insanity.

- When you consider the moon, especially a full moon, as it often appears in popular culture, such as in films, it can symbolize romance, the unknown, or the unapproachable. Sometimes the word *moon* even connotes horrific happenings: Consider the image of a wolf howling at the moon and the derivation of werewolves, as in the tarot card.

- Because almost all gods of the moon are female in traditional cultures, (and therefore appropriately termed *goddesses*), the moon sometimes can symbolize the feminine. It is often connected with the fertility cycle and the female menstrual cycle, which parallel the cycle of the moon, intuition, and the subconscious.

Clearly, we can see that the denotative and connotative meanings of the word *moon* are very different.

Some words have positive connotations; some words have negative connotations. Some words have neutral connotations. The emotional load of a word has to do with personal bias as well as cultural bias. Most people who share a cultural tradition have learned the connotations of certain words. For example, consider these words:

- communism

- democracy

- God

While the words themselves have neutral denotations, what you associate with the word may be either positive or negative, depending on your background and culture. For the majority of U.S. citizens, the first word would have negative connotations (because most of them have been taught that communism is "bad"), and the two following words would have positive connotations.

Some words have connotations that may be positive or negative, depending on a person's point of view and life experience. For example, what kinds of connotations do *dentist, welfare,* and *money* carry for you?

Bias and Tone

In controversial writing—writing in which an author has a point of view about an issue—**bias,** or the side the author takes on an issue, is directly related to the **tone,** or underlying attitude, he or she has about his or her subject. Bias and tone, then, are directly related. If an author has a distinct point of view about an issue, then he or she has an attitude or underlying opinion about that issue. In persuasive or prescriptive writing, an author's primary purpose is to get the reader to agree with his or her point of view. In neutral or objective writing, the author conveys facts with little or no underlying attitude.

The author has two elements at his or her disposal to persuade the reader to accept his or her point of view about an issue: the choice of words and the style of writing.

In a persuasive piece of writing, an author's choice of words, or diction, is extremely important. After all, the author has only words to convince the reader! Because the author only has words and a style in which those words are arranged, he or she will be very deliberate in selecting particular vocabulary to covey his or her message. Most authors are acutely aware of the connotations of the words and phrases they choose.

Loaded Language

Heavily biased words and phrases are referred to as **loaded language,** or words and phrases that an author chooses to convey a point of view and that reveal bias. A word or phrase is considered loaded if it suggests strong connotations—whether negative or positive—beyond its strict dictionary, or denotative, definition (see Table 3.2). A reader who is not aware of loaded language can misconstrue the author's point. Persuasive writing is manipulative, which is not always a negative. After all, it is the author's job to persuade. He or she will use whatever means are available to do so.

Loaded language reveals a great deal about an author's attitude or tone. You can tell whether an author is angry, sad, frustrated, excited, arrogant, disturbed by, or disgusted with a subject from her or

TABLE 3.2 Looking at Language Critically

CONNOTATION	DENOTATION	LOADED LANGUAGE	TONE	BIAS
The suggested implications of a word or phrase, either positive or negative, based on cultural conditioning or individual experience	The dictionary or literal interpretation of a word without symbolic or emotional load	A word or phrase carries connotation—either positive or negative associations—beyond its strict denotative meaning	The author's underlying attitude or emotion toward the subject as revealed by words or writing style	The author's side on an issue as revealed by choice of words and tone

Word choice and writing style → **Connotation** or suggested meaning → **Loaded language**—strongly evocative words or phrases → **Tone**—author's attitude → **Bias**—author's position or preference

his diction—her or his choice of words. Also, you can make an inference about the author's political position or social position, level of education, worldview, and so on from the sort of language that she or he uses. Furthermore, the author's choice of words and style of writing may reveal the nature of the audience for whom her or his writing is intended.

Consider this extract from a reading presented earlier in this chapter. Determine the author's underlying attitude, or tone, as well as which words in particular have connotations that reveal his feelings about the issue, or loaded language:

> At a time when Americans have embraced the death penalty with unseemly enthusiasm, this question ought to haunt prosecutors, judges, and juries.

Here, the author is certainly not objective. He is clearly opposed to the death penalty. His tone is one of horror regarding the errors made in death penalty cases. How do we know this? Consider the phrases "this question ought to haunt prosecutors" and "unseemly enthusiasm." *Haunt* is an interesting word to choose—it implies that some grave injustice has been done and that those in error shall not rest and will be tormented by their unjust deeds. *Haunt* is a heavily loaded word that tells us that the author is opposed to the death penalty. Similarly, *unseemly* means "not decent or proper." Here, the writer clearly is critical of those Americans who support the death penalty, isn't he? Again, the author chose to use words that convey disgust and horror at the justice system and toward Americans who support the death penalty. His tone is one of anger and outrage as well as horror and shock.

Consider the following examples. What do the loaded words or phrases imply about the author's attitude toward the subject?

> What do you say when you have spent more than 20 years in prison for a crime you didn't commit? Scott Fappiano simply said he was glad his ordeal was over and that the injustice had come to an end. His 69-year-old mother said she felt that her son had been kidnapped, but finally had returned.

What is the author's tone? The tone evident in this passage is one of anger. In this case, the state is regarded as a criminal.

> The staff and lawyers of this not-for-profit legal clinic deserve the gratitude of all who pray for justice, for the clinic's mission is nothing less than the overturning of injustice.

What is the author's tone? The tone in this passage is one of thankfulness and gratitude toward those who serve justice over injustice.

> Soon afterward, Texas exonerated Ernest Willis from his arson/murder death sentence when prosecutors agreed with the same expert and science offered in Willingham's case. Nothing could be done for Willingham—likely an innocent man—because the state had already killed him.

What is the author's tone? The tone in this passage is one of anger: The state is guilty of murder.

On Your Own RECOGNIZING LOADED LANGUAGE

Independently or with a partner, consider the following passages. What is the author's tone in each? What loaded language reveals that tone? Underline loaded words or phrases that suggest tone. Write the tone suggested by the words in the space provided. Be prepared to discuss your ideas with the class.

1. How many of those two million have been wrongly convicted? The number certainly is small, but the presence of even one innocent person in prison mocks the very notion of justice.

    Tone: _____

2. All of this, of course, takes on even greater import when the death penalty becomes part of the equation. We know, thanks to the Innocence Project, that people have been wrongly convicted of crimes. Shouldn't that give death penalty supporters pause? Do they believe that the system is flawless, or do they believe that the occasional innocent executed in the name of justice is the tragic price we must pay for law and order?

    Tone: _____

(Continued)

3.   And for all those who are thinking that it might be a good idea to reinstate capital punishment in this state, please, please, please look at the evidence in front of you.

Tone: _____

4.   The evidence in front of New Yorkers—in front of all of us—was a live human being wrongly sent to prison for murder he didn't commit. He lost 15 years of his life thanks to a miscarriage of justice.

Tone: _____

5.   Forensic scientists and prosecutors presented fraudulent, exaggerated, or otherwise tainted evidence to the judge or jury, which led to the wrongful conviction.

Tone: _____

EVALUATING ARGUMENTS

What is the goal of a critical reader? A critical reader goes beyond understanding what is written and makes a judgment about the strengths and weaknesses of a piece of writing. You learned how to map an argument and determine its different parts, using the critical thinking skill of analysis. Now you will develop skills in synthesis and evaluation. Synthesis is drawing conclusions from two of more sources in order to put them together, either in developing a clear thought about an issue, or in writing or speaking about two or more related topics. In this chapter, you will also consider how to evaluate an argument—that is, to make a critical judgment not only about the contents of a reading and the use of propaganda (a deliberate attempt to convince a reader of a specific agenda), but also about the relevance and soundness of the author's support for his or her point of view. You'll also learn the most common errors in reasoning.

Medical research has yielded complex and controversial ethical dilemmas that society grapples with every day. With what we know about genetics, medical technology, and the brain, we are rapidly expanding our insight into what we *can* do medically versus what we *should* do ethically. Do some of our new medical technologies cross the ethical line? What is the ethical line? Just because we have the knowledge to launch exploration into the frontier of modern medical science, should we?

PRE-ASSESSMENT   ONLINE SCIENCE MAGAZINE

Read the passage and then answer the questions that follow. Don't worry if you do not know what all the terms mean yet. The purpose of this Pre-Assessment is to find out how much you already know about the reading skills and strategies introduced in this chapter.

Designer Babies: Ethical? Inevitable?
by Robert Roy Britt

1   A baby born in England recently was chosen in the embryonic stage to be free of a gene linked with certain types of cancer.

2   "This little girl will not face the specter of developing this genetic form of breast cancer or ovarian cancer in her adult life," said Paul Serhal, medical director of the assisted conception unit at University College hospital, London.

3   The case is not the first of its kind.

4   In the United States, a man with a 50 percent chance of passing on a gene for deadly colon cancer used the technique, too. He and his wife had embryos screened prior to implanting one in her womb, resulting in a daughter that won't get the disease.

5   The British woman, who has remained anonymous, made the decision in June to undergo screening of 11 embryos, each three days old, because her husband's female relatives suffered cancers, according to *The Guardian*. "We felt that, if there was a possibility of eliminating this for our children, then that was a route we had to go down," she said at the time.

6   The same genetic testing, called pre-implantation genetic diagnosis (PGD), has been used to test for inherited disorders such as cystic fibrosis and Huntington's disease, life-shortening diseases known to be certainly acquired by those carrying a single gene. What's new in this case is that the gene tested for, called BRCA1, does not inevitably lead to cancer in someone who carries it and if the cancers do develop they are potentially treatable.

7   Women who carry the BRCA1 gene have an 80 percent chance of developing breast cancer and a 60 percent chance of developing ovarian cancer during their lifetime. They also have a 50 percent chance of passing the gene on to each of their children.

8   The events might presage other screenings designed to create <u>designer babies</u> based on gender, IQ or athletic ability, some ethicists fear.

9   "There are many complex issues to take into account and the decision will finally come down to an individual's personal ethics," said Kath McLachlan, a clinical nurse specialist at the charity Breast Cancer Care.

10   Some fear the worst if laws are not crafted to corral the burgeoning field of "<u>reprogenetics</u>," as it is called—combining reproductive technologies with genetic screening.

11   "If misapplied, [these technologies] would exacerbate existing inequalities and reinforce existing modes of discrimination . . . the development and commercial marketing of human genetic modification would likely spark a techno-eugenic rat-race," Richard

(Continued)

Hayes, executive director of the Center for Genetics and Society. "Even parents opposed to manipulating their children's genes would feel compelled to participate in this race, lest their offspring be left behind."

12   The polar opposite argument is made by Dartmouth College ethics professor Ronald M. Green, who envisions a nearly disease-free future in which the information gleaned from reprogenetics allows genes to be tweaked, producing healthier humans without discarding embryos. "Why not improve our genome?" Green asks.

13   A report last year in the journal *Nature* predicted a host of changes to human fertility technology in 30 years' time: Artificial wombs and experiments on human embryos grown in the lab will be commonplace, several scientists said. With embryos grown in labs, mutations could be corrected and improvements could be engineered. The same researcher said there would be no designer babies, however, because no single gene is that predictive of a perfect child.

14   Meanwhile, the British mother and daughter are said to be doing well.

SOURCE: Robert Roy Britt, "Designer Babies: Ethical? Inevitable?", *Live Science*, July 2009 (from http://www.livescience .com/3213-designer-babies-ethical-inevitable.html). Reprinted with permission of TechMediaNetwork, Inc.

COMPREHENSION CHECK

Circle the best answer to the following questions.

Reading Comprehension

1   **What is the issue in this reading?**

A. Whether or not pre-implantation genetic diagnosis (PGD) is ethical

B. Whether or not pre-implantation genetic diagnosis (PGD) causes health concerns

C. Whether or not pre-implantation genetic diagnosis (PGD) should be legal

D. Whether or not pre-implantation genetic diagnosis (PGD) can help us improve our genome

2   **What is the author's point of view?**

A. Yes, pre-implantation genetic diagnosis (PGD) is ethical.

B. Yes, the government will endorse continued use of pre-implantation genetic diagnosis (PGD).

C. No, pre-implantation genetic diagnosis (PGD) is not ethical.

D. The author does not take a side on the issue.

3   **Which of the following arguments is *against* pre-implantation genetic diagnosis (PGD)?**

A. If misused, such technology could lead to more inequality and discrimination.

B. The technique could lead to the marketing of human genetic modification.

C. The technique could lead to competition between parents for "flawless" babies.

D. All of the given are answers.

4 **What type of support is used for arguments *against* pre-implantation genetic diagnosis (PGD)?**

A. Facts

B. Testimony

C. Examples

D. Reasons

5 **Which of the following arguments is used to *support* the use of pre-implantation genetic diagnosis (PGD)?**

A. PGD is unethical and may pose social hazards.

B. PGD can lead to healthier people.

C. PGD can compromise privacy.

D. PGD may pose health risks.

6 **Which of the following is a reasonable assumption underlying the argument in *favor* of pre-implantation genetic diagnosis (PGD)?**

A. Having medical intervention with PGD can save lives.

B. This treatment will not unfairly impact people or be abused.

C. Both a and b are reasonable assumptions.

D. None of the stated assumptions is reasonable.

7 **What type of support is used for the argument *in favor* of pre-implantation genetic diagnosis (PGD)?**

A. Facts

B. Testimony

C. Examples

D. Reasons

8 **What is the ethical dilemma with the specific case of the British couple and the genetic testing of their embryo?**

A. Some people feel that they should take their chances with passing on the gene called BRCA1.

B. They only wanted the perfect child.

C. The BRCA1 gene is predictive of certain cancers but not everyone who has the gene will get the cancer, and, even if they did, there are treatments.

D. The BRCA1 gene is only found in male embryos.

(Continued)

Vocabulary Comprehension

9 **What does the word *reprogenics* mean in paragraph 10?**

A. Combining reproductive technologies with genetic screening

B. Pre-implantation genetic diagnosis

C. Genetic testing

D. Embryonic research

10 **What does the euphemism "*designer babies*" mean?**

A. Babies who grow up to design their own futures

B. Babies who were designed by their parents

C. The medical community's word for embryonic studies

D. Genetically tested embryos selected for the absence of mutations that link to disease

Recognizing Deductive and Inductive Reasoning

To evaluate an argument, first and foremost you need to identify the issue, point of view, and supporting arguments—you have to understand *what* an author has said. However, to judge an author's argument, you need to understand how the author constructed the argument—you have to understand *how* an author has put the argument together. When an author tries to convince a reader of his or her point of view, he or she follows a form of reasoning to try to persuade the reader to agree. There are two types of reasoning. **Deductive reasoning** follows from the general to the specific. **Inductive reasoning,** in contrast, follows from the specific to a conclusion or generality. Recognizing deductive and inductive reasoning, in short, is another way to read critically.

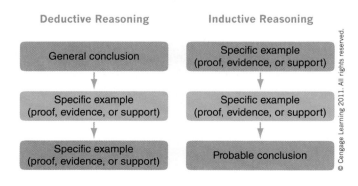

DEDUCTIVE REASONING

Deductive reasoning occurs when general principles are used to reach specific conclusions. The conclusion *leads to* proof, data, or reasons. Deductive reasoning is used when the author begins with a general statement that is assumed to be true. The general point leads to determining the specifics. This would be the type of reasoning used by a lawyer who is defending a client. His or her stance is that the client is not guilty. The conclusion is stated and evidence is garnered to support the conclusion. Scientists use deductive reasoning to prove a generality by conducting different experiments. This could be called a "top-down" approach. One of the most common types of deductive reasoning is called a **syllogism.** A syllogism is a specific form of deductive argument that has three basic steps.

X is Y.

B is X.

Therefore, B is also Y.

All dogs are mammals.

Goldie is a dog.

Therefore, Goldie is a mammal.

In this example, the conclusion is that all dogs are mammals. The fact that Goldie is a mammal follows from the generality that all dogs are mammals.

INDUCTIVE REASONING

Inductive reasoning occurs when specific information leads to a general conclusion. Proof, data, or support makes the conclusion reached logical. This would be the type of reasoning used by a jury to pass judgment on a defendant of guilt or innocence beyond a reasonable doubt. The jury has not formed a prior conclusion in hearing the case and must weigh the evidence to reach a verdict. This type of reasoning might be called a "bottom-up" approach. This is the most common form of reasoning. For example, we assume that tomorrow the sun will rise because each morning in the past it has risen. While it is not certain this will occur again tomorrow, the outcome or conclusion is likely.

The sun rose this morning.

The sun has risen for all the mornings I can remember.

Therefore, the sun will probably rise tomorrow.

The likelihood of the conclusion following from the supporting arguments, then, is what makes an argument inductive. Assume that a child has had only negative experiences with dogs in the past. It is reasonable for that child to assume that all dogs will bring negative experiences.

The neighbor's dog barked at me.

Our new friends have a dog.

Therefore, their dog will (probably) bark at me.

Look at how Frank is behaving.

He's out of control.

He must be mad.

The conclusion that Frank must be mad is arrived at from the evidence that precedes it.

Deductive or inductive reasoning does not have to do with whether the thesis of a reading is at the beginning or end of a passage. Instead, whether a passage uses deductive or inductive reasoning has to do with *how* the conclusion is reached. Just as you focus on recognizing the pattern of organization in an informative text that an author uses to construct and present his information, recognizing how an author constructs his argument—whether inductive or deductive—reveals the author's reasoning and approach in writing persuasive text. Paying attention to the author's thought process adds to your arsenal of skills in comprehending the author's point of view.

QUICK TIPS RECOGNIZING DEDUCTIVE AND INDUCTIVE REASONING

Deductive reasoning occurs when

☑ The conclusion *leads to* proof, evidence, or support.

☑ General principles are used to reach specific conclusions.

Inductive reasoning occurs when

☑ Proof, evidence, or support *leads to* a *probable* conclusion by a process of logic.

☑ The specific supporting points *lead* to the generality.

On Your Own RECOGNIZING DEDUCTIVE AND INDUCTIVE REASONING

Below are arguments or puzzles using either deductive or inductive reasoning. Write an *I* beside examples of inductive reasoning and a *D* beside examples of deductive reasoning.

_____ 1. Justin is a man. All men are actors. Therefore, Justin is an actor.

_____ 2. Miranda used a cookie sheet for three batches of cookies that all came out burned. So, the next batch on that cookie sheet will be burned.

_____ 3. 3, 5, and 7 are prime numbers, so all prime numbers are odd numbers.

_____ 4. Our dog Etch ran away. He has run away before and has always come back. Don't worry—Etch will come back.

_____ 5. All *a* are *c,* and all *b* are *c;* therefore, all *a* are *b.*

Evaluating Arguments

When you watch a sports match, you probably have a favorite team. However, the fact that you favor one team over the other may not influence your opinion about which team played the best game. Furthermore, if you're a serious sports fan, you could see errors in your team's game that made them the unsuccessful team by the end of the game. While you may not endorse the other team, you probably could see why they won—their strategy, moves, and teamwork resulted in the outcome that they were the best players in that game. This sports analogy can be applied to critical reading.

Just because you agree with an author's point of view doesn't mean you have to agree that his or her argument was well constructed. To think critically, it is very important that you can identify, deconstruct, and evaluate arguments. As a college student, you know not to believe everything you read. But how do you back up your judgment about whether an argument is good or bad?

One way to determine if an argument is good or bad is to think about whether you agree with the author's position on the issue. While this may influence your decision, a critical reader also has tools to help him or her make a judgment about an author's argument not based on emotion, but rather on logic and reasoning. Deconstructing an argument means analyzing it to see how the parts fit together and make an informed judgment about the strengths and weaknesses of the argument.

EVALUATING REASONING IN AN ARGUMENT

An author's argument is made up of two parts: the main point or point of view and the support or supporting arguments that provide evidence for the author's main point. The purpose of an argument is to persuade the reader to accept the point of view of the author. As a critical reader, you must consider who the author's intended audience is for the reading. The author's goal is to persuade the reader with a well-organized argument in which the point of view is clearly stated and the supporting evidence is relevant and sufficient to prove the point of view. The author persuades the reader with supporting evidence in the form of facts, reasons, examples, or testimony. The author can also use counterargument as a technique to persuade the reader. The first step in evaluating an argument is to identify the components of the argument, or to *map* the argument. Mapping involves identifying the

- issue;
- author's point of view on the issue;
- supporting arguments;
- type of support used to persuade the reader.

Once you have determined the components of the argument, you need to evaluate the argument as a whole. As a reader, you will have to decide if an author's point of view is sufficiently supported by the supporting arguments. To be a critical reader, you need to dissect an argument to make sure the information is logical and reasonable. A **relevant argument** is one in which the point of view is proven by the supporting arguments; in other words, the support is relevant, or directly relates to the point of view expressed. When the supporting arguments are complete, believable, and consistent with the point of view, we judge the argument to be **sound.**

However, an argument will not be sound if the supporting evidence is not complete, if it is not believable, or if it is not consistent with the author's point of view. You can have a relevant argument with relevant support, but if that support is not complete, believable, or consistent with the arguer's point of view, it will not be a sound argument. Sound arguments are strong arguments. To see errors in reasoning in an argument, you need to map the argument first. Then you need to evaluate the reasoning in the argument.

QUICK TIPS STEPS TO EVALUATING AN ARGUMENT

1. Map the argument.

2. Evaluate the reasoning.
   a. Determine if the reasoning is deductive or inductive.
   b. Determine if the supporting arguments are relevant.

3. Determine if the argument is sound.
   a. Determine if the argument is complete.
   b. Determine if the argument is believable.
   c. Determine if the argument is consistent.

Determining If Support Is Relevant

Evaluating an argument involves first deciding if the support is relevant to the point of view. In other words, does the support directly back up the point the author is making? Whether or not a supporting argument is relevant has to do with whether there are errors in the author's reasoning that make you question if the supporting argument directly relates to the point of view. If you are a fan of courtroom drama in novels, movies, or television, you may have read or seen how lawyers approach the judge when the other side presents evidence that is not relevant, shouting, "Irrelevant, your Honor!" Based on whether the newly submitted evidence relates directly to the issue at hand, the judge may choose to allow or not allow that evidence to be heard.

There are many types of errors in reasoning that logicians, those who study logic, have categorized; literally dozens of subcategories have been outlined by experts. These logical errors are also known as **fallacies.** A fallacy, from the Latin word meaning deceitful or false, is a flaw in reasoning that, at first glance, may appear to be reasonable or logical. Upon closer inspection, however, you will discover that the logic behind the argument is absent or confused. These errors in reasoning are not necessarily intentional, as is propaganda.

Logical Fallacies: Unintentional Errors in Reasoning

Often, the error in reasoning is that an author is operating from certain assumptions, or beliefs, that render the argument unsound. **Assumptions** are beliefs that an author holds true, often unstated, that inform his or her argument. Assumptions may take the form of bias, prejudice, and stereotyping. Assumptions may also make the author "jump to conclusions" rather than clearly and sufficiently explain the support for his or her argument. When an author's assumptions disrupt his or her argument, the result is a logical fallacy. A **logical fallacy** occurs when the premises or supporting arguments do not support the conclusion directly, which makes an argument either irrelevant, not sound, or both. An author may make an unintentional error in reasoning if she makes an error in calculation, judgment, opinion, or has insufficient knowledge.

Propaganda: Intentional Errors in Reasoning

Unlike logical fallacies, propaganda is an error in reasoning that an author makes deliberately in order to sway the opinion of the reader or to manipulate the reader. Propaganda is defined as

1. words or ideas that are used deliberately to harm a person, institution or group

2. the spreading of rumor or slander

3. doctrines or principles used by a source to manipulate or obfuscate

To help make their argument, authors may use intentional errors in reasoning to support their point of view, showing a one-sided, biased position on an issue. As you can see from the definition, propaganda is intended to harm and is deliberate.

The opposite of propaganda is impartiality. While all arguments promote one side of the issue (after all, the purpose is to persuade the reader of the author's point of view), propaganda has negative connotations because the term implies that an author deliberately manipulates the reader by confusing the issue and using deceptive tactics. While all persuasive text seeks to manipulate or convince the reader to some extent, the *purpose* of propaganda is to manipulate the reader.

An example of propaganda is literature promoting a helpline or help center for teenage pregnancies, suggesting that all options for the teenager are presented in deciding what to do about the pregnancy. In truth, the help center has a pro-life agenda and seeks to manipulate the teenager into continuing the pregnancy using inaccurate and biased information in order to manipulate the outcome. This one-sidedness, promoting a specific agenda and obscuring the alternative while posing as an impartial resource, is propaganda. This has nothing to do with the merits of pro-choice or pro-life perspectives but with deliberate obfuscation—not presenting all options while representing that the agency presents itself as offering all options but, in reality, does not.

There are eight common propaganda devices, or fallacies of relevance.

1. **Card stacking** is a device whereby the author presents information in support of one side of the argument but not the other. Card stacking is a propaganda device. The name derives from magicians appearing to present a clean deck of cards for a trick when, in reality, the deck has been rigged. This device is common in persuasion and is difficult to recognize because the purpose of an argument is to support one side of an issue and convince the reader to accept that particular point of view. An example of card stacking is when a television channel or biased print media source presents one side of political perspective without representing the

other point of view. This is card stacking since the audience does not get to consider all sides of the argument.

2. **Glittering generalities** are sweeping statements that are unsupported by hard evidence. The positive support is vague and usually has to do with abstract concepts such as love, honor, freedom, and other positive, but abstract, values. No concrete argument is made.

> Smokers have rights. We have the right to freedom and the right to the pursuit of happiness like everyone else. Those who seek to take away your rights are taking away your liberty. That is un-American.

Issue: Whether or not smokers have rights

Author's Point of View: Yes, smokers have rights.

Supporting Arguments:
 1. We have the right to freedom and the right to pursue happiness.
 2. Opponents take away our liberty, which is un-American.

By declaring smoking laws un-American and by equating smoking with the exercise of freedom, the author is making sweeping statements using vague abstractions like "freedom" and "happiness." The argument is weak and without clear support.

3. **Personal attack,** or *ad hominem* (from the Latin for "argument to the person"), is a technique of attacking the opponent with name-calling rather than addressing the issue at hand.

> How can we trust the eyewitness who claims that Mr. Smith is not guilty of the crime for which he is accused? This witness is a known drug user and, therefore, her testimony is irrelevant.

Issue: Whether or not the witness can be trusted

Author's Point of View: No, the witness cannot be trusted.

Supporting Argument: She is a known drug user.

Here, the issue of the eyewitness testimony is avoided and, instead, "mud is slung" at the eyewitness. Not taken into consideration is whether the eyewitness has recovered from her problems or may be a credible witness. The content of the testimony is dismissed through name-calling. The testimony is dismissed before it is even considered.

4. **Appeal to authority,** or **testimonial** is the opposite of a personal attack. Here, an individual's testimony is considered "proof" of the point of view simply because the person is considered an authority. However, the person's authority is questionable; he or she is not qualified to be an authority on the subject in question.

> Our Founding Fathers would never have tolerated the war over a citizen's right to bear arms. They felt and wrote that all people should have this constitutional right, and so we must listen to their sound judgment.

Issue: Whether or not citizens have a right to bear arms

Author's Point of View: Yes, citizens should have the right to bear arms.

Supporting Arguments:
1. The Founding Fathers would not approve of the opposition to bearing arms.
2. Their judgment is sound.

Here, the basis of the argument relies on the opinions of the Founding Fathers. No actual support as to why we should continue to support the constitutional right is offered. The Founding Fathers' point of view is an appeal to authority. While the right to bear arms may have been necessary at the time of the Founding Fathers, are social conditions the same today?

5. **Bandwagon** is an error in reasoning where the author claims that "everyone's doing this," so you ought to as well. This term derives from the expression "hopping on the bandwagon," which refers to joining a popular movement. Politicians used to ride on large wagons while campaigning. Bands would play atop the wagons, and people would jump on in excitement.

> Bry Carter has proven to be an excellent choice for mayor. Everyone's voting for her, and we all know she will be the best person for the job.

Issue: Whether or not Bry Carter should be mayor

Author's Point of View: Yes, Bry Carter should be elected mayor.

Supporting Argument: Everybody's voting for her.

The implication of this message is that because everyone's voting for Bry Carter for mayor, you should, too.

6. **Plain folk** is an error in reasoning in which an author tries to convince the reader that a person is trustworthy. The author wants you to trust this character because he or she is a "regular" person, just like you and me. This technique is used frequently in political campaigns.

> The secretary of state loves to go fishing and attend local meetings when he is back on his ranch in his hometown. Isn't he what America needs in the White House?

Issue: Whether or not the secretary of state is good for the position

Author's Point of View: Yes, the secretary of state is good for the position.

Supporting Argument: The secretary of state likes to go fishing and attend his hometown meetings when he can.

The fact that the secretary of state likes to attend hometown meetings and fish is not relevant to his position in the government. But the author manipulates you, the reader, by making you think the secretary of state is "just a regular guy" and, therefore, will do a good job for you.

7. A **straw man fallacy** occurs when an opponent's argument is misrepresented and then it is argued that the original point of view has been addressed. This error in reasoning oversimplifies, misconstrues, or misrepresents the original argument. Sometimes, quotations are used out of context as evidence for an opponent's position. This position is, then, counterargued. The problem is that what is counterargued is not the original position of the opponent in the first place. The name derives from the idea of attacking a straw man and claiming victory while the real opponent has not been defeated at all. Straw man is, in short, a diversion tactic to divert attention from the real issue.

> Cassandra thinks that parents should carefully monitor their children's TV viewing. That's ridiculous; you cannot place children in a vacuum their whole lives.

Issue: Whether or not children's TV should be monitored

Author's Point of View: Children's TV viewing should not be monitored.

Supporting Argument: Children cannot be kept in a vacuum, away from daily life.

You can see from this example that the position of the opponent, Cassandra, is simply to monitor children's TV watching. To prove her wrong, the author has made a straw man argument by suggesting that Cassandra's original intent was to keep children from experiencing real life. This is not at all what Cassandra intended.

8. An **appeal to emotion** is used to evoke a strong emotion in a reader in order to give power to the author's point of view. The appeal is to emotion instead of to logic. The author uses loaded and emotionally charged language and manipulates the reader. This often takes the form of **appeal to fear,** where the danger of a situation is stressed in order to convince the reader that the author's point of view is reasonable. **Appeal to pity** is a manipulative technique to convince you to support the underdog or someone in need. The support does not directly relate to the issue. Instead, the author is "tugging on your heartstrings" to convince you to go along with his or her point of view. In addition, an author may use an appeal called **the slippery slope,** which means that unless you adopt the point of view of the author, you are doomed.

> If we do not do something now about the war on terror, we will be at the mercy of those who want nothing more than to see us perish. Thousands will suffer at the hands of the terrorists. Many will be women and children—unless you take action at once.

Issue: Whether or not you should take action on the war on terror

Author's Point of View: You must take action on the war on terror.

Supporting Arguments:
1. If we don't act now, the terrorists will kill us.
2. Thousands of women and children will suffer.

In this example, notice how emotionality is the main component of the support. Rather than offer specific support as to how the war on terror should be launched, the author just appeals to our fear and our pity for potential victims.

QUICK TIPS RECOGNIZING ERRORS IN REASONING: PROPAGANDA

Question to Ask Yourself	Type of Error in Reasoning
■ Does the author make an undeliberate argument where the support does not back up the conclusion?	Logical fallacy
■ Does the author present one point of view on an issue while claiming to be unbiased?	Card stacking
■ Does the author make sweeping statements about abstract values?	Glittering generalities
■ Does the author use an authority figure as the basis of support for a point of view?	Appeal to authority
■ Does the author contend that you should agree because everyone else does?	Bandwagon
■ Does the author suggest that someone is trustworthy just because he or she acts like a "regular" person?	Plain folk
■ Does the author attack the opponent rather than address the issues?	Personal attack
■ Does the author attack an opponent's argument by distorting the original argument?	Straw man
■ Does the author manipulate the reader with emotional appeals?	Appeal to emotion

For more errors in reasoning, please see pp.146–147 in Chapter 6 ("Judging a Writer's Logic").

On Your Own IDENTIFYING ERRORS IN REASONING

Here are statements that have an error in reasoning related to relevance. Identify the error from the list of possibilities below. Be ready to support your reasoning.

    A. Glittering generalities
    B. Bandwagon
    C. Personal attack
    D. Appeal to authority
    E. Plain folk
    F. Straw man
    G. Appeal to emotion
    H. Card Stacking
    I. Logical Fallacy

_____ 1. You always tell me not to smoke. How can you say this when you smoke a pack of cigarettes a day?

(Continued)

_____ 2. I am not a doctor, but I play one in the television drama *Medical Maelstrom*. I find that Relief Tabs always work on my headache. You should try them, too.

_____ 3. Sean tells his new peer group that Heat Wave is his favorite band. Everyone looks at him and smirks at his comment. "Really?" they say. "We like Smash Freak. They are by far the best band to come along in years." Sean looks embarrassed. Finally, he says, "I was just kidding; Smash Freak is way better!"

_____ 4. Travie asks her parent if she can attend a party late one Saturday night. Her parent disapproves of this idea. "You never let me do anything," Travie responds.

_____ 5. The Dove beauty campaign "Real Beauty" doesn't promise to make you look like a supermodel if you use their products. But Dove will make you look like a "regular" person who is very wholesome and attractive.

_____ 6. Bryonie, misinformed in her knowledge of literature, argues that we should read more American literature at school since *Hamlet* has so much wisdom from which students can benefit.

_____ 7. We have to stop the rising tuition costs at our school. If we don't, we will soon be paying the same amount as students at private colleges: $30,000 per year!

_____ 8. Miranda is heading a debate on the merits of the American versus Canadian health care systems—yet only provides American health care facts, while claiming to be unbiased.

_____ 9. Kristen drives by a billboard that features a picture of a car. The caption reads, "Chevrolet, an American Revolution."

_____ 10. Cassandra is asked to help her friend Jeff decide whether to get a cat or a dog as a pet; Cassandra, uninformed on the facts, tells Jeff that cats are the most popular pets in the United States.

QUICK TIPS HOW TO EVALUATE AN ARGUMENT

☑ Map the argument.

☑ Determine if the reasoning is inductive or deductive.

☑ Identify the type of support.

☑ Check the credentials of the author.

☑ Determine if any type of error in reasoning is present.

☑ Check the arguments for relevance.

☑ Is the argument sound? Check to see if the arguments are consistent, believable, and complete.

☑ Determine the intended audience.

Thinking It Through EVALUATING AN ARGUMENT

Preview this article, identifying the issue and the author's point of view (POV). Then read the article through, identifying the supporting arguments and noting them in the margins. Next, identify the type of support in brackets after the supporting argument. After you read the article, determine if the reasoning in the argument is inductive or deductive and whether the arguments are relevant and sound. If they are not, refer to the Quick Tips on page 99 to identify the propaganda or errors in reasoning. Make sure to consider the author's credentials and authority when you evaluate the argument. In addition, consider whom the author intends as the audience.

The "conscience clause" laws protect medical professionals who refuse to perform medical procedures or in any way engage in medical practices that are in opposition to their ethical, moral, or religious personal beliefs. The majority of the ethical debate concerns abortions, nonresuscitation issues, prescriptions for contraceptives, or opposition to stem cell research and/or procedures. While traditionally medical bodies support the conscience clause in theory, many are concerned with the issues where a pharmacist, doctor, or other medical professional may refuse service and also refuse to refer patients to appropriate bodies that may perform or fulfill a service. James O'Neill, the principal associate deputy secretary of the Department of Health and Human Services in 2008, wrote this editorial that was published in *USA Today* in 2009.

Medical Workers Deserve Robust "Conscience Clause"
by James O'Neill

1   Over three decades, Congress has passed laws (often collectively called the **"conscience clause"**) that prohibit hospitals and other institutions that accept federal funds from forcing employees to act against their moral or religious convictions—such as providing sterilization or Plan B, or coercing them to perform or refer for abortions.

Issue: Whether or not medical personnel should be able to act on the conscience clause.

POV: Yes, medical personnel should be able to act on the conscience clause (refuse to perform certain medical procedures because of personal ethical or moral objections).

Right to Object

2   As a Department of Health and Human Services official, I discovered that many doctors didn't even know that they had the right to conscience protection. How could they be expected to defend such a right? In fact, a quasi-governmental certification organization, the American Board

Argument 1: As a Department of Health and Human Services official, I discovered that many doctors didn't even know that they had the right to conscience protection. (Reason or testimony, but sources are not identified)

(Continued)

of Obstetrics and Gynecology, warned OB/GYNs in 2007 that "disqualification or diplomate revocation . . . may occur whenever" their practices conflict with the ethical code of the American College of Obstetricians and Gynecologists, which proposed to add a requirement that "health care professionals have the duty to refer patients" to abortion providers, regardless of conscience objections.

3   Many U.S. health professionals have been asked to suppress their moral objections, including a medical school applicant interrogated about abortion views, a medical student who was sent without warning to assist in a second-trimester abortion, and a nurse at a podiatry surgery center whose boss announced one day that the center would start performing abortions, and that nurses would assist or be fired.

Argument 2: Many U.S. health professionals have been asked to suppress their moral objections. (Reason or testimony, but sources are not identified)

Setting Guidelines

4   While at HHS, I led a team that designed a regulation to enforce the laws for the first time. We based it on the common-sense principle that patients and doctors have the right to agree on treatments and compensation. Neither should force the other to do something. As fellow human beings, their rights are equal.

Argument 3: Both patients and doctors have the right to agree on treatments and payment where one does not force the other to do something against their will. (Reason)

5   Critics suggest the goal of the regulation was to deny women access to abortions. But doctors and nurses at abortion clinics choose to work there.

Argument 4: This issue is not anti-abortion related but a matter of choice of participation in abortions. (Reason, but supported by fact)

6   America could use more doctors and nurses, especially OB/GYNs, so that patients can have greater access. But when 52% of doctors object to abortion for failed contraception, as The *New England Journal of Medicine* reported in 2007, a signal from the

Argument 5: Doctors who oppose abortion ought to be respected—the government should not penalize doctors for their ethics. (Reason)

president that they and medical students like them are not wanted would send the wrong signal.

7   This is not a liberal or conservative issue but individual conscience. As the president has said, "I believe in vigorous enforcement of our non-discrimination laws." Now he has a chance to back up those words with action—or in this case, inaction.

Argument 6: The right to act on the conscience clause is not political but is in accord with non-discrimination laws.

Issue: Whether or not medical personnel should be able to act on the conscience clause.

Point of View: Yes, medical personnel should be able to act on the conscience clause (refuse to perform certain medical procedures because of personal ethical or moral objections).

Supporting Argument 1: As a Department of Health and Human Services official, I discovered that many doctors didn't even know that they had the right to conscience protection.

a. The American College of Obstetricians and Gynecologists proposed to add a requirement that "health care professionals have the duty to refer patients" to abortion providers, regardless of conscience objections.

This argument does not directly support the author's point of view. While it may be related in topic, it does not back up the author's point that medical personnel ought to be able to act according to their conscience. This argument is not relevant. While the supporting point that the American College of Obstetricians and Gynecologists proposed forcing medical professionals to adhere to an agenda that provided referrals to abortion providers does support the point of view that medical professionals are being forced into participating in medical referrals with which they don't agree, this support does not directly prove the point that many medical professionals are not aware of the conscience clause.

Supporting Argument 2: Many U.S. health professionals have been asked to suppress their moral objections.

a. A medical school applicant was interrogated about abortion views.

b. A medical student was sent without warning to assist in a second-trimester abortion.

c. A podiatry surgery center nurse's boss decided that the center would start performing abortions, and that nurses would assist or be fired.

(Continued)

This argument does directly support the author's point of view. Since the author argues in support of a conscience clause, evidence that suggests that medical personnel are being compelled to engage in unethical treatment directly backs up the author's argument with examples. This argument is relevant.

Supporting Argument 3: Both patients and doctors have the right to agree on treatments and payment where one does not force the other to do something against their will.

While at first glance, this argument appears to support the author's point of view, careful thought reveals that this supporting argument, in fact, restates the author's point of view. Saying that medical professionals ought to be able to act according to their conscience is the same as saying that they ought to be able to refuse to do something against their will. The only additional information in this supporting argument is to include the will of the patient as well. This supporting argument is an example of circular reasoning.

Supporting Argument 4: This issue is not anti-abortion related but a matter of choice of participation in abortions.

The author states that physicians have a right to shun practices they judge immoral. This argument directly supports the author's point of view that the conscience clause should remain intact.

Supporting Argument 5: Doctors who oppose abortion ought to be respected—the government should not penalize doctors for their ethics.

    a. Fifty-two percent of doctors object to abortion for failed contraception, as the *New England Journal of Medicine* reported in 2007.

In this supporting argument, the author again resorts to circular reasoning to restate his position on the conscience clause. Here, however, the author also backs up this supporting argument with fact—that the majority of doctors object to abortion for failed contraception, according to the 2007 journal report. However, the author does not account for medical reaction to abortion for other reasons or due to other circumstances—how do the majority of doctors feel about abortion after rape or incest? Also, just because doctors may "object" to abortion for failed contraception, does this mean that objection is the same as refusal to perform this procedure?

Supporting Argument 6: The right to act on the conscience clause is not political but is in accord with nondiscrimination laws.

    a. The president should uphold this right.

In this last supporting argument, the author presents a new point, equating the conscience clause revocation with discrimination. While the author does not go into detail about this point, he says that the president ought to uphold the conscience clause and not rescind it.

Is the reasoning in the argument deductive or inductive? The argument involves deductive reasoning. The conclusion that "medical personnel should be able to act on the conscience clause" is supported by evidence or leads to the support.

Does each of the supporting arguments back up the point of view directly? Arguments 2, 4, and 6 support the author's point of view. Arguments 1, 3, and 5 do not substantiate the point of view.

Is each of the arguments relevant to the point of view and complete, believable, and consistent? There are three errors in reasoning out of six supporting arguments.

Is the argument sound? No, despite the fact that we may ultimately agree with the author, the argument as it stands is not sound. The author was the Principal Associate Deputy Secretary of the Department of Health and Human Services in 2008, which makes him a credible authority on this issue. However, this argument is too flawed in its reasoning to be either sound or convincing. Because the piece is an editorial for a national newspaper, the intended audience is the general public.

On Your Own EVALUATING AN ARGUMENT

Follow the outline from Thinking It Through to evaluate the following argument. Preview the article, ascertaining the issue and the author's point of view. Then read the article through, identifying the supporting arguments and noting them in the margins. Identify the type of support in brackets after the supporting argument. After you read the article, determine if the reasoning in the argument is inductive or deductive. Next, determine if the arguments are relevant and sound. If not, refer to the Quick Tips on page 99 to identify the propaganda or errors in reasoning. Make sure to consider the author's credentials and authority when you evaluate the argument. In addition, consider whom the author intends as the audience.

Doctors Who Fail Their Patients
Editor, the *New York Times*

1   It was bad enough when pharmacists who call themselves pro-life refused to fill prescriptions for morning-after pills and an emergency medical technician refused to help drive a woman to an abortion clinic. Now a new survey has revealed that a disturbing number of doctors, at the presumed pinnacle of the health professions, feel no responsibility to inform patients of treatments that the doctors deem immoral or to refer them to other physicians for care. Although the close-mouthed doctors claim a right to follow their consciences, they are grievously failing their patients and seem to have forgotten the age-old admonition to "do no harm."

(Continued)

2   The survey, by researchers at the University of Chicago, was published last week in *The New England Journal of Medicine*. The researchers mailed questionnaires to some 2,000 doctors asking whether they had religious or moral objections to three controversial practices. Of the 1,144 who responded, only 17 percent objected to "terminal sedation" to render dying patients unconscious, but 42 percent objected to prescribing birth control for adolescents without parental approval, and 52 percent opposed abortion for failed contraception.

3   The encouraging news is that substantial majorities thought that doctors who objected to a practice nevertheless had an obligation to present all options and refer patients to someone who did not object. But that left 8 percent who felt no obligation to present all options and an alarming 18 percent who felt no obligation to refer patients to other doctors. Tens of millions of Americans probably have such doctors and are unaware of their attitudes.

4   The researchers put the burden on patients to question their doctors upfront to learn where they stand before a crisis develops. But that lets doctors off the hook. Physicians have a right to shun practices they judge immoral, but they have no right to withhold important information from their patients. Any doctors who cannot talk to patients about legally permitted care because it conflicts with their values should give up the practice of medicine.

Issue: _____

_____

_____

_____

Point of View: _____

_____

_____

_____

Supporting Argument 1: _____

_____

_____

_____

_____

_____

_____

_____

_____

Supporting Argument 2: _____

_____

_____

_____

_____

_____

_____

_____

Supporting Argument 3: _____

_____

_____

_____

_____

_____

_____

_____

Supporting Argument 4: _____

_____

_____

_____

_____

_____

Is the reasoning in the argument deductive or inductive? _____

_____

_____

_____

Does each of the supporting arguments back up the point of view directly? _____

_____

(Continued)

_____
_____
_____
_____
_____
_____
_____

Is each of the arguments relevant to the point of view and complete, believable, and consistent? _____

Is the argument sound? _____
_____
_____
_____
_____
_____
_____
_____
_____
_____
_____
_____

 **VOCABULARY STRATEGY**

Intended Meaning: Euphemisms and Doublespeak

You learned that loaded language reveals bias as well as tone in an author's writing. As a critical reader, you know that the connotations of words and the use of a particular writing style can reveal the author's position on an issue as well as the author's underlying attitude. Sometimes, however, the author may say one thing in writing and mean another. This is called the author's **intended meaning.** Euphemisms and doublespeak are specific kinds of loaded language and exhibit further subtleties of language that can blur what an author says and what that author really means.

EUPHEMISMS

A **euphemism** is a "nice" way of saying something unpleasant or blunt. The root word for *euphemism* is *eu,* the ancient Greek word for "good." So a euphemism is a socially acceptable way of substituting agreeable wording for unpleasant or offensive truths. We use euphemisms all the time. For example, consider the following:

> We put a suffering or aged pet *to sleep* instead of *killing* it.
>
> We say a loved one has *passed away* instead of saying that he or she has *died.*
>
> We say that an employee has been *let go* instead of *fired.*
>
> We refer to the *ladies' room* instead of *toilet.*
>
> We use the word *incident* instead of *fight* to describe a confrontation or showdown.

All these examples use an agreeable term to "disguise" an unpleasant truth. Even though euphemisms cloak unpleasant realities with pleasant terminology, they do function to mislead the reader by manipulating the realities of the situation. Sometimes this is deliberately misleading, as with propaganda, and serves to manipulate for gain. Sometimes euphemisms serve to cushion social situations out of politeness or pleasantry. In any event, while not always sinister, euphemisms deliberately cloak reality under the guise of pleasantry.

DOUBLESPEAK

Doublespeak, a type of euphemism, is the use of language to blunt or nullify a harsh truth. This type of loaded language definitely functions to manipulate and obfuscate (or confuse) the situation. Doublespeak is deliberately constructed to disguise or distort the truth. It can take the form of euphemism or can involve deliberately ambiguous terminology. Like propaganda, doublespeak has one intent: manipulation to serve an agenda. In fact, doublespeak is a type of propaganda technique! Its purpose is to distort thought using language that has neutral or even positive connotations. Doublespeak can be distinguished from euphemisms by its use by large, powerful groups.

Sometimes this type of propaganda is exercised by corporations, governments, the military, social agencies, sports agencies, religious institutions, and other powerful bodies. It functions as a deliberate, manipulative effort to cloud negative connotations of words or phrases and make the terminology neutral. Moreover, this type of euphemism distorts the truth of what it depicts by making an upsetting reality bland and disguised as something not so bad. As the name implies, the language says one thing, but means another. Notice how these examples neutralize the strong emotions that might be evoked when what is being communicated is comprehended.

> *Collateral damage* means killing innocent civilians while attacking an enemy of war.
>
> *Friendly fire* means accidentally killing military personnel on your own side.
>
> *Downsizing* means firing employees.

Ethnic cleansing means genocide.

Person of interest means suspect.

Shock and awe means massive bombing.

Subsidized means welfare.

Outsourced means dismissing local labor to hire cheap labor in other countries.

Human intelligence means spies.

Physical persuasion or pressure means torture.

Aggressive enforcement means racial profiling or harassment.

On Your Own IDENTIFYING EUPHEMISMS AND DOUBLESPEAK

The following terminology makes a negative connotation more acceptable. Decide if the phrase is a euphemism or, if it is more manipulative, an example of doublespeak. Write an *E* next to the phrases that qualify as euphemisms and a *D* next to the phrases that qualify as doublespeak.

___ 1. *Restroom* for lavatory

___ 2. To *take out,* meaning "to assassinate"

___ 3. *Casualty* for those killed or maimed in war

___ 4. *Correctional facility* for prison

___ 5. *Incentive* for bribe

___ 6. *Capital punishment* for executing inmates

POST-ASSESSMENT   PSYCHOLOGY MAGAZINE

Preview the following article. Then, after you have read it all the way through, answer the questions that follow it. This assessment will help you determine your strengths and weaknesses in understanding, learning, and applying the skills and strategies discussed in this chapter.

Hoping for a Girl
by Jeff Grossman

1   In 2002, when Johanna, an Arkansas mom, learned she would give birth to her third baby boy, she decided to investigate high-tech help for her next child, which she hoped would be a girl. Now she's expecting what she thinks will be her first daughter, thanks to MicroSort, a new reproductive technology.

2   The technology, originally developed for farm animals, uses a laser to separate sperm cells by size (X-chromosome cells are larger). At Genetics and IVF Institute, in Fairfax, Virginia, the basic procedure costs between $2,000 and $4,000, says nursing director Mary Fusillo.

3   With about 500 cases by 2004, MicroSort had a 91 percent success rate in sorting for girls, and close to 75 percent for boys, Fusillo says. Because MicroSort is experimental, it is so far offered only as part of a controlled trial. After 750 births, the Food and Drug Administration will rule whether the technique should be widely available. Only two clinics are currently authorized by the FDA to offer MicroSort.

4   So far, only families seeking "<u>balance</u>" or those at risk for gender-related genetic diseases are eligible, a restriction imposed by the company. To qualify, parents must have more than one child of the same gender. A family with two boys and a girl, for example, could only sort for another girl.

5   Nearly all of the families who have used MicroSort are hoping for girls, partially because sex-linked diseases overwhelmingly affect boys. Even those families seeking balance, though, try for daughters up to twice as often as sons.

6   But is MicroSort headed for a collision with medical ethics? Sex selection for nonmedical reasons is already illegal in the United Kingdom, and earlier this year, the American College of Obstetricians and Gynecologists (ACOG) said it contradicts their code of ethics. "The very idea of preferring a child of a particular sex may be interpreted as condoning sexist values, and, hence, [could] create a climate in which sex discrimination can more easily flourish," says ACOG's ethics committee. The American Society of Reproductive Medicine cautiously endorses gender selection, but warns that gender-sorted kids may disappoint parents when the technique fails or feel pressure to conform to their gender role.

(Continued)

COMPREHENSION CHECK

Circle the best answer to the following questions.

Reading Comprehension

1 **What is the issue?**

A. Whether or not girls are favored over boys in the United States
B. Whether or not balancing families is ethical
C. Whether or not the government will endorse sex-selection techniques
D. Whether or not sex-selection techniques are ethical

2 **What is the author's point of view?**

A. Yes, girls are favored over boys in sex-selection procedures.
B. Yes, the government will endorse sex-selection techniques.
C. No, sex-selection techniques are not ethical.
D. The author does not take a side on the issue.

3 **Which of the following is an argument against selecting the sex of a child?**

A. Parents overwhelmingly choose to screen for girls.
B. The technique can screen to achieve "balance" in families.
C. The technique can screen to weed out sex-linked abnormalities.
D. The test is accurate up to 75 percent of the time for boys and 91 percent of the time for girls.

4 **What type of support is used to support the argument that parents should be allowed to select the sex of a child?**

A. Facts and testimony
B. Facts and reasons
C. Reasons and examples
D. Examples and testimony

5 **Which of the following is a reasonable assumption in the arguments in favor of the procedure?**

A. Gender balance in a family is good.
B. Weeding out sex-related abnormalities is ethical.
C. Both a and b are reasonable assumptions.
D. None of the stated assumptions are reasonable.

6 **What would be a strong argument against the use of this procedure that is *not* presented in the article?**

A. Gender selection is unethical.

B. Sex selection for reasons other than medical purposes is illegal in the United Kingdom.

C. Sex-selection techniques are inaccurate.

D. Sex-selection techniques violate the American College of Obstetricians and Gynecologists' code of ethics.

7 **Which of the following is a reasonable assumption in the argument against using the procedure?**

A. Sex selection is cautiously endorsed by the American Society of Reproductive Medicine.

B. Gender selection can be dangerous because of both foreseen and unforeseen reasons.

C. Gender selection will improve the gene pool.

D. Families have a right to determine the sex of their baby if they can afford it.

8 **This statement from paragraph 6 is an example of which of the following errors in reasoning?**

The very idea of preferring a child of a particular sex may be interpreted as condoning sexist values, and, hence, [could] create a climate in which sex discrimination can more easily flourish," says ACOG's ethics committee.

A. Bandwagon

B. Plain folk

C. Straw man

D. Circular reasoning

Vocabulary Comprehension

9 **The word *balance* in this article is enclosed in quotation marks. It is an example of which of the following types of biased language?**

A. Alliteration

B. Euphemism

C. Doublespeak

D. Contradictory language

10 **What does the word *balance* really mean?**

A. Parents want a girl.

B. Parents want a boy.

C. Parents don't want to determine the sex of their child.

D. Parents do not want all children to be of only one sex.

PARAPHRASING AND SUMMARIZING

iStockphoto/Thinkstock

CHAPTER 4 Paraphrasing

CHAPTER 5 Summarizing

4

PARAPHRASING

Paraphrasing is expressing someone else's ideas not merely in your own words but also in your own style—that is, using your own word choice, sentence structure, and organization of ideas.

WHY PARAPHRASE?

Use paraphrasing to make yourself the main speaker, to clarify the source, to add zest to the original, or to extract key points without the problem of excessive ellipses.

Make Yourself the Main Speaker

Your readers primarily want to read your words—to "hear" what you have to say, even when you are using the ideas of others.

Clarify When the Original Source Is Difficult to Understand

Clarification may be necessary to explain difficult concepts or terminology, antiquated language, or unusual phrasing.

Add Stylistic Zest When the Original Source Is Worded Blandly

You probably wouldn't paraphrase famous quotations, such as Kennedy's "Ask not what your country can do for you; ask what you can do for your country." In many other communications, however, it is the meaning—not the means of expression—that is memorable.

QUICK TIPS HOW TO PARAPHRASE

To paraphrase a reading, follow these steps.

1. Read the original passage.

2. Without looking back at the original, try to formulate your rewording of the ideas.

3. Write down your paraphrase.

4. Go back and reread the original, checking to make sure the basic idea is the same.

HOW TO PARAPHRASE

To paraphrase correctly, be true to the source's meaning, state the meaning in your own style, suspend the use of quotation marks, and give credit to the source. An effective paraphrase is true to the original and in your own style, without quotation marks and with due credit to the original source.

Guidelines for Paraphrasing

BE TRUE TO THE ORIGINAL

Don't add facts, opinions, or interpretations unless you are clear that these are your own. The length of the paraphrase usually is similar to the original, unless you have also summarized some parts and/or deleted unnecessary information.

USE YOUR OWN STYLE

The wording is your own, except for words that cannot be changed without losing the original meaning. The sentence structure is your own. When paraphrasing paragraphs, the sequence of ideas is your own.

OMIT THE QUOTATION MARKS

Use quotation marks only with direct quotations—when you have not changed the original source at all. Of course, you'll place quotation marks around any unchanged portions of the original that you might include in the paraphrase.

GIVE CREDIT

Give credit to your source as a tag or as a parenthetical reference following MLA, APA, or other style guidelines. Giving credit is also known as attributing credit, or attribution.

Methods for Paraphrasing

Paraphrasing shares some techniques with quoting: be honest, be concise, give credit. However, paraphrasing has unique methods of its own. Three major techniques are **re-wording, re-sentencing**, and **re-paragraphing**. Employing any one of them in isolation may still result in plagiarism, but using them together will help ensure the writing style is your own.

- Re-word: Use synonyms for words or phrases.
- Re-sentence: Use different sentence patterns.
- Re-paragraph: Use a different paragraph organization.

RE-WORD

Replace words or phrases with synonyms.

- You don't have to change all the words, but your goal is to re-state the passage in your own words.

- If an important word has no equivalent, keep the original word.

- If the original passage contains an important phrase that is the "intellectual property" of the writer, you can quote that phrase. For example, Stephen Colbert invented the word "truthiness" so you would quote that word if you paraphrased something from Colbert.

  Original: "And most hip-hop, whatever its 'message,' is delivered in a cocky, confrontational cadence" (McWhorter).

  Re-worded: According to McWhorter, the majority of rap, regardless of its meaning, is performed in a self-confident, combative style.

RE-SENTENCE

Change sentence patterns.

- Change parts of speech: Turn a noun into a verb or vice versa: this usually forces a significant change in sentence structure.

- Change the order the information emerges in the sentence, as in sentence inversion.

- Change the modification: adjectives, adverbs, various phrases can be added, subtracted, or moved around.

  Original: "The 'in your face' element is as essential to the genre as vibrato to opera, reinforced as rappers press their faces close to the camera lens in videos, throwing their arms about in poses suggesting imminent battle" (McWhorter).

  Re-sentenced, with new subject and predicate that cause other changes: McWhorter describes the performance as aggressive yet as basic to the art form as brush strokes are to painting, with hip-hoppers—thrusting their faces toward the lens of the camera—waving their arms and striking poses like battling warriors.

Misconceptions About Paraphrasing and Plagiarism

An old rule of thumb dictates you do not have to quote a source as long as you don't use more than four consecutive words from it. This guideline has led some students to believe that you can paraphrase by simply changing every fifth word or so. Wrong! Even if you credit the source of your ideas, formulaic word substitution alone will result in a type of plagiarism (literary theft). When you don't use quotation marks when expressing someone's idea, you are claiming that you are speaking in your own voice. To paraphrase honestly—to avoid plagiarism—you will find it necessary to change the original.

RE-PARAGRAPH

Re-arrange the content of multi-sentence paraphrases.

- Re-locate parts of paraphrased sentences by placing them earlier or later in the paragraph.
- Combine two or more sentences into one sentence.
- Split a long sentence into two or more sentences.

> **Original:** And most hip-hop, whatever its "message," is delivered in a cocky, confrontational cadence. The "in your face" element is as essential to the genre as vibrato to opera, reinforced as rappers press their faces close to the camera lens in videos, throwing their arms about in poses suggesting imminent battle. The smug tone expresses a sense that hip-hop is sounding a wake-up call, from below, to a white America too benighted to listen. I can count on hearing about a "hip-hop revolution" from at least one questioner at every talk I give these days.
>
> —Dr. John McWhorter, linguist, and author of "Mean Street Theater"

> **Re-paragraphed (with re-ordered details and sentence combining):** Professor John McWhorter, a linguist who speaks on African-American culture, notes that out-of-touch Caucasians are alarmed by the aggression they see in hip-hop: violent posturing and angry facial expressions backed by a driving rhythm. At presentations given by McWhorter, the concerned citizens invariably ask him if a revolution is on the way.

TABLE 4.1 Comparison of Paraphrases

GOOD PARAPHRASE	POOR PARAPHRASE
• Is the same length as the original	• Is much shorter or longer than the original
• Uses key terms	• Does not use key terms
• References the author and title	• Does not reference the author and title
• Cuts out unnecessary information	• Includes unnecessary information
• Puts ideas into new wording that communicates the same point	• Consistently uses the same wording as the original (therefore doesn't paraphrase)
• Includes all the major and minor supporting details	• Excludes some major and minor details

THE PARAPHRASING PROCESS

Plan

Read, annotate, and make choices.

- **Read critically and annotate.** Identify the major claim and the important supporting points.
- **Make choices.** Determine how much of the source you wish to delete, to quote, to paraphrase, or to summarize. For a paraphrase, list synonyms for keywords and phrases. List major ideas to be expressed in the paraphrase. If sequence is important, organize the ideas by sequence. If not, consider presenting the ideas in an order that differs from the original.

Draft

Write in your own style: re-word, re-sentence, and re-paragraph.

- **Avoid looking at the original.** If you work from memory and notes, you'll be less likely to mimic the original.
- **Don't editorialize.** Be as objective as possible. A paraphrase is not a review: Refrain from evaluating the quality of the information or from reacting personally. Don't distort the meaning of the original.
- **Integrate.** Connect the paraphrase to your text with an introductory lead-in.

Revise

Cross-reference with the original source.

- Are the wordings, sentence structures, and organization **distinctly** your own?
- Is the length about the same as the original? (This is a matter of practicality—it will usually take approximately the same length to convey the same meaning.)
- Is the original meaning complete and undistorted?
- Did you give credit to your source?

Practice 4.1 PARAPHRASE A SENTENCE: RE-WORD AND RE-SENTENCE

1. Paraphrase the following sentence: re-word, re-sentence, and tag. "Reducing plastics, consuming less energy, walking more, traveling more by bus and train, and finding other ways to create value are some steps toward sustainability" (Gupta 18).

2. For your own writing project, select a sentence to paraphrase: re-word, re-sentence, and tag.

Practice 4.2 EVALUATE PARAPHRASED SENTENCES

For each of the following quotation-paraphrase pairs, evaluate the quality. Has the original meaning been preserved? Is the style of the paraphrase different enough? Which techniques were used to change the style?

1. **ORIGINAL:** "Nearly four million Americans are tipping the scales at more than 300 pounds" (Koontz).

    PARAPHRASE: Americans today are more overweight than ever: there are about four million people who weigh more than 300 pounds (Koontz).

2. **ORIGINAL:** "A study in *Obesity Research* found that newlyweds gain an average of six to eight pounds in the first two years of marriage" (Koontz).

    PARAPHRASE: According to Koontz, research indicates that typical newlyweds gain six to eight pounds within two years.

3. **ORIGINAL:** "At the heart of this obesity epidemic is a debate over whether obesity is a biological 'disease'" (Koontz).

    PARAPHRASE: The obesity problem has people arguing about whether it should be called a disease (Koontz).

4. **ORIGINAL:** "The causes of epilepsy are varied, and one seizure alone doth not an epileptic make" (Koontz).

    PARAPHRASE: Epilepsy has varied causes, and one seizure does not make an epileptic (Koontz).

5. **ORIGINAL:** "Both sunlight and tanning beds increase the risk of skin cancer" (Koontz).

    PARAPHRASE: Tanning beds and sunlight pose a threat to skin health by increasing a person's chances of getting skin cancer (Koontz).

Thinking It Through PARAPHRASING A READING

In this exercise, you'll read more from the article that discusses prescription drug use. Determine the topic and pattern of this whole passage. Determining topic and pattern can help you paraphrase the important ideas.

Topic: _____

Pattern of organization: _____

If you said the topic is prescription drug use on campus, you are correct. You can see repeated words clarifying the topic of the passage circled.

If you said that the pattern of organization is problem or cause, you are correct. What is the problem? _____

The problem is clearly prescription drugs abused on campus. The author outlines this epidemic and provides details of this drug abuse.

Now, read the paragraphs in the left column and then read the paraphrase of these paragraphs in the right column. The first paragraph discussed earlier is included.

Prescription Drug Abuse on Campus

1   One of every five teenagers and adults—about 50 million Americans—have used a prescription drug for a nonmedical purpose. Nonmedical use of any prescription medication is highest among young adults between the ages of 18 and 25, compared with other age groups, and opioid painkillers . . . are the most widely misused.

According to the passage on prescription drug abuse on campus, by Dianne Hales from *An Invitation to Health,* one-fifth of the American population, 50 million adults and teenagers, have used prescription drugs without a medical need. Young adults between 18 and 25 are the largest group to use prescription medicine for non-medical reasons, opioid painkillers being the most popular.

2   The abuse of prescription medications on college campuses has increased in the last 15 years. As many as one in five college students misuses or abuses a prescription medication every year. Young adults (between ages 18 and 25) have the highest rates of prescription painkiller abuse of any age group in the country. Only marijuana use is more widespread on campus.

In the last 15 years, prescription drug abuse on college campuses has grown. Each year one-fifth of the college student population is likely to have abused prescription drugs. The most common abusers of prescription drugs are 18- to 25-year-olds. Marijuana is the only drug that is used more widely on college campuses.

(Continued)

3   College men have higher rates of prescription drug abuse than women. White and Hispanic undergraduates are significantly more likely to abuse medications than are African American and Asian students. Many students taking prescription drugs for medical purposes report being approached by classmates seeking drugs. Undergraduates who misuse or abuse prescription medications are much more likely to report heavy binge drinking and use of illicit drugs. College women who do so are at greater risk for sexual victimization and assault.

SOURCE: From HALES, *An Invitation to Health*, 15E. © 2013 Cengage Learning.

The highest abuse of prescription drugs is among college men. Asian and African American students are less likely to abuse prescription drugs than White or Hispanic college students. Reports show that those actually prescribed drugs are often approached by others wanting to acquire these drugs. The use or abuse of prescription drugs coincides with heavy drinking and the use of other illegal substances. Furthermore, prescription drug abuse is linked with sexual victimization and assault for undergraduate females.

On Your Own PARAPHRASING A READING

In your own words, paraphrase three paragraphs of a related passage from Dianne Hale's book about prescription stimulant abuse. Write your paraphrase next to the original paragraph in the column provided. Then discuss your rewording of the paragraphs with a partner. Remember to make your paraphrase as clear as you can without using the author's original words. Follow the steps outlined in the Quick Tips.

Prescription Stimulants

1   The most widely abused prescription drugs are stimulant medications such as Ritalin. Students often view illicit stimulant use as physically harmless and morally acceptable. Many think that stimulants can help them focus, concentrate, and study longer. Yet users of these drugs actually have lower GPAs than nonusers, and there is little evidence that stimulants provide any boost.

Paraphrase:

2   In various studies, 5 to 35 percent of college-age individuals have reported nonprescribed use of stimulants, and 16 to 29 percent of students prescribed stimulants for ADHD reported being asked to give, sell, or trade their medications.

3   Students who are white, are traditional college age (under 24), belong to fraternities or sororities, have lower grade-point averages, and report some symptoms of ADHD are most likely to misuse or pass on stimulants to others. Most illicit users obtain the drugs from friends or peers for free or at a cost of $1 to $5. In a study of 1,550 undergraduates at a large southern university, about four in ten reported illicit stimulant use. These users, along with students with ADHD, reported significantly greater drug use than others.

4   Although proper medical use of this agent appears safe, misuse or abuse of any stimulant medication can be dangerous, even deadly. When taken in high doses, either orally or nasally, the risk of addiction increases. Physical side effects include cardiorespiratory complications, increased blood pressure, and headache. High doses can trigger panic attacks, aggressive behavior, and suicidal or homicidal impulses. Overdoses can kill.

SOURCE: From HALES, *An Invitation to Health*, 15E. © 2013 Cengage Learning.

Paraphrasing is a skill that you will develop through practice. It helps you fully understand the readings you encounter, often very complex, in college-level texts. It also helps move the new information into your long-term memory through repetition—aloud, silently, or in writing. With practice, the skill of paraphrasing will become more automatic. Until that point, it is a good idea to write down your paraphrase of a particularly difficult passage.

5 SUMMARIZING

SUMMARIZING TO EXPRESS MAIN IDEAS AND SUPPORTING DETAILS

There are three main ways to represent an author's ideas in paragraph form. **Paraphrasing** involves rewording the main idea as well as both major and minor supporting details. Another type of summary strategy is the abstract. An **abstract** is a highly condensed summary of a long reading that highlights only the major points in an otherwise detailed passage. Abstracts are usually written as a summary of a research study. The third method of restating an author's ideas is **summarizing.** This involves putting an author's main idea and major supporting details in your own words. A summary, like a paraphrase, represents an author's ideas in your own words. Unlike a paraphrase, a summary consists of only the author's most important point and major supporting points. All minor details, such as lists and examples, are left out of a summary. Be careful not to add information to the summary that the author has not stated. If you must take direct wording from a passage an author has written, be very sure to use quotation marks to announce that these are the author's words and not your words.

Summarizing is an excellent method for learning information because to learn new information, you need to process it in an organized format, so your brain can retrieve it more effectively. Summarizing allows you to do this because you have to put an author's main idea and major supporting details into your own words and use the same pattern of organization the author uses. Also, because you have to be clear on the main idea and major supporting points, summarizing allows you to determine if you *truly* understand what you have read. You cannot summarize without good comprehension. If you cannot summarize, recheck your notes and reread the passage, concentrating again on what's important.

A summary is written in paragraph format. A good rule is to make your summary about one-fourth as long as the original reading. However, the length of any summary depends on the number of details in the original reading. If the original reading is dense with information, your summary will be longer than a quarter of the original piece. If the original reading contains a lot of minor supporting details, your summary may be quite short.

HOW TO WRITE A SUMMARY

To write a summary, you need to apply everything you have learned so far about approaching a reading. In addition, you will need to use your skills of determining the main idea of a passage, as this is the foundation of a summary. Furthermore, you have to separate major details from minor details.

1. Find the topic of the reading.

2. Determine the author's purpose.

3. Determine the patterns of organization.

4. Determine the main idea.

5. Identify the major supporting details.

6. Paraphrase 4 and 5 into your own words, paying attention to the patterns of organization.

In the following pages, you will see the steps involved in summary writing applied to Nancy Shute's article, "His Brain, Her Brain," published in March 2005 in *U.S. News & World Report.*

His *Brain*, Her *Brain*
by Nancy Shute

1   Anyone who's heard a group of men discuss the virtues of high-end stereo equipment will have little trouble believing that men's and women's brains work differently. That's also no surprise to scientists, who have spent the past two decades trying to figure out which aspects of cognition and behavior are determined by nature and which by nurture. The verdict: Female and male brains differ in both structure and function, and many of those variations start in the womb. It's no longer: "Is there a difference?" It's: "What do these differences mean?"

2   Male and female brains differ in how they're built, with some parts larger in men, others larger in women. The variation is most striking in overall size. Women's brains are about 10 percent smaller than men's, a fact that in centuries past provided ammunition for the argument that women were by nature mentally deficient. Yet, despite this difference, women do just as well as men on intelligence tests. Researchers at the University of California–Irvine say they have figured out one possible explanation: In January, they reported that men have more gray matter in the brain, and women have more white matter. Gray matter forms the brain's information-processing centers, and white matter serves as wiring to connect the processing centers. "Female brains might be more efficient," says Richard Haier, the psychologist who led the study. Women also tend to use their frontal lobes for intellectual performance, while the gray matter used by men is distributed throughout the brain. That has implications for treating diseases like stroke and Alzheimer's, Haier says; treatments could be targeted to protect or restore those critical regions.

3   DIVERGENCE. When it comes to putting brains to work, women and men have their own areas of expertise. Men do better than women at spatial tasks such as thinking about rotating or manipulating an object. They're also better at navigating along a route and at high-end mathematical reasoning; men have scored more perfect 800 scores on the math portion of the SAT than women have every year since 1964. Women excel at tests that measure word recall and at other tests of verbal memory. They're also better at remembering landmarks and where objects are located. It used to be thought that these differences in cognitive skills didn't emerge until puberty, but researchers have found the same differences in very young children.

4   The big question, of course, is whether the differences in his and her brains cause the variation in cognitive skills or whether society pushes women toward verbal, people-oriented tasks, and men toward quantitative fields like engineering. Few women in science have forgotten the infamous Teen Talk Barbie of 1992, which chirped, "Math is hard!" And although the number of women in the sciences has increased steadily over the past 30 years—women now compose the majority in medical schools and graduate programs in biology—they are still underrepresented in math, engineering, and physics.

5   In 1980, psychologists Julian Stanley and Camilla Benbow ignited a firestorm when they proposed that gifted boys did better at math than gifted girls because of a "math gene." The nature vs. nurture debate continues 25 years later, but it is becoming more pragmatic as researchers use MRIs and other brain-imaging tools that show differences

in male and female brains even when performance is identical. "In the early 80s, we were worried that sex differences in the brain would be used against us as women," says Jill Becker, a psychologist at the University of Michigan. "We're all more comfortable with diversity these days, and we've come to accept that there are many different ways of solving a problem. No two brains are the same."

SOURCE: *"His Brain, Her Brain."* By Shute, Nancy, *U.S. News & World Report*, 00415537, 3/7/2005, Vol. 138, Issue 8. Reprinted by permission of U.S. News & World Report.

Check Your Answers

1. **What is the topic of the article?** *Men, women, and brains*

2. **What is the pattern of organization suggested by the topic?** *Comparison and contrast*

3. **What is the author's purpose?** *To inform*

4. **What is the author's main idea about the topic (in your own words)?** *Male and female brains are different physically and as evidenced by how we behave.*

5. **Underline the thesis of the article—the sentence that has the same ideas as you wrote in question 4.** *The thesis is in the first paragraph: The verdict: Female and male brains differ in both structure and function, and many of those variations start in the womb.*

Main Ideas and Supporting Details by Paragraph

PARAGRAPH 1

Thesis: *The verdict: Female and male brains differ in both structure and function, and many of those variations start in the womb.*

PARAGRAPH 2

Topic Sentence: *Male and female brains differ in how they're built, with some parts larger in men, others larger in women.*

Supporting Details

1. *Size*
   a. *Women's brains are 10 percent smaller.*
   b. *Women do as well as men on IQ tests.*
2. *Men have more gray matter—the brain's information-processing centers—and women have more white matter, connecting the processing centers.*
3. *Women's brains might be more efficient.*
   a. *Women use their frontal lobes.*
   b. *Men use matter distributed throughout the brain.*

(Continued)

4. *This knowledge impacts treating diseases of the brain.*

PARAGRAPH 3

Topic Sentence: *When it comes to putting brains to work, women and men have their own areas of expertise.*

Supporting Details

1. *Men are better at spatial tasks, navigating, and high-end math.*
2. *Women are better at words, verbal memory, and remembering landmarks and objects.*

PARAGRAPH 4

Topic sentence: *The big question, of course, is whether the differences in his and her brains cause the variation in cognitive skills or whether society pushes women toward verbal, people-oriented tasks, and men toward quantitative fields like engineering.*

Supporting Detail

The number of women in science has increased in the last 30 years, but is not equal to the number of men in math, engineering, and physics.

PARAGRAPH 5

Topic Sentence: *The nature vs. nurture debate continues 25 years later, but it is becoming more pragmatic as researchers use MRIs and other brain-imaging tools that show differences in male and female brains even when performance is identical.*

Supporting Details

1. *In the past, people were concerned that sex differences in the brain would result in discrimination.*
2. *Today, there's more tolerance of differences.*

Thinking It Through SUMMARIZING A READING

Summary writing sounds complicated, but it is not as difficult as it first appears. You will see all the steps of summary writing modeled here, and then you will write a summary of the main points of the article "His Brain, Her Brain," by Nancy Shute from pages 128–129. You have already determined the thesis as well as the main ideas and major supporting points in the reading. Now all you need to do is arrange these points into paragraph form. Because the original article is about a page in length, you will aim for about half a page in length for the summary. A summary begins with the main idea of the entire reading and then moves into the major supporting points. You do not want to be repetitive or add unnecessary details and lists. As you can see, finding the main ideas of paragraphs is an excellent tool in writing a summary because a topic sentence is the main point of a paragraph—*and a main point in a paragraph becomes a major supporting detail of a whole article.*

Remember, in a summary, you aim to paraphrase ideas. So paraphrase the main idea sentences rather than copying a topic sentence. Go back to the article on page 128 where you have underlined the main points and listed the major details of each paragraph. Then write down just the major ideas.

Title and author:_____

THE MAIN IDEAS AS EXPRESSED BY THE AUTHOR	YOUR PARAPHRASED MAIN IDEAS AND MAJOR SUPPORTING DETAILS
Thesis:	
Topic sentence of paragraph 2:	Your paraphrase of the main idea: The supporting details of paragraph 2:
Topic sentence of paragraph 3:	Your paraphrase of the main idea: The supporting details of paragraph 3:
Topic sentence of paragraph 4:	Your paraphrase of the main idea: The supporting details of paragraph 4:
Topic sentence of paragraph 5:	Your paraphrase of the main idea: The supporting details of paragraph 5:

(Continued)

Compare your answers with those that follow.

Title and author: <u>"His Brain, Her Brain," by Nancy Shute</u>

THE MAIN IDEAS AS EXPRESSED BY THE AUTHOR	YOUR PARAPHRASED MAIN IDEAS AND MAJOR SUPPORTING DETAILS
Thesis: The verdict: Female and male brains differ in both structure and function, and many of those variations start in the womb.	*Male and female brains are different physically, and differences are evident from how we behave.*

Topic sentence of paragraph 2: Male and female brains differ in how they're built, with some parts larger in men, others larger in women.	*Male and female brains differ in structure and size.*
	
	1. *Size*
	    a. *Women's brains are 10 percent smaller.*
	    b. *Women do as well on IQ tests.*
	2. *Men have more gray matter—the brain's information-processing centers—and women have more white matter, connecting the processing centers.*
	3. *Women's brains might be more efficient.*
	    a. *Women use their frontal lobes.*
	    b. *Men use matter distributed throughout the brain.*
	4. *This knowledge impacts treating diseases of the brain.*

Topic sentence of paragraph 3: When it comes to putting brains to work, women and men have their own areas of expertise.	*Because of their brain differences, men and women are good at different things.*
	
	1. *Men are better at*
	    ▪ *spatial tasks*
	    ▪ *navigating*
	    ▪ *high-end math*
	2. *Women are better at*
	    ▪ *words and verbal memory*
	    ▪ *remembering landmarks and objects*

THE MAIN IDEAS AS EXPRESSED BY THE AUTHOR	YOUR PARAPHRASED MAIN IDEAS AND MAJOR SUPPORTING DETAILS
Topic sentence of paragraph 4: The big question, of course, is whether the differences in his and her brains cause the variation in cognitive skills or whether society pushes women toward verbal, people-oriented tasks, and men toward quantitative fields like engineering.	*The question is whether differences in the brain cause differences in ability between men and women or whether it is environment or nurture that explains these differences.* 1. *The number of women in science has increased in last 30 years but is still not equal to the number of men in math, engineering, and physics.*
Topic sentence of paragraph 5: The nature vs. nurture debate continues 25 years later, but it is becoming more pragmatic as researchers use MRIs and other brain-imaging tools that show differences in male and female brains even when performance is identical.	*Today, while the nature-versus-nurture debate continues, technology that allows imaging of the brain can confirm gender brain differences, even when the performance is the same.* 1. *In the past, people were concerned that sex differences in the brain would result in discrimination.* 2. *Today, there's more tolerance of differences.*

Put these ideas into paragraph form to create your summary. Be sure to use appropriate transition words to show the connections between the ideas.

_____

_____

_____

_____

_____

_____

_____

_____

_____

_____

_____

_____

_____

_____

(Continued)

Compare your summary with that written by a partner or others in your small group. Do you all have the main points in your summaries? Whose summary seems most precise and clear? Why? Now compare your summary to this example of a summary. Remember, summaries can be worded differently, but they must all contain the main idea and the major supporting details.

In "His Brain, Her Brain," Nancy Shute discusses the differences between male and female brains. Male and female brains are different physically, and these differences are evident from how we behave. <u>First</u>, male and female brains differ in structure and size. Women's brains are 10 percent smaller than men's, but men and women do equally well on IQ tests. <u>Whereas</u> men have more gray matter (which is in the brain's information-processing centers), women have more white matter, connecting the processing centers of the brain. <u>In addition</u>, women's brains might be more efficient <u>because</u> they use their frontal lobes more, <u>whereas</u> men use matter distributed throughout the brain. This information impacts the treatment of diseases of the brain. <u>Second, because</u> of their brain differences, men and women are good at different things. <u>While</u> men generally are better at spatial tasks like navigating and high-end math, women are better at using words and verbal memory, and at remembering landmarks and objects. <u>Third</u>, the question arises about whether differences in the brain cause differences in ability between men and women or whether it is environment that explains these differences. <u>Although</u> the number of women in science has increased in the last 30 years, their numbers still do not equal those of men in the fields of math, engineering, and physics. <u>Last</u>, today, while the nature-versus-nurture debate continues, technology that allows imaging of the brain can confirm gender brain differences, even when the performance is the same. <u>Whereas</u> in the past people were concerned that sex differences in the brain would result in discrimination, today there's more tolerance of differences.

Note the underlined transition words that help create flow in the preceding summary.

To practise your summary-writing skills, please read the following article by Richard Pells, "Does the World Still Care About American Culture?" It was published in March 2009 in *The Chronicle of Higher Education.* After you have carefully read what Pells says, construct an outline for your summary by taking note of and paraphrasing his main ideas and major supporting details. Then use your outline to write the summary. Begin with Pells's thesis and follow his order of presentation. Your completed summary should be in paragraph form.

BEFORE READING

Do you accept the premise that the rest of the world is less interested in American culture today than it was during most of the twentieth century?

Does the World Still Care About American Culture?

RICHARD PELLS*

1   For most of the 20th century, the dominant culture in the world was American. Now that is no longer true. What is most striking about attitudes toward the United States in other countries is not the anti-Americanism they reflect, or the disdain for former President George W. Bush, or the opposition to American foreign policies. Rather, people abroad are increasingly indifferent to America's culture.

2   American culture used to be the elephant in everyone's living room. Whether people felt uncomfortable with the omnipresence of America's high or popular culture in their countries, they could not ignore its power or its appeal. American writers and artists were superstars—the objects of curiosity, admiration and envy. Today they are for the most part unnoticed or regarded as ordinary mortals, participants in a global rather than a distinctively American culture.

3   America's elections still matter to people overseas. As someone who has taught American studies in Europe, Latin America and Asia, I received e-mail messages from friends abroad asking me who I thought would win the presidency in November. But I rarely get queries about what I think of the latest American movie. Nor does anyone ask me about American novelists, playwrights, composers or painters.

4   Imagine any of these events or episodes in the past happening now: In 1928, fresh from having written "Rhapsody in Blue" and the "Piano Concerto in F Major," George Gershwin traveled to Paris and Vienna. He was treated like an idol. As America's most famous composer, he met with many of the leading European modernists: Schoenberg, Stravinsky, Prokofiev, Ravel. At one point, Gershwin asked Stravinsky if he could take lessons from the great Russian. Stravinsky responded by asking Gershwin how much money he made in a year. Told the answer was in six figures, Stravinsky quipped, "In that case . . . I should study with you."

5   In the 1930s, Louis Armstrong and Duke Ellington toured throughout Europe, giving concerts to thousands of adoring fans, including members of the British royal family. In the 1940s and '50s, Dave Brubeck, Miles Davis, Dizzy Gillespie, Benny Goodman and Charlie Parker often gave concerts in Western and Eastern Europe, the

*Richard Pells, who was born in Kansas City, Missouri, in 1941, studied at Rutgers University (B.A., 1963) and Harvard University (M.A., 1964; Ph.D., 1969). He is a professor of history at the University of Texas at Austin. His books include *Radical Visions and American Dreams* (1973), *Not Like Us: How Europeans Have Loved, Hated, and Transformed American Culture Since World War II* (1997), and *Modernist America: Art, Music, Movies, and the Globalization of American Culture* (Yale University Press, 2011). In the following article from the March 6, 2009, issue of *The Chronicle of Higher Education*, Pells examines the causes behind the decline of global interest in American culture.

(Continued)

Soviet Union, the Middle East, Africa, Asia and Latin America. The Voice of America's most popular program in the 1960s was a show called Music USA, specializing in jazz, with an estimated 100 million listeners around the world. In the 1940s and '50s as well, Leonard Bernstein was invited to conduct symphony orchestras in London, Moscow, Paris, Prague, Tel Aviv and Milan.

6   If you were a professor of modern literature at a foreign university, your reading list had to include Bellow, Dos Passos, Faulkner, Hemingway and Steinbeck. If you taught courses on the theater, it was obligatory to discuss *Death of a Salesman, The Iceman Cometh, Long Day's Journey Into Night* and *A Streetcar Named Desire.*

7   If you wanted to study modern art, you did not—like Gene Kelly in *An American in Paris*—journey to the City of Light (all the while singing and dancing to the music of Gershwin) to learn how to become a painter. Instead you came to New York, to sit at the feet of Willem de Kooning and Jackson Pollock. Or later you hung out at Andy Warhol's "factory," surrounded by celebrities from the arts and the entertainment world.

8   If dance was your specialty, where else could you find more creative choreographers than Bob Fosse or Jerome Robbins? If you were an aspiring filmmaker in the 1970s, the movies worth seeing and studying all originated in America. What other country could boast of such cinematic talent as Woody Allen, Robert Altman, Francis Ford Coppola, George Lucas, Martin Scorsese and Steven Spielberg?

9   Of course, there are still American cultural icons who mesmerize a global audience or whose photos are pervasive in the pages of the world's tabloid newspapers. Bruce Springsteen can always pack an arena wherever he performs. The Broadway musical *Rent* has been translated into more than 20 languages. Hollywood's blockbusters still make millions of dollars abroad. America's movie stars remain major celebrities at international film festivals.

10   But there is a sense overseas today that America's cultural exports are not as important, or as alluring, as they once were. When I lecture abroad on contemporary American culture, I find that few of America's current artists and intellectuals are household names, luminaries from whom foreigners feel they need to learn. The cultural action is elsewhere—not so much in Manhattan or San Francisco but in Berlin (the site of a major film festival) and Mumbai (the home of Indian filmmakers and media entrepreneurs who are now investing in the movies of Spielberg and other American directors). The importance of Mumbai was reinforced, spectacularly, when *Slumdog Millionaire* won the Oscar for best picture.

11   What accounts for the decline of interest in American art, literature and music? Why has American culture become just another item on the shelves of the global supermarket?

12   The main answer is that globalization has subverted America's influence. During the 1990s, many people assumed that the emergence of what they called a global culture was just another mechanism for the "Americanization" of the world. Be it

Microsoft or McDonald's, Disney theme parks or shopping malls, the movies or the Internet, the artifacts of American culture seemed ubiquitous and inescapable.

13   Yet far from reinforcing the impact of American culture, globalization has strengthened the cultures of other nations, regions and continents. Instead of defining what foreigners want, America's cultural producers find themselves competing with their counterparts abroad in shaping people's values and tastes. What we have in the 21st century is not a hegemonic American culture but multiple forms of art and entertainment—voices, images and ideas that can spring up anywhere and be disseminated all over the planet.

14   American television programs like *Dallas* and *Dynasty* were once the most popular shows on the airwaves, from Norway to New Zealand. Now many people prefer programs that are locally produced. Meanwhile, cable and satellite facilities permit stations like Al-Jazeera to define and interpret the news from a Middle Eastern perspective for people throughout the world.

15   Since 2000, moreover, American movies have steadily lost market share in Europe and Asia. In 1998, the year *Titanic* was released abroad, American films commanded 64 percent of the ticket sales in France. Ten years later, Hollywood's share of the French market has fallen to 50 percent. Similarly, in 1998, American films accounted for 70 percent of the tickets sold in South Korea. Today that figure has fallen to less than 50 percent.

16   As in the case of television programs, audiences increasingly prefer movies made in and about their own countries or regions. Indian films are now more popular in India than are imports from Hollywood. At the same time, American moviegoers are increasingly willing to sample films from abroad (and not just in art houses), which has led to the popularity in the United States of Japanese cartoons and animated films as well as recent German movies like *The Lives of Others*.

17   After World War II, professors and students from abroad were eager to study in the United States. America was, after all, the center of the world's intellectual and cultural life. Now, with the rise of continental exchange programs and the difficulties that foreign academics face obtaining U.S. visas, it is often easier for a Dutch student to study in Germany or France or for a Middle Eastern student to study in India, than for either of them to travel to an American university. That further diminishes the impact of American culture abroad.

18   Crowds, especially of young people, still flock to McDonald's—whether in Beijing, Moscow or Paris. But every country has always had its own version of equally popular fast food. There are wurst stands in Germany and Austria, fish-and-chips shops in England, noodle restaurants in South Korea and Singapore, kabob outlets on street corners in almost any city (including in America), all of which remain popular and compete effectively with the Big Mac.

19   Finally, cellphones and the Internet make information and culture instantly available to anyone, without having to depend any longer on American definitions of what

(Continued)

it is important to know. Indeed, globalization has led not to greater intellectual and political uniformity but to the decentralization of knowledge and culture. We live today in a universe full of cultural options, and we are therefore free to choose what to embrace and what to ignore.

20   I am not suggesting that America's culture is irrelevant. It remains one—but only one—of the cultural alternatives available to people abroad and at home. Moreover, it is certainly conceivable that President Barack Obama will improve America's currently dreadful image in the world, encouraging people to pay more attention not only to American policies but also to American culture—which the Bush administration, despite its efforts at cultural diplomacy, was never able to do.

21   But it is doubtful that America will ever again be the world's pre-eminent culture, as it was in the 20th century. That is not a cause for regret. Perhaps we are all better off in a world of cultural pluralism than in a world made in America.

SOURCE: Richard Pells, "Does the World Still Care About American Culture?" Originally appeared in *The Chronicle of Higher Education*, March 6, 2009, Volume 55, Issue 26, p. B4. Reprinted by permission of the author.

THINKING ABOUT THE ESSAY

1. What claim does Pells establish in his introductory paragraph? What minor propositions does he provide to support his claim?

2. Where does Pells inject information about himself into this essay? What is his purpose? Do you think his strategy is effective? Justify your response.

3. Does Pells ever establish a clear definition of American culture or does he force us to induce it? Explain. Could there be alternative definitions of American culture that compete with Pells's understanding of the word? Why or why not?

4. Trace the pattern of cause and effect that Pells establishes. According to Pells, what are the primary and secondary causes for the decline of global interest in American culture?

5. Pells alludes to numerous cultural figures and artistic works in this essay. What expectations does he have of his audience here? Would readers be less likely to relate to his essay—or accept his argument—if they were not familiar with Gene Kelly or had not read or seen *The Iceman Cometh*? Explain.

RESPONDING IN WRITING

6. Write an argumentative essay in which you attempt to refute Pells's claim that the world is losing interest in American culture. Provide supporting points and examples to buttress your argument.

7. Write a causal analysis of the impact of globalization on the dissemination of American culture around the world.

8. Reverse Pells's claim and write an essay contending or explaining why Americans are far more interested in the cultures of other nations and regions than they were in the past.

NETWORKING

9. Working in small groups, develop a list of all the references and allusions in Pells's essay and then identify as many as possible. Based on this list, establish what your group thinks that Pells means by American culture.

10. Conduct online research on one American musician, writer, artist, filmmaker, or actor mentioned in the essay—for example, Louis Armstrong, Ernest Hemingway, or Woody Allen—and explore the reception of this individual overseas. What conclusions can you draw from your research?

CRITICAL
RESPONSE

iStockphoto/Thinkstock

CHAPTER 6 Writing a Critique

Writing a
CRITIQUE

THE CONNECTION BETWEEN READING CRITICALLY AND WRITING A CRITIQUE

A critique is the written form of an evaluation of a passage or an entire work. Reading critically is the biggest aid to writing a critique; applying the guidelines for reading critically is a crucial part of preparing to write a critique. You will need to understand not only the purpose of the piece and its central idea but also the main points the writer makes. Reading critically enriches your understanding of a work and its components, enabling you to focus your critique. So the first step in writing a critique is to read critically and, in the process, to determine your opinion of the piece. Look for the thesis and purpose of the writing, who the likely intended audience is, key ideas or supporting evidence for the thesis, the author's use of language, how well the piece is organized, and how successfully the piece has achieved its stated or implied goal. You may need to read the piece several times before you are clear on your own viewpoint and therefore prepared to write.

WRITING A CRITIQUE

When you write a critique, your goal is to make a formal analysis of and response to a piece of writing, whether a selected passage or an entire essay. Your purpose encompasses both explaining and evaluating a piece of writing. In general, a written critique includes these components: (1) an introduction; (2) an objective, concise summary of the work or passage; (3) an objective analysis of the author's presentation; (4) a subjective response detailing your opinion of the author's views; and (5) a conclusion. *A critique differs from a summary, which is an objective restatement in your own words of the original material. When you summarize, you leave out*

> **IT IS A CAPITAL MISTAKE TO THEORIZE BEFORE ONE HAS DATA.**
> **INSENSIBLY ONE BEGINS TO TWIST FACTS TO SUIT THEORIES, INSTEAD OF**
> **THEORIES TO SUIT FACTS.**
>
> SIR ARTHUR CONAN DOYLE's Sherlock Holmes, *A Scandal in Bohemia*

your personal or subjective viewpoint. In a critique, you begin objectively but then add your own subjective response to the work.

Determining Your Position

To convince an audience that your analysis and response are reasonable or valid, you must convey your views confidently. Thus, before you even begin writing your critique, you must have a clear idea of your own viewpoint on the work. A firm conviction of your own position will help persuade an audience that your critique is sensible and fair. How do you arrive at your position? You do so by carefully reading and rereading the piece you are to critique, by thinking seriously about what the piece says and how it says it, and by assessing how persuaded you are as a reader by what the author has said. This stage in the writing process is crucial for helping you formulate and make concrete the points you want to make in the formal assignment.

As with other kinds of writing, any number of tools for generating writing ideas can be used to help you arrive at your position when writing a critique. The following suggestions are no doubt familiar to you from other writing classes, but here they are worded specifically for discovering your response to a piece of writing that you are to critique.

FREE WRITING

As soon as you have read or reread the work, write for 10 minutes on any impressions of any aspect of the piece that occur to you. Write down everything that comes to mind, no matter how jumbled. When your time is up, select a phrase or word that seems important to your purpose, no matter how vaguely, and write a sentence with the phrase or word in it. Put that sentence at the top of another blank piece of paper and repeat the process of writing for 10 minutes without thinking very deeply or long about what you are writing. If you do this several times, you should end up with a fairly good idea of the position you want to take in the analysis/assessment part of your paper.

LISTING

Another way to discover your viewpoint is to simply list terms or phrases describing your response to the piece you are critiquing. Then study your list and group related ideas together. Do you see a pattern? Does one dominant viewpoint emerge from these groupings? If so, write a statement reflecting that pattern or viewpoint. That should give you a sense of your position when it comes to writing your assessment of and response to the work.

ASKING QUESTIONS

Asking questions is a very useful tool for generating ideas, perhaps most useful when thinking about and drafting your response to a piece of writing. See the discussion on analysis on page 145 for a number of useful questions to ask when assessing the success of a writer's argument, language, evidence, and logic. These questions will help you arrive at your overall response to the work and discover your own position in relation to that of the writer whose work you are critiquing. However, because the response section of a critique expresses your personal, subjective reaction to the work, you will want to ask additional questions:

- Do you agree with the writer's position on the subject? Why or why not?

- What reasons can you give for supporting or disagreeing with the writer?

- Are you convinced by the writer's logic, evidence, and language? Why or why not?

- If you are not convinced, can you give other evidence to counter the arguments or evidence of the writer?

You do not need to go into great detail in the response section of your paper, but you do need to explain your reasons for your response. Give careful thought, then, to not only what you think of the piece of writing but also why you think that way. What specific elements of the work influence your reaction to the work? As with free writing and listing, write your questions and answers. Review what you have written and consider whether you have left anything unasked or unanswered.

When you are satisfied with your pre-writing activities and feel that you have generated enough ideas to write your critique confidently, you are ready to write your first draft. As with all writing assignments, you will likely write several drafts of a paper before you reach the final version. The following section lists the components of a formal critique and gives directions for writing each of those components.

Introduction

The first paragraph of your critique should name the author and title of the work that you are critiquing. Do not neglect this information, as it immediately tells readers the subject of your critique. Then give a very brief overview of the piece in two to four sentences. Your intent in the introduction is not to summarize the piece but to tell readers its purpose. Generally, stating the thesis or central idea of the piece along with a highlight or two and/or its major conclusion(s) will be enough to convey its essence and provide background for the rest of your paper. Finally, your introduction should state your own thesis. In one sentence, indicate your assessment of the passage or work that you examined. Your thesis statement should be worded to reveal your position to readers before they begin reading the body of your paper.

Summary

The first section in the body of your critique should offer an objective summary of the piece. This summary states the original author's purpose and includes key ideas and major points. Where appropriate, include direct quotations that are particularly important to the development of the piece. Do not write anything evaluative or subjective at this point. Your purpose here is to give a fair and accurate summary of the intent and main points of the work you are analyzing.

Analysis

Once you have summarized the work by stating its purpose and key points, begin to analyze the work. Your goal is to examine how well the author has achieved the purpose and consider the validity or significance of the author's information. Do not try to look at every point the author makes; rather, limit your focus to several important aspects of the piece. Remain as objective as possible in this section, saving your personal opinion of the author's position for the response section of your critique. Different purposes for writing—persuasive, expository, and expressive—require application of different criteria to judge a writer's success in achieving the intended purpose. In general, however, certain considerations help in the assessment of any piece of writing. Questions about validity, accuracy, significance, and fairness help you to evaluate any author's success or failure.

Assessing Persuasive Writing

Argumentive writing is defined as a mode of persuasion in which the goal is either to convince readers of the validity of the writer's position (argument) or to move readers to accept the author's view and perhaps even act on it (persuasion). This means that the writer must supply evidence or proof to support his or her position in such a way as to convince readers that the position is valid, whether they agree with the position or not. If the purpose is to persuade, the supporting evidence or proof must be so convincing that readers adopt the position themselves. In any event, when assessing the success of another writer's argument, you should gauge how well that writer has used the standard strategies for argumentation. Furthermore, pay attention to the writer's use of language. Finally, assess the validity of the argument by examining the evidence the writer presents to support his position and the logic of his conclusions.

Examining a Writer's Language

In particular, make sure that the writer defines any words or terms that may be unclear, abstract, or ambiguous. Ask yourself if the writer's language seems intended to intimidate or confuse readers or if the writer attempts to manipulate readers by relying on emotionally loaded words. Does the writer make sarcastic remarks or personal attacks? Ultimately, examine a writer's evidence, to evaluate credibility and fairness. Good writers do not rely on manipulative language, unclear terms, or loaded or sarcastic words to achieve their purposes.

Examining a Writer's Evidence

A writer should support any generalizations or claims with ample, relevant evidence. As a critical reader, consider the value or significance of that evidence. Evidence may be supplied in the form of statistics, facts, examples, or appeals to authorities. Keep in mind that statistics can be manipulated to conform to the needs of the person using them, so make sure that they are based on a large and representative sample, that the method of gathering the statistics yields accurate results, and that the statistics come from reliable sources. Look closely at statements of facts, as well; they should give accurate, complete, and trustworthy information. Examples are specific instances or illustrations that reveal a whole type, and they should give believable, relevant, reliable, and representative support for an author's thesis. Finally, authorities are people who have the training or experience needed to make trustworthy and reliable observations on matters relating to their areas of expertise. In completing a critique, make sure, as far as possible, that the piece under study appeals to believable and credible authorities.

Judging a Writer's Logic

Argumentative or persuasive writing must portray a logical, reasonable, and accurate reasoning process supplemented by relevant, sensible supporting proofs. You will be in a good position to evaluate a writer's reasoning process if you are mindful of any pitfalls that undermine the success of the argument. Evaluating the writer's logic is part of the process of critiquing a work. The following list is a summary of some of these flaws in logic that you should look for when writing your critique:

- **Oversimplification.** Offering a solution or an explanation that is too simple for the problem or issue being argued. This fault in logic overlooks the complexity of an issue. Example: Arguing that the crime rate will go down if we just outlaw handguns overlooks such important considerations as crimes committed with weapons other than handguns and the likely probability that the criminal underworld would continue to have access to guns, illegal or not.

- **Stereotyping.** A form of generalization or oversimplification in which an entire group is narrowly labeled or perceived on the basis of a few in the group. Example: Arguing that women are not suited for combat because women are weaker than men is a stereotype based on the fact that the average woman is weaker than the average man. Not all women are weaker than men.

- **False analogy.** Falsely claiming that, because something resembles something else in one way, it resembles it in all ways. Example: Arguing that anti-abortionists cannot favor the death penalty because they view abortion as murder is a false analogy.

- ***Non sequitur.*** Drawing inferences or conclusions that do not follow logically from available evidence. Example: Reminding a child who will not eat her food of all the starving children in the world is a line of reasoning that does not follow: if the child eats her food, will that lessen the starvation of other children? If the child does not eat the food, can the food itself somehow aid those starving children?

- **Circular reasoning or begging the question.** Making a claim that simply rephrases another claim in other words. It assumes as proof the very claim it is meant to support. Example: A parent replying "because I said so" when a child asks why he must do something.

- **Either/or reasoning.** Admitting only two sides to an issue and asserting that the writer's is the only possible correct one. Example: Arguing that if you do not support your country's involvement in war as I do, you are not patriotic. The implication is that "either you are for your country or you are against it and the right way is my way."

- **Red herring.** Diverting the audience's attention from the main issue at hand to an irrelevant issue. Example: Calling attention to the suffering of a victim's family when arguing for the death penalty shifts focus away from the relevant reasons for capital punishment.

- ***Post hoc, ergo propter hoc* reasoning.** Assuming that something happened simply because it followed something else without evidence of a causal relationship. Example: Arguing that an airline is faulty because of flight delays at an airport assumes that the airline caused the delays, when a more important factor might be weather conditions that prevented airplanes from flying.

For more flaws in logic, please review pages 95–99 in Chapter 3 ("Propaganda: Intentional Errors in Reasoning").

Response

In this part of your critique, express your own position relative to that of the writer of the piece and give reasons why you believe as you do. You may find yourself in total agreement or absolutely opposed to the author's position, or you may place yourself somewhere in between. You may agree with some points the author makes but disagree with others. No matter what position you take, you must state your viewpoint clearly and provide reasons for your position. These reasons may be closely linked to your assessment of key elements of the paper, as laid out in your assessment section, or they may spring from ideas that you generated in your pre-writing activities.

WRITING A CRITIQUE: PREPARATION AND EVALUATION

First, read the text critically by

- determining the main point, the chief purpose, and the intended audience;

- identifying arguments that support or develop the main point;

- locating evidence used to support the arguments; and

- determining any underlying biases or unexamined assumptions.

Then evaluate the text by asking

- Has the author clearly stated or implied a thesis, main idea, or position?

- Has the author written to a clearly identifiable audience?

- What rhetorical strategies in the development and organization of the essay does the writer use? Is the development appropriate to the purpose? Is the essay logically and clearly organized?

- If the writing is an argument, does the author use verifiable facts or convincing evidence? If the essay seeks to explain, define, describe, or accomplish some other purpose, has the writer supplied enough details to clearly achieve the stated or implied purpose?

- Are language and word choice accurate, imaginative, correct, and/or appropriate?

- Does the text leave any unanswered questions?

Conclusion

The final paragraph of your critique should reiterate in several sentences your overall assessment of the piece, the conclusions you have drawn from your analysis, and your personal response to the work. This section is not the place to introduce new material; rather, it is an opportunity to provide an overall summary of your paper. You want your readers to feel that you have given them a thorough and thoughtful analysis of the work under consideration, and that you have brought your comments to a satisfying close.

GUIDELINES FOR WRITING A CRITIQUE

- Begin with an introduction. The introduction familiarizes readers with the work under discussion, provides a context for the piece, and states your thesis.

- Summarize main points. The summary tells readers what major points the writer makes to support her position.

- Analyze how well the writer has achieved her purpose. The analysis tells readers what aspects of the work you have examined, depending on the kind of writing you are considering. In general, assess the overall presentation of evidence, judging its validity, accuracy, significance, and fairness.

- Explain your response to the piece. The response section tells readers your personal viewpoint by explaining the extent to which you agree or disagree with the author.

- Conclude with your observations of the overall effectiveness of the piece and your personal views on the subject. The conclusion summarizes for readers the results of your analysis and your overall judgment of the piece.

Exercise

Read Robert N. Sollod's "The Hollow Curriculum" and the sample critique that follows. Prepare for class discussion by answering the questions for response and discussion after the essay and considering how your response to the piece compares to that of the student writer Kari Kolb.

THE HOLLOW CURRICULUM

Robert N. Sollod*

1   The past decade in academe has seen widespread controversy over curricular reform. We have explored many of the deeply rooted, core assumptions that have guided past decisions about which subjects should be emphasized in the curriculum and how they should be approached. Yet I have found myself repeatedly disappointed by the lack of significant discussion concerning the place of religion and spirituality in colleges' curricula and in the lives of educated persons.

2   I do not mean to suggest that universities should indoctrinate students with specific viewpoints or approaches to life; that is not their proper function. But American universities now largely ignore religion and spirituality, rather than considering what aspects of religious and spiritual teachings should enter the curriculum and how those subjects should be taught. The curricula that most undergraduates study do little to rectify the fact that many Americans are ignorant of religious and spiritual teachings, of their significance in the history of this and other civilizations, and of their significance in contemporary society. Omitting this major facet of human experience and thought contributes to a continuing shallowness and imbalance in much of university life today.

3   Let us take the current discussions of multiculturalism as one example. It is hardly arguable that an educated person should approach life with knowledge of several cultures or patterns of experience. Appreciation and understanding of human diversity are worthy educational ideals. Should such an appreciation exclude the religious and spiritually based concepts of reality that are the backbone upon which entire cultures have been based?

4   Multiculturalism that does not include appreciation of the deepest visions of reality reminds me of the travelogues that I saw in the cinema as a child—full of details of quaint and somewhat mysterious behavior that evoked some superficial empathy but no real, in-depth understanding. Implicit in a multicultural approach that ignores spiritual factors is a kind of critical and patronizing attitude. It assumes that we can understand and evaluate the experiences of other cultures without comprehension of their deepest beliefs.

5   Incomprehensibly, traditionalists who oppose adding multicultural content to the curriculum also ignore the religious and theological bases of the Western civilization that they seek to defend. Today's advocates of Western traditionalism focus, for the most part, on conveying a type of rationalism that is only a single strain in Western thought. Their approach does not demonstrate sufficient awareness of the contributions of Western religions and spirituality to philosophy and literature, to moral and legal codes, to the development of governmental and political institutions, and to the mores of our society.

---

*Robert N. Sollod is a professor of clinical psychology at Cleveland State University. He is author of many articles on spirituality, psychology, and related topics, and was a member of the Task Force on Religious Issues in Graduate Education and Training for the American Psychological Association when he wrote this essay for the March 18, 1992, issue of *The Chronicle of Higher Education*, a professional publication for faculty, staff, and administrators in colleges and universities.

6   Nor is the lack of attention to religion and spirituality new. I recall taking undergraduate philosophy classes in the 1960s in which Plato and Socrates were taught
without reference to the fact that they were contemplative mystics who believed in
immortality and reincarnation. Everything that I learned in my formal undergraduate education about Christianity came through studying a little Thomas Aquinas
in a philosophy course, and even there we focused more on the logical sequence
of his arguments than on the fundamentals of the Christian doctrine that he
espoused. I recall that Dostoyevsky was presented as an existentialist with hardly
a nod given to the fervent Christian beliefs so clearly apparent in his writings. I
even recall my professors referring to their Christian colleagues, somewhat dis-
paragingly, as "Christers." I learned about mystical and spiritual interpretations of
Shakespeare's sonnets and plays many years after taking college English courses.

7   We can see the significance of omitting teaching about religion and spirituality in the discipline of psychology and, in particular, in my own field of clinical
psychology. I am a member of the Task Force on Religious Issues in Graduate
Education and Training in Division 36 of the American Psychological Association,
a panel chaired by Edward Shafranske of Pepperdine University. In this work, I
have discovered that graduate programs generally do not require students to learn
anything about the role of religion in people's lives.

8   Almost no courses are available to teach psychologists how to deal with the religious values or concerns expressed by their clients. Nor are such courses required
or generally available at the undergraduate level for psychology majors. Allusions
to religion and spirituality often are completely missing in textbooks on introductory psychology, personality theory, concepts of psychotherapy, and developmen-
tal psychology.

9   Recent attempts to add a multicultural perspective to clinical training almost
completely ignore the role of religion and spirituality as core elements of many
racial, ethnic, and national identities. Prayer is widely practiced, yet poorly understood and rarely studied by psychologists. When presented, religious ideas are
usually found in case histories of patients manifesting severe psychopathology.

10   Yet spiritual and mystical experiences are not unusual in our culture. And
research has shown that religion is an important factor in the lives of many Americans; some studies have suggested that a client's religious identification may
affect the psychotherapeutic relationship, as well as the course and outcome of
therapy. Some patterns of religious commitment have been found to be associated with high levels of mental health and ego strength. A small number of
psychologists are beginning to actively challenge the field's inertia and indiffer-
ence by researching and writing on topics related to religion and spirituality. Their
efforts have not as yet, however, markedly affected the climate or curricula in most
psychology departments.

11   Is it any wonder that religion for the typical psychotherapist is a mysterious
and taboo topic? It should not be surprising that therapists are not equipped even

(Continued)

to ask the appropriate questions regarding a person's religious or spiritual life—much less deal with psychological aspects of spiritual crises.

12   Or consider the field of political science. Our scholars and policy makers have been unable to predict or understand the major social and political movements that produced upheavals around the world during the last decade. That is at least partly because many significant events—the remarkable rise of Islamic fundamentalism, the victory of Afghanistan over the Soviet Union, the unanticipated velvet revolutions in Eastern Europe and in the Soviet Union, and the continuing conflicts in Cyprus, Israel, Lebanon, Northern Ireland, Pakistan, Sri Lanka, Tibet, and Yugoslavia—can hardly be appreciated without a deep understanding of the religious views of those involved. The tender wisdom of our contemporary political scientists cannot seem to comprehend the deep spirituality inherent in many of today's important social movements.

13   Far from being an anachronism, religious conviction has proved to be a more potent contemporary force than most, if not all, secular ideologies. Too often, however, people with strong religious sentiments are simply dismissed as "zealots" or "fanatics"—whether they be Jewish settlers on the West Bank, Iranian demonstrators, Russian Baptists, Shiite leaders, antiabortion activists, or evangelical Christians.

14   Most sadly, the continuing neglect of spirituality and religion by colleges and universities also results in a kind of segregation of the life of the spirit from the life of the mind in American culture. This situation is far from the ideals of Thoreau, Emerson, or William James. Spirituality in our society too often represents a retreat from the world of intellectual discourse, and spiritual pursuits are often cloaked in a reflexive anti-intellectualism, which mirrors the view in academe of spirituality as an irrational cultural residue. Students with spiritual interests and concerns learn that the university will not validate or feed their interests. They learn either to suppress their spiritual life or to split their spiritual life apart from their formal education.

15   Much has been written about the loss of ethics, a sense of decency, moderation, and fair play in American society. I would submit that much of this loss is a result of the increasing ignorance, in circles of presumably educated people, of religious and spiritual world views. It is difficult to imagine, for example, how ethical issues can be intelligently approached and discussed or how wise ethical decisions can be reached without either knowledge or reference to those religious and spiritual principles that underlie our legal system and moral codes.

16   Our colleges and universities should reclaim one of their earliest purposes—to educate and inform students concerning the spiritual and religious underpinnings of thought and society. To the extent that such education is lacking, our colleges and universities are presenting a narrow and fragmented view of human experience.

17   Both core curricula and more advanced courses in the humanities and social sciences should be evaluated for their coverage of religious topics. Active leadership

at the university, college, and departmental levels is needed to encourage and carry out needed additions and changes in course content. Campus organizations should develop forums and committees to examine the issue, exchange information, and develop specific proposals.

18   National debate and discussion about the best way to educate students concerning religion and spirituality are long overdue.

PERSONAL RESPONSE

Describe the degree to which you are spiritual or religious. How important is religion in your life?

QUESTIONS FOR CLASS OR SMALL-GROUP DISCUSSION

1.   Sollod gives examples of how an understanding of religion and spirituality would help someone trained in his field, psychology, and how it would help political scientists. In what other disciplines or fields do you think such training would be important? Explain how it would enhance the understanding of people trained in those fields.

2.   Discuss whether you agree with Sollod that religion and spirituality have a place in the college curriculum.

3.   Sollod calls for campus organizations to develop forums and committees to examine the place of religion and spirituality on the college campus and to develop specific proposals on the issue (paragraph 17). Conduct your own class forum or create a class committee to consider the issues that Sollod raises. Where do people learn about spirituality? How do you think a person could benefit from learning about religion and spirituality in college courses?

ILLUSTRATION: CRITIQUE

Kari Kolb

English 150

September 20, 2005

A Critique of "The Hollow Curriculum"

In his essay "The Hollow Curriculum," Robert Sollod addresses the controversial subject of religion in the public school system, particularly at the college level. Sollod believes that by failing to

Kolb 2

acknowledge religious histories and teachings, universities contribute to the declining morality of society. He recommends an evaluation of course offerings in terms of ways in which courses on religion or spirituality can be integrated into higher education curriculum. Such a project would involve not only university faculty and administrators but also American citizens nationwide. While it may be true that recent years have seen a moral or ethical decline in the general public, Sollod's assertion that this decline is due to religious ignorance is not only unfounded but also untrue.

Sollod begins his piece by exploring the lack of religious and spiritual emphasis in the national curriculum and in the lives of college alumni. After explaining the religious background of America's history, he goes on to look at other cultures as well. Noting that much of multicultural appreciation depends on understanding others' cultures, Sollod points out that many other civilizations have built the foundation of their culture upon religious and spiritual beliefs. He does not endorse one particular faith; rather, he suggests that all-inclusive religious studies would enrich the careers and lives of college students. Sollod continues by warning that a lack of religious studies has resulted in "the loss of ethics, a sense of decency, moderation, and fair play in American society" (45). His proposed solution includes a curriculum assessment of current course offerings in religion and spirituality, active leadership of faculty and administrators across the university to initiate curriculum change, and the

Kolb 3

involvement of students in the form of debates and committees (45).

Sollod has a solid sense of his audience, made up primarily of faculty and staff in higher education. By implication, what he proposes is of interest to students as well. Sollod draws readers into his argument with a series of questions and then offers information in a simple yet authoritative manner. He provides detailed examples, explaining how religious understanding would enhance all areas of study, ranging from the broad fields of political science and psychology to the ideas of Shakespeare and Socrates. This wide-ranging analysis enables Sollod to reach his large and somewhat diverse audience. He bases much of his reasoning upon the idea that "religious and spiritually based concepts . . . are the backbone upon which entire cultures have been based" (43).

Sollod's valid argument is made even more credible when he extends it to include familiar examples, such as conflicts in the former Soviet Union, Ireland, and the Middle East. At times, Sollod relies on emotional appeals, seen most often in his occasional use of loaded words and phrases such as "continuing shallowness and imbalance" (43) and "mysterious and taboo" (44). In general, though, he makes a fair and logical argument, and he concludes with a rational solution to what he sees as a serious problem.

I agree with Sollod when he states that the college curriculum would be greatly enhanced by the addition of courses in religion and spirituality or the incorporation of such material in traditional courses. Such courses would provide a solid grounding for most professions and promote a greater cultural understanding in general. I do believe, however, that Sollod exaggerates in his statement that the loss of ethics in American society is "a result of the increasing ignorance, in circles of presumably educated people, of religious and spiritual world views" (45). Here, Sollod makes an inaccurate generalization, with no evidence or clear reasoning to back up his stance. On the contrary, statistics show that in the past thirty years, religion has not only sustained itself, but it has also diversified. According to a recent survey, "Some 375 ethnic or multiethnic religious groups have already formed in the United States in the last three decades. Sociologists of religion believe the numbers will only increase in the coming years" (Beckman). These religious groups are not only the creations of immigrants, but they also reflect America's growing diversity. In fact, as Joanne Beckman of Duke University explains, almost half of the baby boomer generation has dropped out of their traditional churches and are "just as willing to sample Eastern religions, New Age spiritualism, or quasi-religious self-help groups. . . . [F]or [these] seekers, spirituality is a means of individual expression, self-discovery, inner healing, and personal growth." Although the deterioration of moral values is a frustrating problem in our society, it cannot, as Sollod suggests, be attributed entirely to a lack of religious appreciation and diversity.

Kolb 5

"The Hollow Curriculum" endorses a controversial proposal that has prompted much deliberation: the addition of, or increase in, religious and spiritual studies in our national curriculum. Although Sollod does well in arguing his position on the subject, he assumes, without proof, that much of university life is shallow and that university curricula is unbalanced. Further, he makes a hasty generalization when he places the blame of America's ethical undoing on the lack of "knowledge or reference to those religious and spiritual principles that underline our legal system and moral codes" (45). In this generalization, he neglects to recognize the growing religious and spiritual diversity of the American people. This omission weakens the foundation of his argument—that an increase in religious studies will benefit all areas of life—by overlooking evidence showing that, despite an increase in spiritual awareness, the loss of ethics remains a problem in our society. Sollod thus undermines his own position and leaves his readers, though inspired by his zeal, understandably skeptical.

Works Cited

Beckman, Joanne. "Religion in Post-World War II in America." *Divining America.* October 2000. Duke U. 17 Sept. 2004. <http://uni52v.unity.ncsu. edu:8080/tserve/twenty/tkeyinfo/trelww2.htm>.

Sollod, Robert. "The Hollow Curriculum." *Perspectives on Contemporary Issues: Readings Across the Curriculum,* 4th ed. Ed. Katherine Anne Ackley. Boston, MA: Thomson Wadsworth, 2006. 43-45.

Exercise

Read Linda Lee's "Who Needs College?" and prepare for class discussion by writing a critique of the essay. The questions for response and discussion after the essay may help you in your critique. Your instructor may want you to hand in your critique or use it for class discussion.

WHO NEEDS COLLEGE?

Linda Lee*

1   Do you, like me, have a child who is smart but never paid attention in class? Now it's high school graduation time. Other parents are talking Stanford this and State U. that. Your own child has gotten into a pretty good college. The question is: Is he ready? Should he go at all?

2   In this country two-thirds of high school graduates go on to college. In some middle-class suburbs, that number reaches 90 percent. So why do so many feel the need to go?

3   America is obsessed with college. It has the second-highest number of graduates worldwide, after (not Great Britain, not Japan, not Germany) Australia. Even so, only 27 percent of Americans have a bachelor's degree or higher. That leaves an awful lot who succeed without college, or at least without a degree. Many read books, think seriously about life and have well-paying jobs. Some want to start businesses. Others want to be electricians or wilderness guides or makeup artists. Not everyone needs a higher education.

4   What about the statistics showing that college graduates make more money? First, until the computer industry came along, all the highest-paying jobs *required* a college degree: doctor, lawyer, engineer. Second, on average, the brightest and hardest-working kids in school go to college. So is it a surprise that they go on to make more money? And those studies almost always pit kids with degrees against those with just high school. An awful lot have additional training, but they are not included. Ponder for a moment: Who makes more, a plumber or a philosophy major?

5   These are tough words. I certainly wouldn't have listened to them five years ago when my son was graduating from high school. He had been smart enough to get into the Bronx High School of Science in New York and did well on his SATs. But I know now that he did not belong in college, at least not straight out of high school.

*Linda Lee is an editor and writer for the *New York Times*. An article she wrote for the Education Life supplement of that publication in 1998, called "What's the Rush? Why College Can Wait," was the basis for her book *Success Without College: Why Your Child May Not Have to Go to College Right Now—And May Not Ever Have to Go* (2000). In addition to contributing to the *Times*, Lee is the author of several books. This brief essay, which touches on some of the ideas explained in her book, appeared in the "Full Circle" column of the June 12, 2001, issue of *Family Circle*.

6   But he went, because all his friends were going, because it sounded like fun, because he could drink beer and hang out. He did not go to study philosophy. Nor did he feel it incumbent to go to class or complete courses. Meanwhile I was paying $1,000 a week for this pleasure cruise.

7   Eventually I asked myself, "Is he getting $1,000 a week's worth of education?" Heck no. That's when I began wondering why everyone needs to go to college. (My hair colorist makes $300,000 a year without a degree.) What about the famous people who don't have one, like Bill Gates (dropped out of Harvard) and Walter Cronkite (who left the University of Texas to begin a career in journalism)?

8   So I told my son (in a kind way) that his college career was over for now, but he could reapply to the Bank of Mom in two years if he wanted to go back. Meanwhile, I said, get a job.

9   If college is so wonderful, how come so many kids "stop out"? (That's the new terminology.) One study showed only 26 percent of those who began four-year colleges had earned a degree in six years. And what about the kids who finish, then can't find work? Of course, education is worth a great deal more than just employment. But most kids today view college as a way to get a good job.

10   I know, I know. What else is there to do? Won't he miss the "college experience?" First off, there are thousands of things for kids to do. And yes, he will miss the college experience, which may include binge drinking, reckless driving and sleeping in on class days. He can have the same experience in the Marine Corps, minus the sleeping in, and be paid good money for it and learn a trade and discipline.

11   If my son had gone straight through college, he would be a graduate by now. A number of his friends are, and those who were savvy enough to go into computers at an Ivy League school walked into $50,000-a-year jobs. But that's not everyone. An awful lot became teachers making half that. And some still don't know what they want to do.

12   They may, like my son, end up taking whatever jobs they can get. Over the last two years, he's done roofing, delivered UPS packages and fixed broken toilets. His phone was turned off a few times, and he began to pay attention to details, like the price of a gallon of gasoline.

13   But a year ago he began working at a telecommunications company. He loves his work, and over the last year, he's gotten a raise and a year-end bonus. He tells me now he plans to stay there and become a manager.

14   So, just about on schedule, my son has had his own graduation day. And although I won't be able to take a picture of him in cap and gown, I couldn't be any more proud. He grew up, as most kids do. And he did it, for the most part, in spite of college.

PERSONAL RESPONSE
Respond to the questions posed by Lee in her first paragraph. Were you ready for college? What would you do if you were not in college?

(Continued)

QUESTIONS FOR CLASS OR SMALL-GROUP DISCUSSION

1. Lee states in paragraph 3 that "not everyone needs a higher education." Do you agree with her? Discuss your response to her statement.

2. In paragraph 5, Lee says that her son "did not belong in college, at least not straight out of high school." Explore the implications of that statement by considering the advantages and disadvantages of postponing entry into college after high-school graduation.

3. Summarize Lee's "case against college." What is her strongest argument? How do you respond to that point?

4. What is your reaction to Lee's characterization of "the college experience" in paragraph 10? Is it true of your own experience in college? Would you describe the college experience differently? If so, how would you describe it?

ARGUMENTATIVE WRITING

PART 4

iStockphoto/Thinkstock

CHAPTER 7 The Nature and Process of Argument

CHAPTER 8 Generating Material

CHAPTER 9 Organizing Materials

CHAPTER 10 The Writing Process: Drafting Arguments

CHAPTER 11 The Writing Process: Revising and Editing Arguments

The Nature and
PROCESS OF ARGUMENT

Considering the Disciplines

Students sometimes sign up for a course in argument because friends have told them they'd do well in it since they like to argue over every little thing with their friends. But being argumentative (in the sense of quarrelsome) is not the same as constructing well-thought-out formal arguments. To argue effectively you must focus on the issue, not how to "defeat your opponent." This chapter introduces you to fundamental concepts of argument and its importance to all fields of study. Regardless of your field, you'll find material in this chapter applicable. Specific topics include a formal definition of argument; the reasons for argument; basic argument structure; and the rhetorical frame that situates the communication act in the context of the audience, the topic, the writer, and the purpose of the communication.

The freedom to think for ourselves and the freedom to present and defend our views rank among the most precious rights that we as individuals possess, as the great poet and essayist John Milton knew. The more we know about argument—what it involves, how a strong argument is constructed, and what a weak argument lacks—the more likely we are to benefit from this liberty.

WHY ARGUE?

All of us find occasions to argue every day. Sometimes we argue just to make conversation. We argue casually with friends about which restaurant serves the best food, which movies are the most entertaining, or which automobile performs the best or most reliably for the money. Sometimes we engage in arguments presented in the media, taking positions on topics debated in newspapers and magazines, or on television, radio, and the Internet. And sometimes we argue in a more analytical manner on issues we have thought a lot about, such as which political party is most sympathetic to education reform, whether the Internet is a reliable research tool, or how we might solve a particular problem. When more is at stake, as in this last type of argument, the chances are greater that we will fail to be persuaded by what we hear or read or become frustrated by our own failure to persuade. We often fail to persuade because we lack evidence to back up our claims or because the evidence we do have is inadequate.

In other words, while casual arguments often consist of little more than exchanges of opinions or unsupported generalizations, more formal arguments are expected to include evidence in support of generalizations if they are to succeed in making strong points, solving real problems, or changing minds.

WHAT IS AN ARGUMENT?

People sometimes say that *everything* is an argument. That is quite true in the sense that whatever is communicated represents an individual point of view, one compelling enough to be accepted by the audience. Thus, if you're writing on a seemingly neutral *topic*, such as a day in the life of an emergency room nurse, you are implicitly arguing that your portrayal of the nurse is accurate and that nurses play a vital role in emergency rooms.

But *argument* as we use the term in this textbook is more explicitly an effort to change readers' minds about an issue. Thus, we would generally call a day-in-the-life article mainly explanatory or reportorial writing. However, if your aim is to show that people often have the wrong idea about the role or importance of hospital nurses, you would be engaged in argumentative writing.

An argument must possess three basic ingredients to be successful. First, it must contain as much *relevant information* about the issue as possible. Second, it must present *convincing evidence* that enables the audience to accept the writer's or speaker's claim. The more controversial the claim, the more compelling the evidence must be. Third, it must lay out a *pattern of reasoning*. That is, it must logically progress from thesis to support of thesis to conclusion. Before we examine these three elements, though, let us consider a formal definition of argument.

A Formal Definition of Argument

An argument is a form of discourse in which the writer or speaker tries to persuade an audience to accept, reject, or think a certain way about a problem that cannot be solved by scientific or mathematical reasoning alone. The assertion that the circumference of a circle is a product of its diameter times pi is not arguable because the assertion cannot be disputed; it is a universally accepted mathematical fact. At the other extreme, asserting an unsubstantiated opinion is not stating an argument; it is only announcing a stance on a particular issue. For example, someone in a casual conversation who asserts that public flogging of robbers would be a more effective deterrent than jailing them is voicing an opinion, not presenting an argument. If you respond by saying "Yeah, probably," or "No way—that would contribute to a culture of violence," you are also stating an opinion. If you respond instead by requesting evidence, such as statistics that show a correlation between public punishment and crime rate, you are helping to shape the conversation into a true argument. It is useful to keep in mind that the word *argument* is derived from the Latin word *arguere*, to clarify or prove.

A good argument is not casual. It takes considerable time and effort to prepare. It not only presents evidence to back up its claim but also acknowledges the existence of other claims about the issue before committing to the claim that corresponds most closely to the arguer's convictions. A good argument also guides the audience through a logical, step-by-step line of reasoning from thesis to conclusion. In short, a good argument uses an argumentative structure.

Amplifying the Definition

Let us now amplify our definition of argument: An argument is a form of discourse in which the writer or speaker presents a pattern of reasoning, reinforced by detailed evidence and refutation of challenging claims, that tries to persuade the audience to accept the claim. Let us take a close look at each of the elements in this definition.

"... A PATTERN OF REASONING ..."

This element requires that a good argument disclose its train of thought in a logical progression that leads the reader or listener from thesis to support of thesis to conclusion. It also implies that any unfamiliar terms or concepts are carefully defined or explained, and that enough background information is provided to enable readers or listeners to understand the larger *context* (interacting background elements) contributing to the argument. For example, to make the claim that gas-guzzling sports utility vehicles (SUVs) are selling better than fuel-efficient subcompacts does not qualify as an argument because no context for the claim is given. Readers or listeners would ask, "So what?" But if the assertion is placed in the context of an urgent problem—for example, that the enormous popularity of SUVs is rapidly increasing gasoline consumption nationally, which in turn is leading to greater dependence on foreign oil—then a valid argument is established.

"... REINFORCED BY DETAILED EVIDENCE ..."

In a formal argument, any assertion must be backed up with specific, compelling evidence that is accurate, timely, relevant, and sufficient. Such evidence can be data derived from surveys, experiments, observations, and firsthand field investigations (statistical evidence), or from expert opinion (authoritative evidence).

"... THAT TRIES TO PERSUADE THE AUDIENCE TO ACCEPT THE CLAIM."

This last element of the definition brings to mind the ultimate aim of any argument: to convince the audience that the arguer's point of view is a sensible one, worthy of serious consideration if not outright acceptance. To accomplish this aim, arguers often reinforce their evidence with what are known as *appeals*—appeals to authority and traditional values, to feelings, and to reason. In an ideal world, evidence (the hard facts) alone would be enough to persuade audiences to accept the truth of a claim, but in reality, more persuasive force often is needed and appeals are drawn in.

WHAT IS AN ARGUABLE THESIS?

As we noted in our formal definition of *argument*, statements of fact are not arguable because they are beyond dispute. One cannot challenge the fact that Homer's *Iliad* is about the Trojan War; however, one can challenge the assertion (or claim) that the Trojan War actually occurred. Now, merely to assert that you don't believe the Trojan War occurred would be expressing your *opinion*, but it is not yet an arguable thesis. Consider what is necessary for this opinion to qualify for both criteria.

For an opinion to become a thesis, it must be presented as *a problem capable of being investigated*—for example, "Judging from the latest archaeological evidence, I wish to argue that the fabled Trojan War did not occur." Moreover, the thesis must be counterarguable. In other words, it should at least be conceivable that the evidence used to support the thesis could be interpreted differently, or that new evidence could negate the old or at least lead to a very different interpretation of the old. We now have a thesis because (1) we have characterized the subject matter as a problem (i.e., experts have been trying to determine for a long time whether the Trojan War occurred), (2) it is capable of being investigated at least through archaeological evidence (and perhaps through other forms of evidence as well—accounts by contemporary historians, for example), and (3) the thesis is refutable.

The next step is to ensure that the argument to be presented is substantive. Merely referring to "archaeological evidence" will not do because it is too generalized; it's like the advertising phrase "Doctors everywhere recommend . . ." or "A million satisfied customers prove. . . ." To make the thesis substantive, reference to evidence needs to be more specific: "Archaeological evidence from the latest excavations in Turkey suggest that the fabled Trojan War did not occur."

"Wait," you say. "Doesn't evidence from excavations qualify as 'fact' and therefore beyond dispute?" No. Facts are self-evident: The square root of 144 will always equal 12, no matter who does the calculating. Archaeological findings are subject to interpretation. One archeologist will study newly discovered artifacts and construct one historical scenario; another archaeologist will study the same artifacts yet construct a completely different scenario. That's because the evidence uncovered (a potsherd, a sculpture fragment, etc.) does not shed enough light on the historical event being investigated.

USING EVIDENCE IN ARGUMENT

Argumentative writing uses two kinds of evidence: indisputable (or factual) and disputable. The first kind refers to matters of public record that anyone can verify. No one is going to dispute the fact that the earth revolves around the sun every 365.25 days. How such facts are applied is another matter, but the facts themselves are beyond dispute.

But what about disputable evidence? Imagine that a friend's room is filled with art books and reproductions of paintings. If someone asks about this friend's interests, you would reply, "Art!" without hesitation, and cite as evidence the books and paintings. But that evidence is disputable: The books and paintings could belong to a roommate, could be a mere inheritance, or could represent a former interest only recently abandoned.

Just the fact that evidence is disputable, however, does not mean it is unreliable. Such evidence often represents the closest one can get to the truth. Will banning handguns prevent tragedies like the Columbine school shootings? One researcher might discover statistical evidence of a correlation between banning guns and reduced crime; yet another researcher could find evidence of a contrary correlation. Different parts of the country or the world, different years, different times of year, different age groups—all represent constantly changing variables that can affect such a correlation. The more aware you are of the possible ways in which evidence may be disputed, the less likely you are to reach facile or premature conclusions.

Exercise 7.1

1. Consulting an unabridged dictionary, prepare a critical summary of the terms *argument*, *debate*, *dispute*, and *quarrel*. In what ways do the definitions differ? Where do they overlap, and how do you account for the overlap?

2. Supplement these definitions with examples, drawing from your own experiences.

3. Which of the following assertions could be developed into a formal argument, and which could not? Explain your reasons.
    a. A clear link has been established between secondhand cigarette smoke and lung cancer.
    b. The Surgeon General has determined that smoking is a health hazard.
    c. Studying a foreign language gives children a greater command of their native language.
    d. The more video games children play, the less likely their abstract reasoning skills are to develop properly.

4. List the topics of recent disputes you have had with friends or family. Under each topic, note the claims asserted by each side, followed by any support that had been attempted for each. Next, go back over these topics and list additional support you would give to one or more of these claims if you had been asked to elaborate on them in a more formal manner.

5. Discuss the kinds of evidence writers would want to use to resolve the following controversial assumptions. What problems with definitions might arise in some of these claims?
    a. Adults are safer drivers than teenagers.
    b. The many species of birds that still inhabit the Everglades suggest that this ecosystem is not as endangered as environmentalists say it is.
    c. The greater number of violent shows you watch, the more likely you are to commit acts of violence.
    d. Male smokers are three times more likely to become impotent than male nonsmokers.
    e. Obscene books should be banned from public school libraries.

8

Generating
MATERIAL

TECHNIQUES FOR GENERATING ARGUMENTS

Brainstorming: Rapid listing of ideas, words, or phrases suggested by a topic

Critical thinking: Interpretation, application, analysis, synthesis, and evaluation

Discussing: Vocal or Internet exchanges with others on a topic

Writing: Using prose to generate ideas, not necessarily to produce a draft

- Focused freewriting: Full-sentence rapid writing on a topic
- Journaling: Full-sentence reflective writing on a topic
- Blogging: Journal or log entries posted on the Web ("weblogging")

Sketching and scrapbooking: Collecting visual materials on a topic

Discovering: Using lists of points or questions as guidelines

Researching: Gathering information

- Primary research: Generating new information
- Secondary research: Finding information generated by others

Much the same way that a carpenter gathers tools and materials before beginning to build a house, the process of generating material helps you gather claims and support before beginning to write a draft. Some scholars refer to this process of jotting notes and getting ideas down on paper as the "zero draft" in preparation for writing the first complete draft. On an intuitive level, you might think anything that keeps you from immediately starting your first draft is a waste of time; in practice, you'll find that generating materials makes drafting proceed more quickly and easily. Generating techniques include brainstorming, critical thinking, discussing, writing, sketching and scrapbooking, discovering, and researching.

BRAINSTORMING

Brainstorming involves the rapid listing of ideas on a given topic. Its goal is quantity: Worries about quality are postponed until after the brainstorming session, when each idea is evaluated. Brainstorming is the most basic and versatile of all planning techniques.

Brainstorming can be performed individually or in any sized group. When performed individually, it is a silent writing activity. In contrast, a group working collaboratively is highly vocal, with a designated person recording the ideas as words or phrases (not complete sentences) because speed is of the essence. Discussion of the ideas is suspended until the brainstorming session ends.

A typical brainstorming session lasts five to ten minutes, but it can be expanded or contracted to suit the situation. For a short writing assignment, a minute of brainstorming might suffice, whereas committees or think tanks may brainstorm for hours, days, or longer on major issues. For many writers, brainstorming recurs quite frequently: A writer may first brainstorm possible topics, then select an issue, and finally brainstorm terms, ideas, and claims specific to the selected issue.

Guidelines for Brainstorming

Brainstorming is the rapid listing of ideas, questions, and information about a topic. It produces a collection of words and phrases that later can be reflected upon, organized, and expanded.

- **Aim for quantity.** Don't stop for any reason. State (orally or in writing) as many ideas as possible in a given period of time.

- **Aim for speed.** Write as quickly as you can. Record your ideas in brief fashion— words, phrases, abbreviations. Don't let recording slow down your generation of ideas.

- **Build from the ideas already recorded.** When the initial stream of ideas starts to slow, expand on things you've already written.

- **Don't worry.** Suspend your inhibitions, never stopping to critique an idea. Write whatever comes to mind. Evaluate later.

Following is a list of terms and ideas that Hetal Shah (see the essay on page 227) produced during a two-minute brainstorming session on her topic of plagiarism:

writing is hard	paraphrasing	quoting	MLA
APA	punishment	flunking	Pressure
Deadlines	too many papers	ethics	Morality
tough teachers	Internet papers	Turnitin.com	paper mill
Footnotes	bibliography	works cited	Guilt
academic dishonesty	cheating	unfair	F

Practice 8.1 BRAINSTORMING

Choose a topic, perhaps one you may later argue. With a watch or clock in view, brainstorm and record a list of issues, terms, facts, ideas, and individuals associated with the topic. You are not limited to controversy: At this stage, simply list anything you know (or want to know) about the topic.

CRITICAL THINKING

Critical thinking involves "reading between the lines," looking beneath the surface meaning of a subject. A productive way to think critically is to ask and answer questions such as those modeled after Bloom's taxonomy. Questions can guide your brainstorming, freewriting, journaling, discussion, or research.

Here is a list of terms and ideas produced by Hetal Shah's ten-minute critical thinking session on the topic of plagiarism. These questions, which are derived from Bloom's taxonomy, also can be used to discover explanations for supporting evidence. (See the "Discovering" section later in this chapter.)

1. **Knowledge and clarification:** Plagiarism is considered cheating or theft. It's easy to plagiarize through Web sites—old student essays are there for the taking. Internet sources also sell customized essays. It's easy to take a published article and turn it into an essay. Penalties can be severe: failure, suspension, expulsion. Not sure what the school's policy is. Not sure how to completely avoid plagiarizing.

2. **Comprehension and interpretation:** Plagiarism can get you into trouble—a short-term fix that can backfire and end your education and maybe your future. But sometimes it's the last resort for desperate students out of time. Sometimes it's the only resort for students who don't know any other way to use sources.

3. **Application:** Plagiarism can get you out of trouble—a deadline or an overload of work. If you're not caught, it can get you a good grade. If you're caught, it's just the opposite: You're in trouble and you get a bad grade. Knowing how to use sources properly makes it possible to get the benefits and avoid penalties.

4. **Analysis:** The "parts" of plagiarism are materials taken from a source—a book or article—that you pretend you wrote yourself. Or it can be a whole essay someone else wrote, using articles and books legitimately. Or you can pretend you're paraphrasing, when you're really quoting without using quotation marks. Guilt and fear are parts of it—sometimes you're caught years after you plagiarized, so you're never in the clear. It's a decision made to go over to the dark side.

5. **Synthesis:** It's a form of cheating—"academic dishonesty." It's like stealing from someone (except the person may never miss what you've stolen!). It's also like a lifesaver for a drowning person—someone who might sink academically without it. It's similar to downloading music without paying royalties or copying answers from someone else's test.

6. **Evaluation:** It gets the job done, in a way. It's efficient—you get a grade without much work. It's scary but kind of a rush, like committing a crime and hoping no one knows it was you. Once you realize how bad some people think it is, you start feeling bad about yourself, like you're a fake. The worst thing is you never learn how to write your own stuff in a way that will help you in life.

Guidelines for Critical Thinking (from Bloom's Taxonomy)*

1. **Knowledge and clarification:** What facts do you know or perhaps need to know?
2. **Comprehension and interpretation:** What is its significance? What does it imply or really mean?
3. **Application:** What uses does it have to you or to others?
4. **Analysis:** What are its parts? How do they work together?
5. **Synthesis:** How does it relate to other things?
6. **Evaluation:** What is its importance? How good is it?

---

*From Benjamin S. Bloom et al., *Taxonomy of Educational Objectives*, Book 1, *Cognitive Domain* (Boston: Allyn & Bacon). Copyright © Pearson Education. Adapted by permission.

Practice 8.2 THINKING CRITICALLY

Choose an issue, perhaps one that emerged from brainstorming or freewriting about a topic. Respond to the following questions and record your answers.

1. **Knowledge and clarification:** What facts do you know or perhaps need to know?

2. **Comprehension and interpretation:** What is its significance? What does it imply or *really* mean?

3. **Application:** What uses does it have to you or to others?

4. **Analysis:** What are its parts? How do they work together?

5. **Synthesis:** How does it relate to other things?

6. **Evaluation:** What is its importance? How good is it?

DISCUSSING

Talking about a subject can be a powerful method for discovering ideas. Interactive, focused discussions often reveal that you know more—or less—about a subject than expected. In either case, it can guide you to the next steps for planning. Discussion adds a social dimension to reading and writing, often making the process more enjoyable because it is interactive and sometimes dramatic. Sometimes discussion is structured around a prepared list of questions, such as those that guide critical thinking or audience profiling, but it can also be freewheeling and spontaneous.

Discussions can range from cooperative (a team effort to understand issues and solve problems) to adversarial (a debate that reveals points of contention, support, and rebuttals). They can occur in large groups, small groups, or pairs; before, during, or after reading or writing—whenever they are useful. Although discussions often occur in classroom settings, they may also take place through e-mail, chat rooms, and instant messaging.

Guidelines for Discussing

The following guidelines are adapted from conflict resolution techniques. They can help make discussion more productive and civil.

- Take turns introducing topics or issues.
- Don't interrupt.
- Respond positively.
- Ask for clarifications.
- Listen for omissions or evasions.

Practice 8.3 DISCUSSING

In a small or large group, discuss a controversial issue of your choice. Argue first as adversaries, taking opposite sides in a point-counterpoint fashion. Then change your approach, working collaboratively to solve the issue by finding common ground and making concessions.

WRITING

Writing can be used as a planning technique. This kind of writing is intended not so much to draft a text but rather to generate ideas before you begin putting the ideas into the form you want. Freewriting, journaling, and blogging are writing techniques used to generate ideas.

Freewriting

Freewriting, also known as stream of consciousness writing or rambling, involves nonstop composing on a particular topic. Freewriters usually write in complete sentences, unlike the word-or-phrase listing of brainstorming. Freewriting sessions typically last five to ten minutes but can be expanded or contracted to fit the particular circumstances. Indeed, some essay tests may ask you to perform focused freewriting for an hour or more.

The most important goal while freewriting is to compose nonstop without worrying about anything except volume: The motto here is "The more, the better." To be able to write rapidly, freewriters suspend their "internal editor," ignoring concerns about errors, disorganization, poor word choice, or lack of ideas. Freewriting offers benefits that might not be achieved through other kinds of writing activities:

- Confidence that might otherwise be diminished by self-editing. If you burden yourself with concerns about saying something "just right," you may never get the idea on paper.

- Fluency through writing with a flow resembling conversation. When we speak, we seldom take long pauses and we almost never run to a dictionary to look up words. Freewriting can help a writer capitalize on the ease of oral communication.

- Freedom from "writer's block." You have no choice except to write. If you are stuck, write something like "I'm stuck, I'm stuck..." until you find something better to write.

Focused freewriting takes the technique a little further, requiring that you write nonstop on a particular topic or issue. Focused freewriters attempt to make their writing coherent—logically flowing from sentence to sentence—but off-topic drifting is natural and acceptable. The following example is a five-minute focused freewrite on the topic of plagiarism by a student in Hetal Shah's collaborative learning group:

> I hope nobody reads this because I'm about to confess! I've plagiarized most of my life. In grade school, teachers would assign reports, and most of the time my report was copied straight out of an encyclopedia. It was never questioned, and I always got a good grade when I turned it in. LOL Book reports were a little harder, except sometimes you could copy a summary straight from the cover of the book! In high school they taught about citing sources and how to make a bibliography, but the English teacher was the only one watching how we used the sources. The biology teacher, the history teacher—I think they were more concerned with what we learned about their subjects and not so much about the actual writing. They never questioned how I came up with the wording while I just took the stuff straight from a book but dummied it down into my own style.

Guidelines for Focused Freewriting

Focused freewriting involves writing nonstop about a topic or issue.

1. **Aim for quantity.** Don't stop for any reason.
2. **Aim for speed.** Write as quickly as you can. It's probably better (faster) if you use cursive rather than printing. If you can't think of something to write, then write something like "I'm stuck" until you're not stuck.
3. **Build from the ideas already recorded.** When the initial stream of ideas starts to slow, expand on things you've already written.
4. **Don't worry.** Suspend your inhibitions, never stopping to solve problems with spelling or word choice—settle for approximate spellings. Write whatever comes to mind about the topic or issue. Evaluate your writing later.

Practice 8.4 FOCUSED FREEWRITING

Freewrite for a set amount of time on a subject or issue you plan to argue.

Journaling

A *journal* is your record of your experiences and reflections. Also known as a log and resembling a diary, journals can be freewritten. In this textbook, however, we distinguish between journaling and freewriting based on how the passage is produced. Journaling is more meditative, allowing you to pause as needed to think about what to write and even to revise what you have already written. Freewriting is nonstop writing and consequently more spontaneous.

The rhetorical context of a journal is defined by its personal nature: for the purposes of reflection, exploration, and self-expression; for an audience of one (the author); through a freeform structure; and in a style that is precisely the voice of the writer. Although *journal* contains a root word from the French *jour* (meaning "day"), writers do not strictly have to write daily. They do need to write regularly, however.

Practice 8.5 JOURNALING

Keep a journal for an extended period of time—days, weeks, or months. Focus the journal on an issue you plan to argue. You may wish to use freewriting as a means for writing the journal, or you may prefer to employ a slower, more reflective technique.

Blogging

A *blog* (a contraction of *Weblog*) is a personal journal made public by posting on a Web page. In the planning phase of writing, a blog may function like a journal while offering some additional benefits: It provides an audience that can respond, creating a community of learners that extends beyond the walls of a classroom to potentially anywhere on the planet. Anything that can be digitalized can be added to the blog—any form of writing, visuals, or music. The public nature of a blog changes the journal's rhetorical context.

Purpose: While the purposes for writing a journal tend to be personal, exploratory, and tentative, a blog may have an effect on other readers, essentially becoming an argument.

Audience: The audience of a journal initially is oneself, whereas the audience of a blog is, potentially, the world.

Structure: Although a blog may retain the relaxed organization of a journal entry, a blogger often will rewrite for the sake of clarifying ideas for an audience.

Style: A blog usually retains the voice of the author. However, because this writing is public, a blogger should observe certain conventions of public discourse, such as avoiding profanity and refraining from the expression of inflammatory ideas such as attacks based on race, culture, gender, or religion. Once a journal becomes public, the writer can be held ethically and legally responsible for its content.

BLOG: CHEATING AND COMMON KNOWLEDGE

I think the problem of cheating in schools is significant and important to address, and we must be aware of the ways that technologies can be used to facilitate cheating. But it would be wrong-headed to see either technologies or the commons as the source of cheating. Instead, we should try to understand the larger social context within which students live (a context that appears to reward cheating on a regular basis) and to develop ways of addressing those issues to encourage more ethical behavior. We should speak out against unethical behavior in all its guises. We should also develop processes within the academic sphere that reward creative behavior rather than promoting obsession with grades and similar phenomenal outputs.*

*Frederick Emrich, Blog: Cheating and Common Knowledge, Info-Commons.org. Reprinted by permission of the author.

Practice 8.6 BLOGGING

Find a blogsite related to an issue you plan to argue. Read through the ongoing discussion and then join in if access is possible—in other words, post a response.

SKETCHING AND SCRAPBOOKING

Writers sometimes keep sketchbooks to help them remember experiences. Sketching often occurs as part of a journal entry, joining images with verbal reflections. Scrapbooks can include photos, clippings, and artifacts (such as a pressed flower or a ticket stub). Nonprint materials sometimes will be the object of your claims or the substance of your evidence. For example, if you were researching sexism in children's toys, you might clip images of Barbie dolls from magazines, photograph the doll or children playing, or download images from Web sources into a file. A scrapbook can be digital, consisting of pictures scanned or copied from Web sources. Digital materials can easily be integrated into a draft of an essay.

Practice 8.7 VISUAL SCRAPBOOKING

Begin a scrapbook or sketchbook on an issue you wish to argue. Try to include examples from a variety of sources.

DISCOVERING

Discovery techniques help you find ideas and facts that are accessible but unnoticed; they remind you where to direct your thoughts. Also known as *heuristics* (from the Greek *eureka*, meaning "I found it"), discovery techniques consist of routines or formulas, such as a list of questions.

Some discovery techniques are generic (all-purpose), such as the "reporter's formula," also known as the "five Ws and an H": who, what, when, where, why, and how. The leads of most news stories answer these questions. Other discovery techniques are geared toward a specific purpose, such as questions focused on an argument's claims, support, and rhetorical context.

Following are questions designed to help you discover claims, evidence, and rhetorical context. The student responses are focused on the topic of plagiarism.

Discovering Claims: What Are You Trying to Argue?

Fact: Is or was it real? Does or did it actually exist? The theft of ideas has been around for a long time. Copyrights and patents haven't always been part of the law and aren't respected everywhere in the world. Plagiarism may not be as one-sided as instructors think, though—it may be "factual" that instructors contribute to the problem.

Identity: What is it? Cheating. Theft. Borrowing. The sincerest form of flattery. An efficient way to get what you want. A misunderstanding. An epidemic.

Cause and effect: How does it work? Too much pressure on students. Unrealistic expectations. Poor instruction. Lack of ethics or morals.

Value: How is it judged? Harshly by instructors, with stiff penalties when formally investigated and tried. Lightly by students, many of whom don't see it as wrongful conduct.

Proposal: Should something be done? Better teaching not only about how to write but also about the policies that guide and procedures that enforce ethical conduct. Policies and pedagogy should be reviewed and revised.

Guidelines for Discovering Claims

Fact: Is or was it real?

Identity: What is it?

Cause and effect: How does it work?

Value: How is it judged?

Proposal: Should something be done?

Practice 8.8 DISCOVERING CLAIMS

For an issue you wish to argue, try to make each kind of claim: fact, identity, value, cause or effect, and proposal.

Discovering Evidence: How Will You Support Your Argument?

Expert opinions: Research shows many experts, mostly instructors and school administrators, comment on the "epidemic" of academic dishonesty. Example: "When Academic Dishonesty Happens on Your Campus" by Karen L. Clos, Dean of Learning and Instructor at Barton County Community College.

Facts and statistics: Number of studies available on why students cheat. Many articles with figures on the increase in cheating, such as "A Culture of Copy-and-Paste" by Jessica Durkin.

History: Apparently Shakespeare borrowed ideas from sources, and imitation has a long intellectual history. In "So, Is It the Real Thing?" Atul Prakash quotes Picasso as saying "a great artist steals."

Personal experience: Careful: I don't want to get into trouble for something I did a long time ago! Better to report what I know others have done or make up a scenario.

Scenarios: I can make up an example about a student under pressure who resorts to plagiarism. I can put a lot of sob-story elements that mitigate things: He wasn't taught properly, she'll lose her scholarship if she fails or if she's punished when caught, etc.

Specific examples: Brief interviews with other students; my observations of cheating by others; my observations of instructors; examples of policies and procedures related to cheating.

Guidelines for Discovering Evidence

Expert opinions:

Facts and statistics:

History:

Personal experience:

Scenarios:

Specific examples:

Practice 8.9 DISCOVERING EVIDENCE

For a claim you wish to make, predict the kinds of evidence you might research or actually do this research.

Guidelines for Discovering Rhetorical Context

Purpose: What effect on the audience are you seeking?

Audience: Who will be reading (or hearing or viewing)?

Structure: What form or organization will the argument take?

Style: How formally will you present your argument?

Practice 8.10 DISCOVERING RHETORICAL CONTEXT

For a particular assignment, determine the rhetorical context: purpose, audience, structure, and style.

RESEARCHING

Primary Research

Evidence is considered primary when it comes not from other researchers but rather from your own activities: experiences or discoveries made through field work such as in a lab, an archaeological dig, a survey, or an interview. Sometimes the best source of evidence is actual experience, such as eating particular foods over a period of time to understand a popular diet. Field excursions may be useful to get a sense of the real world. Some experiences can be vicarious or simulated, as when you attend a realistic war movie to get a sense of real combat.

Secondary Research

Secondary research involves gathering information from the experiences or studies of others. Print materials have long been the mainstay of researchers, but today researchers use a wide variety of sources, including audio recordings, visuals, and electronic texts.

Practice 8.11 EXPERIENCING

List experiences that are relevant to your argument. How practical are they in terms of your ability to attain them? Consider ways of acquiring and using personal experience to support an argument.

Practice 8.12 SEARCHING DATABASES AND LIBRARIES

Find an article, book, and Web source that are relevant to your issue or argument. Copy the bibliographic information, and write a brief summary of each source.

PLAGIARISM
- Not really concrete: words and ideas
- Original author may never know, so no real harm is done.
- Plagiarizer may learn facts, which is why the original was written in the first place.

PLAGIARISM AS THEFT
- Words are a product; they took labor to produce and often have cash value.
- Laws and rules protect the owner of property, including words and ideas.

THEFT
- Concrete: physical possessions and money
- Victims usually know the theft has occurred.

The above Venn diagram shows the relationships between plagiarism and theft.

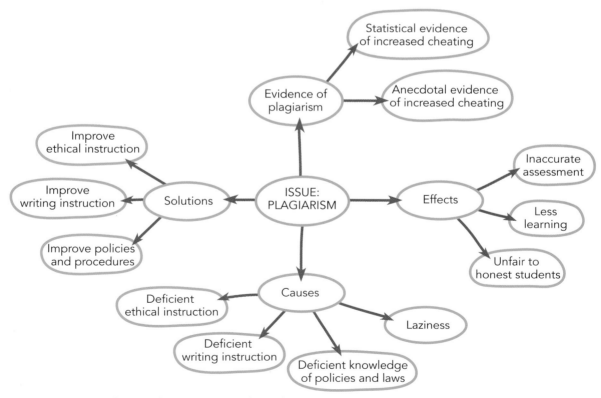

Clustering graphically organizes your supporting points.

Opposition

Students are to blame for giving in to the temptation of an easy way to make a good grade.

The instructor is to blame for not adequately training students in effective use of sources.

The institution is to blame for not adequately informing students about policies against cheating.

Refutation

Some students may not know how plagiarism is wrong. They haven't had adequate ethical education.

It is less a matter of training by teachers and more a matter of students not applying themselves.

Most students already know that they should give credit to their sources. They must take responsibility for knowing the policies.

DIAGRAMMING

Venn diagrams graphically depict how the elements of an argument are related. They show how much (or how little) two or more things (concepts, groups) have in common by depicting those elements as circles that are overlapping, enclosing each other, or separate. These diagrams often are used to explain logical syllogisms and are useful in conceptualizing a comparison and contrast argument. The following Venn diagram shows similarities and differences between plagiarism and theft.

CLUSTERING

Clustering and similar techniques (webbing, mapping) also graphically depict the relationships between ideas. In these diagrams, the major claim (thesis) is located in the center of the page, often inside a circle. Lines radiate from the center circle to secondary circles that represent supporting points or topics.

9

Organizing
MATERIALS

Once you have generated materials to use in an argument, you'll want to organize them in some way that makes sense. This exercise can help with the drafting that comes afterward. Organizing also enhances other planning techniques, perhaps revealing the need for more brainstorming, discovery, or research. In fact, some organization techniques do double duty by helping to generate material. Charts, clusters, diagrams, and outlines are all useful guides for organizing.

CHARTING

Writers sometimes create columns and rows to clarify the connections between parts of their argument. Charts typically use columns to show categories of information and rows to show relationships. The intersection of each column and row forms a box called a cell. Here are some possible headings for charts:

> **CLAIMS AND SUPPORT CHART:** *Claim   Evidence   Explanation*
>
> **PRO AND CON CHART:** *Reasons for   Reasons against*
>
> **REBUTTAL CHART:** *Opposition   Refutation*

A claims and support chart, for example, would state a claim in one cell. The supporting evidence would appear in an adjacent cell. A third cell could hold an explanation of the evidence. Because a claim may have more than one piece of supporting evidence, charts often need expansion or other modifications. Here is an example of a rebuttal chart:

Clustering can be used to organize the information you already have and to reveal where your arguments may need more research. It requires no sequencing of major and minor points, so it is more flexible but less organized than an outline. Clusters, in fact, often are pre-outlines that later are sequenced formally. See the clustering template on the previous page.

OUTLINING

Like clustering, outlining shows the relationships among the various parts of an argument. However, outlining sequences the parts, often labeling them with Roman numbers, uppercase and lowercase letters, Arabic numerals, and so on. A combination of letters, numbers, and indentation can distinguish major and supporting evidence and explanations. Following is a template for a possible outline:

Title (tentative): Curing Plagiarism

I. Introduction

    A. Problem: Increased plagiarism

       1. Anecdotal evidence of plagiarism (brief)

       2. Statistical evidence of plagiarism (brief)

    B. Current "solution" is ill informed and unfair.

       1. Places blame solely on students (brief statement)

       2. Present policies ignore some facts (brief statement)

    C. Thesis: A comprehensive and fair solution is needed

II. A problem really does exist (fuller support than introduction).

    A. Statistical evidence of increase in plagiarism

    B. Anecdotal evidence of plagiarism

    C. Expert testimony about plagiarism

III. Current views of the problem are one-sided.

    A. Places blame solely on students (fuller support)

    B. Present policies ignore some facts (fuller support)

IV. A more balanced view of the causes of plagiarism

    A. Students' responsibility for problem

    B. Instructors' responsibility for problem

    C. Administrators' responsibility for problem

V. Conclusion

    A. Students' responsibility to change

    B. Instructors' responsibility to change

    C. Administrators' responsibility to change

Framework for an Outline

I. First item

II. Second item

   A. Subitem

   B. Subitem

      1. Subsubitem

      2. Subsubitem

III. Third item

Practice 9.1 ORGANIZING

Choose a topic and create a chart, diagram, cluster, or outline that organizes your claims, evidence, and explanations.

The Writing Process:
DRAFTING ARGUMENTS

The word *compose* comes from root words meaning to "place into position" or "put together." Perhaps you are familiar with composing in the musical sense, the process of a musician putting together notes to make a melody. *Composing* also is a synonym for *drafting*, the process of a writer putting together words and the ideas they represent into a unified text—a composition.

Drafting rarely is a straightforward process proceeding sequentially from the first sentence to the conclusion. Experienced writers instead prefer to draft the parts they're clearest about first, in hopes that the other parts will become clearer as the whole takes shape. Sometimes the introduction is written last, because only when the drafting process is complete does the writer fully realize the argument being made.

STRUCTURE OF AN ARGUMENT

An essay's overall structure consists of three major sections: (1) an introduction that provides a thesis statement or otherwise orients the reader toward a major claim, (2) a body consisting of paragraphs that break down the thesis into specific areas and treat each area in detail, and (3) a conclusion that provides closure. As you draft each section, you'll have to make a number of organizational decisions.

Drafting an Introduction

When you meet a stranger in a social situation, an introduction is usually needed before any productive conversation can follow. Most people need a little warming up first, such as sharing interesting personal details and general background information, and perhaps finding a purpose for further conversation. When a reader picks up a composition, there is a similar need for warming up—to pique the reader's interest, establish an issue, and make a claim. An introduction to a

> *" **THE LAST THING ONE DISCOVERS IN COMPOSING A WORK IS WHAT TO PUT FIRST.** "*
> BLAISE PASCAL (1623–1662)

composition accomplishes these goals by providing a lead, background information, and a thesis or major claim.

- A *lead* engages the reader's interest and establishes authority.
- *Background* information lets the reader understand the history, context, and importance of the claim.
- A major *claim* (an argumentative thesis) states or strongly implies what the author intends to argue.

These three components may vary in the order they are presented and in the emphasis each receives: more, less, or none at all, depending on the relevance to the overall composition.

It may help to think of the introduction as a "block of text" rather than as a paragraph. Even though it often lasts for only one paragraph, it can also be composed of two and occasionally even more paragraphs, depending on the length of each part. Introductions often are in proportion to the entire text. Very short writings might embed the introduction into the first body paragraph, often as the first sentence. For example, the one-sentence "lead" in a newspaper column or blog post often acts as the introduction. Longer compositions tend to have more substantive introductions. In fact, nonfiction books usually devote the entire first chapter to the introduction.

DRAFTING A CLAIM

Regardless of which part of the composition you decide to draft, having the major claim written out and visible is essential to keeping yourself on the right track. As you draft your claim, test it by asking these questions:

- Is your claim really a claim? Does it take a position and argue a debatable issue within the "zone of reasonable skepticism"?

- Does your claim fit your audience?
- Is your claim focused?

Is Your Claim Really a Claim?

Is it intended to change the audience's opinions and actions on an issue? Or are you unintentionally writing for another purpose: to inform, to entertain, or to express your feelings? Novice writers sometimes drift into other, nonargumentative purposes.

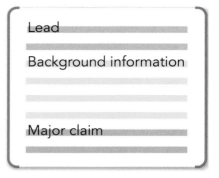

A typical introduction contains a lead, background information, and major claim or thesis.

- **Sometimes an argument shifts into exploratory writing.** An author may think that the audience needs to be led "inductively"—that is, the audience is shown the evidence before being told a conclusion or claim. While exploratory arguments can be very convincing when well-executed, this method often leads to trouble for developing writers. Unfortunately, this practice often results in a rambling "for your information" download of loosely connected facts, with a brief concluding paragraph stating a claim more as an afterthought. Without the perspective of a claim, readers quickly begin to wonder, "What's the point?"

  > To decide whether to support stem-cell research, we should look at the facts.

  This thesis statement leads to facts that lack the perspective of a claim.

- **Sometimes an argument shifts strongly into self-expression.** When an author has strong emotions about an issue, those feelings may erupt into prose that is strong but rings with the wrong "tone of voice"—a strident ranting or perhaps a fawning tribute. Although this kind of writing can be cathartic for the writer, it can be unintentionally amusing for the reader. Because of its charged emotions, the writer can lose the audience's respect (*ethos*) that allows the writer to persuade.

  > It's high time we threw those lying politicians in jail!

  This thesis statement is more suggestive of mob violence than of reasoned action.

Does Your claim Fit Your Audience?

Are you "preaching to the choir"—readers who already believe as you do—or are you "speaking a foreign language"—addressing readers whose beliefs are hopelessly different from yours? Adjust your claim to fit the audience, finding some practical goal worth arguing. Your audience should reside within what we have termed the "zone of reasonable skepticism"—it shouldn't believe your claim as yet, but should be willing to entertain the *possibility* that it *might* be valid.

- **Adjust your claim when you face overwhelming skepticism.** For example, although you might not be able to convince an audience of professors that they share responsibility for plagiarism by students, you might be able to convince them that some student plagiarism stems not from moral weakness but from a lack of knowledge about quoting, paraphrasing, and summarizing.

- **Adjust your claim to address a predisposition of acceptance.** If, for example, you and your audience were already in agreement about the need for improved instruction on using sources, you could argue for staff development to help instructors learn new techniques.

Types of Claims

A major claim is an argument's thesis, the author's position on an issue. Below is a list of kinds of claims.

Fact: Is or was it real?

Identity: What is it?

Cause and effect: How and why does it work?

Value: How is it judged?

Proposal: Should something be done?

Is Your Claim Focused?

An overly broad claim weakens an argument. Novice writers understandably would rather deal with an excess of support rather than a shortage, but they often end up with a claim so broad the composition says very little and consequently is dull to read. Readers often prefer to learn "a lot about a little" rather than a "little about a lot." This goal can be achieved by (1) focusing on only part of a problem rather than many aspects of it or (2) being more specific about details. Consider the following examples:

BROAD, WITH SEVERAL PARTS

Plagiarism can be controlled by instituting an honor code that all students must sign, by strictly enforcing rules and penalties, and by ensuring that instruction on research skills is provided by all instructors.

FOCUSED, WITH FEWER PARTS

The most effective way to curtail plagiarism is staff development to ensure instructors know how to teach research skills.

BROAD, WITH LESS-SPECIFIC DETAILS

There should be a clear policy on plagiarism.

FOCUSED, WITH MORE-SPECIFIC DETAILS

The Office of Student Affairs should articulate and publicize a plagiarism policy that considers not only the offense but also the knowledge and intent of the plagiarist.

Practice 10.1 DRAFTING YOUR MAJOR CLAIM

Write out a major claim (thesis) for an argument. As you draft your claim, test it by asking these questions:

1. Is your claim really a claim?

2. Does your claim fit your audience?

3. Is your claim focused?

DRAFTING THE BACKGROUND INFORMATION

Rarely will a reader have all the prior knowledge needed to understand the issues at stake in your argument. In the introduction, your goal is to provide context, thereby helping the reader understand what the issue is, but without going into too much detail too early. The following suggestions and examples may help as you draft the background information for your introduction.

Emphasize the Importance of an Issue

By establishing the significance of the issue, the reader will be motivated to read on.

> Cheating in college is certainly not a new phenomenon. Underground paper mills, from which students can obtain previously prepared papers to be submitted as their own work, have existed for quite some time. However, with the growth of the Internet has come a concurrent and explosive growth in the number of online paper mills, drastically increasing the accessibility of previously prepared term papers.
>
> —C. R. Campbell, C. O. Swift, and L. T. Denton, "Cheating Goes Hi-Tech"

Present a Quotation Relevant to the Topic

Quotations can be intriguing, can contribute authority, and can hint at the angle your argument will take.

> Picasso once said, "A good artist borrows, a great artist steals.".... Ask any writer, music composer, filmmaker, or designer and they'll tell you nothing is created in a vacuum, all ideas are drawn from outside inspiration. But the problem arises when you infringe on someone else's original work.
>
> —Atul Prakash, "So, Is It the Real Thing?"

Present One or More Examples

Examples make the issue seem real.

> Last year, our college experienced a rash of cheating incidents that caused
> us to reevaluate how prepared we were to deal with academic dishonesty. Within two weeks
> after a seemingly isolated incident in which one of our professors discovered a student
> cheating on a written assignment, four separate incidents of academic dishonesty were
> reported in our online program, in outreach and community education, and in on-campus
> programs as well.
>
> —Karen Clos, "When Academic Dishonesty Happens on Your Campus"

Present Interesting Facts or Statistics

Information your reader does not know can sometimes whet the reader's appetite for more.

> Academic dishonesty, which includes everything from wrongfully getting information by
> looking at a neighbor's test to plagiarizing information in a term paper, is a growing problem
> and concern for higher education. Several recent national surveys have found that more than
> half of all college students in the United States admit to some form of academic dishonesty,
> at least once during their college years. ... Research shows a correlation between academic
> dishonesty and moral development (Barnett and Dalton 1981). That is, individuals with a
> higher level of moral development are less likely to be engaged in academic dishonesty
> because they consider that sort of behavior to be morally wrong.
>
> —Mohammed Y. A. Rawwas, Jamal A. Al-Khatib, and Scott J. Vitell, "Academic Dishonesty"

Pose a Problem or a Mystery

A problem or a mystery gives the issue significance while setting the stage for a solution.

> For years, management educators have learned the tricks of the trade for avoiding academic
> dishonesty by students by changing assignments from semester to semester and even
> requiring in-class writing assignments that could be used as samples and compared to
> writing done outside of class. However, the enhanced opportunities for academic dishonesty
> presented by online term paper mills raise the bar for management educators in devising
> assignments that circumvent the offerings of such term paper services.
>
> —Jeffrey Mello, "Commentary on 'Cheating Goes Hi-Tech'"

Briefly Explain the Issue's History

History can put an issue in context.

> The Internet was still a toddler in the late 1990s. Today, it's a juggernaut. In the last five years,
> instances of plagiarism from webpages have grown perhaps just as rapidly as the Internet itself. In
> fact, some sites even boast "original" essays for sale.
>
> —Jennifer Kabbany, "Educators: Digital Plagiarism Rampant"

Dramatize

Make an issue come to life by providing a real-life story or example or by creating a believable scenario or hypothetical situation.

> Imagine a student who had never cheated before, who works hard and sincerely wants to learn and to better herself. This semester, however, she has taken on far too much work. She can't possibly write all the required research papers in the time by the end of the term. Her GPA hangs in the balance, as does her scholarship and her future. Panicking, she turns to what she sees as her last resort: an online paper mill that will provide what she needs—an instant essay.
>
> —Sam Nguyen, "The Temptation of Instant Essays"

Pose One or More Questions

Questions that are related to your argument can pique readers' interest and help forecast the answers you will reveal.

> What is the relationship between academic dishonesty and workplace dishonesty? If a student is prone to cheating in college, will that same student be prone to cheating in the workplace?
>
> —Sarath Nonis and Cathy Swift, "An Examination of the Relationship Between Academic Dishonesty and Workplace Dishonesty"

Define a Key Concept

A definition can provide good background. However, opening with "According to *Webster's Dictionary*" is a very clichéd lead sentence.

> Indeed, there are many ways to misrepresent the truth. Part of the problem is that not everyone agrees on the definition of lying. Lying by omission, for example, is a form of passive deceit because a person is withholding information or not volunteering the truth…. Plagiarism is another form of lying. Plagiarism is a form of "literary theft," of which I would be guilty, if I didn't tell you that I copied that phrase from the *Merriam-Webster Dictionary*.
>
> —Michael Angelo Caruso, "There Are Many Types of Lies." From *National Driller*, March 1, 2005.
> Reprinted by permission of the author.

Present an Analogy

An analogy helps a reader understand a new issue by comparing it to something more familiar.

> The 1960s gave us, among other mind-altering ideas, a revolutionary new metaphor for our physical and chemical surroundings: the biosphere. But an even more momentous change is coming. Emerging technologies are causing a shift in our mental ecology, one that will turn our culture into the plagiosphere, a closing frontier of ideas.
>
> —Ed Tenner, "Rise of the Plagiosphere"

Present Various Sides of the Issue

Briefly citing several selected sources can show a range of opinions and the extent of differences.

The ease of use of the Internet technology is the number one factor blamed for the increase in academic cheating (Decamp 2001). Another factor is an increasing number of digital paper mills mushrooming on the Internet such as Buyapapers.com…, Term Papers & Term Papers, … and Term Papers Amazon.

—Apiwan D. Born, "How to Reduce Plagiarism" *Journal of Information Systems Education*, Vol. 14(3). Reprinted by permission of the *Journal of Information Systems Management*.

Begin Creatively, with Wit or Word Play

Begin with details that are humorous, or use a creative style.

Teachers do it, journalists do it, even educated priests do it. Cole Porter, composer of "Let's Do It, Let's Fall in Love," was accused of doing it, too—he was sued in 1946. "It," in this case, is not a matter of the heart, but the rather more cerebral issue of plagiarism.

—Katherine Macklem, "Their Cheatin' Hearts"

Practice 10.2 DRAFTING YOUR BACKGROUND INFORMATION

With your major claim in mind, write an introduction that includes background information. You may wish to experiment with the models presented earlier in this chapter.

Drafting Your Lead Sentences

When you write, keep in mind that you maintain your reader's interest only one sentence—if not one word—at a time. The first few words in your argument serve not only to engage your reader's interest, but also to give your reader a hint about the importance of the issue (and possibly even your stand on it). The lead sentence is not a "one off" like the verbal equivalent of the salesman sticking his foot in the door. It should be an integral, comprehensive part of the introduction that nudges the reader in the direction of the claim.

In some ways, the beginning of an essay is the most important part. If the audience members are not engaged immediately, they may never read the rest of the text. A lead can enable you to engage your reader's interest. Of course, the title itself is the first chance you have to catch a reader's attention. Once past the title, a reader will decide very soon whether the text is worth pursuing.

In a typical introduction to a college essay, the lead may or may not be distinguishable from the introduction as a whole, especially when the background information is interesting or when the claim is provocative. However, even in a short piece of writing, the first few sentences can be critical. Consider this opening line from David Glenn's article, "Judge or Judge Not?":

In an ideal world, academe would respond to plagiarism allegations with a sure and swift machinery of justice.

This sentence conveys context—"academe," "plagiarism allegations"—while hinting at frightening, even harsh consequences—"sure and swift machinery of justice." A reader might read on purely for the information, but also might be enticed by the suspense of impending punishment or even by residual guilt from, shall we say, personal plagiaristic indiscretions.

Practice 10.3 ESTABLISHING READER INTEREST WITH LEADS

Below are the opening lines from the models of background information presented earlier in this chapter. How well would they motivate you to read on? Why do they work or not work?

1. "Cheating in college is certainly not a new phenomenon."

2. "Picasso once said, 'A good artist borrows, a great artist steals.'"

3. "Last year, our college experienced a rash of cheating incidents that caused us to reevaluate how prepared we were to deal with academic dishonesty."

4. "Academic dishonesty, which includes everything from wrongfully getting information by looking at a neighbor's test to plagiarizing information in a term paper, is a growing problem and concern for higher education."

5. "For years, management educators have learned the tricks of the trade for avoiding academic dishonesty by students by changing assignments from semester to semester and even requiring in-class writing assignments that could be used as samples and compared to writing done outside of class."

6. "The Internet was still a toddler in the late 1990s. Today, it's a juggernaut."

7. "Imagine a student who had never cheated before, who works hard and sincerely wants to learn and to better herself. This semester, however,…"

8. "What is the relationship between academic dishonesty and workplace dishonesty?"

9. "Indeed, there are many ways to misrepresent the truth."

10. "The 1960s gave us, among other mind-altering ideas, a revolutionary new metaphor for our physical and chemical surroundings: the biosphere."

11. "The ease of use of the Internet technology is the number one factor blamed for the increase in academic cheating."

12. "Teachers do it, journalists do it, even educated priests do it."

Practice 10.4 DRAFTING YOUR LEAD SENTENCE

Examine one of your own introductory paragraphs. Will it catch a reader's interest? Revise your writing, experimenting with alternative ways of engaging the reader's interest.

Practice 10.5 ANALYZING INTRODUCTIONS

Read the two introductory text blocks below, and locate their parts. Place brackets around the leads, and underline the claims. Which parts do you find the most compelling? Why? In what way(s) could they compel an audience to read the rest of the argument?

Excerpt A

In recent years there has been a significant rise in the number of plagiarism cases, both across North America and abroad. For example, the "Plagiarism Advisory Service" issued a report in the summer of 2004 that found one in four British university students to have "copied and pasted material from the Internet into an essay and passed it off as their own work" (Curtis n.p.). While the Internet is blamed by many commentators for the rise in plagiarism, others cite a lack of clarity about what plagiarism is and why it is a serious problem.

—David Rosenwasser, Jill Stephen, Doug Babington, *Writing Analytically with Readings*

Excerpt B

The growth of academic dishonesty is discouraging to faculty, administrators, and ethical students. Faculty, in particular, are often wary of spending time and resources on educating college and university students about academic dishonesty. Administrators, too, are well aware of the costs imposed on the institution by dishonest behavior. And the ethical student knows that rampant cheating can devalue a college degree. But if institutions are to fully educate their students in honesty as well as in particular content areas, they should work to create an ethical campus climate where the rewards of ethical conduct may be as great as mastery of any program of study. Only when institutions treat ethics as an essential element of all conduct—at school, at work, and in personal lives—will students see the importance of infusing ethics in their academic conduct.

—Melanie Stallings Williams and William R. Hosek, *Strategies for Reducing Academic Dishonesty*

Excerpt C

This spring, Jerry Ceppos, vice president for news at Knight Ridder, finished his term as president of the organization that accredits journalism schools. In a speech at the April 30 meeting of the Accrediting Council on Education in Journalism and Mass Communications, Ceppos ticked off a list of plagiarism cases that had cropped up at newspapers over the previous year. They ranged from student papers at the universities of Virginia and Kansas to the *Hartford Courant* and *Milwaukee Journal Sentinel* to *USA Today* and the *New York Times.* "If any outside poked his or her head in this room," Ceppos said, "the first question would obviously be, 'What are you doing about this epidemic of ethical problems in journalism?' "

—Jeff South, "Ethics in the Classroom"

Practice 10.6 DRAFTING INTRODUCTIONS

For an issue that concerns you, draft an introduction that contains a lead, background information, and statement of your major claim.

SHOULD I WRITE MY INTRODUCTION FIRST?

The writing process is both situational and personal: You have your own habits and techniques that must be adapted to different kinds of assignments. You may be comfortable working from beginning to end, or you may prefer to move back and forth through the text as you draft. Here are a few pointers to help you craft your own individual style:

- After planning your argument, write your claim first. Put it on a piece of paper and tape it to the top of your computer screen or in some other visible position. Its presence may serve as a reminder to help you keep your essay focused and on task. (Some word processors will permit you to do this by keeping a window open for notes. You can keep an outline or your claim visible as you write.)

- Don't write your introduction first if you don't feel ready to do so. Jump into the body of the essay after you have figured out your basic organizational strategy.

- Decide how you want to organize your paper—what your main points will be, how you will refute the opposition's arguments, and so on—before you jump into your text. This will save you time reorganizing your text later on.

- If you are composing and the work just isn't moving along, you may need to return to the planning process, generating and organizing material. Do you need to construct a more detailed outline? Would writing out your supporting ideas help?

DRAFTING THE BODY

The body of a composition consists of paragraphs that support the major claim with reasons in the form of evidence and explanations. Sometimes you can comfortably develop one reason per paragraph; at other times, you can devote several paragraphs to one reason or several reasons to one paragraph. This choice depends entirely on the volume of evidence and the amount of explanation it needs.

A paragraph has its own unity of purpose that may be either expressed as an explicitly stated main idea (topic sentence) or implied strongly by the evidence and explanations. As you draft the body, you'll have options about how to arrange the topic sentences and reasons within paragraphs.

Placing Main Ideas

Main ideas (also known as topic sentences) can appear anywhere within a paragraph. For the sake of illustration, we will highlight four paragraph structures:

- **Main idea at top:** You start with the supporting point and follow up by supplying the details that will convince the reader that the claim is valid.

- **Main idea at bottom:** You work through the details first, which allows the reader to accept the claim that is presented at the end as a sort of concluding sentence.

- **Main idea *delayed*:** You delay the claim by "easing into" a paragraph with a sentence or so of transitional material. Sometimes the main idea may not appear until the middle of the paragraph.

- **Main idea *implied*:** Sometimes you might choose to not state the purpose of a block of text, but leave it for the reader to figure out. This approach can be very effective if the block is well written, but can lead to confusion if it is not.

No method is superior to all of the others. In fact, the more you read, the more you will see that many writers mix all of these approaches to organization.

TOP MAIN IDEA

Main idea

Evidence

Discussion

BOTTOM MAIN IDEA

Evidence

Discussion

Main idea

DELAYED MAIN IDEA

Transition

Supporting claim

Evidence

Discussion

IMPLIED MAIN IDEA

Evidence

Discussion

A body paragraph's main idea (also known as topic sentence) can appear in different locations.

Practice 10.7 UNDERSTANDING PARAGRAPHS

Read the paragraphs and then answer the following questions:

1. Does the paragraph have a stated or implied main idea? If stated, where is it located? If implied, what words hint at it?

2. Does the paragraph cohere, effectively supporting a stated or implied main idea? Explain.

3. Is the paragraph engaging? Why or why not?

Excerpt A

U.S. research conducted by Donald L. McCabe, a business professor at Rutgers University in New Jersey, comparing students in 1963 and 1993, shows the percentage of those admitting to copying from a classmate doubled to 52 per cent; those reporting having helped another student cheat jumped to 37 per cent from 23 per cent; and that the use of crib notes in test and exam settings increased to over a quarter from 16 per cent.

—Gulli, Köhler, and Patriquin, "The Great University Cheating Scandal"

Excerpt B

Most people have some idea of what plagiarism is. You already know that it's against the rules to buy a paper from an Internet "paper mill" or to download others' work verbatim and hand them in as your own thinking. And you probably know that even if you change a few words and rearrange the sentence structure, you still need to acknowledge the source. By way of formal definition, plagiarism (as one handbook puts it) gives "the impressions that you have written or though something that you have in fact borrowed from someone else" (Gibaldi 30). It is a form of theft and fraud. Borrowing from someone else, by the way, also includes taking and not acknowledging words and ideas from your friends or your parents. Put another way, any assignment with your name on it signifies that you are the author—that the words and ideas are yours—with any exceptions indicated by source citations and, if you're quoting, by quotation marks.

—David Rosenwasser, Jill Stephen, Doug Babington, *Writing Analytically with Readings*

EVIDENCE

Whenever you make a claim, a skeptical audience will require proof that it is true or reasons to accept it—in short, evidence. Evidence comes in the following forms:

Anecdotes

Narrate or describe real-life accounts of situations or events that have happened to you or to others.

Expert opinions

Quote, paraphrase, or summarize the opinion of an expert or experts on an issue.

Facts and statistics

Provide evidence that an audience will accept at face value.

History

Tell what happened in the past if it is relevant to the present or the future.

Scenario

Produce hypothetical or fictionalized accounts that dramatize typical or possible situations.

Specific example

Offer a sampling of evidence to represent a larger body of evidence.

Organizing Evidence

When you present evidence in an argument, it cannot stand alone. No bit of data is self-evident. It must be explained to establish its validation of the truth of the claim. The explanation of evidence within a block of text is typically organized in one of two ways:

- The *point-by-point method* discusses the evidence one piece at a time. This approach is useful when each piece of evidence needs its own explanation.

- The *block method* is used when either one piece of evidence is followed by several explanations or when several pieces of evidence can be lumped together and explained once.

POINT-BY-POINT METHOD

BLOCK METHOD

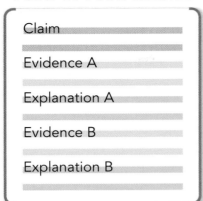

Evidence and explanations can be presented point by point or separated into blocks.

PROVIDING EVIDENCE

While drafting, you must decide what kind of evidence is needed and how much to use. As a rule, provide evidence that is sufficient, relevant, and appealing:

Sufficient

Use only the minimum amount of information you need to establish the truth value of your claim, and no more.

Relevant

Use only evidence that supports your claim; avoid anything that "sort of" or "might" support your claim. If the relationship between evidence and claim is blurry to you, it will be even more blurry to your readers.

Appealing

Use evidence that will be received sympathetically by your readers. Avoid sources or types of evidence they might not respect or might find offensive.

EXPLAINING EVIDENCE

Evidence almost always needs some kind of explanation or discussion to strengthen its connection to the claim. The kinds of explanations below are based on a list of thought processes known as Bloom's Taxonomy.

Clarification (knowledge)

Restate to make sure the evidence is understood. Paraphrase, summary, and emphasis help clarify evidence.

Interpretation (comprehension)

Speculate on its significance. Evidence often requires an interpreter who can "read between the lines" and put it into perspective.

Application

Explain how the evidence applies. Application can show the connection between evidence and claim when the relationship isn't immediately clear.

Analysis

Explain the parts. Analysis divides a whole into its parts and explains how they work separately and in unison.

Synthesis

Relate it to other claims or other forms of evidence. Synthesis brings two or more arguments together, allowing for comparison/contrast, rebuttal, or an accumulation of mutually supporting points.

Evaluation

Explain its value. Evaluation is a kind of qualification, explaining how applicable the evidence is to the claim or how reliable and accurate it is.

Practice 10.8 UNDERSTANDING EVIDENCE AND EXPLANATIONS

Read the excerpt from "The Great University Cheating Scandal" and then answer the following questions.

> "Whatever the policies implemented by universities, cheating is still rampant and getting worse. It would be easy to blame students for their transgressions. Yet it is the universities—the institutions issuing the degrees and guaranteeing educational quality—that must find solutions. Perhaps professors, charged with monitoring their students, don't make good cops. While instructors are 'required to report academic dishonesty,' says Christensen Hughes, 'some don't.' That may understate the problem. While the Guelph study notes that 75 per cent of professors and 80 per cent of teaching assistants thought a student had cheated in the previous year—almost half were absolutely sure of it—less than half said they believed that cheating is a serious problem. In a 2001 paper, U.S. business professors Sarath Nonis and Cathy Owens Swift cited research indicating that while '60 per cent of faculty members observed cheating in their classrooms ... only 20 per cent of them actually met with the student and a higher authority.' Says Nonis, who teaches marketing at Arkansas State University: 'My gut feeling is that number might be even more now.'"
>
> —Cathy Gulli, Nicholas Köhler, and Martin Patriquin,
> "The Great University Cheating Scandal"

1. What is the major claim, and where is it located?

2. What statements could be considered "supporting claims"?

3. Does the paragraph support its claims with evidence and explanations? Where, and how well?

4. Some statements are presented as speculations rather than as facts. Does the evidence support the speculations?

Practice 10.9 DRAFTING BODY PARAGRAPHS

For an issue that concerns you, draft a body paragraph that contains a main idea, evidence, and explanation.

Opposition Arguments and Refutations

The body of an argument argues for a major claim not only by supporting it with reasons (evidence and explanations), but also by rebutting significant alternative arguments.

As your readers consider your argument, they may think of positions and claims that contradict the point you are seeking to prove. These positions, contrary to your own, are sometimes called *opposition arguments* or *alternative arguments*. The process of neutralizing them is called *refutation* or *rebuttal*. Although *refute* means "to prove something is false or in error," you can also advance your claim by showing yours to be better than the opposition's claim or by offering a compromise between your position and the opposition's position.

Refutation can be vital to a successful argument. There are four ways to organize the refutation of alternative arguments:

- *Early refutation* deals with alternative arguments shortly after the introduction or within the introduction.

- *Late refutation* deals with alternative arguments in a separate section near or in the conclusion.

- *Occasional refutation* deals with alternative arguments as they become relevant to topics within the body of the composition.

- *Complete refutation* deals with alternative arguments as the chief purpose of the composition. Typically, this approach entails a point-by-point organization.

Early Refutation

Early refutation meets the opposition "head on," listing and usually discussing the alternative arguments in the early paragraphs and sometimes even in the introduction. Writers who opt for early refutation do so for several reasons:

- When an audience is clearly aware of opposing claims—perhaps even sympathetic to them—there is a danger that readers will resist your own claims until their doubts are allayed. Early acknowledgment of alternative arguments can remove these doubts or at least put your audience in a more receptive frame of mind.

- Acknowledging the opposition is a way to establish your own credibility, your *ethos*. You let the audience know not only that you have done your homework but also that your argument will not be one-sided. The audience will pick up clues from the tone of your writing style about how fairly you will treat the opposition.

- Introductions and early paragraphs often are used to establish the context of an issue, so identifying alternative arguments may be essential for clarifying the purpose and major claims of your composition.

Late Refutation

Sometimes writers postpone dealing with alternative arguments until the conclusion of the composition. This tactic has advantages for some purposes and some audiences:

- When an audience is unaware of the opposing arguments, the composition can become bogged down by introducing topics that have to then be dismissed before proceeding to your major claim.

- When an audience is aware of the opposing arguments but either is unconcerned by them or is sympathetic and receptive toward your claims, the refutation can be delayed.

Sometimes you cannot directly discredit or diminish the opposition. In fact, sometimes the opposition claim is not only valid but also appealing. In such cases, refutation does not prove error but rather offers your claim as being better than the rival claim. You offer the audience the greater of two goods; it is like concluding, "Now that you've seen my claim, isn't it better than my opposition's claim?"

Occasional Refutation

Sometimes you may decide that it is more advantageous to refute alternative arguments as the need arises. This method offers several advantages:

- Many arguments incorporate a number of claims, but not all of these claims have opposing claims needing refutation. Opposing arguments can occur anywhere in the body of your composition, whenever your rhetorical strategy calls for dealing with opposing views.

- Some arguments and opposing arguments have symmetry—for every pro, there is con; for every point, there is a counterpoint. A point-by-point organization can pair up each claim with an opposing claim, perhaps in the same paragraph or in juxtaposed paragraphs. For example, suppose that you have decided to argue against blaming students for their own acts of plagiarism. Your refutation might line up with the opposition's argument something like this:

Opposition's Argument	*Your Refutation*
MAJOR CLAIM	
Students are responsible for their own acts of plagiarism.	Students are not solely to blame. Administrators and teachers are also responsible.
SUPPORT	
It is primarily an issue of character.	It is primarily an issue of ignorance of ways to correctly use sources.
SUPPORT	
Plagiarism can harm others in various ways.	Misunderstanding the cause of plagiarism can cause harm, also.
SUPPORT	
The solution is punishment.	The solution is a combination of ethical awareness, clear policy, and improved instruction.

Complete Refutation

Your argument can be structured completely as a reaction to an opposing argument while not offering an alternative argument of your own. Sometimes it is important enough to expose a misconception or to advise against a course of action. Your argument would be saying, basically, "I don't know what the solution is to Problem X, but I know the opposition's solution is wrong." For example, you might give reasons why a policy against plagiarism is inadequate without offering a policy to replace it.

What's Wrong with Five-Paragraph Form?

Perhaps the best introduction to what's wrong with five-paragraph form can be found in Greek mythology. On his way to Athens, the hero Theseus encounters a particularly surly host, Procrustes, who offers wayfarers a bed for the night but with a catch. If they do not fit his bed exactly, he either stretches them or lops off their extremities until they do. This story has given us the word "procrustean," which the dictionary defines as "tending to produce conformity by violent or arbitrary means."

Five-paragraph form is a procrustean formula that most students learn in high school. While it has the advantage of providing a mechanical format that will give virtually any subject the appearance of order, it usually lops off a writer's ideas before they have the chance to form, or stretches a single idea to the breaking point. In other words, this simplistic scheme blocks writers' abilities to think deeply or logically, restricting rather than encouraging the development of complex ideas.

A complex idea is one that has many sides. To treat such ideas intelligently, writers need a form that will not require them to cut off all of those sides except the one that most easily fits the bed. Most of you will find the basic five-paragraph form (also known as the hamburger model) familiar:

1. An introduction—the top bun—that announces the writer's main idea, about which he or she will make three points.

2. Three paragraphs—the meat patties—each on one of the three points.

3. A conclusion—the bottom bun—beginning "Thus, we see" or "In conclusion" that essentially repeats the introduction.

Here is an example in outline form:

Introduction: The food in the school cafeteria is bad. It lacks variety, it's unhealthy, and it is always overcooked. In this essay I will discuss these three characteristics.

Paragraph 2: The first reason cafeteria food is bad is that there is no variety. (Plus one or two examples—no salad bar, mostly fried food, and so forth)

Paragraph 3: Another reason cafeteria food is bad is that it is not healthy. (Plus a few reasons—high cholesterol, too many hot dogs, too much sugar, and so forth)

Paragraph 4: In addition, the food is always overcooked. (Plus some examples—the vegetables are mushy, the "mystery" meat is tough to recognize, and so forth)

Conclusion: Thus, we see… (Plus a restatement of the introductory paragraph)

Most high school students write dozens of themes using this basic formula. They are taught to use five-paragraph form because it seems to provide the greatest good—a certain minimal clarity—for the greatest number of students. But the form does not promote logically tight and intellectually aggressive writing. It is a meat grinder that can turn any content into sausage. The two major problems it typically creates are easy to see.

1. The introduction reduces the remainder of the essay to *redundancy*. The first paragraph tells readers, in an overly general and list-like way, what they're going to hear; the succeeding three paragraphs tell the readers the same thing again in more detail and carry the overly general main idea along inertly; and the conclusion repeats what the readers have just been told (twice). The first cause of all this redundancy lies with the thesis. As in the example above, the thesis (cafeteria food is bad) is too broad—an unqualified and obvious generalization—and substitutes a simple list of predictable points for a complex statement of idea.

2. The form arbitrarily divides content: why are there three points (or examples or reasons) instead of five or one? A quick look at the three categories in our example reveals how arbitrarily the form has divided the subject. Isn't overcooked food unhealthy? Isn't a lack of variety also conceivably unhealthy? The format invites writers to list rather than analyze, to plug supporting examples into categories without examining the examples or how they are related. Five-para-graph form, as is evident in our sample's transitions ("first," "another reason," and "in addition"), counts things off but doesn't make logical connections. At its worst, the form prompts the writer to simply append evidence to generalizations without saying anything about it.

The subject, on the other hand, is not as unpromising as the format makes it appear. It could easily be redirected along a more productive pathway. (If the food is bad, what are the underlying causes of the problem? Are students getting what they ask for? Is the problem one of cost? Is the faculty cafeteria better? Why or why not?)

Now, let's look briefly at the introductory paragraph from a student's essay on a more academic subject. Here we can see a remarkable feature of five-paragraph form—its capacity to produce the same kind of say-nothing prose on almost any subject.

> Throughout the film *The Tempest,* a version of Shakespeare's play *The Tempest,* there were a total of seven characters. These characters were Calibano, Alonso, Antonio, Aretha, Freddy, the doctor, and Dolores. Each character in the film represented a person in Shakespeare's play, but there were four people who were greatly similar to those in Shakespeare, and who played a role in symbolizing aspects of forgiveness, love, and power.

The final sentence of the paragraph reveals the writer's addiction to five-paragraph form. It signals that the writer will proceed in a purely mechanical and superficial way, producing a paragraph on forgiveness, a paragraph on love, a paragraph on power, and a conclusion stating again that the film's characters resemble Shakespeare's in these three aspects. The writer is so busy *demonstrating* that the characters are concerned with forgiveness, love, and power that she misses the opportunity to analyze the significance of her own observations. Instead, readers are drawn wearily to a conclusion; they get no place except back where they began. Further, the demonstration mode prevents her from analyzing connections among the categories. The writer might consider, for example, how the play and the film differ in resolving the conflict between power and forgiveness (focusing on difference within similarity) and to what extent the film and the play agree about which is the most important of the three aspects (focusing on similarity despite difference).

These more analytical approaches lie concealed in the writer's introduction, but they never get discovered because the five-paragraph form militates against sustained analytical thinking. Its division of the subject into parts, which is only one part of analysis, has become an end unto itself. The procrustean formula insists upon a tripartite list in which each of the three parts is separate, equal, and, above all, *inert.*

Here are two *quick checks* for whether a paper of yours has closed down your thinking through a scheme such as five-paragraph form:

1. *Look at the paragraph openings.* If these read like a list, each beginning with an additive transition like "another" followed by a more or less exact repetition of your central point ("Another example is…" or "Yet another example is…"), you should suspect that you are not adequately developing your ideas.

2. *Compare the wording in the last statement of the paper's thesis (in the conclusion) with the first statement of it in the introduction.* If the wording at these two locations is virtually the same, you will know that your thesis has not responded adequately to your evidence.

An Alternative to Five-Paragraph Form: The All-Purpose Organizational Scheme

Five-paragraph form sacrifices thinking for organization—a losing bargain—but organization does matter. The various analytical techniques and prompts that we offer in its place, from "interesting" and "strange" to looking for difference within similarity, will encourage thinking, but how do you go about organizing that thinking? Let's leap ahead to a template that you can adapt to many kinds of analytical writing. It is constructed upon several premises:

- An analytical writer approaches evidence to refine and sharpen his or her thesis, not just to support it.

- A productive thesis changes (evolves) as it encounters evidence.

- The paper itself should re-enact in more polished form for the reader the chains of thought that led the writer to his or her conclusions.

Some of the steps below will become clearer by the end of the chapter. In any case, here is the template:

1. WRITE AN INTRODUCTION

Begin analytical papers by defining some issue, question, problem, or phenomenon that the paper will address. An introduction is not a conclusion. It lays out something you have noticed that you think needs to be better understood. Use the introduction to get your readers to see why they should be more curious about the thing you have noticed.

2. STATE A WORKING THESIS

Early in the paper, often at the end of the first paragraph or the beginning of the second (depending on the conventions of the discipline you are writing in), make a tentative claim about whatever it is you have laid out as being in need of exploration. The initial version of your thesis, known as *the working thesis*, should offer a tentative explanation, answer, or solution that the body of your paper will go on to apply and develop (clarify, extend, substantiate, qualify, and so on).

3. BEGIN QUERYING YOUR THESIS

Start developing your working thesis and other opening observations with the question "So what?" This question is shorthand for questions like "What does this observation mean?" and "Where does this thesis get me in my attempts to explain my subject?"

4. MUSTER SUPPORTING EVIDENCE FOR YOUR WORKING THESIS

Test its adequacy by seeing how much of the available evidence it can honestly account for. That is, try to prove that your thesis is correct, but also expect to come across evidence that does not fit your initial formulation of the thesis.

5. SEEK COMPLICATING EVIDENCE

Find evidence that does not readily support your thesis. Then explore—and explain—how and why it doesn't fit.

6. REFORMULATE YOUR THESIS

Use the complicating evidence to produce new wording in your working thesis (additions, qualification, and so forth). This is how a thesis evolves: by assimilating obstacles and refining terms.

7. REPEAT STEPS 3 TO 6

Query, support, complicate, and reformulate your thesis until you are satisfied with its accuracy.

8. STATE A CONCLUSION

Reflect on and reformulate your paper's opening position in light of the thinking that your analysis of evidence has caused you to do. Culminate rather than merely restate your paper's main idea in the concluding paragraph. Do this by getting your conclusion to again answer the question "So what?" In the conclusion, this question is shorthand for "Where does it get us to view the subject in this way?" or "What are the possible implications or consequences of the position the paper has arrived at?" Usually the reformulated (evolved) thesis comes near the beginning of the concluding paragraph. The remainder of the paragraph gradually moves the reader out of your piece, preferably feeling good about what you have accomplished for him or her.

As should be apparent, following the template will require you to shift your approach not only to a thesis (abandoning the notion of a fixed and static one) but also to evidence. Let's turn now to consider more carefully the nature and function of evidence.

Linking Evidence and Claims

Evidence matters because it always involves authority: the power of evidence is, well, *evident* in the laboratory, the courtroom, the classroom, and just about everywhere else. Your high school grades are evidence, and they may have worked for or against you. If they worked against you—if you believe yourself smarter than the numbers indicate—then you probably offered alternative evidence, such as extracurricular achievements, when you applied to college. As this example illustrates, there are many kinds of evidence; and whether or not something qualifies as acceptable evidence, as well as what it may show or prove, is often debatable.

The types and amounts of evidence necessary for persuading readers and building authority also vary from one discipline to another, as does the manner in which the evidence is presented. While some disciplines—the natural sciences, for example—will require you to present your evidence first and then interpret it, others (the humanities and some social sciences) will expect you to interpret your evidence as it is presented. But in all disciplines—and virtually any writing situation—it is important to support claims with evidence, to make your evidence lead to claims, and especially to be explicit about *how you've arrived at the connection between your evidence and your claims* (see Figure 10.1).

The first step in learning to explain the connection between your evidence and your claims is to remember that *evidence rarely, if ever, can be left to speak for itself.* When you leave evidence to speak for itself, you are assuming that it can be interpreted in only one way and that others will necessarily think as you do.

Writers who think that evidence speaks for itself generally do very little with it. Sometimes they will present it without making any overt claims, stating, for example, "There was no alcohol at the party," and expecting the reader to understand this statement as a sign of approval or disapproval. Alternatively, they may simply place the evidence next to a claim. Such writers will say, for example, "The party was terrible: there was no alcohol," or "The party was great: there was no alcohol." Merely juxtaposing the evidence to the claim (just putting them next to each other) leaves out the *thinking* that connects them and thereby implies that the logic of the connection is obvious. But even for readers prone to agree with you, just pointing to the evidence, assuming it will speak for itself, is not enough.

Of course, before you can attend to the relationship between evidence and claims, you first have to make sure to include both of them. The two most fundamental problems that writers must surmount, then, are unsubstantiated claims and pointless evidence. Let's pause to take a look at how to remedy these problems.

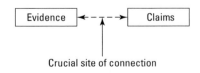

FIGURE 10.1 Linking Evidence and Claims

UNSUBSTANTIATED CLAIMS

Problem: Making claims that lack supporting evidence.
Solution: Learning to recognize and support unsubstantiated assertions.

Unsubstantiated claims occur when you concentrate only on conclusions, omitting the evidence that led to them. At the opposite extreme, pointless evidence results when you offer a mass of detail attached to an overly general claim. To solve both of these problems, remember two rules. Whenever you make a claim, make sure that you (1) offer your readers the evidence that led you to it and (2) explain how the evidence led you to that conclusion. The word "unsubstantiated" means "without substance." An unsubstantiated claim is not necessarily false; it just offers none of the concrete "stuff" upon which the claim is based. When you make an unsubstantiated claim, you assume that readers will believe you just because you say this or that.

Perhaps more important, unsubstantiated claims deprive you of details. Without details, you're left with nothing concrete to think about. If you lack some actual "stuff" to analyze, you can easily get stuck in a set of abstractions, which tend to overstate your position, inhibit your thinking, and leave your readers wondering exactly what you mean. The further away your language gets from the concrete, from references to physical detail—things that you can see, hear, count, taste, smell, and touch—the more abstract it becomes. An aircraft carrier anchored outside a foreign harbour is concrete; the phrase "intervening in the name of democracy" is abstract.

You can see the problem of unsubstantiated assertions not only in papers but also in everyday conversation. It occurs when people get in the habit of leaping to conclusions—forming impressions so quickly and automatically that they have difficulty even recalling what it was that triggered a particular response. Ask such people why they thought a party was boring or a new acquaintance pretentious, and they will rephrase the generalization rather than offer the evidence that led to it: the party was boring because nobody did anything; the person is pretentious because he puts on airs.

Voices Across the Curriculum EARNING YOUR CONCLUSIONS

Typically, when we write analytically, we write for others. What would induce them to read what we've written, grab their attention, make them keep reading? Detail, for one. Too often, feeling inadequate, fearing being mistaken, we hide behind labels, abstract phrases, and technical jargon, refuse to be present in what we write, and—consequently—nothing distinguishes our essay from any other.

Better to step forward, risk being there, making ourselves and our thinking visible. Details do that. As poet, novelist, and writing teacher Natalie Goldberg reminds us: "*Be specific. Not car, but Cadillac. Not bird, but wren. Not a codependent, neurotic man, but Harry, who runs to open the refrigerator for his wife, thinking she wants an apple, when she is headed for the gas stove to light her cigarette. Be careful of those pop-psychology labels. Get below the label and be specific to the person (or to the experience)*" (3).

Details persuade; rather than tell, they show. They make our subsequent abstractions and conclusions count.

—Mark Weisberg, professor of law

Rephrasing your generalizations rather than offering evidence tends to starve your thinking; it also has the effect of shutting out readers. If, for example, you defend your judgment that a person is pretentious by saying that he puts on airs, you have ruled on the matter and dismissed it. (You have also committed a logical flaw known as a *circular argument*, because "pretentious" and "putting on airs" mean virtually the same thing and using one in support of the other is arguing in a circle.) If, by contrast, you include the *grounds* upon which your judgment is based—the fact that he uses big words or that he always wears a bow tie—you have given readers a glimpse of your criteria. Readers are far more likely to accept your views if you give them the chance to think *with* you about the evidence. The alternative—offering groundless assertions—is to expect them to take your word for it.

There is, of course, an element of risk in providing the details that have informed your judgment. You leave yourself open to attack if, for example, your readers wear bow ties or speak in polysyllables. But this is an essential risk to take, for, otherwise, you leave your readers wondering why you think as you do or, worse, unlikely to credit your point of view. Moreover, in laying out your evidence, you will be more likely to anticipate your readers' possible disagreements. This will make you more inclined to think openly and carefully about your judgments.

In order to check your drafts for unsubstantiated assertions, you first have to know how to recognize them. One of the most fundamental skills for a writer to possess is the ability to *distinguish* evidence from claims. It is sometimes difficult to separate facts from judgments, data from interpretations of the data. Writers who aren't practised in this skill can believe that they are offering evidence when they are really offering only unsubstantiated claims. In your own reading and writing, pause once in a while to label the sentences of a paragraph as either evidence (E) or claims (C). What happens if we try to categorize the sentences of the following paragraph in this way?

> The NHL Players Association is ruining professional hockey in North America. Although players claim that they are underpaid, they are really just being greedy. Seventeen years ago, they delayed the start of the season for fifteen weeks, because the commissioner refused to buckle to their demands. Hockey is a sport, not a business, and it is a sad fact that it is being threatened by selfish athletes.

The first and last sentences of the paragraph are claims. They draw conclusions about as yet unstated evidence that the writer will need to provide. The middle two sentences are harder to classify. If particular players have stated publicly that they are underpaid, the existence of the players' statements is a fact. But the writer moves from evidence to claims when he suggests that the players are motivated by greed. As it stands, the assertion is an unsubstantiated claim. Unless the writer proceeds to ground it in evidence—relevant facts—it amounts to little more than name-calling. Similarly, it is a fact that the 1994–95 season was delayed for fifteen weeks, but the assertion that "the commissioner refused to buckle" is another unsubstantiated claim. The writer needs to offer evidence in support of this claim, along with his reasons for believing that the evidence means what he says it does.

Without evidence and the reasoning you've done about it, your writing asks readers to accept your opinions as though they were facts. The central claim of the hockey paragraph—that greedy players are ruining the sport—is an example of an opinion treated as though it were factual information. While many readers might be inclined to accept some version of the claim as true, they should not be asked to accept the writer's opinion as a self-evident truth.

The word "evident" comes from a Latin verb meaning "to see." To say that the truth of a statement is "self-evident" means that it does not need proving because its truth should be plainly seen by all. The problem is that very few ideas—no matter how much you may believe in them—readily attest to their own truth. And precisely because what people have taken to be common knowledge ("Women can't do math," for example, or "Men don't talk about their feelings") so often turns out to be wrong, you should take care to avoid unsubstantiated claims.

You need to be stingy, therefore, about treating your claims and evidence as factual. The more concrete information you gather, the less likely you will be to accept your opinions, partial information, or misinformation as fact. The writer of the hockey paragraph, for example, offers as fact that the players claim they are underpaid. If he were to search harder, however, he would find that his statement of the players' claim is not entirely accurate. The players have not unanimously claimed that they are underpaid; they have acknowledged that the problem has to do with poorer "small-market" teams competing against richer "large-market" teams. This more complicated version of the facts might at first be discouraging to the writer, since it reveals his original thesis ("greed") to be oversimplified. But then, as we have been saying, the function of evidence is not just to corroborate your claims; it should also help you to *test* and *refine* your ideas and to *define* your key terms more precisely.

Try This

> Take an excerpt from your own writing, at least two paragraphs in length—perhaps from a paper you have already written or a draft you are working on—and label each sentence as either evidence (E) or claim (C). For sentences that appear to offer both, determine which parts of the sentence are evidence and which are claim, and then decide which one, E or C, predominates. What is the ratio of evidence to claim, especially in particularly effective or particularly weak paragraphs?

POINTLESS EVIDENCE

Problem: Presenting a mass of evidence without explaining how it relates to the claims.
Solution: Making details speak; explaining how evidence confirms and qualifies the claim.

Your thinking emerges in the way that you follow through on the implications of the evidence you have selected. You need to interpret it for your readers. It is not enough to insert evidence after your claim, expecting readers to draw the same conclusion about its meaning that you have. You cannot assume that the facts can speak for themselves. You have to make the details speak, conveying to your readers why the details mean what you claim they mean.

The following paragraph illustrates what happens when a writer leaves the evidence to speak for itself:

> The use of computers is ruining the concentration powers of most Canadian teenagers today. For example, one of the most popular games, *Diablo II*, throws a confusing array of visual signals in front of the player's eyes. Also of concern is the fact that many young people admit to having no appetite for reading books. It takes a great deal of focus and determination to wade through a 350-page novel. In addition to not appreciating the

insights of our many fine novelists, such as Margaret Atwood and Hugh MacLennan, teenagers seem oblivious to the physical effects of spending countless hours glued to a screen, seated on a chair. Studies suggest that office workers who spend all day at their desks and at their keyboards suffer not only muscle problems but also psychological ones in the long term. Without the ability to concentrate on something other than the kaleidoscope of colours, images, and noise that emanates from high-tech games and other computerized diversions, an entire generation will face years of recuperation, once those teenagers become adults who must work to support a family and to earn a decent living.

Unlike the paragraph on greedy athletes, which was virtually all claims, this one offers a loose parade of evidence that is both preceded and followed by a redundant claim about teenagers and their dwindling powers of concentration. In essence, this paragraph is built like a miniature five-paragraph hamburger. The three meat patties of evidence—*Diablo II*, Canadian literature, and office-worker ailments—are sandwiched between twin buns of interpretation.

Unfortunately, the formula works no better at the paragraph level than it does at the essay level. Lining up evidence in a series of three (or four, or five) will be unconvincing if that evidence is left to speak for itself. If readers are to accept the writer's implicit claim—that teenagers are both inattentive and sedentary—he will have to show *how* and *why* the evidence supports that conclusion. The rule that applies here is that *evidence can almost always be interpreted in more than one way.*

You might, for instance, formulate at least three conclusions from the evidence offered in this hamburger paragraph. You might decide that the writer believes teenagers spend the same number of hours on the computer as office workers do—or that lack of exercise takes away one's ability to concentrate. Quite possibly, you might disagree with his claim and conclude that video games have positive effects on those who enjoy them; *Diablo II* could be read as a stimulant to the imagination. Since the connection between claim and evidence is not clearly stated, readers are left to fend for themselves.

How can you ensure that your readers will at least understand your interpretation of the data? Begin by constantly reminding yourself that the thought connections that have occurred to you will not automatically occur to others. This doesn't mean that you should assume your readers are stupid, but you shouldn't expect them to read your mind and to do for themselves the thinking that you should be doing for them.

You can make the details speak if you take the time to stop and look at them, asking questions about what they imply. The two steps to follow are (1) to say explicitly what you take the details to mean and (2) to state exactly how the evidence supports or qualifies your claims.

The writer of the hamburger paragraph leaves his claim and virtually all of his reasoning about the evidence implicit. What, for example, is the connection between teenagers who don't like to read and teenagers who like to play computer games? Are they one and the same? Does the writer presume that the two activities are mutually exclusive? Due to its overly loose construction, the paragraph generates more questions than it answers.

There is a final lesson to glean from this example. Notice that when you focus on tightening the links between evidence and claim, the result is almost always a "smaller" claim than the one you set out to prove. This is what evidence characteristically does to a claim; it shrinks and restricts its scope. This process, also known as *qualifying a claim*, is the means by which a thesis evolves.

Sometimes it is hard to give up on the large, general assertions that were your first response to your subject. But your sacrifices are exchanged for greater accuracy and validity. The sweeping claims you lose ("an entire generation will face years of recuperation") give way to less resounding but also more informed, more incisive, and less judgmental ideas.

DRAFTING THE CONCLUSION

Conclusions, like introductions, are specialized passages. They let the readers know that the essay is coming to an end and remind them of the main idea of the argument. A writer will often remind the readers of the thesis and sometimes summarize the main points of the essay. In arguments, the conclusion is usually the place to mention the major claim (thesis statement) again and to emphasize again some of the argument's most compelling claims that made up the body of the piece.

If you have difficulty concluding your composition, consider these three techniques: (1) revisit the claim, (2) remind the reader of the argument's central ideas, and/or (3) offer a final parting statement. The first two techniques are relatively easy to understand. Sometimes the third is not. The parting statement may be thought of as the reverse of the lead that you used initially to gain the reader's attention and give some hint of the topic. Like the lead sentences used to pique the reader's interest, the parting statement casts a wide net, but is intended to "ease" the reader out of the argument while at the same time maintaining the reader's continued interest. It is like a train slowing down to let you off at your stop.

Here are some points to remember when writing a conclusion:

- Write the conclusion only after you know the final structure of your essay.

- Restate your claim, but don't quote it verbatim from the introduction. The claim can appear anywhere within the conclusion. When it appears at the bottom, it may serve as the parting statement.

- Summarize the most important supporting points, but don't make the conclusion read like a laundry list. Some writers will restate their response to an alternative argument before reintroducing their overall claim.

- Use transitional words and phrases.

- End with a general statement related to your topic. In most cases, it will be broader than your claim. Its purpose should be to maintain the reader's interest in the issue at hand.

- Don't undermine your efforts by being apologetic (e.g., "...but I'm not really an expert") or cute ("That's my story, and I'm stickin' with it").

OPTIONS FOR CONCLUSIONS

Summarize

Go over your major points, but don't simply repeat the introduction. Add some perspective and vary the phrasing.

Personalize

Explain how the issue affects you or the reader.

Focus

Emphasize a particular point over other points.

Quote

Revisit an earlier quotation in your text, or introduce another quotation that summarizes or provides perspective.

Question

Pose questions that may lead to action or further investigation.

Propose an action

Introduce a call for action, even though the text itself may be more about problems than solutions.

Warn

Caution about consequences.

Encourage

Offer some consolation.

Expand

Put the text in a larger context.

Practice 10.10 UNDERSTANDING CONCLUSIONS

Read the concluding paragraphs and then answer the following questions.

1. What technique of concluding does the author use: summarizing, personalizing, focusing, quoting, questioning, proposing, warning, encouraging, expanding, or some other method?

2. From the conclusion alone, can you guess the main idea of the essay as a whole? Speculate on some of the topics that could have been in the essay.

3. Which conclusion appeals to you most? Least? Explain.

Excerpt A

Knowing what plagiarism is, however, doesn't guarantee that you'll know how to avoid it. Is it okay, for example, to cobble together a series of summaries and paraphrases in a paragraph, provided that you include the authors in the bibliography at the end of the paper? Or what if you insert a single footnote at the end of the paragraph? The answer is that both are still plagiarism, because your reader can't tell where your thinking starts and others' thinking stops. As a basic rule of thumb, *"Readers must be able to tell as they are reading your paper exactly what information came from which source and what information is your contribution to the paper"* (Hult 2003).

—David Rosenwasser, Jill Stephen, Doug Babington, *Writing Analytically with Readings*

Excerpt B

I request every student to keep an electronic journal of how they complete a term paper from the beginning to the end. They need to submit all articles they use in their papers along with highlighted areas from where they borrow ideas or concepts. Student electronic journals are recorded on a course management system called Blackboard where I can access and monitor student progress. One may find this activity very time consuming; however, I schedule my time to access each student's journal only once a week and set aside 15-20 minutes in every class to discuss with individuals about their paper. I believe that this on-going effort helps bring out the best in students.

—Apiwan D. Born, "How to Reduce Plagiarism"

Excerpt C

The Chinese people are eager to achieve a Western standard of living, and they deserve nothing less than to reap the benefits of their labor. But as long as authorities allow property rights and trademarks to be blithely ignored, and as long as academics treat original work as communal property to be pilfered at will, China's economic revolution will rest on a foundation of sand.

—Maclean's Canada Editors, "The China Syndrome: Corruption and Theft"*

---

*Maclean's Canada Editors, "The China Syndrome: Corruption and Theft" May 15, 2005. Reprinted by permission.

TYING IT ALL TOGETHER

Readers expect precision and unity in any kind of writing. In part, this is accomplished through a thesis and topic sentences. In addition, writers use qualifiers and transitions to smooth out the flow of words.

Using Qualifiers

By their very nature, claims tend to be accompanied by a degree of uncertainty. Arguers often must qualify their claims by (1) explaining under which circumstances the claim is true or (2) estimating the probability that a claim is true.

Qualifiers

Qualifiers describe the limits of a claim. Below are some examples:

absolutely	occasionally
probably	always
possibly	sometimes
most of the time	as a rule
seldom	typically
regularly	hardly ever
never	potentially
usually	tentatively
generally	often
least	frequently

CIRCUMSTANTIAL QUALIFIERS

Some claims apply only under certain circumstances.

In the following excerpt, the qualifier is underlined:

> Students think they are less likely to get caught for plagiarism if they submit a purchased essay rather than one that is available for free on the web.
>
> —John Stilla

PROBABILITY QUALIFIERS

So many things in life are unknown, but decisions still must be made based on our "best guess." Sometimes you can find statistical data that will give you a numerical estimate of probability. At other times, you'll have to offer verbal qualifiers ranging from long explanations to simple adverbs such as *possibly, sometimes, potentially,* or *probably.*

In the following excerpts, the qualifier is underlined:

> A student <u>could</u> resort to plagiarism if that student experiences writer's block the night before an essay is due.
>
> —John Stilla

> <u>Sometimes</u> students plagiarize unintentionally because they are unaware of how to construct a proper paraphrase."
>
> —John Stilla

Using Transitions

Readers appreciate when you help them see how the parts of a composition relate to each other. You do this in part by directly stating the relationships in your thesis and topic sentences and in part by showing the relevance of your evidence. In addition, you can use transitions—that is, words or phrases that state how the parts are related. Without transitions, your reader may have to work harder to understand how sentences or whole paragraphs relate to each other and to the thesis.

Consider, for example, one of the most frequently used transitions in this book: "for example." It signals that something concrete will illustrate a generality. In addition, consider the transitional phrase "in addition." It signals that you are being given an additional example. You get the idea.

TRANSITIONS

Addition
again, also, and, as well, besides, in addition, furthermore, moreover

Cause and effect
accordingly, because, consequently, since, so, therefore, thus

Clarification
i.e., in other words, that is to say, to put it another way

Concession
granted that, naturally, of course, to be sure

Comparison
by the same token, comparably, in the same way, likewise, similarly

Contrast
but, conversely, however, in spite of, nevertheless, on the other hand

Emphasis
by all means, certainly, indeed, in fact, no doubt, of course, surely

Illustration
e.g., for example, for instance, specifically, to demonstrate

Purpose
in order that, in order to, intending to, so that

Sequence
finally, first (second, and so on), then, next, numbered list (1., 2., and so on)

Space
above, adjacent, adjoining, beyond, far, here, near, there

Summary
briefly, in conclusion, in the final analysis, to summarize, to sum up

Time
after, before, immediately, later, meanwhile, occasionally, soon

Practice 10.11 USING TRANSITIONS TO ACHIEVE COHERENCE

Read the excerpts about plagiarism and respond to the following questions:

1. Locate each transition. Explain how they function in the paragraph. How do they vary in their functions?
2. Which transitions seems more sophisticated to you? Which type would you be inclined to use? How does the type of transition used affect the style of the piece?
3. Are there places where formal transitions are not needed to move effectively from one sentence to another? How is this effect achieved?

Excerpt A

Knowing what plagiarism is, however, doesn't guarantee that you'll know how to avoid it. Is it okay, for example, to cobble together a series of summaries and paraphrases in a paragraph, provided that you include the authors in the bibliography at the end of the paper? Or what if you insert a single footnote at the end of the paragraph? The answer is that both are still plagiarism, because your reader can't tell where your thinking starts and others' thinking stops. As a basic rule of thumb, *"Readers must be able to tell as they are reading your paper exactly what information came from which source and what information is your contribution to the paper"* (Hult 2003).

—David Rosenwasser, Jill Stephen, Doug Babington, *Writing Analytically with Readings*

Excerpt B

What was Dmitry Yemets thinking when he cloned Harry Potter to create his wizard Tanya Grotter—that they would meet and become friends? They did in fact meet, but it was in an Amsterdam courtroom, when British author J. K. Rowling asserted her plagiarism claim. True enough, the claim was not against Yemets but against the publisher, Byblos, who had set April 2003 as the release date for the first 7,000 copies of a Dutch translation of *Tanya Grotter and the Magic Contrabass.*

—Anna Dymkovets, "Cultural Clones"

Practice 10.12 USING TRANSITIONS

Examine one of your own essays or one of a classmate. Circle all of the transitions. Insert (pencil in) additional transitions wherever a transition would help the flow.

Plagiarism is literary theft.

Student Essay

As you read the following student essay, identify and evaluate its structural features: introduction (lead, background, major claim), supporting and rebutting body paragraphs (types of claims, evidence, and explanations; their organization), and conclusion. What does the author do well, and what could she improve?

Shah 1

Hetal Shah

EN 101

Dr. Everett

February 8, 2012

Curing Plagiarism

Academic dishonesty is spreading like an epidemic across colleges and universities. Its symptoms range from copying a friend's homework to looking at another student's answers during a test to turning in a term paper that is plagiarized. *Plagiarism, which is taking credit for someone else's words or ideas,* in particular has increased at an alarming rate. Schools and colleges seek to understand not only the causes for rampant plagiarism but also ways to treat it more effectively. The remedy lies in cooperation between instructors, administrators, and students: instructors should improve how they teach academic honesty, administrators should revise and publicize policies treating academic misconduct, and students should value ethics over grades.

Statistics show a tremendous increase in academic dishonesty across the nation. According to a study conducted by *Plagiarism.org* 58.3 percent of high school students in 1969 allowed others to copy their work. In 1989, about 97.3 percent allowed their work to be copied by other students. Even more students today are copying homework answers and cheating on tests to maintain high grades.

There are many causes of plagiarism. One reason is the pressure on students to achieve, varying from maintaining a high GPA in high school to get into a good college to keeping up grades while in college to hold on to scholarships (Durkin). A second reason is the competitive nature of grading: a student must be not just acceptable but better than others (Fanning 8). Plagiarism also occurs because it is socially acceptable: many students do not consider it to be cheating because all their friends are doing it. In addition, cheaters are convinced that they are not going to get caught (Gulli, Köhler, and Patriquin 34); 95 percent of high school students who cheated were never found out (Gomez 42). Finally, rigorous course loads have led many students, often those who are near the top of their classes, to cheat in an effort to keep up with the workload.

Acting as a kind of safety valve for the pressures on students, modern technology has contributed greatly to the rise of plagiarism. The Internet has broadened the horizons for those who plagiarize because it is easily accessible and its resources are huge. At least 305 "cheat sites" with names such as "schoolsucks.com" and "lazystudents.com" sell recycled and custom-made papers (Clos 2). A study performed by *Education Week* found that 54 percent of American students admitted using prewritten Internet essays as a source for completing assignments at least once (Durkin).

According to Apiwan D. Born, an educator who specializes in information systems, instructors tend to react to plagiarism after the fact, when instead they should be proactive, stopping it before it starts: "an instructor should focus on 'how to reduce and discourage cheating activities' rather than 'why students cheat and how they did it.'" Proactive measures include teaching writing as a process rather than as a product, using more group rather than solitary activities, conducting more writing activities in class rather than out of class, and educating students better about what plagiarism is and why it is wrong (Born 223).

Establishing a campuswide program for educating students about plagiarism and instructors about plagiarism prevention is an administrative task. Just as campuses provide seminars for faculty members to help them better serve students with handicaps or to avoid practices that might be taken as sexual harassment, training should take place to help faculty understand the causes of *and solutions* to academic dishonesty. Administrative policies regarding cheating should be not only judicial and punitive, as they are now, but also proactive and preventive: writing instruction and ethical instruction need to be highlighted, promoted, and practiced universally.

Shah 3

Finally, students should be held responsible. At present there is a culture of complicity, where honest students tolerate the cheating done by their peers: students who would without hesitation report the theft of physical property instead look the other way when intellectual property is stolen. Something like an honor code needs to be established. Without the support of the average student, any program that promotes academic honesty is doomed to failure.

The epidemic of cheating will continue to plague academia until instructors, administrators, and students work together to treat it. This means more than posting a policy statement in a syllabus or handbook. This means more than assigning the "avoid plagiarism" passage for students to read in their composition textbooks. This means more than using antiplagiarism websites and software to catch plagiarists and then punish them after the fact. It means, instead, a cooperative effort to <u>cure</u> plagiarism through improved instruction, improved administration, and improved student ethics.

Shah 4

Works Cited

Born, Apiwan D. "How to Reduce Plagiarism." *Journal of Information Systems Education* 14.3 (2003): 223–24. Print.

Clos, Karen. "When Academic Dishonesty Happens on Your Campus." *Innovation Abstracts* 24.26 (2002): 1–2. Print.

Durkin, Jessica. "A Culture of Copy-and-Paste." *Spiked Online*. Signet Group, 28 Apr. 2005. Web. 2 Feb. 2011.

Fanning, Karen. "Is Honesty Still the Best Policy?" *Junior Scholastic* 107.17 (2005): 8–9. Print.

Gomez, Dina S. "It's Just So Easy to Cheat." *NEA Today* 19.7 (2001): 42. Print.

Gulli, Cathy, Nicholas Köhler, and Martin Patriquin. "The Great University Cheating Scandal." *Maclean's*. 12 Feb. 2007: 32–36. *ProQuest.Umi*. Web. 8 Feb. 2011.

Plagiarism.org. iParadigms LLC. 2011. Web. 28 January 2011.

Looking Back

- An essay's basic structure consists of three major sections: (1) an introduction that provides a thesis statement or otherwise orients the reader toward a major claim, (2) a body of paragraphs that break down the thesis into specific areas and treat each area in detail, and (3) a conclusion that provides closure.

- A basic introduction to a composition contains a lead, background information, and a thesis or major claim.

- The body of an argument argues for the major claim (1) by supporting it with reasons (evidence and explanations) and (2) by rebutting significant alternative arguments.

- A topic can be stated at the top of a text block or paragraph, at the bottom of a text block or paragraph, as a delayed topic (after a transition sentence), or as an implied topic (not directly stated).

- There are four ways to organize the refutation of alternative arguments: early, late, occasional, and complete.

- Arguers often must qualify their claims by explaining under which circumstances the claim is true or by estimating the probability that a claim is true.

- Conclusions can do many things: summarize, personalize, focus, quote, question, propose, warn, encourage, or expand.

- Transitions help maintain coherence within a composition.

Suggestions for Writing

- Write a journal entry about your own process of drafting.

- After choosing an issue that interests you, follow the suggestions in the chapter as you draft an argument.

The Writing Process:
REVISING AND EDITING ARGUMENTS

Writing is a process of change. Through your efforts, a blank sheet of paper or a computer screen evolves into a text. As you then evaluate and rewrite what you've written, the text undergoes improvements in form and content. The latter changes are the result of revision and editing.

REVISING AN ARGUMENT

The word *revision* is derived from a prefix and root word that mean "see again." Revision is expressed as alterations of your words, phrases, and larger blocks of text. Yet these external, visible changes emerge from invisible thought processes within you. The greater part of "seeing again" is internal, growing with your understanding of the needs of people (an audience), your own needs (your purpose for writing), and the ways in which rhetoric and argument can satisfy those needs.

Looking at your own writing with fresh eyes can be tricky. Some authors find they benefit from putting their texts aside for a while, allowing a kind of "distancing" or perspective. Unfortunately, many writing assignments come with deadlines that rule out a prolonged cooling-off period for works in progress. Fortunately, writers have several methods they can use to quickly re-see and improve their work. For example, revision guides, checklists, and rubrics can all be used to evaluate your own writing. These three methods can also be used to gather and organize feedback from your peers and from your writing instructor, as well as to guide you in giving feedback to other writers in your class.

Revision Isn't Editing

Although the words "revision and editing" often are uttered in the same breath, as though the two are the same activity, they are actually fundamentally different processes. Revision is closely related to planning and drafting, in that these processes are primarily concerned with the content—the meaning or message—of a text. Like planning and drafting, revision is recursive, with the writer repeating this process as often as necessary until he or she is satisfied with what the text has to say. By contrast, editing is nonrecursive, a terminal phase that normally doesn't lead to the production of content. The primary concern of editing is the correctness of technical features—spelling, punctuation, usage, formatting, and other features that affect meaning only if they are performed incorrectly.

Efficient writers postpone editing as long as possible because it slows the writing process: You pause to look up the spelling of a word. Inexperienced writers have difficulty turning off their "internal editor," the part of them that resists writing anything that isn't correct. If your writing has ever come to a screeching halt because of technical matters, your internal editor needs to take a break. To make matters worse, the technical changes that slow down your writing process may end up in the scrap heap later on as you revise.

Revision Guides, Checklists, and Rubrics

Revision guides, checklists, and rubrics all direct you to find and evaluate particular features (criteria) of your draft:

- They present the criteria (characteristics, descriptors) of good writing.
- They assume you can detect particular weaknesses and revise them once your attention is directed that way.
- They can be used to guide an evaluation of your own writings or the writings of others.

These three revision tools differ somewhat in how they are structured and used:

- The revision guide is long and detailed. It will help focus your attention on the many details to be considered while checking an early draft.

- The checklist is brief, a summary of the long revision guide. The checklist works best after you are familiar with the details of the revision guide.

- A rubric adds a grading scale to the criteria featured in both the revision guide and the checklist. Depending on how your instructor structures the activities in class, the rubric may or may not be useful.

Feedback from others also can be directed by a revision guide, checklist, or rubric. Feedback, which will be discussed later in this chapter, can occur in one-on-one discussion sessions (with an instructor or a peer such as another student) and group work or, less personally, through a reviewer's written or recorded comments.

Using a Revision Guide

Here are some suggestions for using a revision guide productively:

- **Consider every question.** Not all questions will be useful, but as a whole the guide should help pinpoint significant strengths and weaknesses or concerns.

- **Mark and annotate.** Show the locations of specific strengths and weaknesses.

- **Evaluate.** Finish by writing a brief statement about the strengths, your concerns, and your recommendations.

REVISION GUIDE

As you read the piece from start to finish, comment on the features of argument and rhetoric. Below are specific questions that might be useful. (A brief version of these features is presented later in this chapter on page 236 as a Revision Checklist.)

ARGUMENT: Claims, Evidence, Explanations, Qualifications, and Refutations

Claims

- What is the major claim? Where is it stated or how is it implied?

- Is the major claim significant (worth arguing), clear, arguable, and relevant to an issue?

- What, if any, are the supporting claims? Where are they stated?

- Are the supporting claims clear, arguable, and relevant to the major claim?

- How could the claim(s) be improved?

Evidence

- What evidence supports the claim(s)? Where is it located?

- Is the evidence adequate, current, credible, and relevant to the claim(s) or supporting points (topic sentences)? Why or why not?

- How could the evidence be improved?

Explanations of Evidence

- What explanations are provided? Where are they located?

- Are the explanations clear, adequate, and relevant to claim(s) and evidence?

- How could the explanations be improved?

Qualifiers

- What qualifiers are provided? Where are they located?

- Are the qualifiers accurate and clearly phrased?

- How could the qualifiers be improved?

Refutations

- What are the opposition arguments? Are the opposition arguments refuted? Where are they stated and refuted?

- Are the opposition arguments presented and refuted fairly and adequately?

- How could the presentation and refutation of opposition arguments be improved?

RHETORIC: Purpose, Audience, Structure, and Style

Purpose

- What does the author want to accomplish? (The purpose may be identical to the major claim, or, more precisely, the change the author seeks in the reader.)

- In what ways could the intended purpose be reconceptualized (broadened, narrowed, redirected) by the author?

Audience

- Who is the audience? Where is the audience stated or how is it implied?

- Is the audience compatible with the other rhetorical features: purpose, structure, and style?

- In what ways could the intended audience be reconceptualized (broadened, narrowed, redirected) by the author?

Structure

- What form does this argument take (e.g., essay, letter, editorial)?

- Is the type of argument appropriate to the assignment and rhetorical context?

- Are the basic organizational features (introduction, body, conclusion, thesis and topic sentences, transitions, paragraphing) present and effective?

(Continued)

- If needed, are specialized organizational features (e.g., for definition, comparison/contrast, narration) present and effective?

- How could the structure be improved?

Style

- **Diction:** Are the word choices appropriate? Why or why not? What might be improved?

- **Voice:** Is the voice appropriately formal or informal? Do you have a sense of the personality of the author? What are the strongest and weakest examples of voice? What might be improved?

- **Tone:** Is the tone appropriate to the other rhetorical considerations: purpose, audience, and structure? Why or why not? What are the strongest and weakest examples of tone? What might be improved?

- **Point of view:** Is the point of view appropriate to the rhetorical context and task specifications? (For example, research papers tend to be written in the third-person perspective, whereas personal narratives such as anecdotes are typically written in the first-person perspective.) What might be improved?

- **Sentence variety:** Are the sentences appropriately varied in length and form (simple, compound, complex)? What might be improved?

Practice 11.1 USING A REVISION GUIDE

Use the revision guide on pages 232–234 as you evaluate the following passage from the rough draft of James Southard's essay "P.S.I.: Plagiarism Scene Investigator." (The complete essay is presented later in this chapter.) Mark, annotate, and evaluate the passage. Focus on strengths, concerns, and suggestions about the claim, support, and technical features.

"The criminal justice system is not altogether cold hearted and can provide means of rehabilitation and redemption. For example, a first time shop-lifter is often given an opportunity to clear their name. Judges have the option to *divert* criminal proceedings under certain circumstances. Under a *diversion*, a judge will assign some sort of community service or class that the offender must attend. After completing this court assigned requirement, and after staying out of any more trouble, the court will expunge the defendant's record. With first time plagiarists, we could adopt a similar plan. It would involve actually charging the individual with theft of property and putting the offender in front of a judge. The judge could then assign a writing course to the plagiarist. Upon completion of the course and a verification that no further plagiarism has occurred, the student or writer could have their record cleared. Of course, if the plagiarist fails to fulfill the requirements of the diversion, he or she should be tried for theft of property and if found guilty, sentenced under the criminal code."

Practice 11.2 REVISING A SAMPLE PARAGRAPH

Revise the paragraph in Practice 11.1, using your evaluation of it as a guide.

Practice 11.3 USING A REVISION GUIDE ON ANOTHER WRITER'S PARAGRAPH

Choose a paragraph from another student's paper (or a paper of your own). Using the revision guide, evaluate the paragraph.

Using a Revision Checklist

A revision checklist contains criteria that are similar to those in a revision guide but presents them in a briefer form. Think of the revision guide as a training program: Using the guide is slow at first, but you eventually internalize the criteria. Once you become familiar with the guide, you can switch to the shorter, quicker checklist. The checklist is also useful for peer evaluation, as we will soon see.

The checklist presented in this book includes criteria for argument and rhetoric. In addition, it includes criteria for technique, which encompasses grammar and usage, mechanics, and task specifications. Technique is a concern of editing. Editing and technique will be discussed more thoroughly later in this chapter.

Use a checklist much as you would a revision guide:

- **Consider every feature listed on the checklist.** Not all points will be useful, but as a whole the checklist should help pinpoint significant strengths and weaknesses or concerns.

- **Mark and annotate.** Show the locations of specific strengths and weaknesses.

- **Evaluate.** Finish by writing a brief statement about the strengths, your concerns, and your recommendations.

Using Rubrics

Checklists and revision/editing guides both present criteria that describe good writing. When you take criteria a step further and add a rating scale, the result is an evaluation tool known as a scoring guide or rubric. Letter grades are a traditional kind of rating scale: A, B, C, D, F. In recent years the trend has been to use a numeric scale—such as 0 to 3, 1 to 5, 1 to 6, or 0 to 9—for the convenience of calculating scores mathematically.

Instructors, institutions, and testing programs (such as AP and ACT) have developed their own rubrics. Although rubrics are most often used for assessments ("grading"), they also can be used by writers in much the same way they use checklists and revision/editing guides. In fact, knowing the value of criteria can be formative (instructional), not just summative (evaluative).

REVISION AND EDITING CHECKLIST

This is a summary of key features of argument, rhetoric, and technique that we explained in the long "Revision Guide" earlier in the chapter and the "Editing Guide" later in the chapter.

Argument

Claims, support (evidence and explanations), qualifications, and refutations are thorough, honest, and convincing.

- **Claim(s):** Clear, significant, arguable, and relevant to the issue.
- **Evidence:** Adequate, current, credible, and relevant to the claim(s).
- **Explanations:** Clear, adequate, and relevant to the claim(s) and evidence.
- **Qualifiers:** Clearly and accurately show to what extent a claim is applicable.
- **Refutation:** Opposition arguments are presented and refuted fairly and adequately.

Rhetoric

Purpose, audience, structure, and style are effective.

- **Purpose:** Author's goal is clearly stated or strongly implied. (Purpose is the major claim plus the change the author seeks in the reader.)
- **Audience:** Appropriate for the purpose, structure, and style.
- **Structure:**
  - Basic organizational features (introduction, body, conclusion, thesis and topic sentences, transitions, paragraphing) are present and effective.
  - If needed, specialized organizational features (e.g., for definition, comparison/contrast, narration) are present and effective.
- **Style:** Diction, voice, tone, point of view, and syntax are appropriate for the purpose, audience, and structure.

Technique

Technical elements are correct.

- **Grammar and usage:** Sentences and their parts are formed according to accepted standards.
- **Mechanics:** Spelling, capitalization, punctuation, and formatting are correct.
- **Format:** The correct conventions of document design are followed, including such elements as line spacing, paragraphing, title page, heading styles, font, documentation style, and appropriate use of tables, graphs, illustrations, photos, and the like.
- **Task specifications:** Topic, deadline, length, sources, and referencing style are as required.

Students sometimes use rubrics (rather than revision guides or checklists) to help them evaluate one another's essays or sample essays provided by instructors. Typically, the instructor will later reveal the actual rubric value for the writing sample, helping the students determine how well they do or do not understand the criteria. Professional evaluators call this kind of training *calibration*: the process of tuning one's ability to assess. Sample essays with established values are called *range finders*.

RUBRIC FOR ARGUMENTS

This rubric features the same criteria featured in the Revision Guide and Revision and Editing Checklist; it adds a grading scale. The rubric is holistic: Each score evaluates all of the qualities as a whole.

Score 5: Essays meriting a score of 5 are of high quality, exhibiting advanced skill with argument, rhetoric, and technique:

- **Argument:** Claims, evidence, explanations, qualifications, and opposition arguments/refutations are presented in a thorough, honest, and convincing manner.

- **Rhetoric:** Purpose, audience, structure, and style consistently work in harmony to advance the argument.

- **Technique:** Grammar, usage, mechanics, and task specifications are nearly flawless.

Score 4: Essays meriting a score of 4 are of good quality, exhibiting proficient skill with argument, rhetoric, and technique. Minor lapses are evident in one category.

Score 3: Essays meriting a score of 3 are of adequate quality, exhibiting passable skill with argument, rhetoric, and technique. Minor lapses are evident in two or more categories.

Score 2: Essays meriting a score of 2 are of inconsistent quality, exhibiting developing skill with argument, rhetoric, and technique. Minor lapses in all categories or a major weakness in one area is evident.

Score 1: Essays meriting a score of 1 are of low quality. Major lapses in all categories are evident.

TASK-SPECIFIC RUBRICS

Because all arguments are bound by rhetorical context—a specific situation framing a contract between a writer and a reader—rubrics can also be specific to a particular type of argument. For example, a rubric used to evaluate the argument made by a newspaper or online editorial would be very different from a rubric used to evaluate an argument made in a proposal to build a new campus student center.

Practice 11.4 USING A RUBRIC: "P.S.I.: PLAGIARISM SCENE
                              INVESTIGATOR"

Using the Rubric for Arguments above, assess the complete draft of "P.S.I.: Plagiarism Scene
Investigator" presented later in of this chapter. In group discussion or a brief writing, justify
your assessment.

FIVE KINDS OF WEAK THESES AND
HOW TO FIX THEM

A *strong thesis* makes a claim that (1) requires analysis to support and evolve it and (2) offers some
point about the significance of your evidence that would not have been immediately obvious to your
readers. By contrast, a *weak thesis* either makes no claim or makes a claim that does not need proving.
As a quick flash-forward, here are the five kinds of weak thesis statements—ones that

1. make no claim ("This paper will examine the pros and cons of ...");

2. are obviously true or a statement of fact ("Exercise is good for you");

3. restate conventional wisdom ("Love conquers all");

4. offer personal conviction as the basis for the claim ("Shopping malls are wonderful places");

5. make an overly broad claim ("Individualism is good").

Weak Thesis Type 1: The Thesis Makes No Claim

The following statements are not productive theses because they do not advance an idea about the
topics the papers will explore.

Problem Examples

I'm going to write about Darwin's concerns with evolution in *The Origin of Species*.

This paper will address the characteristics of a good corporate manager.

The problem examples each name a subject and link it to the intention to write about it, but they
don't make any claim about the subject. As a result, they direct neither the writer nor the reader
toward some position or plan of attack. The second problem example begins to move toward a point
of view through the use of the value judgment "good," but this term is too broad to guide the analysis.
The statement-of-intention thesis invites a list: one paragraph for each quality the writer chooses to
call good. Even if the thesis were rephrased as "This paper will address why a good corporate manager
needs to learn to delegate responsibility," the thesis would not adequately suggest why such a claim
would need to be argued or defended. *There is, in short, nothing at stake, no issue to be resolved.* A

writer who produces a thesis of this type is probably unduly controlled by "banking"—that relatively passive, information in/information out approach to learning.

Solution

Raise specific issues for the essay to explore.

Solution Examples

Darwin's concern with survival of the fittest in *The Origin of Species* initially leads him to neglect a potentially conflicting aspect of his theory of evolution—survival as a matter of interdependence.

The very trait that makes for an effective corporate manager—the drive to succeed—can also make the leader domineering and therefore ineffective.

Some disciplines expect writers to offer statements of method and/or intention in their papers' openings. Generally, however, these openings also make a claim: for example, "In this paper I will examine how the sponsorship scandal undermined Prime Minister Martin's attempt to present the Liberal platform during the 2004 federal election campaign," *not* "In this paper I will discuss the Liberal platform during the 2004 federal election campaign."

Weak Thesis Type 2: The Thesis Is Obviously True or Is a Statement of Fact

The following statements are not productive theses because they do not require proof. A thesis needs to be an assertion with which it would be possible for readers to disagree.

Problem Example

The jeans industry targets its advertisements to appeal to young adults.

If few people would disagree with the claim that a thesis makes, there is no point in writing an analytical paper on it. Though one might deliver an inspirational speech on a position that virtually everyone would support (such as the value of tolerance), endorsements and appreciations don't usually lead to analysis; they merely invite people to feel good about their convictions.

In the second problem example, few readers would disagree with the fact that the issue is "controversial." In the second sentence of that example, the writer has begun to identify a point of view—that the flight from teaching is a "problem"—but her next declaration, that she will "show different views and aspects," is an overly vague statement of intention, not an idea. The phrasing of the claim is noncommittal and so broad that it prevents the writer from formulating a workable thesis.

Solution

Find some avenue of *inquiry*—a question about the facts or an issue raised by them. Make an assertion with which it would be possible for readers to disagree.

Solution Example

By inventing new terms, such as "loose fit" and "relaxed fit," the jeans industry has attempted to normalize, even glorify, its product for an older and fatter generation.

Weak Thesis Type 3: The Thesis Restates Conventional Wisdom

Restatement of one of the many clichés that constitute a culture's conventional wisdom is not a productive thesis unless you have something to say about it that hasn't been said many times before.

Problem Examples

An important part of one's college education is learning to better understand others' points of view.

From cartoons in the morning to adventure shows at night, there is too much violence on television.

"I was supposed to bring the coolers; you were supposed to bring the chips!" exclaimed ex-Beatle Ringo Starr, who appeared on TV commercials for Sun County Wine Coolers a few years ago. By using rock music to sell a wide range of products, the advertising agencies, in league with corporate giants such as Pepsi, Michelob, and Ford, have corrupted the spirit of rock and roll.

All of these examples say nothing worth proving because they are clichés. ("Conventional wisdom" is a polite term for cliché.) Most clichés were fresh ideas once, but over time they have become trite, prefabricated forms of nonthinking. Faced with a phenomenon that requires a response, many inexperienced writers rely on a knee-jerk reaction: they resort to a small set of culturally approved "answers." In this sense, clichés resemble statements of fact. So commonly accepted that most people nod to them without thinking, statements of conventional wisdom make people feel a comfortable sense of agreement with one another. The problem with this kind of packaged solution is that because conventional wisdom is so general and so conventional, it doesn't teach anybody—including the writer—anything. Worse, since the cliché masquerades as an idea, it prevents the writer from engaging in a fresh, open-minded exploration of his or her subject.

There is some truth in all of the problem examples above, but none of them *complicates* its position. A thoughtful reader could, for example, respond to the claim that advertising has corrupted the spirit of rock and roll by suggesting that rock and roll was highly commercial long before it colonized the airwaves. The conventional wisdom that rock and roll is somehow pure and honest while advertising is phony and exploitative invites the savvy writer to formulate a thesis that overturns these clichés. As our solution example demonstrates, one could argue that rock actually has improved advertising, not that ads have ruined rock—or, alternatively, that rock has shrewdly marketed idealism to a gullible populace. At the least, a writer deeply committed to the original thesis would do better to examine what it was that Ringo was selling—what he stands for in this particular case—than to discuss rock and advertising in such general terms.

Solution

Seek to complicate—see more than one point of view on—your subject. Avoid conventional wisdom unless you can qualify it or introduce a fresh perspective on it.

Solution Examples

While an important part of one's college education is learning to better understand others' points of view, a persistent danger is that the students will simply be required to substitute the teacher's answers for the ones they grew up uncritically believing.

While some might argue that the presence of rock and roll soundtracks in TV commercials has corrupted rock's spirit, this point of view not only falsifies the history of rock but also blinds us to the ways that the music has improved the quality of television advertising.

Weak Thesis Type 4: The Thesis Offers Personal Conviction as the Basis for the Claim

A statement of one's personal convictions or one's likes or dislikes does not alone supply sufficient grounds for a productive thesis.

Problem Examples

The songs of the punk rock group Minor Threat relate to the feelings of individuals who dare to be different. Their songs are just composed of pure emotion. Pure emotion is very important in music, because it serves as a vehicle to convey the important message of individuality. Minor Threat's songs are meaningful to me because I can identify with them.

Sir Thomas More's *Utopia* proposes an unworkable set of solutions to society's problems because, like communist Russia, it suppresses individualism.

Although I agree that environmentalists and business should work together to ensure the ecological future of the world, and that this cooperation is beneficial for both sides, the indisputable fact is that environmental considerations should always be a part of any decision that is made. Any individual, if he looks deeply enough into his soul, knows what is right and what is wrong. The environment should be protected because it is the right thing to do, not because someone is forcing you to do it.

Like conventional wisdom, personal likes and dislikes can lead inexperienced writers into knee-jerk reactions of approval or disapproval, often expressed in a moralistic tone. The writers of the problem examples above assume that their primary job is to judge their subjects, or testify to their worth, not to evaluate them analytically. As a result, such writers lack critical detachment not only from their topics but, crucially, from their own assumptions and biases. They have *taken personal opinions for self-evident truths*. You can test a thesis for this problem by asking if the writer's response to questions about the thesis would be "because I think so."

The most blatant version of this tendency occurs in the third problem example, which asserts, "Any individual, if he looks deeply enough into his soul, knows what is right and what is wrong. The environment should be protected because it is the right thing to do." Translation (only slightly exaggerated): "Any individual who thinks about the subject will obviously agree with me because my feelings and convictions feel right to me and therefore they must be universally and self-evidently true." The problem is that this writer is not distinguishing between his own likes and dislikes (or private convictions) and what he takes to be right, real, or true for everyone else. Testing an idea against your own feelings and experience is not an adequate means of establishing whether something is accurate or true.

Solution

Try on other points of view honestly and dispassionately; *treat your ideas as hypotheses to be tested rather than obvious truths.* In the following solution examples, we have replaced opinions (in the form of self-evident truths) with ideas—theories about the meaning and significance of the subjects that could be supported and qualified with evidence.

Solution Examples

Sir Thomas More's *Utopia* treats individualism as a serious but remediable social problem. His radical treatment of what we might now call "socialization" attempts to redefine the meaning and origin of individual identity.

While cooperation between environmentalists and business is essential to the ecological future of the world, what matters most is that pressure be applied to private corporations—to ensure that they confront environmental concerns that may not benefit them in the short run.

It is fine, of course, to write about what you believe and to consult your feelings as you formulate an idea. But the risk you run in arguing from your unexamined feelings and convictions is that you will prematurely dismiss from consideration anything that is unfamiliar or does not immediately conform to what you already believe. The less willing you are to test these established and habitual convictions, the less chance you will have to refine or expand the ways in which you think. You will continue to play the same small set of tunes in response to everything you hear. And without the ability to think from multiple perspectives, you will be less able to defend your convictions against the ideas that challenge them because you won't really have examined the logic of your own beliefs—you just believe them.

At the root of this problem lurks an anti-analytical bias that predisposes many writers to see any challenge to their habitual ways of thinking as the enemy and to view those who would raise this challenge as cynics who don't believe in anything. Such writers often feel personally attacked, when in fact the conviction they are defending is not really so personal after all. Consider, for example, the first two problem examples above, in which both writers take individualism to be an incontestable value. Where does this conviction come from? Apparently, neither of the writers arrived at the thesis independent of the pervasive American culture to which they were exposed, permeated as it is by the "rugged individualism" of John Wayne and Sylvester Stallone movies.

In other words, "individualism" as an undefined blanket term verges on *cultural cliché.* That it is always good or positive is a piece of conventional wisdom. But part of becoming educated is to take a look at such global and undefined ideas that one has uncritically assimilated.

The writers of the first two problem examples would have to question *to what extent* they should attack a book or support a rock band merely on the basis of whether or not each honours individualism. If the author of the second problem example had been willing to explore how Thomas More conceives of and critiques individualism, he or she might have been able to arrive at a revealing analysis of the tension between the individual and the collective rather than merely dismissing the entire book.

This is not to say that the first requirement of analytical writing is that you abandon all conviction or argue for a position in which you do not believe. But we are suggesting that the risk of remaining trapped within a limited set of culturally inherited opinions is greater than the risk that you will run by submerging your personal likes or dislikes and instead honestly and dispassionately trying on different points of view. The energy of analytical writing comes not from rehearsing your convictions but from treating them as hypotheses to be tested, as scientists do—from finding the boundaries of your ideas, reshaping parts of them, seeing connections you have not seen before.

When a writing assignment asks for your ideas about a subject, it is usually not asking for your opinion—what you think *of* the subject—but for your reasoning on *what* and *how* the subject means. *An idea is not the same thing as an opinion.* The two are closely related, since both, in theory, are based on reasoning. Opinions, however, often take the form of judgments, the reflections of our personal attitudes and beliefs. While having ideas necessarily involves your attitudes and beliefs, it is a more disinterested process than is opinion making. The formulation of ideas, which is one of the primary aims of analysis, involves questioning. By contrast, opinions are often habitual responses, mental reflexes that kick in automatically when an answer seems to be called for.

Weak Thesis Type 5: The Thesis Makes an Overly Broad Claim

An overly general claim is not a productive thesis because it oversimplifies and is too broad to direct development. Such statements usually lead either to say-nothing theses or to reductive either/or thinking.

Problem Examples

Violent revolutions have had both positive and negative results for man.

There are many similarities and differences between the Carolingian and the Burgundian Renaissances.

Othello is a play about love and jealousy.

It is important to understand why leaders act in a leadership role. What is the driving force? Is it an internal drive for the business or group to succeed, or is it an internal drive for the leader to dominate over others?

Overly generalized theses avoid complexity. At their worst, as in our first three examples, they settle for assertions broad enough to fit almost any subject and thus say nothing in particular about the subject at hand. A writer in the early stages of his or her drafting process might begin working from a general idea, such as what is positive and negative about violent revolutions or how two historical periods are like and unlike, but these formulations are not specific enough to guide the development of a paper. Such broad categories are likely to generate listing, not thinking. We can, for example, predict that the third thesis will prompt the writer to produce a couple of paragraphs demonstrating that *Othello* is about love and then a couple of paragraphs demonstrating that *Othello* is about jealousy, without analyzing what the play says about either.

Our fourth problem example, inquiring into the motivation of leaders in business, demonstrates how the desire to generalize can drive writers into logical errors. Because this thesis overtly offers readers two possible answers to its central question, it appears to avoid the problem of oversimplifying a complex subject. But this appearance of complexity is deceptive because the writer has reduced the possibilities to only two answers—an either/or choice: Is "the driving force" of leadership a desire for group success or a desire to dominate others? Readers can only be frustrated by being asked to choose between two such options when the more logical answer probably lies somewhere in between or somewhere else altogether.

The best way to avoid the problem evident in the first three examples is to sensitize yourself to the characteristic phrasing of such theses: "both positive and negative," "many similarities and differences," or "both pros and cons." Virtually everything from meatloaf to taxes can be both positive and negative.

Solution

Convert broad categories and generic (fits anything) claims to more specific, more qualified assertions; find ways to bring out the complexity of your subject.

Solution Examples

Although violent revolutions begin to redress long-standing social inequities, they often do so at the cost of long-term economic dysfunction and the suffering that attends it.

The differences between the Carolingian and Burgundian Renaissances outweigh the similarities.

Although *Othello* appears to attack jealousy, it also supports the skepticism of the jealous characters over the naïveté of the lovers.

Try This

You can learn a lot about writing strong thesis statements by analyzing and rewriting weak ones. Rewrite the following three weak theses. As in the case of our solution examples, revising will require you to add information and thinking to the weak theses. Try, in other words, to come up with some interesting claims that most readers would not already have thought of to develop the subject of television violence. (The third thesis you will recognize as a problem example for which we offered no solution.)

1. In this paper I will discuss police procedures in recent domestic violence cases.

2. The way that the media portrayed the events of April 30, 1975, when Saigon fell, greatly influenced the final perspectives of the American people toward the end result of the Vietnam War.

3. From cartoons in the morning to adventure shows at night, there is too much violence on television.

GUIDELINES FOR ADDRESSING OTHER POINTS OF VIEW

1. *Restate the other claim to show that you understand it.* This is often easier to do in a face-to-face discussion than in writing, but it is important in any argument. Sometimes misunderstandings can be uncovered by this technique. Restatements can also lead to finding common ground. A restatement should be made in a nonjudgmental, respectful tone.

2. *Find areas of agreement, or common ground, at the outset of the argument.* This, too, is sometimes easier to do in a face-to-face discussion than in writing. It is a technique often used in negotiations and mediation. However, in a written argument, you should try whenever you can to establish common ground with those who have other beliefs about the issue that you are addressing. Often identifying warrants can lead parties to find areas of agreement. When people see that they agree about some parts of an issue, they can establish mutual respect and then examine their differing opinions carefully.

3. *Identify which differences are important and which are trivial.* This, too, is more easily done when people talk with each other, but it is also something that can be attempted in written argument. Here, too, identifying warrants sometimes clarifies the significance of some parts of an argument.

4. *Concede points that you cannot uphold.* Sometimes you will have to concede that some of your opponents' ideas are so strong that you cannot counter them, even if you do not agree with them.

5. *Compromise.* At times, accepting a middle position or a partial achievement of your purpose is better than arguing for its complete achievement.

6. *Rebut.* This means to refute or to present opposing evidence. Rebuttal often seems necessary. It is part of the debate tradition and is important in legal arguments, but it maintains adversarial positions. If you have to rebut an opposing point, do so courteously.

7. *Be sensitive to different argumentative philosophies.* Some cultures, some groups, and some individuals prefer indirect methods of argumentation while others want to get to the point quickly. Sometimes a direct approach is seen as rude or overly aggressive; sometimes an indirect approach is seen as weak, sneaky, or confusing. In the United States, directness is often considered as the best approach. If your audience is from a different culture, however, be sure that you understand that culture's argumentative style.

POINT / COUNTERPOINT

Introduction

Forecast (optional)

(1) Refutation

(1) Argument

(2) Refutation

(2) Argument

(3) Refutation

(3) Argument

Conclusion

Point and counterpoint organization.

RANGE OF STYLES

Style in writing is analogous to style in dress, ranging from informal to formal. Research papers tend to be formal, written in an "academic style" that prefers third-person point of view and avoids contractions. In other words, you avoid the use of *I* or *you*, and you write out terms such as *should not* instead of using *shouldn't*. The rules are not hard and fast, however, and they depend upon the rhetorical context and the contract between the author and the audience.

> **Informal:** I think we should all work together so plagiarism doesn't mess up our school.

> **Formal:** Students, instructors, and administrators should cooperate in promoting a healthy atmosphere of academic honesty.

You have probably noticed that this textbook uses a less formal style, assuming a second-person point of view (POV) to address *you* directly.

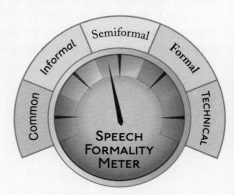

Style can range in degrees of formality.

Second-person POV fits our purpose of acting as your mentor: We want to convey a tone that is friendlier than third-person POV will allow. Also, we would argue that the textbook itself is not a research paper—so cut us some slack, okay? (You wouldn't use slang phrases like "cut us some slack, okay" in a formal research paper.)

While there are no absolute cutoff points distinguishing degrees of formality in writing, you could think of your choices as a continuum, as displayed in the imaginary "formality meter."

Common

Language is specific to the community where it is used. Incomplete sentences, alternative grammar, and idiomatic expressions are freely employed in some communities. Slang and other "unofficial" words may also be used.

Example of word choice expressing "amount": a bunch.

Informal

Language is used broadly outside of one's immediate family, neighborhood, or peer group to communicate with the world at large. Incomplete sentences and contractions are freely used, although alternative grammar, idiomatic speech, slang, and other expressions that might impede communication are avoided.

Example of word choice expressing "amount": a lot.

Semiformal

This language is commonly used to communicate, both in writing and speech, at work and in school. Incomplete sentences, alternative grammar, and idiomatic expressions are usually avoided. The writing in newspapers and magazines represents this level of formality.

Example of word choice expressing "amount": many.

Formal

This language is carefully written. Rules of punctuation and grammar are strictly followed. Contractions and other signs of informality are avoided. Words are carefully chosen to communicate specific ideas. Generally, a more complex vocabulary is employed.

Example of word choice expressing "amount": an abundance.

Technical

Sentences and paragraphs must follow a specific format. Words are often the jargon used by specialists and have very precise meanings. This language is typical of legal documents and technical manuals.

Example of word choice expressing "amount": 6.74 liters.

GIVING AND RECEIVING FEEDBACK

Feedback is the advice you give to or receive from others. Advice can come from face-to-face exchanges, from written or recorded comments, or from a combination of these encounters. In a classroom setting, advice often comes from other students. This kind of feedback goes by many names, often including the word *peer* followed by another term: peer conferencing, peer response, peer review, or peer editing. *Peer evaluation* is the preferred term in this textbook.

When you evaluate the writing of others, additional guidelines should be followed to ensure the advice is constructive: Be positive and be specific.

Be Positive

Even the best examples of writing likely will contain flaws, especially in earlier drafts, and sooner or later those flaws will have to be addressed. Nevertheless, it is vitally important to be constructive and considerate when giving feedback.

Any writer who has made a serious attempt at producing a piece of writing will be sensitive about its reception. It is unrealistic to expect complete emotional "detachment" of an author from a work.

Unfortunately, evaluators tend to have a keener eye for flaws than for virtues: *Error marking* traditionally is synonymous with *paper grading*. Fortunately, there are several ways to make criticism more constructive:

- **Limit the number of critical "summary" remarks.** Few people are able to assimilate more than three or four new concepts in a feedback session. Also, you don't want to make the person despair.

Working Effectively with Others

When you work with other students in groups, whether to create an original project (such as a group presentation) or to receive feedback about something you bring to the group (such as a rough draft of a paper you have written), this activity is often termed collaborative learning or cooperative learning. Such activities give students an opportunity to learn from one another in a way that is not possible in a whole-class activity. You should take advantage of this time by doing the following:

- **Come prepared to your group meeting.** When you come unprepared, you affect the performance of the entire group.
- **Be an active participant.** Passive group members hinder the learning of everyone involved.
- **Avoid dominating the group.** When one person dominates the conversation, others do not have as much of a chance to contribute.
- **Respect other group members.** Treating others with respect contributes to group cohesion and makes the experience more pleasant for everyone involved.

GIVING FEEDBACK

When giving advice to other writers, your major goals are to be positive and to be specific. One way to accomplish both these goals is to phrase advice as questions. This method also lets you indicate problems (being descriptive) without offering solutions (being prescriptive). In fact, it is better if the writer is the one who figures out the solution.

Below is a list of problems typically faced by writers and examples of questions that can lead to solutions. The list is not comprehensive; you'll have to react to other problems with questions (feedback) of your own creation.

PROBLEM	QUESTION
Thesis isn't a claim.	What kind of change in the reader do you want? Where do you state your major claim or thesis? Can you turn this thesis into a fact claim? Identity claim? Cause and effect claim? Value claim? Proposal claim?
Claim is too broad.	**Which part of the issue is most significant?** **Are you arguing more than one major claim?**
Evidence is insufficient.	What are some reasons you could give? Where do you give some support? Can you restate? Interpret? Apply? Analyze? Synthesize? Evaluate?
Evidence is irrelevant.	**How does that evidence fit your claim?** **Could you delete part of that quotation?**
Evidence is excessive.	Do you need all that information to support your claim?
Quotations need work.	**Who is the source, and why is he or she worth quoting?** **Could you paraphrase some of these quotations?** **Could some of the quotation be deleted?**
Evidence needs explaining.	How does the evidence fit your claim? What does this statement mean?
Explanation isn't clear.	**How could you make this clearer?** **Should you restate? Interpret? Apply? Analyze? Synthesize? Evaluate?**
Style is inappropriate.	How will a reader react to your tone? Is your word choice appropriate to the reader? Is a first-person point of view appropriate for this writing?
Writing is disorganized.	**What is the main idea of this paragraph? Does that point fit?** **Would a forecast statement in the introduction help show your organization?** **How does this idea or sentence lead to the next one?**
Wording is repetitive.	Could you eliminate some repeated phrases or ideas? Could you combine some related sentences? Could you vary the way you say this?

- **Balance the negative with the positive.** Always find positive traits in the writing: People tend to learn very well from positive feedback.

- **Soften criticism by phrasing an observed weakness as a question.** For example, instead of saying "Your evidence is outdated," you could ask, "Have you looked for more recent data?"

Be Specific

Broad, generic feedback is quick and easy to give and receive, but it has little constructive value. For example, labeling an entire piece of writing as "good" or "I don't like it" seldom tells the author enough to lead to better writing. A writer needs to know very specifically *what* is effective or ineffective: a particular word, a particular example, or a particular sequence of sentences. It is even more useful if the writer knows *why* something works or fails.

Learning to evaluate writing may be one of the best ways to grow as a writer: *Identifying* quality can take you most of the way toward *producing* quality. At first it may be easier to evaluate others' writing than to evaluate your own work, probably because you are "too close" to your own material. As you learn to spot the best and worst qualities of other people's writings, you begin to "internalize" those criteria and to understand them better in your own work.

James Southard shared an early draft of his essay "P.S.I.: Plagiarism Scene Investigator" with a peer-evaluation group in his writing class. Here is the introduction to his essay, with annotations James made during discussion of his draft. (The complete version of the rough draft is presented later in this chapter.)

Plagiarism is <u>defined</u> as "stealing somebody's work or idea: the process of copying another person's idea or written work and claiming it as original." (<u>Bing/Encarta</u>) This is a simple definition. So, let's be a little more specific. When a person copies and pastes from an internet or written source without giving the original author credit for the work, they are committing plagiarism. When a person recycles <u>an old</u> essay and calls it an original work, they are committing plagiarism. When a person directly quotes the words of a speech or interview without crediting the speaker, they are committing plagiarism. Any college student <u>knows</u> about plagiarism and the possible consequences of committing the offense, but is plagiarism really that serious? What's the big <u>deal? When</u> committing plagiarism, that person is committing a <u>crime</u>.

Good to define key terms. Sometimes better to postpone the definition until you've established the issue or hooked the reader's attention.

Check MLA

Interesting parallel structure in three consecutive sentences.

Do you mean someone else's essay?

This is a fact claim. Support and document here or later in the essay.

Unclear how "big deal" leads to the crime claim. If crime is your thesis, re-organize to lead up to it.

Literally or figuratively? Perhaps compare to other theories or metaphors.

James's writing teacher reviewed a very rough draft of "P.S.I.: Plagiarism Scene Investigator" and sent him an e-mail with the following suggestions about his introduction.

FROM: Rob Lamm

TO: James Southard

DATE: 4/26/2012 09:22 AM

CC:

BCC:

SUBJECT: Your essay draft

Dear James,

I've read the rough draft of your essay, "P.S.I.: Plagiarism Scene Investigator."

It's coming along nicely. Below are some suggestions to help you make it even better.

Strengths
- Your intro displays some elements of a good introduction: It establishes an issue—a problem to be solved.
- The issue or problem has significance and a sense of urgency.
- Stylistically, it uses a technique of parallelism called symploce: you repeat the beginnings and endings of a series of sentences for emphasis and intensification: "When a person ... they are committing."

Concerns
- Can you think of a better opening than the definition? A definition is useful, but other leading sentences can hook a reader's interest more effectively.
- Your thesis seems to be that plagiarism is a crime. Do you mean literally or figuratively? Perhaps the intro could contrast the crime metaphor with other ways that scholars view plagiarism, such as a form of ignorance or as a disease.
- Consider also using transitions. What transitional word, phrase, or sentence can show the connection between the last two sentences: "What's the big deal? When committing plagiarism, that person is committing a crime."

After reflecting on the feedback from his classmates and instructor, James revised the introduction to his essay:

Educators often speak of plagiarism as if it were a disease: "The whole world . . . is worried about what is often regarded as 'the plagiarism epidemic'" (Howard). The same educators seem to think the vaccine is as simple as educating students concerning the rules of how to properly document works and the consequences of failing to follow these rules. Indeed, many plagiarists plead ignorance (Shafer). Yet it's hard to believe that college students have had no prior education about plagiarism. The health metaphor is flawed and thus is unlikely to lead to a "cure" or any other kind of solution. Instead of using a disease metaphor, I propose that educators and students use a crime metaphor.

Practice 11.5 USING A REVISION GUIDE OR CHECKLIST TO GIVE FEEDBACK

Using the revision guide or checklist discussed earlier in the chapter, evaluate the complete rough draft of the following essay by James Southard. Mark, annotate, and evaluate, focusing on strengths, concerns, and suggestions. Phrase some suggestions in the form of questions. Share your comments and suggestions with your classmates. What are the most useful and constructive ways to deliver feedback? At what points does it become challenging to evaluate someone else's writing?

Practice 11.6 BEFORE YOU READ

Working individually or in a group, consider the problem of plagiarism.

1. If you were given a job to prevent plagiarism, what actions would you take?

2. How severely should plagiarists be punished?

3. Examine the essay's title. What does it suggest about the author's thesis?

Student Essay

James Southard

Dr. Lamm

Composition

25 April 2012

P.S.I.: Plagiarism Scene Investigator

Educators often speak of plagiarism as if it were a disease: "The whole world . . . is worried about what is often regarded as 'the plagiarism epidemic'" (Howard). The same educators seem to think the vaccine is as simple as educating students concerning the rules of how to properly document works and the consequences of failing to follow these rules. Indeed, many plagiarists plead ignorance (Shafer). Yet it's hard to believe that college students have had no prior education about plagiarism. The health metaphor is flawed and thus is unlikely to lead to a "cure" or any other kind of solution. Instead of using a disease metaphor, I propose that educators and students use a crime metaphor.

Specifically, I propose that we look to the criminal justice system as a model for ways to understand and to combat plagiarism. A plagiarist is more like shoplifter stealing a candy bar or a car thief stealing a car: some people will break the rules even though they know stealing is wrong and even though they know how *not* to steal.

Plagiarism is defined as "stealing somebody's work or idea: the process of copying another person's idea or written work and claiming it as original" (Bing/Encarta). When a person copies and pastes from an internet or written source without giving the original author credit for the work, they are committing plagiarism. When a person recycles an old essay and calls it an original work, they are committing plagiarism. When a person directly quotes the words of a speech or interview without crediting the speaker, they are committing plagiarism but more specifically, they are stealing.

Proverbial wisdom and probably many plagiarists say "no harm, no foul." Is plagiarism really that serious? Ideas aren't physical objects, so what's the big deal? This question is answered in criminal codes across the country. Take for example Arkansas' theft of property statute:

> A person commits theft of property if he or she knowingly takes or exercises unauthorized control over or makes an unauthorized transfer of interest in, the property of another person, with the purpose of depriving the owner of the property. (A.C.A. 5-36-103)

This statute covers more than stealing physical items. It includes theft of property that "has inherent, subjective or idiosyncratic value to the owner or possessor even if the property has not market value or replacement cost" (A.C.A. 131). This offense is considered a Class A misdemeanor and carries with it a possible punishment of a year in jail with up to a $1000.00 fine. However, if the offense is repeated against the same individual, the crime can be raised to the status of a Class D felony. This level of felony carries the possibility of a prison sentence with up to a $10,000.00 fine. The law doesn't exclude the possibility of a civil suit being brought against a person for this type of theft.

Stealing intellectual property can cost a person a lot. Just ask the people that have stolen music online and been caught. Ask the people who have been caught making illegal copies of movies. Individuals who have been convicted of these crimes have been forced to pay thousands for the offenses. Depending on what is plagiarized, the cost can be high. Even though the people stealing music and movies aren't necessarily calling the works their own, the theft is similar in nature.

Southard 3

What plagiarism-fighting tips can we gain from the criminal justice system? First, there must be penalties to fit the crimes. Colleges and universities usually mete out justice in terms of grade reductions, suspensions, and expulsions, but perhaps that is not enough. Fines, community service, permanent records, and embarrassing publicity (such as releasing names to the press) may be appropriate. For thieves, it often is the deterrent of severe punishment that makes them think twice and follow the straight and narrow.

The criminal justice system is not altogether cold hearted and can provide means of rehabilitation and redemption. For example, a first time shoplifter is often given an opportunity to clear their name. Judges have the option to *divert* criminal proceedings under certain circumstances. Under a *diversion*, a judge will assign some sort of community service or class that the offender must attend. After completing this court assigned requirement, and after staying out of any more trouble, the court will expunge the defendant's record. With first time plagiarists, we could adopt a similar plan. It would involve actually charging the individual with theft of property and putting the offender in front of a judge. The judge could then assign a writing course to the plagiarist. Upon completion of the course and a verification that no further plagiarism has occurred, the student or writer could have their record cleared. Of course, if the plagiarist fails to fulfill the requirements of the diversion, he or she should be tried for theft of property and if found guilty, sentenced under the criminal code.

By the strict enforcement of rules and laws against plagiarism, educators can make a real difference. Students will be motivated to pay attention when they are taught the ways to properly use sources, and would-be plagiarists will become upright intellectual citizens. Above all, fewer victims will be shouting, "Call the Police, I've been plagiarized!"

Southard 4

Works Cited

Devine, Joseph. "Fighting Back Against Intellectual Property Theft."
EzineMark.com, 19 Apr. 2010. Web. 19 Apr. 2011.

Howard, Rebecca Moore. "The Search for a Cure: Understanding the
'Plagiarism Epidemic.'" McGrawHillHigherEducation.com, 2003. Web.
22 Apr. 2011.

Kohn, Alfie. "Standardized Testing and Its Victims" *Education Week*,
27 Sep. 2000. Web. 15 Apr. 2011.

Plagiarism defined. *Bing/Encarta Dictionary*. Web. 20 April. 2011.

Shafer, Jack. "Why Plagiarists Do It." *Slate*, 26, April 2006. Web.
23 Apr. 2011.

"Theft of Property." A.C.A. 5-36-103 (2010). Print.

Practice 11.7 RESPONDING TO THE ESSAY

1. Do you agree or disagree with the author's claim and supporting ideas? Did the author change your prior opinion in any way? How?

2. Where is the author's support stronger? Where is it weaker? Explain.

3. Does the author's treatment of other points of view affect your willingness to believe what he has to say? In what way?

4. What, if anything, would you change about the essay's organization and content? Is there anything missing that you would add?

5. Which of the appeals (logic, authority, emotion) do you think was strongest in this essay? Which was weakest? Why do you think so?

6. Name the essay's greatest strength and most significant weakness. Explain your answer.

EDITING AN ARGUMENT

Editing is a process of tidying up the technical and mechanical features of a piece of writing—that is, "dotting the 'Is' and crossing the 'Ts.'" Known sometimes as proofreading, most editing can be postponed until a draft is completed, although fastidious people may have trouble ignoring errors even temporarily. Whether sooner or later, eventually the editing must be done.

Over the years you probably have been taught many rules about spelling, punctuation, grammar/usage, and formatting. As you edit, your personal storehouse of knowledge is your primary resource. However, so many rules exist that you'll probably supplement your own body of knowledge with reference books—a dictionary, a thesaurus, and a writer's handbook (for usage and mechanics). If you use a word processor, these resources may be part of your software package.

A final aspect of editing involves formatting and document design. This means that your final document has the correct appearance—the title page, pagination, paragraph spacing, font choice, headings, and so on conform to the documentation style you are following (such as MLA or APA). Formatting can also involve the correct placement and formatting of photos, illustrations, maps, and more.

Editing on a Word Processor

Electronic versions of dictionaries, thesauruses, and handbooks often are integrated into word processors. These tools alert you to potential errors as you write, highlighting misspelled words or faulty sentences. Clicking on a highlighted passage summons a menu of suggestions and additional tools. At other times, you may choose to activate proofreading and editing software by clicking on typed words or a toolbar. You can also use the document map to help you view the structure of the essay as a whole and move sections around. Some specialized word processors like Scrivener also have note-taking and research functions you might find useful.

COMMANDS AND FUNCTIONS

Word processors allow you to issue commands and perform functions important in editing and proofreading: copy, count (words, pages), find and replace, delete, move, search. A person who is skilled in the use of a word processor can apply these functions to great advantage, making changes much more rapidly than is possible with pen and paper. You should always check the checker, because it will accept any correctly spelled word, regardless of meaning.

SPELLING CHECKER

A checker can spot possible problems and enable you to choose from a menu of suggested spellings or add new spellings to its list. Auto-correct is an option that will empower your word processor to make some changes automatically. A spelling checker, however, can make mistakes. Its lexicon may be limited, omitting some words that are acceptable: The words *prewrite* and *freewrite,* for example, are accepted in the English profession but are not recognized by many spelling checkers. Also, a checker will accept a properly spelled word even when it is the wrong word. If, for example, you mistyped "spell" as "spiel," the spelling checker would not catch the error because "spiel" is the correct spelling for another word.

GRAMMAR CHECKER

A word processor can check for lapses in accepted grammar and usage. A grammar checker can also give you short lessons in style, explaining why some things are incorrect and offering alternatives. Like spelling checkers, grammar checkers have limitations and sometimes must be ignored or overruled.

DICTIONARY

This resource can be activated by clicking on a word in your text or by clicking onto an icon displayed on a toolbar. Although useful, these dictionaries may be less complete than hardcover collegiate dictionaries.

SYNONYMS (THESAURUS)

Highlighting a word and clicking will activate this resource. The list of synonyms may be useful yet less complete than a print version of a thesaurus.

TRANSLATOR

Some software provides English-to-foreign language translations. Also, a number of Web sites provide this service. While these programs are useful for gaining an understanding of basic information from a foreign-language Web site or other source, they are notorious for making mistakes in their translations. Don't trust the accuracy of the translation unless it has been checked by someone fluent in the language.

EVALUATOR

Some software programs will "grade" your writing. This kind of evaluation is not a substitute for a human editor, but it can give you feedback by evaluating features such as sentence and paragraph length and the average words per sentence or paragraph and can highlight words that might be used improperly.

Note: It is important to note that none of these programs can "read" your writing or make contextual decisions about your prose. It is unwise to assume that a grammar checker or other device can "fix" your writing for you. If you use any of these tools, remember that you, as a writer, have to make the final decision.

CANDIDATE FOR A PULLET SURPRISE *JERROLD H. ZAR*

This poem was originally published in the January–February 1994 issue of the *Journal of Irreproducible Results.* By the author's count, 127 of the 225 words in the poem are incorrect (although all words are correctly spelled).

I have a spelling checker, It came with my PC.

It plane lee marks four my revue Miss steaks aye can knot sea.

Eye ran this poem threw it, Your sure reel glad two no.

Its vary polished in it's weigh.

My checker tolled me sew.

A checker is a bless sing, It freeze yew lodes of thyme.

It helps me right awl stiles two reed, And aides me when eye rime.

Each frays come posed up on my screen Eye trussed too bee a joule.

The checker pours o'er every word To cheque sum spelling rule.

Bee fore a veiling checker's Hour spelling mite decline, And if we're lacks oar have a laps, We wood bee maid too wine.

Butt now bee cause my spelling Is checked with such grate flare, Their are know fault's with in my cite, Of nun eye am a wear.

Now spelling does knot phase me, It does knot bring a tier.

My pay purrs awl due glad den With wrapped word's fare as hear.

To rite with care is quite a feet Of witch won should bee proud, And wee mussed dew the best wee can, Sew flaw's are knot aloud.

Sow ewe can sea why aye dew prays Such soft wear four pea seas, And why eye brake in two averse Buy righting want too pleas.

Jerry Zar, "Candidate for a Pullet Suprise." From *Journal of Irreproducible Results*, Jan–Feb, 1994. Reprinted by permission.

Practice 11.8 EDITING "CANDIDATE FOR A PULLET SURPRISE"

Revise the humorous poem "Candidate for a Pullet Surprise" by replacing all the incorrect words and phrases with ones that are correct.

EDITING GUIDE: TECHNIQUE

Grammar and Usage

Sentences: Are the sentences formed correctly? Are there any "fused sentences" (comma splices or run-ons) or fragments?

Words: Are the forms of words correct? Are there incorrect singular or plural nouns or verbs? Do all of the pronouns have antecedents? Do all verbs agree with their subjects?

Meaning of words: Do the words mean what they are intended to mean? Are there errors in diction, "wrong words"?

Positions of words: Are words arranged in correct order? Are any modifiers placed in a way that could be misread (dangling, squinting, misplaced)? Are instances of "parallelism" correct or faulty?

Mechanics: Are spelling, capitalization, punctuation, and formatting correct?

Task Specifications: Did you use the required topic, deadline, length, sources, and referencing style?

Ironic Rules for Writing

1. Don't abbrev.
2. No sentence fragments.
3. Implement the vernacular.
4. Dump the slang. It sucks.
5. Avoid clichés like the plague.
6. Try to never split an infinitive.
7. Don't never use double negatives.
8. Passive voice should be made active.
9. Avoid redundant punctuation!!! Okay???
10. And do not start sentences with conjunctions.
11. Prepositions are words you shouldn't end with.
12. Use parallelism when you speak and in writing.
13. Fix comma splices, use a conjunction or semicolon.
14. Each of the pronouns should agree with their antecedent.
15. Mixed metaphors are like a disease that must be ironed out.

Editing Guides

An editing guide, like a revision guide, directs you to find and evaluate particular features of your draft. It aims specifically at correctness: grammar/usage, mechanics, and task specifications. This kind of guide often is joined with a revision guide, forming a dual-purpose "revision and editing guide."

Editing Marks

Professional editors use a variety of symbols and abbreviations to show where and how a text should be corrected. Known as *editing marks* or *proofreading marks,* they are fairly easy to learn and very handy for shortening the time it takes to mark a paper.

The passage below is a paragraph from a student essay. Errors have been added to help illustrate the use of editing marks.

¶ Statistics support the claim of a tremendous increase in academic

dishonesty across the nation. For example, according to a study

conducted by The State of Americans: This Generation and the Next, 5.3

(Tense)

percent of high school students in 1969 allow others to copy their work. In

(Frag) *(Dgl mod)*

1989, about 97.3 percent. Copyright their homework, high grades are all

(Sp)

that students seem to care about. Bassed on these disturbing statistics,

(Wdy) *(Awk)*

it is relevant that pressures are negatively affecting the maintenance

(lc) *(lc)*

of Academic Integrity in the many schools. Plagiarism and cheating are

also on the rise in schools because many students do not think, or rather

(SVA)

do not even understand, that such acts are illegal. A student don't feel

(Sp) *(CS)*

that copying someone else's work is socially inacceptible, all their friends

(Ref?)

are going it. They are convinced that they are not going to get caught

(Lincoln 47). Ninety-five percent of high school students who cheat

(Tense)

admitted that they do not get caught (Gomez 42).

EDITING AND PROOFREADING MARKS

Can you think of a way to correct each of the examples?

Symbol	Meaning	Example
Abr	Abbreviation problem	*(Abr)* Doct. Peterson is the best pharmacy professor on campus.
Agr	Agreement problem	*(Agr)* Salar and Won Ho is going to Law Vegas next month for a seminar.
Ante? or Ref?	Pronoun antecedent missing or unclear	*(Ante?)* My friends Phil and Dave painted his apartment last weekend.
Awk	Awkward language	*(Awk)* The earthquake was a really awful bad disaster.
Cap (X)	Faulty capitalization	*(Caps)* Next year I'm going to study at the university of london.
C/S	Comma splice	*(C/S)* I'm going to the store, I'm going to buy bread.
Delete (⌿)	Problem word or phrase	*(Del)* Next month five students are going before the the academic discipline board for plagiarism incidents.
Dic	Diction problem (word choice)	*(Dic)* I performed really good on the test.
Dgl mod	Dangling or misplaced modifier	*(Dgl mod)* Lying beside the street in a drainage ditch, I discovered a wallet walking home.
-ed	Problem with -ed verb ending	*(-ed)* If you had jog with Fred every morning like you had planned, you would be in better shape these days.
Frag	Sentence fragment	Dealing with angry people on a daily basis at my job at the police department. *(Frag)*
F/S	Fused sentence or run-on	*(F/S)* I'm going to the store I'm going to buy bread.
Insert (∧)	Missing word or phrase	Next month five students are going before ^the academic discipline board for plagiarism incidents.
lc	Improper capitalization	One of the most important influences on modern life is Market Capitalism. *(lc)*
//	Problem with parallelism	In college, I'm planning on majoring in English and to play football. *(//)*
P/A	Pronoun agreement problem	*(P/A)* The average student gets their chance at success if he studies hard.
Para. (¶)	Make a new paragraph	My supervisor said, "I'll have to let you go if you don't lose weight. It's bad for the company's image." *(¶)* "Try it," I said. "Try it, and I'll sue."
Rep.	Repeated word or phrase	Technically, I'm having trouble understanding technical technology. *(Rep)*
SP	Spelling error	*(SP)* My favorite professer is Dr. Roberts.
-s	Problem with -s ending	*(-s)* Dr. Stephens plan to run for public office.

Symbol	Meaning	Example
SVA	Subject and verb agreement problem	(SVA) The committee, which includes Aditi and Kareem, are voting in favor of the amendment.
Tense	Verb tense problem	In Shakespeare's Hamlet, the title character will lecture his mother on morality after he killed Polonius. (Tense)
Wdy	Wordy phrase needs to be simplified	One of the really major problems with not only American, but the society of the world in general today is the lack of civility and the tendency to be curt and impolite to others. (Wdy)
WW	Wrong word	(WW) One affect of higher gas prices is that some people get more exercise.

Practice 11.9 USING AN EDITING GUIDE AND EDITING MARKS: "P.S.I.: PLAGIARISM SCENE INVESTIGATOR"

Using the editing guide and editing marks, annotate the errors in the following passage from James Southard's rough draft. (Errors have been added to the original draft.)

"What plagiarism fighting tips can we gains from the criminal justice system. First, their must be penalties to fit the crimes, colleges and universities usually meet out justice in terms of grade reductions, suspensions, and expulsions. Ignoring their conscience, punishments such as fines, community service, permanent records, and embarrassing publicity (such as as releasing names to the press) may be appropriate for plagiarists. For a thief, it often is the deterrent of severe punishment that makes them think twice. And follow the straight and narrow."

Looking Back

- Revising is "re-seeing." One way to re-see is to understand the qualities that characterize good writing.

- Checklists, revision guides, and rubrics can not only help you re-see and revise but also can help you advise others.

- Postpone editing until you are satisfied with the rhetorical and argumentative features of your draft.

- Use the tools of the trade. A dictionary and thesaurus are basic resources that are typically available as books or as word processing software.

- Word processors offer many tools and commands that facilitate revision.

- Rubrics can help you understand which qualities characterize good writing and how those qualities are evaluated.

Suggestions for Writing

- In both your current and later writing assignments, use a revision/editing guide, checklist, or rubric as you critically read and revise your work.

- In both your current and later writing assignments, use a revision/editing guide, checklist, or rubric as you give feedback to other writers.

GRAMMAR AND
MECHANICS

PART
5

CHAPTER 12 Parts of Speech

CHAPTER 13 Sentence Basics

CHAPTER 14 Simple, Compound, and Complex Sentences

CHAPTER 15 Agreement

CHAPTER 16 Sentence Problems

CHAPTER 17 Comma

CHAPTER 18 Quotation Marks and Italics

CHAPTER 19 Other Punctuation

12

Parts of
SPEECH

The words that make up sentences can be classified into nine grammatical categories or word classes. The function of a word in a sentence determines what part of speech it is. The word *rock*, for example, can belong to any one of three categories, depending on its context.

> We stopped to rest in the shadow of an enormous *rock*. (noun)

> The baby will usually stop fussing if you *rock* her. (verb)

> I used to listen only to *rock* music, but now I prefer rap. (adjective)

Here's another example, illustrating three functions of the word *since*.

> We have not seen Lucy *since* Saturday. (preposition)

> We haven't seen Lucy *since* she left. (subordinate conjunction)

> We haven't seen Lucy *since*. (adverb)

NOUNS

A noun is a word that names a person, place, object, quality, or concept.

Common nouns are general names for persons, places, and objects: e.g., *artist, politician; city, suburb; train, computer.*

- **Concrete** nouns name things that can be seen and touched: *telephone, sister, puppy.*

- **Abstract** nouns name thoughts, emotions, qualities, or values—things that cannot be seen or touched: e.g., *ambition, success, honesty.*

Proper nouns name specific persons, places, and things and are capitalized: *Queen Elizabeth, Homer Simpson, Bugs Bunny, CN Tower, Calgary, General Motors.*

Collective nouns name groups of people or things that act as a single unit: *jury, class, committee, herd.*

VERBS

A verb is a word or phrase that tells what the subject of the clause is or does.

- **Action verbs** tell what the subject does:

    The <u>driver</u> <u>braked</u> suddenly.

- **Linking** (or **copula**) **verbs** connect the subject to a word or phrase identifying or describing the subject of a sentence:

    The <u>driver</u> <u>was</u> my older brother. <u>He</u> <u>felt</u> sleepy.

All verbs have different forms (called tenses) to indicate past, present, or future time.

Our team <u>played</u> badly last night. (action verb in past tense)

Mario <u>thinks</u> that we <u>will win</u> tonight. (present tense, future tense)

I <u>am</u> not so confident. (linking verb in present tense)

Auxiliary (or **helping**) **verbs** are used with a main verb to show tense or voice. The auxiliary verbs are *be, have, do, may, can, ought, must, shall, will,* and their various forms.

By November, <u>we</u> <u>will have spent</u> six months in Canada. (future perfect tense)

The way verbs interact with their subjects is shown through a quality called **voice**. Active voice and passive voice verbs give different messages to the reader.

- **Active voice** verbs show the subject doing or acting:

  A <u>woman</u> in a BMW <u>took</u> my parking place.

  The <u>tornado</u> <u>destroyed</u> everything in its path.

- **Passive voice** verbs show the subject being acted upon:

  My parking <u>place</u> <u>was taken</u> by a woman in a BMW.

  Our <u>home</u> <u>was destroyed</u> by the tornado.

PRONOUNS

Pronouns are words that substitute for nouns. They can act as subjects or objects. There are seven classes of pronouns:

1. Personal Pronouns

	Singular (Subject/Object)	Plural (Subject/Object)
1st person	I/me	we/us
2nd person	you/you	you/you
3rd person	he, she, it/him, her, it	they/them

We would like *you* to come with *us*, but *they* can fit only four people into the car.

2. Possessive Pronouns

	Singular	Plural
1st person	mine	ours
2nd person	yours	yours
3rd person	his, hers, its	theirs

The wonton soup is *yours;* the chicken wings are *hers;* the spareribs are *mine;* and the spring rolls are *ours* to share.

3. Indefinite Pronouns

Singular	Plural
any, anyone, anybody, anything	some, all, many
everyone, everybody, everything	some, all, many
someone, somebody, something	some people, some things
no one, nobody, nothing, none (sing.)	none (pl.)
one	several
each	both
either, neither	few, several, many

Is *no one* curious about *anything someone* is doing for the good of us *all*?

4. Demonstrative Pronouns

Singular	Plural
this	these
that	those

This paper is mine; *these* papers are yours.

That is my magazine; I've read *those*, so you can have them.

5. Relative Pronouns

**Singular and Plural
(Subject/Object)**

who/whom; whoever/whomever; which/whichever;
what/whatever; that; whose

The Order of Canada, *which* was created in 1967, is awarded each year to Canadians *who* have distinguished themselves in the arts and sciences, politics, or community service, and *whose* contributions in *whatever* field are deemed worthy of national honour.

6. Interrogative Pronouns

**Singular and Plural
(Subject/Object)**

who?/whom?
which? what?/which? what?

Jan is the leader on *whom* the team depended. *Who* could take her place? *What* can the team do now?

7. Reflexive/Emphatic Pronouns

	Singular	Plural
1st person	myself	ourselves
2nd person	yourself	yourselves
3rd person	himself, herself, itself	themselves

We had planned to go by *ourselves*, but since Sharon invited *herself* along, Leo and Jon should have included *themselves* on the outing, too.

ADJECTIVES

An adjective is a word that modifies or describes a noun or pronoun.

- Adjectives usually answer one of these questions: "What kind?" "Which?" "How many?"

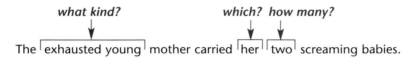

- Pay special attention to the possessive pronoun adjectives: *my, our; your; his, her, their.* These words follow the same rules for agreement that govern the possessive pronouns listed above.

- Most adjectives have three forms:

  Positive (Base) Form: e.g., short, brief, concise

  Comparative Form:

  - Add *-er* to one-syllable words: e.g., shorter, briefer
  - Use *more* + base form for adjectives of two or more syllables: e.g., more concise

  Superlative Form:

  - Add *-est* to one-syllable words: e.g., shortest, briefest
  - Use *most* + base form for adjectives of two or more syllables: e.g., most concise

A few adjectives such as *bad* have irregular comparatives (*worse*) and superlatives (*worst*). Your dictionary will list these irregular forms.

ADVERBS

An adverb is a word that modifies or describes a verb, an adjective, or another adverb.

- Adverbs commonly answer the questions "When?" "Where?" "How?"
- Adverbs often—but not always—end in *-ly.*

Rocco *foolishly* challenged the police officer. (adverb modifies verb)

The baby is an *extremely* fussy eater. (adverb modifies adjective)

My elderly father drives |*very slowly.*| (adverb modifies another adverb; adverb phrase modifies verb)

PREPOSITIONS

A preposition is a word (or words) such as *in, on, among, to, for, according to, instead of* that introduces a prepositional phrase. A prepositional phrase = preposition + object of the preposition (a noun or pronoun).

Prepositional phrases can function as adjectives, adverbs, or nouns.

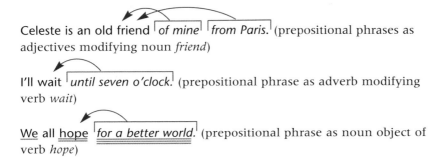

Celeste is an old friend *of mine* *from Paris.* (prepositional phrases as adjectives modifying noun *friend*)

I'll wait *until seven o'clock.* (prepositional phrase as adverb modifying verb *wait*)

We all hope *for a better world.* (prepositional phrase as noun object of verb *hope*)

CONJUNCTIONS

Conjunctions are connecting words used to join two words, two phrases, or two clauses.

- **Coordinating conjunctions** (*and, but, or, for, so, nor, yet*) join grammatically equal elements in a sentence (e.g., the two parts of a compound subject; two independent clauses).

  Moreen *and* Gina are coming, *but* Tessa is not.

- **Subordinating conjunctions** are dependent clause cues: *because, although, when, since,* etc. They link dependent (or subordinate) clauses to independent clauses.

  Tom must go home early *because* he promised to cook dinner.

- **Conjunctive adverbs** are transitional expressions (e.g., *however, therefore, nevertheless, in fact*) usually used after a semicolon to join two independent clauses.

  I would like to go to the club tonight; *however,* I have no money.

- **Correlative conjunctions** are conjunctions used in pairs: e.g., *both . . . and, not only . . . but (also), either . . . or, neither . . . nor*. These constructions are intensifiers. They make the meaning of a statement more emphatic by focusing the reader's attention on each element separately.

For example,

Helen is beautiful *and* intelligent. (coordinating conjunction = statement)

Helen is *both* beautiful *and* intelligent. (correlative conjunctions = emphatic statement)

Luca invited all his friends to the party *and* gave everyone a gift. (coordinating conjunction = statement)

Not only did Luca invite all his friends to the party, *but (also)* he gave everyone a gift. (correlative conjunctions = emphatic statement)

ARTICLES

An article precedes the noun it modifies. The **definite article**, *the*, may be used with a singular or a plural noun; it denotes a particular person or thing. The **indefinite article,** *a/an,* is generally used with a singular, countable noun, and signals an unspecified one of a number of others. (Use *an* before vowel *sounds,* not just vowels: e.g., *an apple, an honest* person.)

The student sitting next to you is asleep. (a particular student)

A student in the back row is snoring. (one of a number of students)

A number of factors determine the use or non-use of articles.

EXPLETIVES

Here and *There* are expletives, which are words used at the beginning of a sentence to postpone the subject until after the verb and thus emphasize it.

Here is your mail. (= Your mail is here.)

There are hundreds of copies still available. (= Hundreds of copies are still available.)

13

"We cannot always build the future for our youth,
but we can build our youth for the future."
—Franklin Delano Roosevelt

Sentence Basics

As you know, sentences are built from some very simple parts—nouns, verbs, and modifiers. Every sentence has, at its base, the pairing of a noun and a verb, or a few of them. The other words in the sentence merely modify the noun and verb.

These are sentence basics—the building blocks of thought. With these blocks, you can build tiny towers or magnificent mansions. It all comes down to understanding how to put the pieces together and deciding what you want to create. This chapter can help.

Learning Outcomes

LO1 Understand subjects and predicates.

LO2 Work with special subjects.

LO3 Work with special predicates.

LO4 Understand adjectives.

LO5 Understand adverbs.

LO6 Use prepositional phrases.

LO7 Use clauses.

LO8 Apply sentence basics in a real-world context.

What do you think?

How do we "build our youth for the future," as Roosevelt suggests in the quotation above? What part do language and writing play in building our youth?

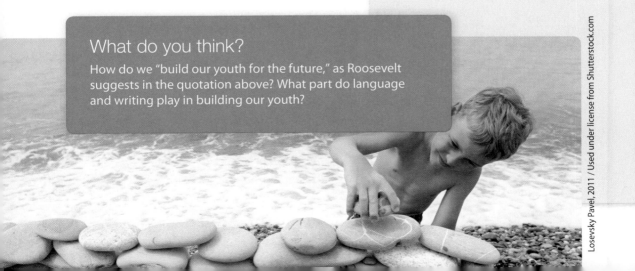

Losevsky Pavel, 2011 / Used under license from Shutterstock.com

LO1 Subjects and Verbs (Predicates)

The subject of a sentence tells what the sentence is about. The verb (predicate) of a sentence tells what the subject does or is.

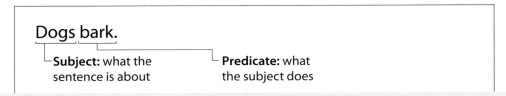

Dogs bark.

Subject: what the   Predicate: what
sentence is about   the subject does

Simple Subject and Simple Predicate

The **simple subject** is the subject without any modifiers, and the **simple predicate** is the verb and any helping verbs without modifiers or objects.

The black and white Schnauzer barked all day long.
                    simple subject simple predicate

Complete Subject and Complete Predicate

The **complete subject** is the subject with modifiers, and the **complete predicate** is the predicate with modifiers and objects.

The black and white Schnauzer barked all day long.
        complete subject   complete predicate

Implied Subject

In commands, the subject *you* is implied. Commands are the only type of sentence in English that can have an **implied subject**.

(You)   Stop barking!
implied subject   complete predicate

Inverted Order

Most often in English, the subject comes before the predicate. However, in questions and sentences that begin with *here* or *there*, the subject comes after the predicate.

        subject   subject
Why are you so loud?   Here is a biscuit.
    predicate   predicate

Creating Subjects and Verbs (Predicates)

Identify/Write For each sentence below, identify the simple subject (SS) and simple predicate (SP). Then write a similar sentence of your own and identify the simple subject and simple predicate in the same way.

1. For thousands of years, humans bred dogs.

   _____

2. All dog breeds descended from wolf ancestors.

   _____

3. At the end of the Ice Age, humans lived nomadically with their dogs.

   _____

4. Ever since that time, dogs enjoyed going for walks.

   _____

Identify/Write For each sentence below, identify the complete subject (CS) and complete predicate (CP). Then write a similar sentence of your own and identify the complete subject and complete predicate in the same way.

1. An Irish wolfhound stands as tall as a small pony.

   _____

2. Wolfhounds were bred to hunt their ancestors.

   _____

3. Wolfhounds also were used for hunting boar.

   _____

4. Why are boars extinct in Ireland?

   _____

5. There were too many wolfhounds.

   _____

Vocabulary

simple subject
the subject without any modifiers

simple predicate
the verb and any helping verbs without modifiers or objects

complete subject
the subject with modifiers

complete predicate
the predicate with modifiers and objects

implied subject
the word *you* implied in command sentences

LO2 Special Types of Subjects

As you work with subjects, watch for these special types.

Compound Subjects

A **compound subject** is two or more subjects connected by *and* or *or*.

My <u>sister and I</u> swim well. <u>Terri, Josh, and I</u> love to dive.
   compound subject   compound subject

"To" Words (Infinitives) as Subjects

An **infinitive** can function as a subject. An infinitive is a verbal form that begins with *to* and may be followed by objects or modifiers.

<u>To become a park ranger</u> is my dream.
      infinitive subject

"Ing" Words (Gerunds) as Subjects

A **gerund** can function as a subject. A gerund is a verb form that ends in *ing* and may be followed by objects or modifiers.

<u>Hiking</u> builds strong calves.   <u>Hiking the Appalachian trail</u> is amazing.
gerund subject   gerund subject

Noun Clause as Subject

A **noun clause** can function as a subject. The clause itself has a subject and a verb but cannot stand alone as a sentence. Noun clauses are introduced by words like *what, that, when, why, how, whatever,* or *whichever.*

<u>Whoever hikes the trail</u> should bring replacement boots.
   noun clause subject

<u>Whatever you need</u> must be carried on your back.
noun clause subject

CONSIDER THE TRAITS

Note that each of these special subjects still functions as a noun or a group of nouns. A sentence is still, at root, the connection between a noun and a verb.

Say It

Pair up with a partner and read each sentence aloud. Take turns identifying the type of subject—compound subject, infinitive subject, gerund subject, or noun-clause subject. Discuss your answers.

1. You and I should go hiking sometime.
2. To reach the peak of Mount Rainier would be amazing.
3. Whoever wants to go should train with mountaineering.
4. Hiking the Rockies at altitude is challenging.

Creating Special Subjects

Identify/Write   For each sentence below, identify the complete subject as a compound subject (CS), infinitive (I), gerund (G), or noun clause (NC). Then write a similar sentence of your own and identify the complete subject in the same way.

1. Planning for success is the key to success. _____

2. To complete the course in two years is my main goal. _____

3. The fan and the air conditioner are running. _____

4. Working through our differences won't be easy. _____

5. A donut, a cup of coffee, and good conversation make my morning. _____

6. Lifting the ban on street parking will help the neighborhood. _____

7. To live life to its fullest is not as easy as it sounds. _____

8. Whoever finds the money will keep it. _____

9. Are Hannah, Michelle, and Sharissa going? _____

10. Whenever he arrives is the starting time. _____

Olena Simko, 2011 / Used under license from Shutterstock.com

Vocabulary

compound subject
two or more subjects connected by *and* or *or*

infinitive
a verb form that begins with *to* and can be used as a noun (or as an adjective or adverb)

gerund
a verb form that ends in *ing* and is used as a noun

noun clause
a group of words beginning with words like *that, what, whoever,* and so on; containing a subject and a verb but unable to function as a sentence

LO3 Special Verbs (Predicates)

As you work with predicates, watch for these special types.

Compound Predicates

A **compound predicate** consists of two or more predicates joined by *and* or *or*.

I watched and laughed. My cat stalked, pounced, and tumbled.
   compound predicate   compound predicate

Predicates with Direct Objects

A **direct object** follows a transitive verb and tells what or who receives the action of the verb.

I pointed the laser. My cat saw the spot. He batted it and nipped the ground.
      direct object   direct object   direct objects

Predicates with Indirect Objects

An **indirect object** comes between a transitive verb and a direct object and tells to whom or for whom an action was done.

I gave him a rest. My cat shot me a puzzled look.
   indirect object   indirect object

Passive Predicates

When a predicate is **passive**, the subject of the sentence is being acted upon rather than acting. Often, the actor is the object of the preposition in a phrase that starts with *by*. To make the sentence **active**, rewrite it, turning the object of the preposition into the subject.

Passive

My cat was exhausted by the game.
subject   passive verb   object of the preposition

Active

The game exhausted my cat.
subject   active verb   direct object

Say It

Pair up with a partner and read each sentence aloud. Take turns identifying the sentence as active or passive. If the sentence is passive, speak the active version out loud.

1. My cat was mesmerized by the laser.
2. The light danced in his paws.
3. The laser glowed red on the wall.
4. The light was chased all down the hallway by my cat.

Creating Special Predicates

Identify/Write For each sentence below, write and label any compound predicate (CP), direct object (DO), and indirect object (IO). Then write a similar sentence of your own and identify the compound predicate and direct or indirect object in the same way.

1. Our pet rabbits hopped and thumped. _____

2. The lop-ear leaped the gate. _____

3. I gave her a carrot. _____

4. She crouched and nibbled. _____

5. The lionhead sniffed and bounded. _____

6. I gave him some dried banana. _____

7. Those rabbits give me hours of entertainment. _____

Identify/Write For each passive sentence below, write and label the simple subject (SS), the simple predicate (SP), and the object of the preposition *by* (O). Then rewrite each sentence, making it active. (See "Passive Predicates" on the previous page.)

1. The rabbits are fed by my sister. _____

2. Their cages are cleaned by her as well. _____

3. She is seen by them as their food goddess. _____

Vocabulary

compound predicate
two or more predicates joined by *and* or *or*

direct object
a word that follows a transitive verb and tells what or who receives the action of the verb

indirect object
a word that comes between a transitive verb and a direct object and tells to whom or for whom an action was done

passive
the voice created when a subject is being acted upon

active
the voice created when a subject is acting

LO4 Adjectives

To modify a noun, use an adjective or a phrase or clause acting as an adjective.

Adjectives

Adjectives answer these basic questions: *which, what kind of, how many, how much.*

To modify the noun **athletes,** ask . . .

Which athletes? ⟶ college athletes

What kind of athletes? ⟶ female athletes

How many athletes? ⟶ ten athletes

ten female college athletes

Adjective Phrases and Clauses

Phrases and clauses can also act as adjectives to modify nouns.

To modify the noun **athletes,** ask . . .

Which athletes? ⟶ athletes who are taking at least 12 credit hours

What kind of athletes? ⟶ athletes with a 3.0 average

The administration will approve loans for athletes with a 3.0 average who are taking at least 12 credit hours.

INSIGHT

It's less important to know the name of a phrase or clause than to know how it functions. If a group of words answers one of the adjective questions, the words are probably functioning as an adjective.

Say It

Pair up with a classmate to find adjectives—words, phrases, or clauses—that modify the nouns below. Take turns asking the questions while the other person answers.

1. **Sports**
   Which sports?
   What kind of sports?
   How many sports?

2. **Classes**
   Which classes?
   What kind of classes?
   How many classes?

Using Adjectives

Answer/Write For each noun, answer the questions using adjectives—words, phrases, or clauses. Then write a sentence using two or more of your answers.

1. **Tournaments**

   Which tournaments? _____

   What kind of tournaments? _____

   How many tournaments? _____

   Sentence: _____

   _____

2. **Opponents**

   Which opponents? _____

   What kind of opponents? _____

   How many opponents? _____

   Sentence: _____

   _____

3. **Victories**

   Which victories? _____

   What kind of victories? _____

   How many victories? _____

   Sentence: _____

   _____

LO5 Adverbs

To modify a verb, use an adverb or a phrase or clause acting as an adverb.

Adverbs

Adverbs answer these basic questions: *how, when, where, why, how long,* and *how often.*

To modify the verb **dance,** ask . . .

How did they dance? ⟶	danced vigorously
When did they dance? ⟶	danced yesterday
Where did they dance? ⟶	danced there
How often did they dance? ⟶	danced often

Yesterday, the bride and groom often vigorously danced, there in the middle of the floor.

Adverb Phrases and Clauses

Phrases and clauses can also act as adverbs to modify verbs.

To modify the verb **dance,** ask . . .

How did they dance? ⟶	danced grinning and laughing
When did they dance? ⟶	danced from the first song
Where did they dance? ⟶	danced all around the room
Why did they dance? ⟶	danced to celebrate their wedding
How long did they dance? ⟶	danced until the last song

Grinning and laughing, the bride and groom danced all around the room from the first song until the last song to celebrate their wedding.

CONSIDER SPEAKING AND LISTENING

Read the last sentence aloud. Though it may look imposing on the page, it sounds natural, probably because adverbs and adjectives are a common part of our speech. Experiment with these modifiers in your writing as well.

Using Adverbs

Answer/Write   For each verb, answer the questions using adverbs—words, phrases, or clauses. Then write a sentence using three or more of your answers.

1. Ran

How did they run? _____

When did they run? _____

Where did they run? _____

Why did they run? _____

How long did they run? _____

How often did they run? _____

Sentence: _____

_____

2. Jumped

How did they jump? _____

When did they jump? _____

Where did they jump? _____

Why did they jump? _____

How long did they jump? _____

How often did they jump? _____

Sentence: _____

_____

LO6 Prepositional Phrases

One of the simplest and most versatile types of phrases in English is the **prepositional phrase**. A prepositional phrase can function as an adjective or an adverb.

Building Prepositional Phrases

A prepositional phrase is a preposition followed by an object (a noun or pronoun) and any modifiers.

Preposition	+	Object	=	Prepositional Phrase
at		noon		at noon
in		an hour		in an hour
beside		the green clock		beside the green clock
in front of		my aunt's vinyl purse		in front of my aunt's vinyl purse

As you can see, a propositional phrase can be just two words long, or many words long. As you can also see, some prepositions are themselves made up of more than one word. Here is a list of common prepositions.

Prepositions

aboard	back of	except for	near to	round
about	because of	excepting	notwithstanding	save
above	before	for	of	since
according to	behind	from	off	subsequent to
across	below	from among	on	through
across from	beneath	from between	on account of	throughout
after	beside	from under	on behalf of	'til
against	besides	in	onto	to
along	between	in addition to	on top of	together with
alongside	beyond	in behalf of	opposite	toward
alongside of	but	in front of	out	under
along with	by	in place of	out of	underneath
amid	by means of	in regard to	outside	until
among	concerning	inside	outside of	unto
apart from	considering	inside of	over	up
around	despite	in spite of	over to	upon
as far as	down	instead of	owing to	up to
aside from	down from	into	past	with
at	during	like	prior to	within
away from	except	near	regarding	without

INSIGHT

A preposition is pre-positioned before the other words it introduces to form a phrase. Other languages have post-positional words that follow their objects.

Using Prepositional Phrases

Create   For each item below, create a prepositional phrase by writing a preposition and an object (and any modifiers). Then write a sentence using the prepositional phrase.

1. | Preposition | + | Object (and any modifiers) |

Sentence: _____

2. | Preposition | + | Object (and any modifiers) |

Sentence: _____

3. | Preposition | + | Object (and any modifiers) |

Sentence: _____

4. | Preposition | + | Object (and any modifiers) |

Sentence: _____

5. | Preposition | + | Object (and any modifiers) |

Sentence: _____

Vocabulary

prepositional phrase
a group of words beginning with a
preposition and including an object (noun
or pronoun) and any modifiers

LO7 Clauses

A clause is a group of words with a subject and a predicate. If a clause can stand on its own as a sentence, it is an **independent clause**, but if it cannot, it is a **dependent clause**.

Independent Clause

An independent clause has a subject and a predicate and expresses a complete thought. It is the same as a simple sentence.

Clouds piled up in the stormy sky.

Dependent Clause

A dependent clause has a subject and a predicate but does not express a complete thought. Instead, it is used as an **adverb clause**, an **adjective clause**, or a **noun clause**.

An adverb clause begins with a subordinating conjunction (see below) and functions as an adverb, so it must be connected to an independent clause to be complete.

CONSIDER SPEAKING AND LISTENING

In each example below, read the dependent clause out loud. (The dependent clause is in red.) Can you hear how each dependent clause sounds incomplete? Read it to another person, and the listener will probably say, "What about it?" These clauses depend on a complete thought to make sense.

after	as long as	given that	since	unless	where
although	because	if	so that	until	whereas
as	before	in order that	that	when	while
as if	even though	provided that	though	whenever	

Even though the forecast said clear skies, the storms rolled in.

An adjective clause begins with a relative pronoun *(which, that, who)* and functions as an adjective, so it must be connected to an independent clause to be complete.

I don't like a meteorologist who often gets the forecast wrong.

A noun clause begins with words like those below and functions as a noun. It is used as a subject or an object in a sentence.

| how | what | whoever | whomever |
| that | whatever | whom | why |

I wish he had known what the weather would be.

Using Clauses

Identify/Write For each sentence below, write and label any adverb clauses (ADVC), adjective clauses (ADJC), or noun clauses (NC). Then write a similar sentence of your own and identify the clauses.

1. I wonder why weather is so unpredictable.

2. Storms still surprise meteorologists who have years of experience.

3. Many different factors determine what will happen in the sky.

4. Until we can track all factors, we can't predict perfectly.

5. Whoever gives a forecast is making a guess.

6. Since weather is so uncertain, predictions have percentages.

7. A 50 percent chance of rain means that there is a 50 percent chance of fair weather.

8. When air crosses a large lake, it picks up moisture.

9. Because of lake-effect rain, Valparaiso is called "Vapor Rain Snow."

10. Buffalo gets whatever moisture Lake Erie dishes up.

Vocabulary

independent clause
a group of words with a subject and predicate that expresses a complete thought

dependent clause
a group of words with a subject and predicate that does not express a complete thought

adverb clause
a dependent clause beginning with a subordinating conjunction and functioning as an adverb

adjective clause
a dependent clause beginning with a relative pronoun and functioning as an adjective

noun clause
a dependent clause beginning with a subordinating word and functioning as a noun

LO8 Real-World Application

Identify In the e-mail below, write and identify simple subjects (SS), simple predicates (SP), and dependent clauses (DC).

Send	Attach	Fonts	Colors	Save As Draft

To: Terri Bell

Subject: Revision Suggestions

Hi, Teri: *1*

I enjoyed your article, "What Is New in *BattleTown 2*," which you submitted for publication on MMORPNews2.com. We like your article but request a few revisions before we send contracts.

This is a quick rundown of our revision suggestions: *5*

1. The opening could be more gripping. The title works well to grab the reader's interest, but the opening feels flat. Perhaps you could provide a glimpse of new features of game play, or even give a scenario that wasn't possible in *BattleTown 1*.

2. A direct quotation from Todd Allen would strengthen the center section.   *10* Though you allude to your interview on many occasions, Todd never speaks for himself, and he is a definite name in the industry.

3. Can you get permission to use the visuals? AssemblyArts would love the free publicity, but you need written permission to include the screenshots.

If you could make these changes, we would be very interested in publishing   *15* your article. Once I see the revised piece, I can send a contract for you to sign.

Thanks,

Richard Prince

Expand Answer the adjective and adverb questions below. Then expand the sentence using some of the words, phrases, and clauses you have created.

The agent called.

Which agent? _____

What kind of agent? _____

Called *when?* _____

Called *how?* _____

Sentence: _____

14

> "A complex system that works is invariably found to have evolved from a simple system that works."
> —John Gaule

Simple, Compound, and Complex Sentences

Most leaves have a central stem with veins extending from it. Sometime this structure forms a simple oval, but at other times, two or more ovals connect to form a compound leaf. And the shape of some leaves is complex, as if a number of leaves were fused together.

Sentences are similar. All have a noun and a verb, but some stop at this simple structure. In other cases, two or more sentences combine to make a compound sentence. And when a sentence has one or more dependent clauses fused to it, it becomes complex.

This chapter shows how to create simple, compound, and complex sentences. As with leaves, variety makes sentences beautiful.

Learning Outcomes

LO1 Create simple sentences.
LO2 Create simple sentences with compound subjects.
LO3 Create simple sentences with compound verbs (predicates).
LO4 Create compound sentences.
LO5 Create complex sentences.
LO6 Create complex sentences with relative clauses.
LO7 Apply simple, compound, and complex sentences in a real-world document.

What do you think?

Which type of leaf is most beautiful—a simple, compound, or complex leaf? Why?

LO1 Simple Sentences

A **simple sentence** consists of a subject and a verb. The subject is a noun or pronoun that names what the sentence is about. The verb tells what the subject does or is.

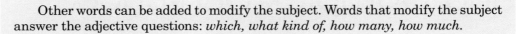

Rachel sang.
subject verb

Modifiers

Other words can be added to modify the subject. Words that modify the subject answer the adjective questions: *which, what kind of, how many, how much.*

My new roommate Rachel sang. *(Which Rachel do you mean?)*

Other words can also modify the verb. These words and phrases answer the adverb questions: *how, when, where, why, to what degree,* and *how often.*

Rachel sang in the shower at the top of her lungs.
                    (Where and how did Rachel sing?)

Direct and Indirect Objects

The verb might also be followed by a noun or pronoun that receives the action of the verb. Such a word is called the **direct object**, and it answers the question *what* or *whom?*

Rachel sang "I Need a Hero." *(What did Rachel sing?)*

Another noun or pronoun could come between the verb and the direct object, telling *to whom* or *for whom* an action is done. Such a word is the **indirect object**.

I gave her a picture of Chuck Norris.
        (I gave a picture of Chuck Norris to whom?)

Vocabulary

simple sentence
a subject and a verb that together form a complete thought

direct object
a noun or pronoun that follows a verb and receives its action

indirect object
a noun or pronoun that comes between a verb and a direct object, telling *to whom* or *for whom* an action is done

newphotoservice, 2011 / Used under license from Shutterstock.com

Say It

Team up with a partner and follow these steps: One of you speaks the sentence aloud, and the other asks the question in italics. Then the first person says the sentence again, inserting an answer.

1. We sang songs. *(Where did you sing songs?)*
2. The song was our favorite. *(Which song was your favorite?)*
3. Rachel sang. *(What did Rachel sing?)*
4. I sang a song. *(To whom did you sing a song?)*

INSIGHT

In item 1, you are adding modifiers to the verb and in item 2, you are adding modifiers to the subject. In item 3, you are adding a direct object, and in item 4, you are adding an indirect object.

Creating Simple Sentences

Create Provide a noun for a subject and a verb for a predicate. Then write a sentence with the noun and verb, adding details that answer the questions asked.

1. | Subject | Verb |

   Which? _____

2. | Subject | Verb |

   What kind of? _____

3. | Subject | Verb |

   When? _____

4. | Subject | Verb |

   Where? _____

5. | Subject | Verb |

   How? _____

LO2 Simple Sentences with Compound Subjects

A simple sentence can have a **compound subject** (two or more subjects).

A Simple Sentence with Two Subjects

To write a simple sentence with two subjects, join them using *and* or *or*.

One Subject: Lee worked on the Rube Goldberg machine.
Two Subjects: Lee and Jerome will add the lever arm that tips the bucket.
Lee or Jerome will add the lever arm that tips the bucket.

One Subject: Ms. Claymore will help them attach the flywheel.
Two Subjects: Ms. Claymore and her aide will help them attach the flywheel.
Either Ms. Claymore or her aide will help them attach the flywheel.

A Simple Sentence with Three or More Subjects

To write a simple sentence with three or more subjects, create a series. List each subject, placing a comma after all but the last, and place an *and* or *or* before the last.

Three Subjects: Jerome, Lee, and Sandra are finishing the machine soon.
Five Subjects: Jerome, Lee, Sandra, Ms. Claymore, and her aide will enter the machine in a contest.

NOTE: When a compound subject is joined by *and,* the subject is plural and requires a plural verb. When a compound subject is joined by *or,* the verb should match the last subject.

Ms. Claymore and her aide need to submit the entry form.

Ms. Claymore or her aide needs to submit the entry form.

CONSIDER THE TRAITS

A compound subject does not make the sentence compound. As long as both (or all) of the subjects connect to the same verb or verbs, the sentence is still considered simple.

Say It

Speak each of the following sentences out loud.
1. Jerome *loves* the Rube Goldberg project.
2. Jerome *and* Sandra *love* the Rube Goldberg project.
3. Jerome *or* Sandra *works* on it every day after school.
4. Jerome, Sandra, *and* Lee *have* contributed most.
5. Jerome, Sandra, *or* Lee *has* contributed most.

Using Compound Subjects

Create   Write subjects for each of the boxes provided. Then write a sentence that includes the subjects as a compound subject using *and* or *or*.

1. | Subject | Subject |

2. | Subject | Subject |

3. | Subject | Subject | Subject |

4. | Subject | Subject | Subject |

5. | Subject | Subject | Subject | Subject |

6. | Subject | Subject | Subject | Subject |

Vocabulary

compound subject
two or more subjects in a simple sentence

LO3 Simple Sentences with Compound Verbs

A simple sentence can also have two or more verbs (predicates). Remember that the predicate tells what the subject is doing or being, so as long as both predicates connect to the same subject, the sentence is still a simple sentence.

A Simple Sentence with Two Verbs

To create a **compound predicate** with two parts, join two verbs using *and* or *or*.

One Verb: The band rocked.

Two Verbs: The band rocked and danced.

Remember that the predicate includes not just the verbs, but also words that modify or complete the verbs.

One Predicate: The band played their hit single.

Two Predicates: The band played their hit single and covered other songs.

A Simple Sentence with Three or More Verbs

To create a compound predicate with three or more parts, list the verbs in a series, with a comma after each except the last, and the word *and* or *or* before the last.

Three Verbs: The singer crooned, wailed, and roared.

Five Verbs: The fans clapped, screamed, danced, cheered, and swayed.

If each verb also includes modifiers or completing words (direct and indirect objects), place the commas after each complete predicate.

The crowd members got to their feet, waved their hands back and forth, and sang along with the band.

CONSIDER THE TRAITS

A compound verb does not make the sentence compound. As long as both (or all) of the verbs connect to the same subject or subjects, the sentence is still considered simple.

Using Compound Predicates

Create For each subject below, create predicates. Then write a simple sentence that joins the compound predicates with *and* or *or*.

1. The reporters

> Predicate

> Predicate

2. The police

> Predicate

> Predicate

3. The manager

> Predicate

> Predicate

4. The bouncer

> Predicate

> Predicate

> Predicate

Vocabulary

compound predicate
two or more predicates in a
simple sentence

LO4 Compound Sentences

A **compound sentence** is made out of simple sentences joined by a coordinating conjunction: *and, but, or, nor, for, so,* or *yet.*

Compound of Two Sentences

Most compound sentences connect two simple sentences, which are also called independent clauses. Connect the sentences by placing a comma after the first sentence and using a coordinating conjunction after the comma.

Two Sentences: We ordered pizza. I got just one piece.

Compound Sentence: We ordered pizza, but I got just one piece.

Compound of Three or More Sentences

Sometimes, you might want to join three or more short sentences in a compound sentence.

Three Sentences: Tim likes cheese. Jan likes veggie. I like pepperoni.

Compound Sentence: Tim likes cheese, Jan likes veggie, and I like pepperoni.

You can also join the sentences using semicolons. Authors sometimes use this approach to describe a long, involved process or a flurry of activity.

Tim ate the cheese pizza; Jan ate the veggie pizza; Ray showed up and ate the pepperoni pizza; I got back in time for the last slice.

NOTE: Remember that a compound sentence is made of two or more complete sentences. Each part needs to have its own subject and verb.

CONSIDER THE TRAITS

The word *and* indicates that the second clause provides additional information. The words *but, or, nor,* and *yet* create a contrast. The words *for* and *so* indicate that one clause is the cause of the other.

Creating Compound Sentences

Write   Write a simple sentence for each prompt; then combine them as a compound sentence.

1. What pizza do you like? _____

   What pizza does a friend like? _____

   Compound Sentence: _____

   _____

2. Where do you go for pizza? _____

   What other place do people go? _____

   Compound Sentence: _____

   _____

3. Who likes thin crust pizza? _____

   Who likes pan pizza? _____

   Who likes stuffed pizza? _____

   Compound Sentence: _____

   _____

4. What is the weirdest pizza? _____

   What is the grossest pizza? _____

   What is the stinkiest pizza? _____

   Compound Sentence: _____

   _____

5. When do you eat pizza? _____

   When do your friends eat pizza? _____

   When does your family eat pizza? _____

   Compound Sentence: _____

   _____

Vocabulary

compound sentence
two or more simple sentences
joined with a coordinating
conjunction

LO5 Complex Sentences

A **complex sentence** shows a special relationship between two ideas. Instead of connecting two sentences as equal ideas (as in a compound sentence), a complex sentence shows that one idea depends on the other.

Using a Subordinating Conjunction

You can create a complex sentence by placing a subordinating conjunction before the sentence that is less important. Here are common subordinating conjunctions:

after	before	so that	when
although	even though	that	where
as	if	though	whereas
as if	in order that	till	while
as long as	provided that	'til	
because	since	until	

> **CONSIDER SPEAKING AND LISTENING**
>
> Read the example complex and compound-complex sentences aloud. Despite their daunting names, these sentences aren't that complicated. You use them all the time in speech. Experiment with them in your writing.

The subordinating conjunction shows that this sentence depends on the other sentence and can't stand without it.

Two Sentences:	We played strong offense. We won the football game.
Complex Sentence:	Because we played strong offense, we won the football game.
	We won the football game because we played strong offense.

NOTE: The subordinating conjunction goes at the beginning of the less important clause, but the two clauses could go in either order. When the dependent clause comes second, it usually isn't set off with a comma.

Compound-Complex

You can create a **compound-complex sentence** by placing a subordinating conjunction before a simple sentence and connecting it to a compound sentence.

Simple Sentence:	I threw two touchdowns.
Compound Sentence:	Jake kicked the extra points, and the other team couldn't catch up.
Compound-Complex:	After I threw two touchdowns, Jake kicked the extra points, and the other team couldn't catch up.

Creating Complex Sentences

Write Write a simple sentence for each prompt. Then select a subordinating conjunction from the facing page, place it at the beginning of one sentence, and combine the two sentences into a single complex sentence.

1. What did you play? _____

    Did you win or lose? _____

    Complex sentence: _____

    _____

2. Who did you play? _____

    Why did you play the opponent? _____

    Complex sentence: _____

    _____

3. Who won the game? _____

    Why did that side win? _____

    Complex sentence: _____

    _____

4. Where did you play? _____

    Where else could you have played? _____

    Complex sentence: _____

    _____

5. What surprised you? _____

    Why did it surprise you? _____

    Complex sentence: _____

    _____

6. How long did you play? _____

    When did you stop? _____

    Complex sentence: _____

    _____

Vocabulary

complex sentence
a sentence with one independent clause and one or more dependent clauses

compound-complex sentence
a sentence with two or more independent clauses and one or more dependent clauses

LO6 Complex Sentences with Relative Clauses

In a complex sentence, one idea depends on the other. You've seen how a dependent clause can start with a subordinating conjunction. Another type of dependent clause starts with a relative pronoun.

Relative Clauses

A **relative clause** is a group of words that begins with a **relative pronoun** *(that, which, who, whom)* and includes a verb and any words that modify or complete it:

Relative Clauses:	that leads into the garden
	which usually leans against the shed
	who planted the scallions
	whom I asked to help me weed

Each relative clause above has a subject and a verb, but none of the clauses is a complete sentence. All need to be connected to a complete sentence.

Complex Sentences:	I followed the path that leads into the garden.
	I looked for the shovel, which usually leans against the shed.
	We have many onions thanks to a friend who planted the scallions.
	I worked with Tina, whom I asked to help me weed.

That and *Which*

The pronoun *that* signals that the information after it is necessary to the sentence. The pronoun *which* signals that the information is not necessary, so the clause is set off with a comma.

That: The scallions that we planted this spring taste strongest. (*That* defines the scallions.)

Which: I love scallions, which I eat raw or fried. (*Which* does not define the scallions but just adds more information about them.)

Who and *Whom*

The pronoun *who* is the subject of the relative clause that it introduces. The pronoun *whom* is a direct object of a clause it introduces.

Who: I helped the woman who harvested scallions. (*Who* is the subject.)

Whom: I thanked the woman whom I helped. (*Whom* is the direct object.)

Using Relative Clauses

Create   For each item, write a relative clause beginning with the pronoun provided. Then write a complex sentence that includes the relative clause. In case you need a topic idea, think of a party you have attended or one that you would like to attend.

1. Relative clause: _____that_____

   Complex sentence: _____

   _____

2. Relative clause: _who_____

   Complex sentence: _____

   _____

3. Relative clause: _which_____

   Complex sentence: _____

   _____

4. Relative clause: _whom_____

   Complex sentence: _____

   _____

5. Relative clause: _that_____

   Complex sentence: _____

   _____

6. Relative clause: _which_____

   Complex sentence: _____

   _____

INSIGHT

In some languages, if the relative pronoun is the object of the clause it introduces, another pronoun is inserted in the clause: *I liked the gift that my boss gave it to me.* In English, no additional pronoun is inserted: *I liked the gift that my boss gave to me.*

Vocabulary

relative clause
a group of words that begins with a relative pronoun and includes a verb but cannot stand alone as a sentence

relative pronoun
a word *(that, which, who, whom)* that relates a relative clause with another word in the sentence

LO7 Real-World Application

Rewrite   Read the following message about a meeting. Note how every sentence is a simple sentence. Rewrite the message, combining sentences into some compound or complex sentences and improving the flow.

Dear Mr. Lindau:

You asked about the Monday production meeting. I will summarize it. The production staff met with the editors. The writers explained their new project. It focuses on twenty-first-century skills. The writers presented two chapters. They will become a prototype.

The new project needs to be visual. It should appeal to students and teachers. The design needs to make text accessible. The writing has an open quality. It still feels academic. The book should be available for sale in the fall. A teacher's edition will follow.

The designers are beginning work on a prototype. The writers continue to create chapters.

Dear Mr. Lindau:

_____

_____

_____

_____

_____

_____

_____

_____

_____

CONSIDER THE WORKPLACE

Using a variety of sentences in workplace writing will help ideas flow and will present a polished image.

15

"My idea of an agreeable person is a person who agrees with me."

—Benjamin Disraeli

Agreement

When two people agree, they can work together. They have the same goals and outlook, and they can become a team.

Subjects and verbs are much the same. If the subject is plural, the verb needs to be as well, or they can't work together. Pronouns also need to agree with their antecedents in terms of number. Without agreement, these words fight each other, and instead of conveying ideas, they disrupt communication.

This chapter focuses on the agreement between subjects and verbs and between pronouns and antecedents. It also tackles other pronoun problems. After you work through the exercises here, you'll find it easy to write agreeable sentences.

Learning Outcomes

LO1 Make subjects and verbs agree.

LO2 Make two subjects agree with verbs.

LO3 Practice agreement with *I* and *you*.

LO4 Practice agreement with indefinite pronouns.

LO5 Practice pronoun-antecedent agreement.

LO6 Correct other pronoun problems.

LO7 Check agreement in a real-world context.

What do you think?

What makes a person agreeable? What makes subjects and verbs agreeable?

LO1 Subject-Verb Agreement

A verb must **agree in number** with the subject of the sentence. If the subject is singular, the verb must be singular. If the subject is plural, the verb must be plural.

| singular subject | + | singular verb | = agreement | | plural subject | + | plural verb | = agreement |

The truck needs a tune-up.

The trucks need tune-ups.

NOTE: Plural subjects often end in *s*, but plural verbs usually do not. Also note that only present tense verbs and certain *be* verbs have separate singular and plural forms.

Present:	**singular**	**plural**	**Past:**	**singular**	**plural**
	walks	walk		walked	walked
	sees	see		saw	saw
	eats	eat		ate	ate
	is/am	are		was	were

To make most verbs singular, add just an *s*.

run—runs   write—writes   stay—stays

The verbs *do* and *go* are made singular by adding an *es*.

do—does   go—goes

When a verb ends in *ch, sh, x,* or *z,* make it singular by adding *es*.

latch—latches   wish—wishes   fix—fixes   buzz—buzzes

When a verb ends in a consonant followed by *a y,* change the *y* to *i* and add *es*.

try—tries   fly—flies   cry—cries   quantify—quantifies

INSIGHT

The "Say It" activity on the next page will help you become familiar with the subject-verb agreement patterns in English. Practice it aloud, and for added practice, write the sentences as well.

Say It

Read the following sentences aloud, emphasizing the words in italics.
1. The bird *sings*. The birds *sing*. The phone *rings*. The phones *ring*.
2. The person *is*. The people *are*. The child *is*. The children *are*.
3. He *works*. They *work*. She *learns*. They *learn*.
4. The woman *does*. The women *do*. The man *goes*. The men *go*.
5. She *wishes*. They *wish*. He *boxes*. They *box*.

Correcting Basic Subject-Verb Agreement

Write   For each sentence below, write the correct form of the verb in parentheses.

1. A philosophy major _____ about thinking. (know)
2. A philosopher _____ to find philosophical work. (try)
3. An employer rarely _____ to hire philosophers. (wish)
4. But such students _____ able to think (is).
5. My roommate _____ philosophy. (study)
6. He also _____ to study the want ads for jobs. (need)
7. He _____ employers need thinkers. (say)
8. That idea _____ sense. (make)
9. But that idea doesn't _____ people hire him. (make)
10. At his job, he _____ lawn mowers very philosophically. (fix)

Correct   Correct any agreement errors you find by writing the line number and the verb you would change. Cross it out and write the correct present tense verb.

> The philosopher Plato say the material world aren't the real world.   *1*
> He say we sees shadows on a cave wall. Plato believe in eternal forms of
> perfection. Every real table in the world are patterned after the perfect
> form of a table. In that way, people too is patterned after the perfect form
> of people. Though Plato live more than three hundred years before Jesus,   *5*
> many Christian thinkers likes his concept of eternal forms. The idea fit
> well with the ideas of a soul and a creator. Many modern thinkers, though,
> has the opposite idea. They says that only physical things is real. Plato, of
> course, disagree.

Write   For each plural verb below, write one sentence using the verb in its singular form.

1. fly _____
2. do _____
3. fish _____
4. wax _____

Vocabulary

agree in number
match, as when a subject and verb are both singular, or when they are both plural

LO2 Agreement with Two Subjects

Sentences with **compound subjects** have special rules to make sure that they agree.

When a sentence has two or more subjects joined by *and,* the verb should be plural.

plural subject **+** plural verb **=** agreement

Jumbo and Dumbo march.

When a sentence has two or more subjects joined by *or, nor,* or *but also,* the verb should agree with the last subject.

singular subject **+** singular verb **=** agreement

Either Jumbo or Dumbo trumpets.

Not only Jumbo but also Dumbo trumpets.

 or

CJimenez, 2011 / Used under license from Shutterstock.com

Say It

Read the following sentences aloud, emphasizing the words in *italics.*

1. Jumbo *and* Dumbo *perform*. Jumbo *or* Dumbo *performs*.
2. The man *and* woman *dance*. The man *or* woman *dances*.
3. The Democrat *and* the Republican *agree*. The Democrat *or* the Republican *agrees*.
4. Not only Dave *but also* Tim *writes*.
5. The dog, cat, *and* guinea pig *greet* me. The dog, cat, *or* guinea pig *greets* me.

CONSIDER TEST TAKING

For more practice with compound subjects, see pages 294–295.

Fixing Agreement with Two Subjects

Write For each sentence below, write the correct form of the verb in parentheses.

1. The acrobat and clown _____ the crowd. (entertain)

2. The acrobat or clown _____ a pie in the face. (get)

3. A trapeze artist and a tightrope walker _____ an ovation. (receive)

4. Not only the acrobat but also the clown _____ highly paid. (are)

5. Neither the lion tamer nor the sword swallower _____ insurance. (have)

6. The human cannonball or the lion tamer _____ the scariest job. (have)

7. Either Todd or Lewis _____ to join the circus. (plan)

8. Thrills and hard work _____ Todd or Lewis. (await)

9. Not only Todd but also Lewis _____ a daredevil. (are)

10. The clowns or the ringmaster _____ each act. (introduce)

Correct Correct any agreement errors you find by writing the line number and incorrect verb, crossing it out, and writing the correct present tense verb.

> Childhood dreams and fantasies rarely comes true. A firefighter   *1*
> or police officer are what many children dream of being. Imagine a
> world filled with firefighters and police! Neither the accountant nor the
> landscaper figure big in childhood plans. A princess or a wizard are also
> a popular choice for kids. Job openings and pay for both careers is pretty   *5*
> slim. Even the job of astronaut or explorer have become scarce. The trials
> of joblessness and the responsibilities of adulthood conspires to convince
> people to seek other careers. Childhood stars sometimes get "real" jobs, too.
> Johnny Whitaker and Wil Wheaton works with computers. They traded
> childhood dreams for adult ones.   *10*

Write Write a sentence with a compound subject joined by *and*. Write a sentence with a compound subject joined by *or*. Check subject-verb agreement.

_____

Vocabulary

compound subject
two or more subjects that share the same verb or verbs

LO3 Agreement with *I* and *You*

The pronouns *I* and *you* usually take plural verbs, even though they are singular.

plural verb

Correct: I go to Great America and ride roller coasters. You do too.

singular verb

Incorrect: I goes to Great America and rides roller coasters. You does too.

NOTE: The pronoun *I* takes the singular verbs *am* and *was*. **Do not** use *I* with *be* or *is*.

Correct: I am excited. I was nervous. I am eager to ride the roller coaster.

Incorrect: I are exited. I were nervous. I is eager to ride the roller coaster.

Quick Guide

Using *am, is, are, was,* and *were*

	Singular	Plural
Present Tense	I *am* you *are* he *is* she *is* it *is*	we *are* you *are* they *are*
Past Tense	I *was* you *were* he *was* she *was* it *was*	we *were* you *were* they *were*

INSIGHT

The word *am* exists for one reason only, to go along with the word *I*. There is no other subject for the verb *am*. In academic or formal writing, *I* should never be used with *be* or *is*. Think of René Descartes saying, "I think, therefore I am."

Say It

Read the following word groups aloud, emphasizing the words in *italics*.
1. I *laugh* / You *laugh* / She *laughs* / They *laugh*
2. I *work* / You *work* / He *works* / They *work*
3. I *do* / You *do* / He *does* / They *do*
4. I *am* / You *are* / She *is* / They *are*
5. I *was* / You *were* / He *was* / They *were*

Correcting Agreement with *I* and *You*

Write   For each blank below, write the correct forms of the verb in parentheses. (Do not change the tense.)

1. I _____ louder than he _____ . (laugh)

2. You _____ as well as she _____ . (climb)

3. We _____ together, or you _____ alone. (work)

4. Stan _____ silverware while I _____ pans. (wash)

5. I _____ often, but he _____ rarely. (help)

6. The group _____ on Sunday, but I _____ later. (watch)

7. I _____ first, and she _____ after. (eat)

8. You _____ tired, and I _____ too. (is)

9. Last year, I _____ short, but you _____ tall. (was)

10. You _____ helpful; I hope I _____ also. (is)

Correct   Correct any agreement errors you find by writing the line number and incorrect verb. Cross it out and write the correct verb.

     I is starting a class in astronomy, and I wonders if I can borrow your   *1*
telescope. You rarely uses it anymore, and I needs it to be able to look at
the moons of Jupiter. My professor says that even a moderate-size telescope
will show the moons. She have instructions for finding Jupiter. I knows
how to use the telescope, but if you is afraid I would break it, you could set   *5*
it up for me.

     Another idea would be for us to stargaze together. I has a place away
from city lights, and I has lawn chairs and blankets we could use. If you
agrees to come along and set up the telescope, I agrees to bring snacks for
us.   *10*

     What do you think? I hopes I'm not asking too much and that you isn't
mad about the request. I just is excited to see Jupiter's moons, and I thinks
you might like to see them, too.

Write   Write two sentences using "I" as the subject. Then write two more using "you" as the subject. Check your subject-verb agreement.

_____

_____

LO4 Agreement with Singular Indefinite Pronouns

An **indefinite pronoun** is intentionally vague. Instead of referring to a specific person, place, or thing, it refers to something general or unknown.

Singular Indefinite Pronouns

Singular indefinite pronouns take singular verbs:

Someone cooks every night.

No one gets out of kitchen duty.

Everyone benefits from the chore schedule.

Note that indefinite pronouns that end in *one, body,* or *thing* are singular, just as these words themselves are singular. Just as you would write, "That thing is missing," so you would write "Something is missing." The words *one, each, either,* and *neither* can be tricky because they are often followed by a prepositional phrase that contains a plural noun. The verb should still be singular.

One of my friends is a great cook.

Each of us wants to cook as well as he does.

Remember that a compound subject joined with *and* needs a plural verb, and a compound subject joined with *or* needs a verb that matches the last subject.

Anything and everything taste terrific in his meals.

No one or nothing keeps him from making a wonderful meal.

Singular

someone
somebody
something

anyone
anybody
anything

no one
nobody
nothing

everyone
everybody
everything

one
each
either
neither

Say It

Read the following word groups aloud, emphasizing the words in *italics*.

1. No one *is* / Nobody *has* / Nothing *does*

2. Everyone *is* / Everybody *has* / Everything *does*

3. One of my friends *is* / Each of my friends *has* / Either of my friends *does*

Correcting Indefinite Pronoun Agreement I

Write For each sentence below, write the correct form of the verb in parentheses. (Do not change the tense.)

1. Everyone _____ an application. (complete)

2. Somebody _____ to get the job. (have)

3. Each of the jobs _____ available. (are)

4. Neither of the applicants _____ qualified. (are)

5. Either of the prospects _____ to be trained. (hope)

6. Nobody _____ to go home empty-handed. (want)

7. Everybody _____ bills to pay. (have)

8. Someone or something _____ to give. (have)

9. Either of the positions _____ well. (pay)

10. One of my friends _____ for word on the job. (wait)

Write Write sentences using each indefinite pronoun as a subject. Choose present tense verbs and check subject-verb agreement.

1. Someone _____

_____

2. Nothing _____

_____

3. Neither _____

_____

4. Everyone _____

_____

5. Each _____

_____

6. Anybody _____

_____

Vocabulary

indefinite pronoun
a special type of pronoun that does not refer to a specific person or thing

Agreement with Other Indefinite Pronouns

Other indefinite pronouns are always plural, or have a singular or plural form, depending on how they are used.

Plural Indefinite Pronouns

Plural indefinite pronouns take plural verbs:

Plural
both
few
many
several

Many of us follow classical music.

Several are big fans.

Singular or Plural Indefinite Pronouns

Some indefinite pronouns or quantity words are singular or plural. If the object of the preposition in the phrase following the pronoun is singular, the pronoun takes a singular verb; if the object is plural, the pronoun takes a plural verb.

Singular or Plural
all
any
half
part
most
none
some

Most of the song thrills us.

Most of the songs thrill us.

Notice the shift in meaning, depending on the prepositional phrase. "Most of the song" means that one song is mostly thrilling. "Most of the songs" means that all but a few of many songs are thrilling. Here's another startling difference.

Half of the concert features Tchaikovsky.

Half of the concerts feature Tchaikovsky.

In the first example, half of one concert features the Russian master. In the second example, half of many concerts feature Tchaikovsky's music. What a difference one *s* can make!

Say It

Read the following word groups aloud, emphasizing the words in *italics*.
1. Both *are* / Few *have* / Many *do* / Several *were*
2. All of the piece *is* / Any of the pieces *are* / Half of the piece *does*
3. Part of the song *is* / Most of the songs *are* /
   None of the instruments *are* / Part of the instrument *is*

Correcting Indefinite Pronoun Agreement II

Write For each blank below, write the correct form of the verb in parentheses. (Do not change the tense.)

1. Several _____ attending, but all of us _____ listening. (are)

2. All of the songs _____ dramatic, but all of the drama _____ intentional. (is)

3. Everyone _____ Tchaikovsky, but few _____ only him. (likes)

4. One of my friends _____ to classical radio; several _____ to MP3's. (listen)

5. Half of the album _____ symphonies, and half of the symphonies _____ brass fanfares. (feature)

6. Most of us _____ about music, and some of us _____ music, too. (read)

7. Of the music fans, several _____ hard-core, but none of them _____ a composer. (is)

8. One of my friends _____ trombone, and some of my friends _____ piano. (play)

9. Few _____ played in an orchestra, but one of us _____ played in a band. (has)

CONSIDER SPEAKING AND LISTENING

After completing the sentences in the first exercise, say them aloud, emphasizing the underlined verbs.

Write Write sentences using each indefinite pronoun as a subject. Choose present tense verbs and check subject-verb agreement.

1. Part _____

2. Most _____

3. Few _____

4. Several _____

5. Both _____

6. All _____

LO5 Pronoun-Antecedent Agreement

A pronoun must agree in **person**, **number**, and **gender** with its **antecedent**. (The antecedent is the word the pronoun replaces.)

The woman brought her briefcase but forgot her computer.

antecedent
(third person singular feminine)

+

pronoun
(third person singular feminine)

=

agreement

Quick Guide

	Singular	Plural
First Person:	I, me (my, mine)	we, us (our, ours)
Second Person:	you (your, yours)	you (your, yours)
Third Person: masculine feminine neuter	 he, him (his) she, her (her, hers) it (its)	 they, them (their, theirs) they, them (their, theirs) they, them (their, theirs)

Two or More Antecedents

When two or more antecedents are joined by *and,* the pronoun should be plural.

Kali and Teri filled their baskets with eggs.

When two or more singular antecedents are joined by *or, nor,* or *but also,* the pronoun or pronouns should be singular.

Kali or Teri filled her basket with eggs.

Not only Kali but also Teri filled her basket with eggs.

NOTE: Avoid sexism when choosing pronouns that agree in number.

Sexist: Each child should bring his basket.
Correct: Each child should bring her or his basket.
Correct: Children should bring their baskets.

Correcting Pronoun-Antecedent Agreement

Write For each blank below, write the pronoun that agrees with the underlined word or words.

1. <u>Ted</u> has written a patriotic poem and _____ will read _____ poem at the Fourth of July festival.

2. <u>Shandra</u> and <u>Shelli</u> will bring _____ lawn chairs to the fireworks display.

3. Either <u>John</u> or <u>Grace</u> will play _____ or _____ favorite marches over the sound system.

4. Not only <u>John</u> but also <u>Dave</u> plays trombone and will bring _____ instrument to play with the band.

5. Each <u>person</u> should bring _____ or _____ own flag.

6. <u>Mayor Jenny White</u> or <u>Congressperson Mark Russell</u> will give the invocation, and then _____ or _____ will introduce the main speaker.

7. <u>Rick</u> and <u>Linda</u> will sing _____ rendition of the national anthem.

8. <u>Acrobats</u> will stroll through the park on _____ ten-foot-tall stilts.

9. Each <u>acrobat</u> will have to keep _____ or _____ balance on uneven ground among running children.

10. <u>Ducks</u> and <u>ducklings</u> in the lake will have to make _____ way to quieter waters when the fireworks begin.

Revise Rewrite each of the following sentences to avoid sexism.

1. Every acrobat should check his equipment.

   _____

2. Each acrobat must keep her balance.

   _____

3. One of the acrobats left his stilts at the park.

   _____

Vocabulary

person
the person speaking (first person—*I, we*), the person being spoken to (second person—*you*), or the person being spoken about (third person—*he, she, it, they*)

number
singular or plural

gender
masculine, feminine, neuter, or indefinite

antecedent
the noun (or pronoun) that a pronoun refers to or replaces

LO6 Other Pronoun Problems

Missing Antecedent

If no clear antecedent is provided, the reader doesn't know what or whom the pronoun refers to.

Confusing: In Illinois, they claim Lincoln as their own.
(Who does "they" refer to?)
Clear: In Illinois, the citizens claim Lincoln as their own.

Vague Pronoun

If the pronoun could refer to two or more words, the passage is **ambiguous**.

Indefinite: Sheila told her daughter to use her new tennis racket.
(To whom does the pronoun "her" refer, Sheila or her daughter?)
Clumsy: Sheila told her daughter to use Sheila's new tennis racket.
Clear: Sheila lent her new tennis racket to her daughter.

Double Subject

If a pronoun is used right after the subject, an error called a double subject occurs.

Incorrect: Your father, he is good at poker.
Correct: Your father is good at poker

INSIGHT

Use *my* before the thing possessed and use *mine* afterward: *my cat,* but *that cat is mine.* Do the same with *our/ours, your/yours,* and *her/hers.*

Incorrect Case

Personal pronouns can function as subjects, objects, or possessives. If the wrong case is used, an error occurs.

Subject	Object	Possessive
I	me	my, mine
we	us	our, ours
you	you	your, yours
he	him	his
she	her	her, hers
it	it	its
they	them	their, theirs

Incorrect: Them are funny videos.

Correct: They are funny videos.

The list on the right tells you which pronouns to use in each case.

Correcting Other Pronoun Problems

Write For each blank below, write the correct pronoun from the choices in parentheses.

1. _____ need to help_____ with the taxes.

   (I, me, my, mine)   (you, your, yours)

2. _____ should help_____ and see what_____ needs.

   (you, your, yours)   (she, her, hers)   (she, her, hers)

3. _____ can show _____ that account of _____ .

   (he, him, his)   (I, me, my, mine)   (you, your, yours)

4. _____ gave_____ permission for_____ to see.

   (you, your, yours)   (you, your, yours)   (I, me, my, mine)

5. _____ asked_____ accountant to help _____ .

   (we, us, our, ours)   (we, us, our, ours)   (we, us, our, ours)

Revise Rewrite each sentence below, correcting the pronoun problems.

1. Bob and Josh took his assignment to class.

   _____

2. Lupita needed to visit with Kelly, but she had no time.

   _____

3. Before climbing in, it broke.

   _____

4. They say that a cure for cancer is coming.

   _____

5. Trina and Lois, they bought frozen custard.

   _____

6. Carl asked Tim to cook his lunch.

   _____

Vocabulary

ambiguous
unclear, confusing

M. Unal Ozmen, 2011 / Used under license from Shutterstock.com

LO7 Real-World Application

Correct In the letter below, correct the agreement errors. Write the line number and any word you would change. Then show the change. Use the correction marks at the bottom of the page.

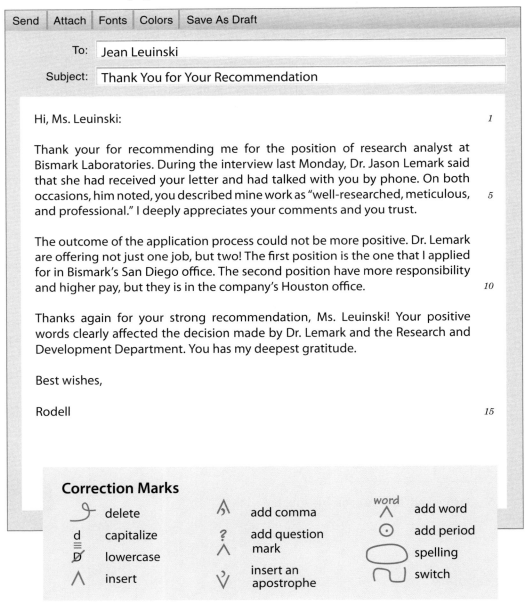

| Send | Attach | Fonts | Colors | Save As Draft |

To: Jean Leuinski

Subject: Thank You for Your Recommendation

Hi, Ms. Leuinski: 1

Thank your for recommending me for the position of research analyst at Bismark Laboratories. During the interview last Monday, Dr. Jason Lemark said that she had received your letter and had talked with you by phone. On both occasions, him noted, you described mine work as "well-researched, meticulous,   5 and professional." I deeply appreciates your comments and you trust.

The outcome of the application process could not be more positive. Dr. Lemark are offering not just one job, but two! The first position is the one that I applied for in Bismark's San Diego office. The second position have more responsibility and higher pay, but they is in the company's Houston office.   10

Thanks again for your strong recommendation, Ms. Leuinski! Your positive words clearly affected the decision made by Dr. Lemark and the Research and Development Department. You has my deepest gratitude.

Best wishes,

Rodell   15

Correction Marks

- ⌓ delete
- d̲ capitalize
- ꝃ lowercase
- ⋀ insert
- ⌐⁄ add comma
- ? add question mark
- ⌄̓ insert an apostrophe
- word ⋀ add word
- ⊙ add period
- ⟳ spelling
- ⟳ switch

16

> "I say that what we really need is a car that can be shot when it breaks down.'"
> —Russell Baker

Sentence Problems

Cars are great when they go, but when a car breaks down, it is a huge headache. There's going to be a look under the hood, a bit of scrabbling beneath the thing, maybe a push, maybe a jack, and probably a tow truck and a big bill.

Sentences also are great until they break down. But you don't have to be a skilled mechanic to fix sentences. This chapter outlines a few common sentence problems and shows how to fix them. You'll be on your way in no time!

Learning Outcomes

LO1 Correct common fragments.

LO2 Correct tricky fragments.

LO3 Correct comma splices.

LO4 Correct run-on sentences.

LO5 Correct rambling sentences.

LO6 Correct misplaced and dangling modifiers.

LO7 Correct shifts in sentence construction.

LO8 Check for fragments in a real-world context.

LO9 Correct comma splices and run-ons in a real-world context.

LO10 Correct sentence problems in a real-world context.

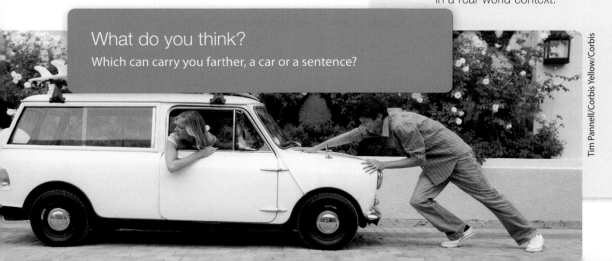

What do you think?

Which can carry you farther, a car or a sentence?

Tim Pannell/Corbis Yellow/Corbis

LO1 Common Fragments

In spoken communication and informal writing, sentence fragments are occasionally used and understood. In formal writing, fragments should be avoided.

Missing Parts

A sentence requires a subject and a predicate. If one or the other or both are missing, the sentence is a **fragment**. Such fragments can be fixed by supplying the missing part.

Fragment:	Went to the concert.
Fragment + Subject:	We went to the concert.
Fragment:	Everyone from Westville Community College.
Fragment + Predicate:	Everyone from Westville Community College may participate.
Fragment:	For the sake of student safety.
Fragment + Subject and Predicate:	The president set up a curfew for the sake of student safety.

Incomplete Thoughts

A sentence also must express a complete thought. Some fragments have a subject and a verb but do not express a complete thought. These fragments can be corrected by providing words that complete the thought.

Fragment:	The concert will include.
Completing Thought:	The concert will include an amazing light show.
Fragment:	If we arrive in time.
Completing Thought:	If we arrive in time, we'll get front-row seats.
Fragment:	That opened the concert.
Completing Thought:	I liked the band that opened the concert.

> **Say It**
>
> Read these fragments aloud. Then read each one again, but this time supply the necessary words to form a complete thought.
> 1. The student union building.
> 2. Where you can buy used books.
> 3. Walked to class every morning.
> 4. When the instructor is sick.
> 5. The cop was.

Correct Add words to correct each fragment below. Write the complete sentence on the lines provided.

1. Went to the office.

_____

2. The photographer, standing at the door.

_____

3. Will debate the pros and cons of tanning.

_____

4. Native Americans.

_____

5. Is one of the benefits of art class.

_____

Correct The following paragraph contains numerous fragments. Either add what is missing or combine fragments with other sentences to make them complete. Use the correction marks shown below.

> Some people are good at memorizing facts. They piece things together. *1*
> Like the inside of a jigsaw puzzle. Slowly build a big picture. Others are
> better at grasping overall shapes. Then filling in the middle with facts.
> Either way, have to finish the puzzle.

Correction Marks

ℐ delete	⋏ add comma	word ∧ add word
d capitalize	? add question mark	⊙ add period
⊘ lowercase	∧	spelling
∧ insert	⌄ insert an apostrophe	switch

Correct On your own paper or orally, correct the following fragments by supplying the missing parts. Use your imagination.

1. In the newspaper.
2. We bought.
3. The purpose of sociology class.
4. Somewhere above the clouds tonight.
5. Was the reason.

Vocabulary

fragment
a group of words that is missing a subject or a predicate (or both) or that does not express a complete thought

LO2 Tricky Fragments

Some fragments are more difficult to find and correct. They creep into our writing because they are often part of the way we communicate in our speaking.

Absolute Phrases

An **absolute phrase** looks like a sentence that is missing its helping verb. An absolute phrase can be made into a sentence by adding the helping verb or by connecting the phrase to a complete sentence.

Absolute Phrase (Fragment):	Our legs trembling from the hike.
Absolute Phrase + Helping Verb:	Our legs were trembling from the hike.
Absolute Phrase + Complete Sentence:	We collapsed on the couch, our legs trembling from the hike.

Informal Fragments

Fragments that are commonly used in speech should be eliminated from formal writing. Avoid the following types of fragments unless you are writing dialogue.

Interjections:	Hey! Yeah!	**Questions:**	How come? Why not? What?
Exclamations:	What a nuisance! How fun!		
Greetings:	Hi, everybody. Good afternoon.	**Answers:**	About three or four. As soon as possible.

NOTE: Sentences that begin with *here* or *there* have a **delayed subject**, which appears after the verb. Other sentences (commands) have an **implied subject** (*you*). Such sentences are not fragments.

> **Delayed Subject:**   Here are some crazy fans wearing wild hats.
> **Implied Subject:**   Tackle him! Bring him down!

Say It

Read these fragments aloud. Then add words to form a complete thought.
1. Are three types of laptop computers.
2. Our instructor explaining the assignment.
3. About three in the morning.
4. Is my favorite Web site.
5. My friend working at a half-priced disk shop.

Complete   Rewrite each tricky fragment below, making it a sentence.

1. Our boisterous behavior announcing our approach.

   _____

2. A tidy hedge surrounding the trimmed lawn.

   _____

3. The owner's gaze tracking us from the front porch.

   _____

4. His dogs barking loudly from the backyard.

   _____

5. Our welcome feeling less likely with each step.

   _____

Delete   The following paragraph contains a number of informal fragments. Identify and delete each one. Reread the paragraph and listen for the difference.

> Wow! It's amazing what archaeologists can discover from bones.   *1*
> Did you know that Cro-Magnon (our ancestors) and Neanderthal tribes
> sometimes lived side by side? Sure did! In other places, when climate
> change drove our ancestors south, Neanderthals took their place.
> Neanderthals were tough and had stronger arms and hands than Cro-   *5*
> Magnons had. Neanderthal brains were bigger, too. What? So why aren't
> there any Neanderthals around now? Huh? Well, although Neanderthal
> tribes used spears and stone tools, our ancestors were much better
> toolmakers. Yeah! Also, Neanderthals mainly ate big animals, while Cro-
> Magnon ate anything from fish to pigs to roots and berries. So in the long   *10*
> run, Cro-Magnon hominids prospered while Neanderthal tribes dwindled
> away.

Vocabulary

absolute phrase	**delayed subject**	**implied subject**
a group of words with a noun and a participle (a word ending in *ing* or *ed*) and the words that modify them	a subject that appears after the verb, as in a sentence that begins with *here* or *there* or a sentence that asks a question	the word *you*, assumed to begin command sentences

LO3 Comma Splices

Comma splices occur when two sentences are connected with only a comma. A comma splice can be fixed by adding a coordinating conjunction (*and, but, or, nor, for, so,* or *yet*) or a subordinating conjunction (*while, after, when,* and so on). The two sentences could also be joined by a semicolon (;) or separated by a period.

Comma Splice: The Eiffel Tower was a main attraction at the Paris Exposition, the Ferris wheel was its equivalent at the Chicago Exposition.

Corrected by adding a coordinating conjunction:	The Eiffel Tower was a main attraction at the Paris Exposition, and the Ferris wheel was its equivalent at the Chicago Exposition.
Corrected by adding a subordinating conjunction:	While the Eiffel Tower was a main attraction at the Paris Exposition, the Ferris wheel was its equivalent at the Chicago Exposition.
Corrected by replacing the comma with a semicolon:	The Eiffel Tower was a main attraction at the Paris Exposition; the Ferris wheel was its equivalent at the Chicago Exposition.

INSIGHT

A comma is not strong enough to join sentences without a conjunction. A semicolon can join two closely related sentences. A period or question mark can separate two sentences.

Comma Splice: An engineer named George Washington Gale Ferris planned the first Ferris wheel, many people thought he was crazy.

Corrected by adding a coordinating conjunction:	An engineer named George Washington Gale Ferris planned the first Ferris wheel, but many people thought he was crazy.
Corrected by adding a subordinating conjunction:	When an engineer named George Washington Gale Ferris planned the first Ferris wheel, many people thought he was crazy.
Corrected by replacing the comma with a period:	An engineer named George Washington Gale Ferris planned the first Ferris wheel. Many people thought he was crazy.

Correcting Comma Splices

Practice A   Correct the following comma splices by adding a coordinating conjunction (*and, but, yet, or, nor, for, so*), adding a subordinating conjunction (*when, while, because,* and so on), or replacing the comma with a semicolon or period. Use the approach that makes the sentence read most smoothly.

1. We set out for a morning hike, it was raining.

2. The weather cleared by the afternoon, we hit the trail.

3. Both Jill and I were expecting wonderful scenery, we were not disappointed.

4. The view of the valley was spectacular, it was like a portrait.

5. We snacked on granola bars and apples, we enjoyed the view.

6. Then we strapped on our backpacks, the final leg of the hike awaited us.

7. The trail became rockier, we had to watch our step.

8. We reached the end of our hike, the sun was setting.

9. We're on the lookout for a new trail, it will be tough to beat this one.

10. We're done with our physical activities, it is time to watch a movie.

Practice B   Correct any comma splices in the following e-mail message.

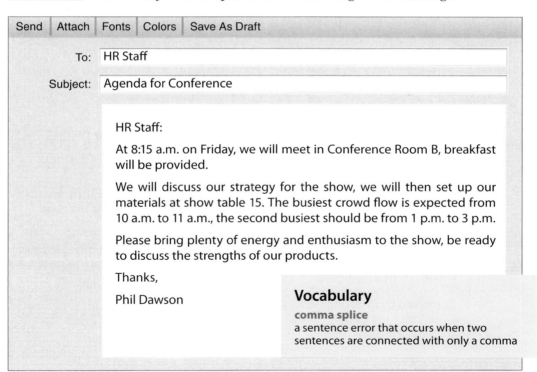

| Send | Attach | Fonts | Colors | Save As Draft |

To: HR Staff

Subject: Agenda for Conference

HR Staff:

At 8:15 a.m. on Friday, we will meet in Conference Room B, breakfast will be provided.

We will discuss our strategy for the show, we will then set up our materials at show table 15. The busiest crowd flow is expected from 10 a.m. to 11 a.m., the second busiest should be from 1 p.m. to 3 p.m.

Please bring plenty of energy and enthusiasm to the show, be ready to discuss the strengths of our products.

Thanks,

Phil Dawson

Vocabulary

comma splice
a sentence error that occurs when two sentences are connected with only a comma

LO4 Run-On Sentences

A **run-on sentence** occurs when two sentences are joined without punctuation or a connecting word. A run-on can be corrected by adding a comma and a conjunction or by inserting a semicolon or period between the two sentences.

Run-On: Horace Wilson taught in Tokyo in 1872 he introduced the Japanese to baseball.

Corrected by adding a comma and coordinating conjunction:	Horace Wilson taught in Tokyo in 1872, and he introduced the Japanese to baseball.
Corrected by adding a subordinating conjunction and a comma:	While Horace Wilson taught in Tokyo in 1872, he introduced the Japanese to baseball.
Corrected by inserting a semicolon:	Horace Wilson taught in Tokyo in 1872; he introduced the Japanese to baseball.

CONSIDER THE TRAITS

Here's an additional way to correct a run-on sentence: Turn one of the sentences into a phrase or series of phrases; then combine it with the other sentence.

> *The first team in Japan was formed in 1878 without a thought about how popular the sport would become.*

Run-On: The first team in Japan was formed in 1878 no one knew how popular the sport would become.

Corrected by adding a comma and a coordinating conjunction:	The first team in Japan was formed in 1878, yet no one knew how popular the sport would become.
Corrected by adding a subordinating conjunction and a comma:	When the first team in Japan was formed in 1878, no one knew how popular the sport would become.
Corrected by inserting a period:	The first team in Japan was formed in 1878. No one knew how popular the sport would become.

Correcting Run-On Sentences

Correct   Correct the following run-on sentences. Use the approach that makes the sentence read most smoothly.

1. In 1767 English scientist Joseph Priestley discovered a way to infuse water with carbon dioxide this invention led to carbonated water.

2. Carbonated water is one of the main components of soft drinks it gives soft drinks the fizz and bubbles we enjoy.

3. The first soft drinks in America were dispensed out of soda fountains they were most often found at drug stores and ice-cream parlors.

4. Interestingly, soda was sold at drug stores it promised healing properties.

5. Most of the formulas for American soft drinks were invented by pharmacists the idea was to create nonalcoholic alternatives to traditional medicines.

6. The first carbonated drink bottles could not keep bubbles from escaping it was more popular to buy a soda from a soda fountain.

7. A successful method of keeping bubbles in a bottle was not invented until 1892 it was called a crowned bottle cap.

8. The first diet soda to be sold was known as "No-Cal Beverage" in 1959 the first diet cola hit the stores.

Rewrite   Rewrite the following paragraph, correcting any run-on sentences that you find.

> Arbor Day is an undervalued holiday in America. On this holiday, people are encouraged to plant trees it is celebrated on the fourth Friday of April. It was created by J. Sterling Morton he was President Grover Cleveland's Secretary of Agriculture. The holiday is now observed in a number of other countries.
>
> 1
>
> 5

Vocabulary

run-on sentence
a sentence error that occurs when two sentences are joined without punctuation *or* a connecting word

LO5 Rambling Sentences

A **rambling sentence** occurs when a long series of separate ideas are connected by one *and, but,* or *so* after another. The result is an unfocused sentence that goes on and on. To correct a rambling sentence, break it into smaller units, adding and cutting words as needed.

Rambling: When we signed up for the two-on-two tournament, I had no thoughts about winning, but then my brother started talking about spending his prize money and he asked me how I would spend my share so we were counting on winning when we really had little chance and as it turned out, we lost in the second round.

Corrected: When we signed up for the two-on-two tournament, I had no thoughts about winning. Then my brother started talking about spending the prize money. He even asked me how I would spend my share. Soon, we were counting on winning when we really had little chance. As it turned out, we lost in the second round.

Say It

Read the following rambling sentences aloud. Afterward, circle all of the connecting words (*and, but, so*), and be prepared to suggest different ways to break each rambling idea into more manageable units.

1. I enjoyed touring the hospital and I would enjoy joining the nursing staff and I believe that my prior work experience will be an asset but I also know that I have a lot more to learn.

2. The electronics store claims to offer "one-stop shopping" and they can take care of all of a customer's computer needs and they have a fully trained staff to answer questions and solve problems so there is really no need to go anywhere else.

Losevsky Pavel, 2011 / Used under license from Shutterstock.com

Correcting Rambling Sentences

Correct Correct the following rambling sentences by dividing them into separate sentences. Afterward, share your corrections with a classmate.

1. The dancer entered gracefully onto the stage and she twirled around twice and then tiptoed to the front of the stage and the crowd applauded.

   _____

2. I went to the movies last night and when I got to the theater, I had to wait in a super-slow line and when I finally got to the front, the show I wanted to see was sold out.

   _____

3. I like to listen to music everywhere but I especially like to rock out in my car so I scream and dance and I don't care if anyone sees me through the windows.

   _____

CONSIDER EXTENDING

Share your corrections with a classmate. Did you change each rambling sentence in the same way?

Answer Answer the following questions about rambling sentences.

1. How can you recognize a rambling sentence?

   _____

2. Why is a rambling sentence a problem?

   _____

3. How can you correct one?

   _____

Vocabulary

rambling sentence
a sentence error that occurs when a long series of separate ideas are connected by one *and, but,* or *so* after another

LO6 Misplaced/Dangling Modifiers

Dangling Modifiers

A modifier is a word, phrase, or clause that functions as an adjective or adverb. When the modifier does not clearly modify another word in the sentence, it is called a **dangling modifier**. This error can be corrected by inserting the missing word and/or rewriting the sentence.

Dangling Modifier: After strapping the toy cowboy to his back, my cat stalked sullenly around the house.
(The cat could strap the toy cowboy to his own back?)

Corrected: After I strapped the toy cowboy to his back, my cat stalked sullenly around the house.

Dangling Modifier: Trying to get the cowboy off, the bowl got knocked off the shelf. *(The bowl was trying to get the cowboy off?)*

Corrected: Trying to get the cowboy off, the cat knocked the bowl off the shelf.

Misplaced Modifiers

When a modifier is placed beside a word that it does not modify, the modifier is misplaced and often results in an amusing or **illogical** statement. A **misplaced modifier** can be corrected by moving it next to the word that it modifies.

Misplaced Modifier: My cat was diagnosed by the vet with fleas.
(The vet has fleas?)

Corrected: The vet diagnosed my cat with fleas.

Misplaced Modifier: The vet gave a pill to my cat tasting like fish.
(The cat tastes like fish?)

Corrected: The vet gave my cat a pill tasting like fish.

INSIGHT

Avoid placing any adverb modifiers between a verb and its direct object.
  Misplaced: I will throw quickly the ball.
  Corrected: I will quickly throw the ball.
Also, do not separate two-word verbs with an adverb modifier.
  Misplaced: Please take immediately out the trash.
  Corrected: Please immediately take out the trash.

Say It

Read the following sentences aloud, noting the dangling or misplaced modifier in each one. Then tell a classmate how you would correct each error.
1. After tearing up the couch, I decided to get my cat a scratching post.
2. I have worked to teach my cat to beg for three weeks.

Correcting Dangling and Misplaced Modifiers

Rewrite Rewrite each of the sentences below, correcting the misplaced and dangling modifiers.
1. I bought a hound dog for my brother named Rover. _____
2. The doctor diagnosed me and referred me to a specialist with scoliosis. _____
3. The man was reported murdered by the coroner. _____
4. Please present the recommendation that is attached to Mrs. Burble. _____
5. Jack drove me to our home in a Chevy. _____
6. I couldn't believe my brother would hire a disco DJ who hates disco. _____
7. We saw a fox and a vixen on the way to the psychiatrist. _____
8. I gave the secretary my phone number that works in reception. _____
9. I found a pair of underwear in the drawer that doesn't belong to me. _____
10. We offer jackets for trendy teens with gold piping. _____

Correct For each sentence, correct the placement of the adverb.
1. Give quickly the report to your boss. _____
2. We will provide immediately an explanation. _____
3. Fill completely out the test sheet. _____

INSIGHT

When a modifier comes at the beginning of the sentence or the end of the sentence, make sure it modifies the word or phrase closest to it. Ask yourself, "Who or what is being described?"

Vocabulary

dangling modifier
a modifying word, phrase, or clause that appears to modify the wrong word or a word that isn't in the sentence

illogical
without logic; senseless, false, or untrue

misplaced modifier
a modifying word, phrase, or

clause that has been placed incorrectly in a sentence, often creating an amusing or illogical idea

LO7 Shifts in Sentences

Shift in Person

A **shift in person** is an error that occurs when first, second, and/or third person are improperly mixed in a sentence.

Shift in person:	If you exercise and eat right, an individual can lose weight. (The sentence improperly shifts from second person—*you*—to third person—*individual*.)
Corrected:	If you exercise and eat right, you can lose weight.

Shift in Tense

A **shift in tense** is an error that occurs when more than one verb tense is improperly used in a sentence.

Shift in tense:	He tried every other option before he agrees to do it my way. (The sentence improperly shifts from past tense—*tried*—to present tense—*agrees*.)
Corrected:	He tried every other option before he agreed to do it my way.

Shift in Voice

A **shift in voice** is an error that occurs when active voice and passive voice are mixed in a sentence.

Shift in voice:	When she fixes the radiator, other repairs may be suggested. (The sentence improperly shifts from active voice—*fixes*—to passive voice—*may be suggested*.)
Corrected:	When she fixes the radiator, she may suggest other repairs.

Say It

Read the following sentences aloud, paying careful attention to the improper shift each contains. Then tell a classmate how you would correct each error.

1. David exercises daily and ate well.
2. Marianne goes running each morning and new friends might be met.
3. After you choose an exercise routine, a person should stick to it.
4. Lamar swam every morning and does ten laps.
5. The personal trainer made a schedule for me, and a diet was suggested by her.

Correcting Improper Shifts in Sentences

Rewrite   Rewrite each sentence below, correcting any improper shifts in construction.

1. You should be ready for each class in a person's schedule. _____

2. I work for my brother most days and classes are attended by me at night.___

3. When you give me a review, can he also give me a raise? _____

4. As we walked to school, last night's football game was discussed by us. _____

5. I hoped to catch the bus until I see it leave. _____

Correct   Correct the improper shifts in person, tense, or voice in the following paragraph. Use the correction marks below when you make your changes.

> Some people are early adopters, which means technology is adopted   *1*
> by them when it is new. Other people are technophobes because you are
> afraid of technology, period. I am not an early adopter or a technophobe,
> but a person has to see the value in technology before I use it. Technology
> has to be cheap, intuitive, reliable, and truly helpful before you start using   *5*
> it. I let others work out the bugs and pay the high prices before a piece
> of technology is adopted by me. But when I decide it is time to get a new
> gadget or program, you buy it and use it until it is worn out. Then I look
> for something else that is even cheaper and more intuitive, reliable, and
> helpful, which is then bought by me.   *10*

Correction Marks

℘ delete	⅄ add comma	⌄̂ᵂᵒʳᵈ add word
d̳ capitalize	? add question	⊙ add period
∅̶ lowercase	∧ mark	⌒ spelling
∧ insert	⌄ insert an apostrophe	∪ switch

Vocabulary

person
first person (*I* or *we*—the person speaking), second person (*you*—the person spoken to), or third person (*he, she, it,* or *they*—the person or thing spoken about)

voice of verb
whether the subject is doing the action of the verb (active voice) or is being acted upon (passive voice)

shift in person
an error that occurs when first, second, and third person are improperly mixed in a sentence

shift in tense
an error that occurs when more than one verb tense is improperly used in a sentence

shift in voice
an error that occurs when active voice and passive voice are mixed in a sentence

LO8 Real-World Application 1

Correct Correct any sentence fragments in the following business memo. Use the correction marks below.

Slovik Manufacturing   *1*

Date: August 8, 2011

To: Jerome James, Personnel Director

From: Ike Harris, Graphic Arts Director

Subject: Promotion of Mona Veal from Intern to Full-Time Graphic Artist   *5*

For the past five months, Mona Veal as an intern in our Marketing Department. I recommend that she be offered a position as a full-time designer. Are the two main reasons behind this recommendation.

1. Mona has shown the traits that Slovik Manufacturing values in a graphic designer. Creative, dependable, and easy to work with.   *10*

2. Presently, we have two full-time graphic designers and one intern. While this group has worked well. The full-time designers have averaged 3.5 hours of overtime per week. Given this fact. Our new contract with Lee-Stamp Industries will require more help, including at least one additional designer.   *15*

If you approve this recommendation. Please initial below and return this memo.

Yes, I approve the recommendation to offer Mona Veal a full-time position.

Attachment: Evaluation report of Mona Veal   *20*

cc: Elizabeth Zoe
    Mark Moon

Correction Marks

Mark	Meaning	Mark	Meaning	Mark	Meaning
⟍	delete	⋀	add comma	word ∧	add word
d ≡	capitalize	? ∧	add question mark	⊙	add period
∅	lowercase	∧			spelling
∧	insert	∨	insert an apostrophe		switch

LO9 Real-World Application 2

Correct Correct any comma splices or run-on sentences in the following e-mail message. Use the correction marks on the previous page.

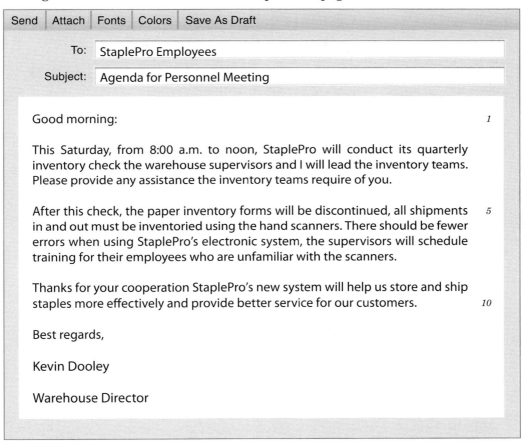

| Send | Attach | Fonts | Colors | Save As Draft |

To: StaplePro Employees

Subject: Agenda for Personnel Meeting

Good morning: *1*

This Saturday, from 8:00 a.m. to noon, StaplePro will conduct its quarterly inventory check the warehouse supervisors and I will lead the inventory teams. Please provide any assistance the inventory teams require of you.

After this check, the paper inventory forms will be discontinued, all shipments   *5*
in and out must be inventoried using the hand scanners. There should be fewer errors when using StaplePro's electronic system, the supervisors will schedule training for their employees who are unfamiliar with the scanners.

Thanks for your cooperation StaplePro's new system will help us store and ship staples more effectively and provide better service for our customers.   *10*

Best regards,

Kevin Dooley

Warehouse Director

Reflect Reflect on what you have learned about comma splices and run-on sentences by answering the following questions.

1. What is the difference between a comma splice and a run-on sentence?

2. How can you correct comma splices and run-on sentences? (Name at least three ways.)

3. What are three common coordinating conjunctions that you can use to connect two sentences?

LO10 Real-World Application 3

Correct Correct any dangling modifiers, misplaced modifiers, or shifts in construction in the following message. Use the correction marks below.

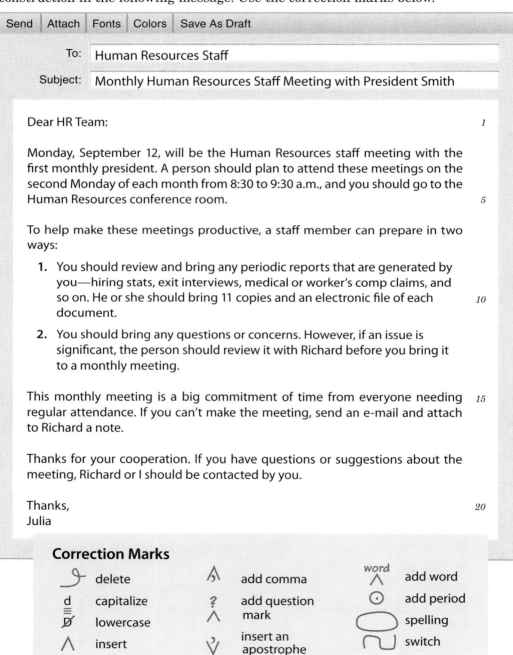

| Send | Attach | Fonts | Colors | Save As Draft |

To: Human Resources Staff

Subject: Monthly Human Resources Staff Meeting with President Smith

Dear HR Team: *1*

Monday, September 12, will be the Human Resources staff meeting with the
first monthly president. A person should plan to attend these meetings on the
second Monday of each month from 8:30 to 9:30 a.m., and you should go to the
Human Resources conference room.   *5*

To help make these meetings productive, a staff member can prepare in two
ways:

1. You should review and bring any periodic reports that are generated by
    you—hiring stats, exit interviews, medical or worker's comp claims, and
    so on. He or she should bring 11 copies and an electronic file of each   *10*
    document.

2. You should bring any questions or concerns. However, if an issue is
    significant, the person should review it with Richard before you bring it
    to a monthly meeting.

This monthly meeting is a big commitment of time from everyone needing   *15*
regular attendance. If you can't make the meeting, send an e-mail and attach
to Richard a note.

Thanks for your cooperation. If you have questions or suggestions about the
meeting, Richard or I should be contacted by you.

Thanks,   *20*
Julia

Correction Marks

ℐ	delete	⋀	add comma	⋀ *word*	add word
d̲̲	capitalize	? ⋀	add question mark	⊙	add period
D̸	lowercase			⌒	spelling
⋀	insert	⌄	insert an apostrophe	⌒	switch

Rewrite The sentences that follow come from church bulletins and are amusing due to misplaced or dangling modifiers or other sentence problems. Rewrite each sentence to remove these problems.

1. Remember in prayer the many who are sick of our church and community.

   _____

2. For those of you who have children and don't know it, we have a nursery downstairs.

   _____

3. The ladies of the church have cast off clothing of every kind. They can be seen in the church basement Saturday.

   _____

4. The third verse of "Blessed Assurance" will be sung without musical accomplishment.

   _____

Write Write the first draft of a personal narrative (true story) in which you share a time when you misplaced or lost something important to you or to someone else. Here are some tips for adding interest to your story:

- Start right in the middle of the action.
- Build suspense to keep the reader's interest.
- Use dialogue.
- Use sensory details (what you heard, saw, felt, and so on).

Afterward, exchange your writing with a classmate. Read each other's narrative first for enjoyment and a second time to check it for the sentence errors discussed in this chapter.

CONSIDER THE WORKPLACE

Journalists and publishers need to be especially careful to avoid mistakes in their writing. But errors in writing reflect badly on all professionals.

17

"The writer who neglects punctuation, or mispunctuates, is liable to be misunderstood for the want of merely a comma. "

—Edgar Allan Poe

Comma

When you speak, you communicate with much more than words. You pause, raise or lower your pitch, change your tone or volume, and use facial expressions and body language to get your point across.

When you write, you can forget about pitch or volume, facial expressions or body language. You're left with the tone of your words and with the pauses that you put in them. Commas give you one way to create a soft pause. They help to show which words belong together, which should be separated, and which line up in parallel. Commas are key to being understood.

In this chapter you will learn about the conventional use of commas. Understanding the correct comma usage is an important step in becoming a college-level writer.

Learning Outcomes

LO1 Use commas in compound sentences.

LO2 Use commas with introductory phrases and equal adjectives.

LO3 Use commas between items in a series.

LO4 Use commas with appositives and nonrestrictive modifiers.

LO5 Use commas in real-world writing.

What do you think?

Imagine reading a book or newspaper without punctuation. What difficulties may you encounter? Explain.

Monkey Business Images, 2011 / Used under license from Shutterstock.com

LO1 In Compound Sentences and After Introductory Clauses

The following principles will guide the use of commas in your writing.

In Compound Sentences

Use a comma before the coordinating conjunction *(and, but, or, nor, for, yet, so)* in a compound sentence.

Heath Ledger completed his brilliant portrayal as the Joker in *The Dark Knight*, **but** he died before the film was released.

NOTE: Do not confuse a compound verb with a compound sentence.

Ledger's Joker became instantly iconic and won him the Oscar for best supporting actor. *(compound verb)*

His death resulted from the abuse of prescription drugs, but it was ruled an accident. *(compound sentence)*

After Introductory Clauses

Use a comma after most introductory clauses.

Although Charlemagne was a great patron of learning, he never learned to write properly. (adverb dependent clause)

When the clause follows the independent clause and is not essential to the meaning of the sentence, use a comma. This comma use generally applies to clauses beginning with *even though, although, while,* or some other conjunction expressing a contrast.

Charlemagne never learned to write properly, **even though he continued to practice.**

NOTE: A comma is *not* used if the dependent clause following the independent clause is needed.

CONSIDER THE TRAITS

Make sure to use both a comma and a coordinating conjunction in a compound sentence, or you will create a comma splice or a run-on.

Correcting Comma Errors

Correct   If the clause on each side of the coordinating conjunction could stand alone as a sentence, add a comma. Write the words before and after the comma, showing the comma between them. Write "correct" if the conjunction separates word groups that can't stand alone.

1. Catherine had questions about her class schedule so she set up an appointment with her academic adviser.   _____

2. I was going to play in the sand volleyball league but it conflicted with my work schedule.   _____

3. Trisha picked up some groceries and stopped by the bank.   _____

4. I normally don't listen to jazz music yet I love going to summer jazz concerts in the park.   _____

5. Should I finish my essay a day early or should I go to my friend's house party?   _____

6. Kevin has a job interview at the advertisement agency and he hopes he can make a good impression.   _____

7. Creativity is his best quality but leadership is not far behind.   _____

Correct   If an introductory clause needs to be followed by a comma, write the words before and after the comma, showing it between them. If no comma is needed, write "correct."

1. Even though digital books are the craze I prefer paperbacks.   _____

2. Although the crab dip appetizer was delicious my entrée left something to be desired.   _____

3. Because I'm starved for time online shopping is a convenient alternative to mall shopping.   _____

4. I toggled through radio stations while I waited at the tollbooth.   _____

5. Erin worried about giving her speech even though she had practiced for weeks.   _____

LO2 With Introductory Words and Equal Adjectives

After Introductory Phrases

Use a comma after introductory phrases.

In spite of his friend's prodding, Jared decided to stay home and study.

A comma is usually omitted if the phrase follows an independent clause.

Jared decided to stay home and study **in spite of his friend's prodding.**

You may omit a comma after a short (four or fewer words) introductory phrase unless it is needed to ensure clarity.

At 10:32 p.m. he would quit and go to sleep.

To Separate Adjectives

Use commas to separate adjectives that equally modify the same noun. Notice in the examples below that no comma separates the last adjective from the noun.

You should exercise regularly and follow a **sensible, healthful** diet.

A good diet is one that includes lots of **high-protein, low-fat** foods.

To Determine Equal Modifiers

To determine whether adjectives modify a noun equally, use these two tests.

1. Reverse the order of the adjectives; if the sentence is clear, the adjectives modify equally. (In the example below, *hot* and *crowded* can be switched, but *short* and *coffee* cannot.)

   Matt was tired of working in the **hot, crowded** lab and decided to take a **short coffee** break.

2. Insert *and* between the adjectives; if the sentence reads well, use a comma when *and* is omitted. (The word *and* can be inserted between *hot* and *crowded*, but *and* does not make sense between *short* and *coffee*.)

Correcting Comma Errors

Correct If a comma is needed after the introductory phrase, write the words before and after the comma, with it between them. If no comma is needed, write "correct."

1. Before you send the e-mail make sure you reread it for errors in clarity. _____

2. In accordance with the academic code plagiarism is deemed a major offense. _____

3. After hitting the 10-mile jogging plateau Heather felt a great rush of adrenaline. _____

4. Heather felt a great rush of adrenaline after hitting the 10-mile jogging plateau. _____

5. Thankfully DeMarcus stopped the leak before it could do any real damage. _____

6. Based on his past experience Wilson decided against going to the concert. _____

7. To train for the triathlon Brent altered his diet. _____

8. At the end of the day Erin recorded her favorite show. _____

Correct For each sentence below, determine whether or not a comma is needed to separate the adjectives that modify the same noun. Write the two adjectives with the comma between them. Write "correct" if a comma is not needed.

1. I'm expecting this to be a **rocking after** party. _____

2. There's nothing like the **warm emerald** water off the Florida Gulf Coast. _____

3. The exercise program included a **calorie-burning cardio** session. _____

4. My **surly economics** professor is one of a kind. _____

5. I'm in desperate need of a **relaxing summer** vacation. _____

6. Marathon runners favor **light comfortable** shorts. _____

Photosani, 2011 / Used under license from Shutterstock.com

LO3 Between Items in a Series and Other Uses

Between Items in Series

Use commas to separate individual words, phrases, or clauses in a series. (A series contains at least three items.)

Many college students must balance studying with **taking care of a family, working, getting exercise, and finding time to relax.**

Do not use commas when all the items are connected with *or, nor,* or *and.*

Hmm . . . should I study **or** do laundry **or** go out?

To Set Off Transitional Expressions

Use a comma to set off conjunctive adverbs and transitional phrases.

Handwriting is not**, as a matter of fact,** easy to improve upon later in life; **however,** it can be done if you are determined enough.

If a transitional expression blends smoothly with the rest of the sentence, it does not need to be set off.

If you are **in fact** coming, I'll see you there.

To Set Off Dialogue

Use commas to set off the words of the speaker from the rest of the sentence. Do not use a comma before an indirect quotation.

"Never be afraid to ask for help," advised Ms. Kane

"With the evidence that we now have," Professor Thom said**, "many scientists believe there could be life on Mars."**

To Enclose Explanatory Words

Use commas to enclose an explanatory word or phrase.

Time management**, according to many professionals,** is an important skill that should be taught in college.

Correcting Comma Errors

Correct   Indicate where commas are needed. Write the words before and after the comma, showing the comma between them.

1. I considered becoming a lawyer; however law school wasn't for me.

2. "Don't give up, don't ever give up" advised the late Jim Valvano.

3. MGMT's music is infused with electronic beats, catchy lyrics and a pop-friendly sound.

4. Western Wisconsin as opposed to Illinois is relatively hilly.

5. In Boston I visited Fenway Park the U.S.S. *Constitution,* and Old North Church.

6. Thomas as you may have noticed is eager to share his vast knowledge of random facts.

7. In regard to public transportation, you may decide between the subway buses or taxicabs.

8. "While it certainly offers a convenient alternative to paper maps" said Emilie "my car's navigational system more often gets me lost."

9. Avocados the key ingredient of guacamole are a good source of fiber.

10. Secondly determine if weather price or transportation will factor into your decision.

Correct   Indicate where commas are needed. Write the line number and the words before and after the comma, showing the comma between them.

> On an early summer morning in July I sat slumped in a terminal   *1*
> at JFK airport, reminiscing about my time in Washington D.C. It had
> been a fun trip. I visited all the usual landmarks, including the Lincoln
> Memorial, Arlington National Cemetery and the Smithsonian Institute.
> However my favorite landmark was Mount Vernon the home and former   *5*
> estate of President George Washington. It's easy to see why Washington
> adored the location. The estate located in Alexandria, Virginia, is nestled
> above the Hudson River. Besides Washington's plantation home, the estate
> also included a distillery a blacksmith shop and acres of farmland. If you're
> ever in Washington D.C., I highly recommend a trip to Mount Vernon.   *10*

LO4 With Appositives and Other Word Groups

To Set Off Some Appositives

A specific kind of explanatory word or phrase called an **appositive** identifies or renames a preceding noun or pronoun.

Albert Einstein**, the famous mathematician and physicist,** developed the theory of relativity.

Do not use commas if the appositive is important to the basic meaning of the sentence.

The famous physicist **Albert Einstein** developed the theory of relativity.

With Some Clauses and Phrases

Use commas to enclose phrases or clauses that add information that is not necessary to the basic meaning of the sentence. For example, if the clause or phrase (in boldface) were left out of the two examples below, the meaning of the sentences would remain clear. Therefore, commas are used to set off the information.

The locker rooms in Swain Hall**, which were painted and updated last summer,** give professors a place to shower. (nonrestrictive clause)

Work-study programs**, offered on many campuses,** give students the opportunity to earn tuition money. (nonrestrictive phrase)

Do not use commas to set off necessary clauses and phrases, which add information that the reader needs to understand the sentence.

Only the professors **who run at noon** use the locker rooms. (necessary clause)

Using "That" or "Which"

Use *that* to introduce necessary clauses; use *which* to introduce unnecessary clauses.

Campus jobs **that are funded by the university** are awarded to students only. (necessary)

The cafeteria**, which is run by an independent contractor,** can hire nonstudents. (unnecessary)

Correcting Comma Errors

Correct   Indicate where commas are needed in the following sentences. Write the words before and after the comma and show the comma between them. If no commas are needed, write "correct."

1. The U.S.S. *Constitution* a wooden-hulled ship named by George Washington is the world's oldest floating commissioned naval vessel.   _____

2. Gordon Ramsay the fiery chef and television star specializes in French, Italian, and British cuisines.   _____

3. Hall of Fame baseball player and notable philanthropist Roberto Clemente died in a plane crash while en route to Nicaragua to deliver aid to earthquake victims.   _____

4. The concert hall which is on the corner of Meridian Ave and 1st Street is expected to revitalize the downtown district.   _____

5. Press passes that allow for backstage access are given out to special media members.   _____

6. John Quincy Adams who later became the sixth president of the United States authored the Monroe Doctrine in 1823.   _____

Write   The following sentences contain clauses using *that.* Rewrite the sentences with clauses using *which,* and insert commas correctly. You may need to reword some parts.

1. The mechanical issue that delayed the flight should be corrected within 25 minutes.

   _____

2. The wind farm that was built along I-95 is scheduled to double in size by 2016.

   _____

3. Scholarships that are sponsored by the Kiwanis Club are awarded to local high school students.

   _____

Vocabulary

appositive
a noun or noun phrase that renames another noun right beside it

LO5 Real-World Application

Correct Indicate where commas are needed in the following e-mail message. Write the line number and the words before and after the comma, showing it between them.

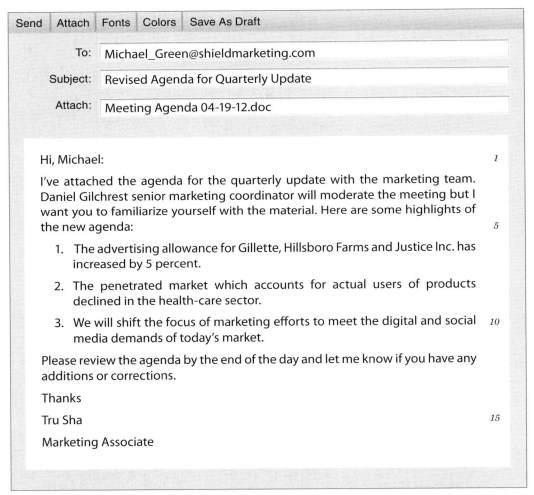

| Send | Attach | Fonts | Colors | Save As Draft |

To: Michael_Green@shieldmarketing.com

Subject: Revised Agenda for Quarterly Update

Attach: Meeting Agenda 04-19-12.doc

Hi, Michael: *1*

I've attached the agenda for the quarterly update with the marketing team. Daniel Gilchrest senior marketing coordinator will moderate the meeting but I want you to familiarize yourself with the material. Here are some highlights of the new agenda: *5*

1. The advertising allowance for Gillette, Hillsboro Farms and Justice Inc. has increased by 5 percent.

2. The penetrated market which accounts for actual users of products declined in the health-care sector.

3. We will shift the focus of marketing efforts to meet the digital and social   *10* media demands of today's market.

Please review the agenda by the end of the day and let me know if you have any additions or corrections.

Thanks

Tru Sha   *15*

Marketing Associate

CONSIDER THE WORKPLACE

Correct comma use is critical for clear business communication.

18

"Sometimes people give [book] titles to me, and sometimes I see them on a billboard."
—Robert Penn Warren

Quotation Marks and Italics

Broadway is plastered with billboards five stories high and is jammed with marquees that flash in the night. They advertise plays and movies, books and magazines, albums and TV shows—all in spotlights or neon trying to make people take notice.

In writing, there are no spotlights, there is no neon. Instead of writing the names of plays, movies, books, and so forth in giant, flashing letters, writers set them off with *italics*. This chapter will show you how to correctly punctuate titles of works big and small and words used as words.

Learning Outcomes

LO1 Understand the use of quotation marks.

LO2 Understand the use of italics.

LO3 Apply quotation marks and italics in a real-world document.

What do you think?

How are quotation marks and italics like flashing lights in writing? How are they different?

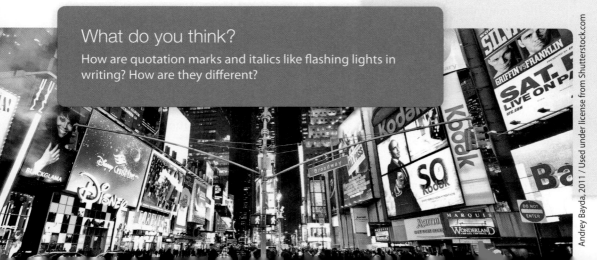

LO1 Quotation Marks

To Punctuate Titles (Smaller Works)

Use quotation marks to enclose the titles of smaller works, including speeches, short stories, songs, poems, episodes of audio or video programs, chapters or sections of books, unpublished works, and articles from magazines, journals, newspapers, or encyclopedias.

Speech:	"Ain't I a Woman?"
Song:	"California Girls"
Short Story:	"The Tell-Tale Heart"
Magazine Article:	"Is Google Making Us Stupid?"
Chapter in a Book:	"The Second Eve"
Television Episode:	"The Empty Child"
Encyclopedia Article:	"Autoban"

Placement of Periods and Commas

When quoted words end in a period or comma, always place that punctuation inside the quotation marks.

"When you leave the kitchen," Tim said, "turn out the light."

Placement of Semicolons and Colons

When a quotation is followed by a semicolon or colon, always place that punctuation outside the quotation marks.

I finally read "The Celebrated Jumping Frog of Calaveras County"; it is a hoot!

Placement of Exclamation Points and Question Marks

If an exclamation point or a question mark is part of the quotation, place it inside the quotation marks. Otherwise, place it outside.

Shawndra asked me, "Would you like to go to the movies?" What could I say except, "That sounds great"?

For Special Words

Quotation marks can be used (1) to show that a word is being referred to as the word itself; (2) to indicate that it is jargon, slang, or a coined term; or (3) to show that it is used in an ironic or sarcastic sense.

(1) The word "chuffed" is British slang for "very excited."
(2) I'm "chuffed" about my new computer.
(3) I'm "chuffed" about my root canal.

Using Quotation Marks

Correct   For the following sentences, write down words that should be in quotation marks, and show the marks.

1. Tim loves the short story Cask of Amontillado by Edgar Allan Poe.
2. Stephen King's short story The Body was made into a movie.
3. Anna Quindlen wrote the article Uncle Sam and Aunt Samantha.
4. Lisa told Jennie, Tonight is the pizza and pasta buffet.
5. Jennie asked, Isn't it buy one, get one free?
6. Was she thinking, That's a lot better than cooking?
7. Here is the main conflict of the story To Build a Fire: man versus nature.
8. I read an article entitled The Obese Fruit of Capitalism; it suggested that our modern obesity epidemic demonstrates the tremendous achievements of fast food and agribusiness.
9. What does the word hypertrophy mean?
10. I was thrilled to receive the unexpected bill.

Write   Write a sentence that indicates the actual meaning of each sentence below.

1. The fully loaded logging truck "tiptoed" across the one-lane bridge.

   _____

   _____

   _____

2. Enjoy our "fast" and "friendly" service.

   _____

   _____

   _____

3. We had a "fun" time at our IRS audit.

   _____

   _____

   _____

LO2 Italics

To Punctuate Titles (Larger Works)

Use italics to indicate the titles of larger works, including newspapers, magazines, journals, pamphlets, books, plays, films, radio and television programs, movies, ballets, operas, long musical compositions, CD's, DVD's, software programs, and legal cases, as well as the names of ships, trains, aircraft, and spacecraft.

Magazine: *The Week*	**Newspaper:** *Chicago Tribune*
Play: *Cat on a Hot Tin Roof*	**Journal:** *Nature*
Film: *Casablanca*	**Software Program:** *Final Draft*
Book: *Death's Disciples*	**Television Program:** *Doctor Who*

For a Word, Letter, or Number Referred to as Itself

Use italics (or quotation marks) to show that a word, letter, or number is being referred to as itself. If a definition follows a word used in this way, place that definition in quotation marks.

The word *courage* comes from the French word *cour,* which means "heart."

In the handwritten note, I couldn't distinguish an *N* from an *M*.

For Foreign Words

Use italics to indicate a word that is being borrowed from a foreign language.

The phrase *et cetera ad nauseum* is a Latin phrase meaning "and so on until vomiting."

For Technical Terms

Use italics to introduce a technical term for the first time in a piece of writing. After that, the term may be used without italics.

Particle physicists are seeking the elusive *Higgs boson*—a subatomic particle thought to provide mass to all other particles. The Higgs boson has become a sort of Holy Grail of quantum mechanics.

NOTE: If a technical term is being used within an organization or a field of study where it is common, it may be used without italics even the first time in a piece of writing.

Using Italics

Correct   For the following sentences, write down or underline words that should be in italics.

1. One of my favorite novels is The Curious Incident of the Dog in the Night-Time by Mark Haddon.

2. Have you seen the amazing movie Memento?

3. The name of the paso doble dance comes from the Spanish word for "double step."

4. In 1945, the bomber called the Enola Gay dropped the first atomic bomb, a weapon predicted in 1914 in the H. G. Wells novel The World Set Free.

5. She always has a real joie de vivre.

6. To look at the PDF, you need Adobe Reader or Adobe Acrobat.

7. In this context, the words profane and profanity do not refer to swearing but simply to things that are not divine.

8. The television show Project Runway pits fashion designers against each other.

9. In the musical A Funny Thing Happened on the Way to the Forum, the slave Pseudolus spells out his hope to be F – R – E – E.

10. The enlargement of muscles through weight lifting is known as hypertrophy.

Write   Write three sentences, each demonstrating your understanding of one or more rules for using italics.

1. _____

   _____

   _____

2. _____

   _____

   _____

3. _____

   _____

   _____

LO3 Real-World Application

Practice If a word in the following e-mail should be italicized or in quotation marks, write the line number and the word and show the correct punctuation.

| Send | Attach | Fonts | Colors | Save As Draft |

To: Will McMartin

Subject: Metrameme Author Bio

Hi, Will: *1*

Here is the author bio you requested from me to be published in my next book, War Child:

John Metrameme has published over a dozen novels, most recently the historical epic Sons of Thunder and the romp Daddy Zeus. He has written articles also for   *5*
The Atlantic and The New Yorker, and his short story Me and the Mudman won the Rubel Prize. Metrameme is perhaps best known for his novel Darling Buds of May.

In his spare time, Metrameme enjoys acting in productions at his community theater. He played himself in the three-man show The Complete Works of   *10*
William Shakespeare (Abridged). He also starred as Kit Gill in No Way to Treat a Lady and as Jonathan in Arsenic and Old Lace.

Will, please let me know if you need anything more from me.

Thanks,

John   *15*

Correction Marks

ℐ	delete	⅍	add comma	ᴡᴏʳᵈ ∧	add word
d̲	capitalize	?	add question mark	⊙	add period
ⱷ	lowercase	∧		⌒	spelling
∧	insert	ⱽ	insert an apostrophe	∿	switch

19

Other Punctuation

> "Once in a while you have to take a break and visit yourself."
> —Audrey Giorgi

Work is important, of course. Progress. Motion. Getting somewhere. And yet, sometimes it's important to pause and take a breath. Breaks allow you to work even more effectively afterward.

Written materials need pauses and breaks, too. It doesn't have to be a full stop (a period); maybe something softer will do. Semicolons, colons, and dashes can give the reader just the right break to be refreshed and to set out again. This chapter covers these three punctuation marks as well as the useful hyphen.

Learning Outcomes

LO1 Use apostrophes for contractions and possessives.

LO2 Use semicolons and colons correctly.

LO3 Understand hyphen use.

LO4 Use dashes well.

LO5 Apply apostrophes in real-world documents.

LO6 Apply punctuation in real-world documents.

What do you think?

Do you deserve a break? What kind? What kind of break does this sentence deserve if any?

Yuri Arcurs, 2011 / Used under license from Shutterstock.com

LO1 Contractions and Possessives

Apostrophes are used primarily to show that a letter or number has been left out, or that a noun is possessive.

Contractions

When one or more letters are left out of a word, use an apostrophe to form the **contraction**.

don't	he'd	would've
(*o* is left out)	(*woul* is left out)	(*ha* is left out)

Missing Characters

Use an apostrophe to signal when one or more characters are left out.

class of '16	rock 'n' roll	good mornin'
(*20* is left out)	(*a* and *d* are left out)	(*g* is left out)

Possessives

Form possessives of singular nouns by adding an apostrophe and an *s*.

Sharla's pen	the man's coat	*The Pilgrim's Progress*

Singular Noun Ending In *s* (One Syllable)

Form the possessive by adding an apostrophe and an *s*.

the boss's idea	the lass's purse	the bass's teeth

Singular Noun Ending In *s* (Two Or More Syllables)

Form the possessive by adding an apostrophe and an *s*—or by adding just an apostrophe.

Kansas's plains	*or*	Kansas' plains

Plural Noun Ending In *s*

Form the possessive by adding just an apostrophe.

the bosses' preference	the Smiths' home
the girl's ball	the girls' ball
(*girl* is the owner)	(*girls* are the owners)

Plural Noun Not Ending In *s*

Form the possessive by adding an apostrophe and an *s*.

the children's toys	the women's room

Forming Contractions and Possessives

Write   For each contraction below, write the words that formed the contraction. For each set of words, write the contraction that would be formed.

1. you're _____

2. John is _____

3. would have _____

4. she'd _____

5. you would _____

6. shouldn't _____

7. I had _____

8. they are _____

9. we've _____

10. it is _____

Rewrite   Rework the following sentences, replacing the "of" phrases with possessives using apostrophes.

1. I'm going to the house of Jeremy.

   _____

2. The ice cream of the corner stand is amazing.

   _____

3. The pace of the track star is impressive.

   _____

4. I like the early work of the Rolling Stones.

   _____

5. The persona of Texas is well represented in the slogan "Everything is bigger in Texas."

   _____

6. The paintings of the artist were outstanding.

   _____

7. I discovered the best pizza spot of Portland.

   _____

8. She reviewed the notes of Kimbra.

   _____

9. The contractor assessed the structure of the house.

   _____

10. The position of the politician on health care remained firm.

   _____

Vocabulary

contraction
word formed by joining two words, leaving out one or more letters (indicated by an apostrophe)

LO2 Semicolons and Colons

Semicolons and colons have specific uses in writing.

Semicolon

A **semicolon** can be called a soft period. Use the semicolon to join two sentences that are closely related.

> The mosquitoes have returned; it must be August in Wisconsin.

Before a Conjunctive Adverb

Often, the second sentence will begin with a conjunctive adverb *(also, besides, however, instead, meanwhile, therefore)*, which signals the relationship between the sentences. Place a semicolon before the conjunctive adverb, and place a comma after it.

> The outdoor mosquito treatment was rated for six weeks; however, it lasted only four.

With Series

Use a semicolon to separate items in a series if any of the items already include commas.

> Before the party, I'll cut the grass and treat the lawn; buy a bug zapper, citronella candles, and bug spray; and get ready to swat and scratch.

Colon

The main use of a **colon** is to introduce an example or a list.

> Here's one other mosquito treatment: napalm.
> I have one motto: No bug is going to use my blood to reproduce!

After Salutations

In business documents, use a colon after **salutations** and in memo headings.

> Dear Ms. Alvarez: To: Tawnya Smith

Times and Ratios

Use a colon to separate hours, minutes, and seconds. Also use a colon between the numbers in a ratio.

> 8:23 a.m.   4:15 p.m.   14:32:46   The mosquito-person ratio is 5:1.

Using Semicolons and Colons

Correct Rewrite the following sentences, adding semicolons and commas as needed.

1. Mosquitoes here are a nuisance however in some places they are deadly.

2. Malaria kills many in Africa and South America it is carried by mosquitoes.

3. Each year, mosquito-borne illnesses affect 700 million victims many of them die.

4. Mosquitoes breed in stagnant water they need only a small amount.

5. Ponds would produce more mosquitoes however, many fish eat mosquito eggs and larva.

6. A female mosquito inserts her proboscis, injects an anti-clotting agent, and draws blood into her abdomen then she uses the blood proteins to create her eggs.

7. A mosquito bites you and gets away afterward she uses your blood to create more little horrors.

8. Bats rely on mosquitoes for much of their food frogs and birds eat them as well.

9. A friend of mine says a bug zapper does not get rid of mosquitoes it only reduces the "mosquito pressure."

10. The oldest known mosquito was trapped in amber in the Cretaceous period 73 million years ago perhaps it inspired the dinosaur mosquito in *Jurassic Park.*

Correct Rewrite the following sentences, adding colons as needed.

1. Mosquitoes in Egypt can carry a deadly disease yellow fever.

2. Here's the real shame the mosquitoes don't catch the disease.

3. Thankfully, mosquitoes don't pass along one terrible disease AIDS.

4. A mosquito can, however, pass along another nasty payload parasites.

5. Millions die per year because of one critter the mosquito.

6. A world without mosquitoes would be utterly different for one species Homo sapiens.

Vocabulary

semicolon
a punctuation mark (;) that connects sentences and separates items in some series

colon
a punctuation mark (:) that introduces an example or list and has other special uses

salutation
the formal greeting in a letter; the line starting with "Dear"

LO3 Hyphens

A **hyphen** joins words to each other or to letters to form compounds.

Compound Nouns

Use hyphens to create **compound nouns**.

city-state	fail-safe	fact-check	one-liner	mother-in-law

Compound Adjectives

Use hyphens to create **compound adjectives** that appear before the noun. If the adjective appears after, it usually is not hyphenated.

peer-reviewed article   an article that was peer reviewed
ready-made solution   a solution that is ready made

NOTE: Don't hyphenate a compound made from an -*ly* adverb and an adjective, or a compound that ends with a single letter.

newly acquired songs	grade B plywood

Compound Numbers

Use hyphens for **compound numbers** from twenty-one to ninety-nine. Also use hyphens for numbers in a fraction and other number compounds.

twenty-two	fifty-fifty	three-quarters	seven thirty-seconds

With Letters

Use a hyphen to join a letter to a word that follows it.

L-bracket	U-shaped	T-shirt	O-ring	G-rated	x-ray

With Common Elements

Use hyphens to show that two or more words share a common element included in only the final term.

We offer low-, middle-, and high-coverage plans.

Using Hyphens

`Correct` Rewrite the following sentences, adding hyphens as needed.

1. The United Nations secretary general ruled the vote fifty fifty.

2. I replaced the U bend and made a new P trap under the sink.

3. He guessed the board was three eighths inch thick.

4. Would you like to purchase low , medium , or high deductible insurance?

5. The double decker sandwich includes low fat ham and fat free mayonnaise.

6. The ham is low fat, and the mayonnaise is fat free.

7. In your graph, make sure to label the x and y axes.

8. The sales tax percentage is at an all time high.

9. My father in law is an attorney at law.

10. The T shirt showed the x ray of a ribcage.

Vocabulary

hyphen
a short, horizontal line (-) used to form compound words

compound noun
a noun made of two or more

words, often hyphenated or spelled closed

compound adjective
an adjective made of two or more words, hyphenated

before the noun but not afterward

compound numbers
two-word numbers from twenty-one to ninety-nine

LO4 Dashes

Unlike the hyphen, the **dash** does more to separate words than to join them together. A dash is indicated by two hyphens with no spacing before or after. Most word-processing programs convert two hyphens into a dash.

For Emphasis

Use a dash instead of a colon if you want to emphasize a word, phrase, clause, or series.

> Donuts—they're not just for cops anymore.
>
> There's only one thing better than a donut—two donuts.
>
> I like all kinds of donuts—fritters, crullers, and cake donuts.

To Set Off a Series

Use a dash to set off a series of items.

> Elephant ears, Danish, funnel cakes—they just aren't as cool as donuts.
>
> They have many similarities—batter, frosting, and sugar—but where's the hole?

With Nonessential Elements

Use a dash to set off explanations, examples, and definitions, especially when these elements already include commas.

> The hole—which is where the "dough nut" got its name originally—is a key component.

To Show Interrupted Speech

Use a dash to show that a speaker has been interrupted or has started and stopped while speaking.

> "I'd like a—um—how about a fritter?"
>
> "You want an apple—"
>
> "Yes, an apple fritter, well—make it two."

INSIGHT

In most academic writing, use dashes sparingly. If they are overused, they lose their emphasis.

Using Dashes

Correct Rewrite the following sentences, adding dashes where needed.

1. Which would you prefer a cruller, a glazed donut, or a long john?

2. I love a nice blintz basically like a crepe but from Eastern Europe.

3. Donuts or do you prefer the spelling "doughnuts" are yummy.

4. "Could I have a dozen of Do you have a sale on donuts or on" "Today our sale is on wait, let me check yes, on donuts. Get a dozen for $3.00."

5. Batter, hot fat, frosting, sprinkles that's how you make a donut.

6. Making your own donuts is fun fattening, too!

7. A deep-fat fryer basically a deep pot filled with oil is needed to make donuts.

8. Let the donut cool before taking a bite extremely hot!

9. Decorate your donut with frosting, cinnamon, jelly whatever you want.

10. Don't eat too many donuts you'll end up with one around the middle.

Correct Write your own sentence, correctly using dashes for each of the situations indicated below:

1. For emphasis:

_____

2. To set off a series:

_____

3. With nonessential elements:

_____

Vocabulary

dash
long horizontal line that separates words, creating emphasis.

LO5 Real-World Application 1

Correct The following letter sounds too informal because it contains too many contractions. For any contractions you find, write the line number and full form of the word. Also, if you find any errors with apostrophes, write the line number and show the correct punctuation.

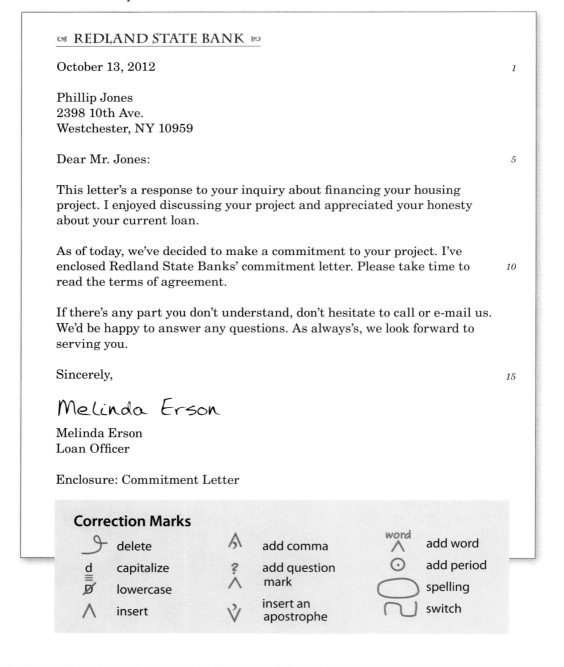

ଓ **REDLAND STATE BANK** ଞ

October 13, 2012   *1*

Phillip Jones
2398 10th Ave.
Westchester, NY 10959

Dear Mr. Jones: *5*

This letter's a response to your inquiry about financing your housing project. I enjoyed discussing your project and appreciated your honesty about your current loan.

As of today, we've decided to make a commitment to your project. I've enclosed Redland State Banks' commitment letter. Please take time to   *10* read the terms of agreement.

If there's any part you don't understand, don't hesitate to call or e-mail us. We'd be happy to answer any questions. As always's, we look forward to serving you.

Sincerely,   *15*

Melinda Erson

Melinda Erson
Loan Officer

Enclosure: Commitment Letter

Correction Marks

⌐ delete	⅄ add comma	word ∧ add word
d̲ capitalize	? add question mark	⊙ add period
ⱡ lowercase		spelling
∧ insert	⌄ insert an apostrophe	switch

LO6 Real-World Application 2

Correct Rewrite the following e-mail message, inserting semicolons, colons, hyphens, and dashes where necessary.

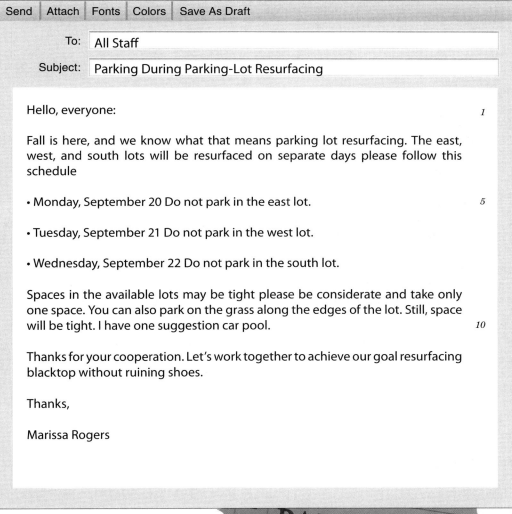

| Send | Attach | Fonts | Colors | Save As Draft |

To: All Staff

Subject: Parking During Parking-Lot Resurfacing

Hello, everyone: 1

Fall is here, and we know what that means parking lot resurfacing. The east, west, and south lots will be resurfaced on separate days please follow this schedule

• Monday, September 20 Do not park in the east lot.   5

• Tuesday, September 21 Do not park in the west lot.

• Wednesday, September 22 Do not park in the south lot.

Spaces in the available lots may be tight please be considerate and take only one space. You can also park on the grass along the edges of the lot. Still, space will be tight. I have one suggestion car pool.   10

Thanks for your cooperation. Let's work together to achieve our goal resurfacing blacktop without ruining shoes.

Thanks,

Marissa Rogers

INDEX

a/an, 272
Absolute phrase, 322
Abstract, 56, 57
Abstract noun, 266
"Academic Dishonesty" (Rawwas et al.), 193
Academic style, 246
Action verb, 267
Active voice, 268, 278
Ad hominem attack, 96
Addressing other points of view, 245–246
Adjective, 270, 280
Adjective clause, 286
Adjective phrases/clauses, 280
Adverb, 270, 282
Adverb clause, 286
Adverb phrases/clauses, 282
Agreement, 303–318
   pronoun-antecedent, 314–315
   subject-verb (*see* Subject-verb agreement)
All-purpose organizational scheme, 210–212
Alternative argument, 206
am, 308
Analogy, 194
Analysis, 27, 204
Anecdote, 202
Angelou, Maya, 267
Antecedent, 314–316
Apostrophe, 356
Appeal to authority, 96–97
Appeal to emotion, 98
Appeal to fear, 98
Appeal to pity, 98
Application, 204
Appositive, 346
Arguable thesis, 165–166
Argument
   argumentative structure, 164
   basic ingredients, 164
   casual *vs.* formal, 163
   deconstructing, 93
   defined, 164–165

   evaluating, 86–108
   mapping, 62–65, 93
   parts, 93
   purpose, 62, 93
   relevance, 93, 94
   soundness, 93, 94
   supporting evidence, 70–75, 146
   thesis, 165–166
   See also Argumentative writing
Argument mapping, 62–65, 93
Argumentative writing, 161–264
   addressing other points of view, 245–246
   all-purpose organizational scheme, 210–212
   argumentative features, 232–233, 236
   body (*see* Body)
   conclusion, 217–219
   defined, 145
   diversity of argumentative philosophies, 245
   editing (*see* Editing)
   evidence, 166
   five-paragraph form, 208–210
   generating material (*see* Generating material)
   introduction (*see* Introduction)
   organizing materials, 182–186
   qualifiers, 220–221
   revising (*see* Revising)
   rhetorical features, 233–234, 236
   technique, 236, 260
   thesis, 238–244
   transitions, 221–223
   See also Argument
Articles, 272
Asking questions, 144, 194
Assumptions, 94–95
Authorities, 146
Author's point of view, 61
Author's writing patterns, 10. *See also* Patterns of organization
Auto-correct, 257
Auxiliary verb, 267

Background information, 192–195
Bacon, Francis, 53
Baker, Russell, 319
Bandwagon, 97
Begging the question, 147
Bias, 83, 84
Block method (organizing evidence), 192, 203
Blog, 175
Blogging, 176
Bloom's taxonomy, 171, 172, 204
Body, 198–217
    evidence and explanations, 202–205
    linking evidence and claims, 212–217
    main idea, 199–200
    refutation of alternative argument, 206–208
    what it does, 228
Bottom main idea, 200
Bottom-up approach (inductive reasoning), 91
Brainstorming, 169–170

Calibration, 237
"Candidate for a Pullet Surprise" (Zar), 259
Card stacking, 95–96
Cause and effect patterns, 29–33
"Causes of Wrongful Conviction, The" (Innocence
    Project), 63–64
Charting, 182–183
"Cheating Goes Hi-Tech" (Campbell et al.), 192
"China Syndrome: Corruption and Theft, The," 219
Chronological order, 19
Circular argument, 214
Circular reasoning, 147
Circumstantial qualifiers, 220
Claim, 189–192, 217
Claims and support chart, 182
Clarification (knowledge), 204
Clarification pattern of organization, 24
Clause
    adjective, 286
    adverb, 286
    defined, 286
    dependent, 286
    independent, 286
    noun, 286
    relative, 300
Clustering, 183–185
Collective noun, 267
Colon, 358
.com sites, 59

Comma, 339–348
    adjectives, 342
    appositive, 346
    clauses/phrases, 346
    compound sentence, 340
    dialogue, 344
    equal modifiers, 342
    explanatory words, 344
    introductory clause, 340
    introductory phrase, 342
    series, items in, 344
    that, which, 346
    transitional expressions, 344
Comma splice, 324–325
"Commentary on 'Cheating Goes Hi-Tech'" (Mello), 193
Common language, 247
Common noun, 266
Comparative form (adjective), 270
Comparison and contrast pattern, 33–34
Complete predicate, 274
Complete refutation, 206, 208
Complete subject, 274
Complex idea, 208
Complex sentence, 298–301
Complicating evidence, 211
Composing, 188. See also Drafting arguments
Compound adjective, 360
Compound-complex sentence, 298, 299
Compound noun, 360
Compound number, 360
Compound predicate, 277, 294
Compound sentence, 296
Compound subject, 276, 292
Conan Doyle, Arthur, 143
Conclusion, 217–219
Concrete noun, 266
Conjunction, 271–272
Conjunctive adverb, 271
Connotation, 82–84
Constructive criticism, 248–252
Contraction, 356
Controversial issue, 54
Cooling-off period, 230
Coordinating conjunction, 271
Copula verb, 267
Correlative conjunction, 272
Counterargument, 70
Critical thinking, 171–172
Critique, 142–160

asking questions, 144
assessment/analysis section, 145–147
components, 142
conclusion section, 149
defined, 142
determining your position, 143
free writing, 144
guidelines/tips, 149
introduction section, 145
language, 146
limit your focus, 145
listing, 144
logic, 146–147
objective summary, 145
purpose, 142
read critically, 142
response section, 148
sample, 153–157
steps in process, 148
summary, compared, 142–143
supporting evidence, 146
"Cultural Clones" (Dymkovets), 223
"Curing Plagiarism" (Shah), 225–228

Dangling modifier, 330, 331
Dash, 362
Deconstructing an argument, 93
Deductive reasoning, 90–92
Definite article, 272
Definition, 194
Definition pattern of organization, 25
Delayed main idea, 200
Delayed subject, 322, 323
*Demon-Haunted World: Science as a Candle in the Dark,
     The* (Sagan), 5
Demonstrative pronoun, 269
Denotation, 82, 84
Dependent clause, 286
Descartes, René, 308
Descriptive writing, 25–26, 61
"Designer Babies: Ethical? Inevitable?" (Britt), 87–88
Diagramming, 183, 184
Diction, 83
Direct object, 277, 290
Discovering, 177–179
Discussing, 173
Disputable evidence, 166
Disraeli, Benjamin, 303
Diversity of argumentative philosophies, 245
Division/classification pattern, 28–29

"Doctors Who Fail Their Patients" *(New York Times),*
     105–106
"Does the World Still Care About American Culture?"
     (Pells), 135–138
Double subject, 316
Doublespeak, 109–110
Drafting arguments, 188–228
     body (*see* Body)
     conclusion, 217–219
     introduction (*see* Introduction)
     overview, 228
     qualifiers, 220–221
     transitions, 221–223
Dramatize, 194
Drawing, 55, 56

Early refutation, 206
Editing, 257–263
     dictionary, 258
     editing guide, 261
     editing/proofreading marks, 261–263
     evaluator, 258
     formatting/document design, 257
     grammar and usage, 260
     grammar checker, 258
     postpone the process, 231, 257, 264
     spelling checker, 257
     synonyms (thesaurus), 258
     technical elements, 260
     translator, 258
     what is it, 231, 257
Editing/proofreading marks, 261–263
Editorial, 54
.edu sites, 59
"Educators: Digital Plagiarism Rampant" (Kabbany), 193
Either/or reasoning, 147
Eliot, George, 183
Emotional load of a word, 83
Emphasis, 362
Emphatic order, 17
Emphatic pronoun, 269
English-to-foreign language translator, 258
Errors in reasoning, 94–99, 146–147
Essay structure, 188
"Ethics in the Classroom" (South), 197
Euphemism, 109
Evaluating arguments, 86–108
Evaluation, 204
Evidence

claims, and, 212–217
complicating, 211
explaining, 204
forms of, 202
indisputable/disputable, 166
make it appealing to audience, 203
organizing, 202–203
pointless, 213, 215–217
relevance, 203
sufficiency, 203
supporting, 70–75, 146
"Examination of the Relationship Between Academic Dishonesty and Workplace Dishonesty, An" (Nonis/Swift), 194
Example/illustration pattern of organization, 24–25
Examples, 70, 146, 193
Experiencing, 180
Expert opinion, 202
Expert witness/testimony, 70
Explaining evidence, 204
Expletives, 272
Exploratory writing, 190
Eyewitness testimony, 70

Fact(s), 66–70, 165, 166
Fallacies of relevance, 95. *See also* Propaganda devices
Fallacy, 94–95. *See also* Propaganda devices
False analogy, 147
Feedback, 248–252
Field excursions, 180
Figure and ground, 55
First person, 314
Five-paragraph form, 208–210
Flaws in logic, 94–99, 146–147
Focused freewriting, 174–175
Focusing, 191–192
for example, 221
Foreign words, 352
Formal language, 246–247
Formality meter, 246
Formatting/document design, 257
Fraction, 360
Fragment, 320–323
Free writing, 144
Freewriting, 174–175

Galileo, 8
"Gambling on Campus," 43–44
Gathering information (researching), 180

Gaule, John, 289
"Gender Differences Among Adolescents with Gambling-Related Problems" (Ellenbogen et al.), 47–48
Generating material, 168–180
blogging, 176
brainstorming, 169–170
critical thinking, 171–172
discovering, 177–179
discussing, 173
freewriting, 174–175
journaling, 175
researching, 180
scrapbooking, 177
sketching, 177
Gerund, 276
Gerund subject, 276
Giorgi, Audrey, 355
Glittering generalities, 96
Goldberg, Natalie, 213
Goldwyn, Samuel, 231
.gov sites, 59
"Government Misconduct" (Innocence Project), 64–65
Grammar and mechanics, 265–365
agreement, 303–318
parts of speech, 266–272
punctuation (*see* Punctuation)
sentence (*see* Sentence)
Grammar checker, 258
"Great University Cheating Scandal, The" (Gulli et al.), 201, 205
Guidelines/tips. *See* Quick tips

Hamburger model, 208
Hamburger paragraph, 216
"Hand of Man on America, The" (Plowden), 56
"Harsh Punishment Is the Best Way to Prevent Juvenile Crime" (Sukhia), 79–80
Helping verb, 267
Here, 272
Heuristics, 177
High-inference language, 82
"His Brain, Her Brain" (Shute), 128–129
History, 193, 202
"Hollow Curriculum, The" (Sollod), 150–153
"Hoping for a Girl" (Grossman), 111
"How to Reduce Plagiarism" (Born), 195, 219
Hyphen, 360
Hypothesis, 57

I, 308
Impartiality, 95
Implied main idea, 200
Implied subject, 274, 322, 323
in addition, 221
Incomplete thought, 320
Indefinite article, 272
Indefinite pronoun, 269, 310–313
Independent clause, 286
Indirect object, 277, 290
Indisputable evidence, 166
Inductive reasoning, 90–92
Infinitive, 276
Infinitive subject, 276
Informal fragment, 322
Informal language, 239, 246–247
Informative writing, 61
Innocence Project, 62–65, 72–76
"Insights: Hoping for a Girl" (Grossman), 111
Intended meaning, 108
Intentional errors in reasoning, 95. *See also* Propaganda
    devices
Interesting facts, 193
Internal editor, 231
Internet sources, credibility of, 59, 60
Interpretation (comprehension), 204
Interrogative pronoun, 269
Interrupted speech, 362
Introduction, 188–198
    background information, 192–195
    lead sentence, 195–196
    major claim, 189–192
    when to write it?, 198
Inverted order, 274
Ironic rules of writing, 260
Issue, 61
Italics, 352

Jotting notes, 169
Journal, 175
Journaling, 175

Lao-Tzu, 169
Late refutation, 206–207
Lead sentence, 195–196
Lead statement, 53
Lee, Linda, 158
"Life Without Parole For Juveniles: Morally Wrong"
    (Coleman), 76–78

Linking evidence and claims, 212–217
Linking verb, 267
List, 22
Listing, 144
Listing patterns, 16–23
Literal language, 82
Loaded language, 83–85
Log, 175
Logical errors, 94–99, 146–147
Logical fallacy, 95
Lottery, The (Jackson), 26

Main idea, 199–200
Major claim, 189–192, 217
Major details, 13, 14
Manguel, Alberto, 3
Mapping, 183
Mapping arguments, 62–65, 93
"Medical Workers Deserve Robust 'Conscience Clause'",
    101–103
Milton, John, 162, 163
Minor details, 13, 14
Misplaced modifier, 330, 331
Mixed pattern of organization, 36–38
Modifier
    comma, 342
    dangling, 330
    misplaced, 330
    simple sentence, 290
Montaigne, 117
my, mine, 316

.net sites, 59
Non sequitur, 147
Noun, 266–267
Noun clause, 276, 286
Noun clause subject, 276
Number compound, 360

Occasional refutation, 206, 207
Op-ed section (newspaper), 54
Opinion, 66
Opposition argument, 206
Order of importance, 17–18
.org sites, 59
Organizational patterns, 10. *See also* Patterns of
    organization
Organizing evidence, 202–203
Organizing materials, 182–186

charting, 182–183
clustering, 183–185
diagramming, 183, 184
outlining, 185–186
Other points of view, 245–246
Outlining, 185–186
Oversimplification, 146

Paraphrasing, 116–125
defined, 116, 126
good/poor paraphrase, compared, 120
guidelines/tips, 118
plagiarism, 119
plan, draft, revise, 121
quick tips, 117
re-paragraphing, 120
re-sentencing, 119
re-wording, 118–119
why paraphrase?, 116
Parts of speech, 266–272
adjective, 270
adverb, 270
articles, 272
conjunction, 271–272
expletives, 272
noun, 266–267
preposition, 271
pronoun, 268–269
verb, 267–268
Pascal, Blaise, 189
Passive predicate, 277
Passive voice, 268, 278
Patterns of organization, 10–50
cause and effect, 29–33
chronological order, 19
comparison and contrast, 33–34
definition and example, 25
description, 25–26
division and classification, 28–29
example/illustration, 24–25
listing patterns, 16–23
longer readings, 43–45
mixed pattern, 36–38
order of importance, 17–18
overview, 15
patterns that analyze, 27–35
patterns that explain, 23–27
patterns that list, 16–23
problem and solution, 31–33
quick tips, 36, 45

sequence or process order, 20
simple listing, 16–17
spatial order, 20–21
Patterns that analyze, 27–35
Patterns that explain, 23–27
Patterns that list, 16–23
Peer evaluation, 248
Pells, Richard, 135
Personal attack, 96
Personal pronoun, 268
Persuasive writing, 61, 83
Photograph, 55, 56
Place order, 20–21
Plagiarism, 119
Plain folk, 97
Plural indefinite pronoun, 312
Poe, Edgar Allan, 339
Point-by-point method (organizing evidence), 202, 203
Pointless evidence, 213, 215–217
Positive (base) form (adjective), 270
Possessive pronoun, 268
Possessives, 356
Post hoc, ergo propter hoc reasoning, 147
Powell, Colin, 11
Predicate, 274, 278
Premises, 61
Preposition, 271, 284
Prepositional phrase, 271, 284
Prescriptive writing, 60–61
Primary research, 180
Pro and con chart, 182
Probability qualifiers, 221
Problem and solution, 31–33
Problem or a mystery, 193
Process order, 20
Pronoun, 268–269
antecedent, and, 314–316
defined, 268
demonstrative, 269
double subject, 316
incorrect case, 316
indefinite, 269
interrogative, 269
personal, 268
possessive, 268
reflexive, 269
relative, 269
vagueness/ambiguity, 316
Pronoun-antecedent agreement, 314–315

Pronoun possessive, 356
Proofreading, 257
Proofreading marks, 261–263
Propaganda, 95
Propaganda devices, 95–99
   appeal to authority, 96–97
   appeal to emotion, 98
   bandwagon, 97
   card stacking, 95–96
   glittering generalities, 96
   personal attack, 96
   plain folk, 97
   quick tips, 99
   straw man, 97–98
Proper noun, 266
"P.S.I.: Plagiarism Scene Investigator" (Southard), 250,
   251, 253–256, 263
Psychology (Bernstein et al.), 27, 35, 38, 49
Punctuation
   apostrophe, 356
   colon, 358
   comma (*see* Comma)
   dash, 362
   hyphen, 360
   quotation marks, 350
   semicolon, 358

Qualifiers, 220–221
Qualifying a claim, 216
Questions, asking, 144, 194
Quick tips
   deductive and inductive reasoning, 92
   evaluating an argument, 94, 100
   evaluating an outline source for quality, 60
   facts and opinions, 66
   list, 22
   organizational pattern, 36, 45
   paraphrasing, 117
   propaganda errors, 99
   reading a newspaper article, 54
   reading a research study, 58
   reading an editorial, 54
   reading an essay, 53
Quotation, 192
Quotation marks, 350

Rambling, 174
Rambling sentence, 328
Range finders, 237

Ratio, 358
Re-paragraphing, 120
Re-sentencing, 119
Re-wording, 118–119
Reasoning
   deductive, 90–92
   errors in, 94–99, 146–147
   evaluating, 93–94
   inductive, 90–92
Reasons, 70
Rebuttal, 206–208
Rebuttal chart, 182, 183
Red herring, 147
Reflexive/emphatic pronoun, 269
Refutation, 206–208
Relative clause, 300
Relative pronoun, 269, 300, 301
Relevant argument, 93, 94
Researching, 180
Revising, 230–237
   checklist, 235, 236
   recursive, 231
   revision guide, 232–235
   rubrics, 235–237
   what is it, 230–231
Revision and editing guide, 261
Revision checklist, 235, 236
Revision guide, 232–235
Rhetorical features (argumentative writing), 233–234, 236
Rhetorical modes, 10. *See also* Patterns of organization
"Rise of the Plagiosphere" (Tenner), 194
Roosevelt, Franklin Delano, 273
Rubrics, 235–237
Run-on sentence, 326–327

Sagan, Carl, 5
Salutation, 358, 359
Scandal in Bohemia, A (Conan Doyle), 143
Scenario, 202
Scoring guide (rubrics), 235–237
Scrapbooking, 177
Second person, 314
Secondary research, 180
Semicolon, 358
Semiformal language, 247
Sensory details, 25–26
Sentence
   comma splice, 324–325
   complex, 298–301

compound, 296
compound-complex, 298
fragment, 320–323
inverted order, 274
rambling, 328–329
run-on, 326–327
shifts, 332–333
simple, 290–295
subject-verb agreement (*see* Subject-verb agreement)
subjects and predicates, 274–279
Sentence fragment, 320–323
Sequence or process order, 20
Series
comma, 344
dash, 362
semicolon, 358
Sexism, 314
Shah, Hetal, 225
Shift in person, 332
Shift in tense, 332
Shift in voice, 332
Signal words/phrases, 12. *See also* Transitional words/
phrases
Simple listing, 16–17
Simple predicate, 274
Simple sentence, 290–295
compound predicate, 294
compound subject, 292
defined, 290
direct/indirect object, 290
modifiers, 290
Simple subject, 274
Singular indefinite pronoun, 310
Sketching, 177
Slippery slope, 98
"So, Is It the Real Thing?" (Prakash), 192
Sollod, Robert N., 150
Sound argument, 94
Southard, James, 250, 253
Spatial order, 20–21
Special words, 350
Specific example, 202
Spelling checker, 257
Statement of fact, 146, 165. *See also* Fact(s)
Statistics, 70, 146, 193
Stereotyping, 147
Stilla, John, 220, 221
Strategies for Reducing Academic Dishonesty (Wlliams/
Hosek), 197

Straw man fallacy, 97–98
Stream of consciousness writing, 174
Strong thesis, 238
Style of writing, 246–247
Subject, 274–277
Subject-verb agreement, 304–313
agreement in number, 304
compound subject, 306
I, 308
indefinite pronoun, 310–313
you, 308
Subordinating conjunction, 271, 298
Summarizing, 126–139
comprehension, 126
critique, compared, 142–143
defined, 126
length, 127
paragraph format, 127
quotation marks, 126
sample summary, 134
steps in process, 127
transition words, 134
Superlative form (adjective), 270
Supporting arguments, 61, 71
Supporting details, 11, 13–15
Supporting evidence, 70–75, 146
Syllogism, 91
Synonyms (thesaurus), 258
Synthesis, 86, 204

Task-specific rubrics, 237
Technical language, 247
Technical terms, 352
Technique, 236, 260
"Teens and Drugged Driving," 45
"Temptation of Instant Essays, The" (Nguyen), 194
Testimonial, 96
Testimony, 70
that, 300, 346
the, 272
"Their Cheatin' Hearts" (Macklem), 195
There, 272
"There Are Many Types of Lies" (Caruso), 194
Thesis, 52, 238–244. *See also* Weak thesis
Thesis statement (major claim), 189–192, 217
Thinking critically, 171–172
Third person, 314
Time, 358
Time order, 19

Tips/guidelines. *See* Quick tips
Titles
    larger works, 352
    smaller works, 350
Tone, 83–85
Top-down approach (deductive reasoning), 91
Top main idea, 200
Topic sentence, 5, 199, 200
Transitional words/phrases
    achieving coherence, 221–223
    addition, 222
    cause, 28
    cause and effect, 222
    chronological order, 16
    clarification, 24, 222
    comparison, 28, 222
    concession, 222
    contrast, 28, 222
    definition and example, 24
    description, 24
    division/classification, 28
    effect, 28
    emphasis, 222
    example/illustration, 24
    functions, 12
    illustration, 222
    order of importance, 16
    problem and solution, 28
    purpose, 222
    sequence or process order, 16, 222
    simple listing, 16
    spatial order, 16, 222
    summarizing, 134, 222
    time, 222
"Tugging on your heartstrings," 98

Unintentional errors in reasoning, 94–95, 146–147
Unsubstantiated claim, 213–215

Vague pronoun, 316
Van Allen, James, 127
Venn diagram, 183, 184
Verb, 267–268
Visual scrapbooking, 177
Vocabulary strategy
    bias/tone, 83
    connotation/denotation, 82–83
    euphemisms/doublespeak, 109–110
    intended meaning, 108
    loaded language, 83–85
Voice, 268

Warren, Robert Penn, 349
Weak thesis, 238–244
    conventional wisdom, 240–241
    no claim, 238–239
    obviously true/statement of fact, 239–240
    overly broad claim, 243–244
    personal conviction, 241–243
Webbing, 183
Weisberg, Mark, 213
"When Academic Dishonesty Happens on Your Campus"
    (Clos), 193
which, 300, 346
"Who Needs College?" (Lee), 158–159
who/whom, 300
Working thesis, 211
Writing Analytically with Readings (Rosenwasser et al.),
    197, 201, 219, 223
Writing structure, 10. *See also* Patterns of organization
"Wrongly Convicted" (Golway), 72–76

you, 308

Zero draft, 169
Zone of reasonable skepticism, 190